DYNAMIC ... IC
HEA ...

DYNAMIC ENERGETIC HEALING®

INTEGRATING CORE SHAMANIC PRACTICES WITH ENERGY PSYCHOLOGY APPLICATIONS AND PROCESSWORK PRINCIPLES

HOWARD BROCKMAN, LCSW

COLUMBIA

CP LLC

PRESS

Columbia Press, LLC
1620 Commercial St. SE
Salem, Oregon 97302

Dynamic Energetic Healing® and are registered trademarks of Howard Brockman and The Heart Center Incorporated (an Oregon corporation).

Callahan Techniques and Thought Field Therapy are registered trademarks of Dr. Roger Callahan.

Editor: Linda Jenkins
Cover image: Willow Arlenea
Illustrations: Andrea Carlson
Cover and book design: Jerry Soga
Composition: William H. Brunson Typography Services
Proofreader: Marvin Moore

ISBN-13 978-0-9766469-8-3
ISBN-10 0-9766469-8-6

Library of Congress Control Number 2005903096

DISCLAIMER

Shamanic healing methods, energy psychology techniques, and other described methods presented in this book should not be considered an exclusive approach for confronting psychological and/or medical problems.

This book is intended as an informational guide only. The remedies, approaches, and techniques described herein are meant to supplement, and not to be a substitute for, professional medical care or treatment. Proper use of the methods described in this book requires a thorough understanding, proper analysis, and supervised training. They should not be used to treat a serious ailment without prior consultation with a qualified healthcare professional. All matters regarding your health require medical supervision.

Neither the author nor anyone else who has been involved in the creation, production, or support of the book shall be liable for any direct, incidental, economic, non-economic, punitive, or consequential damages.

DEDICATION

*To my parents, whose support in all kinds of ways
they can never know of enabled me to get to
where I am today and write this book*

C O N T E N T S

List of Illustrations   xv

Preface   xvii

Acknowledgments   xxi

Introduction   xxiii

Part 1:
The Strands That Weave Dynamic Energetic Healing® Together

Chapter 1   Beginnings   3

Chapter 2   Antecedents of Dynamic Energetic Healing®   27

Chapter 3   My Role within the Context of Dynamic
               Energetic Healing®   41

Chapter 4   Therapeutic Presence   47

Chapter 5   Integrating the Second Attention into Dynamic Energetic
               Healing®: Acknowledging the Dreamingbody   53

Chapter 6   The Compassionate Spirits: Moving into the
               Dreamtime Experience   61

Chapter 7   Collaborating with the Compassionate Spirits:
               Embracing a New Paradigm   67

Chapter 8   Living Life Intentionally   71

Chapter 9   The Mysterious Phenomenon of Psychoenergetic
               Reversal   83

Chapter 10   Understanding Trauma within Dynamic
              Energetic Healing®   91

Chapter 11   Soul Loss   107

Chapter 12   Energetic Practice   119

Chapter 13   Energetic Origins from a Hypnotic Perspective 133

Chapter 14   Energetic Boundaries   139

Chapter 15   Working with Supernatural Energies   145

Chapter 16   Intrusions   157

Chapter 17   Creating a Sacred Space   167

Chapter 18   Living Life Free of Trauma   171

Part 2:
The Dynamic Energetic Healing® Interventions

Introduction to Part 2   177

Chapter 19   Tapas Acupressure Technique   183

Chapter 20   Emotional Freedom Techniques, Modified   187

Chapter 21   Tapping the Temporal Curve   195

Chapter 22   The Chakra Interventions   199

Chapter 23   Negative Affect Erasing Method   215

Chapter 24   Frontal Occipital (F/O) Holding   219

Chapter 25   Sound as Vibrational Healing   227

Chapter 26   Shamanic Healing Approaches   239

Chapter 27   Focused Prayer   249

Conclusion to Part 2   251

Part 3:
The Dynamic Energetic Healing® Protocol

Introduction to Part 3   255

Chapter 28   Preparing to Work on a Specific Intention   257

Chapter 29   Establishing a Clear Intention   265

Chapter 30   Working at the Energetic Origin   271

Chapter 31   Dealing with Trauma   289

Chapter 32   Integration and Completion   301

Conclusion to Part 3   309

Part 4:
Case Histories

Introduction to Part 4   313

Case 1   Eliminating Panic Attacks Related to the Fear of
          Having a Colonoscopy: Clearing an Intrusion   315

Case 2   Metamorphizing Post-Surgical Depression: Conscious
          Applications of Circulating Chi   319

Case 3   Resolving Depression, Insomnia, and Suicidal Thoughts:
          Healing the Aftermath of Childhood Abuse and Trauma   323

Case 4   Neutralizing Present-Day Allergy Symptoms: Learning
          Psychopomp Work in a Past-Life Origin   329

Case 5   Healing the Roots of Melanoma Skin Cancer:
          Disidentifying from Two Negative Archetypes   333

Case 6   Transforming the Fear of Bulimic Purging:
          Shamanic Spirit Releasement   341

Case 7   Transmuting the Trauma of Early Sexual Abuse:
          Correcting a Lifetime of Disembodiment   345

Case 8   Relieving Acid Reflux and Preparing for Labor and
          Delivery: Energetic Boundary Work and Past-Life
          Regression   351

Case 9   Alleviating the Loss and Guilt of Giving a Baby Up for
          Adoption: Finding Power through Past-Life Regression   357

Case 10   Releasing Old Trauma and Alleviating Symptoms of
          Fatigue: Allergy Antidoting Techniques   371

Case 11   Shifting Lifelong Persistent Despair: Dreamtime
          and Frontal Occipital Holding   375

Case 12   Overcoming Compulsive Overeating: Healing the
          Wounded Inner Child   379

Case 13   Restoring Healthy Immune Function: Establishing
          Energetic Boundaries with an Ancestral
          Earthbound Spirit   387

Case 14   Confronting Psychic Attack: Reestablishing the
          Reliability of Muscle Testing   391

Case 15   Mitigating Depression: Uncovering an Energetic
          Origin Outside of Worldly Time   399

Case 16   Validating Empirically the Existence of Past Lives:
            Recovering Power and Terminating Therapy   403

Case 17   Treating Long-Term Panic Disorder: Resolving
            Recurrent Spirit Intrusion and Learning to
            Honor All Parts of the Self   409

Conclusion to Part 4   427

Final Thoughts   431

Appendix 1 Concerns Regarding the Pharmacological Model   433

Appendix 2 DSM-IV Descriptions of Dissociative Disorders   441

Appendix 3 Dynamic Energetic Healing® Protocol Checklist   443

Bibliography   445

Index   453

ILLUSTRATIONS

Figure 1   Tapas Acupressure Technique (TAT)   (Ch. 19)   184

Figures 2a, 2b Emotional Freedom Techniques (EFT)   (Ch. 20)   188, 189

Figure 3   Summary of EFT Treatment Points   (Ch. 20)   191

Figure 4   Tapping the Temporal Curve   (Ch. 21)   196

Figure 5   The Chakras   (Ch. 22)   200

Figure 6   Negative Affect Erasing Method (NAEM)   (Ch. 23)   216

Figure 7   Frontal Occipital Holding (F/O Holding) (Ch. 24)   220

Figure 8   Kirtan Kriya Meditation   (Ch. 25)   229

Figure 9   Manual Muscle Testing   (Ch. 28)   260

PREFACE

I have gone through many changes over the years, both personally and professionally. These changes, and the accompanying paradigm shifts, are described in chapter 1, "Beginnings." As a model for psychotherapeutic change, Dynamic Energetic Healing® is as innovative and distinctive as it is remarkably effective. This book has been written for healthcare professionals and those who are interested in finding reliable ways to make long-lasting, positive changes in their lives.

As explained in chapter 1, I have learned many spiritual practices in my pursuit of heightened awareness and expanding consciousness. By integrating these insights and experiences, the Dynamic Energetic Healing® model helps people to change and extricate themselves from the binding effects of past trauma.

As a clinician and psychotherapist, I am a licensed clinical social worker in private practice in the state of Oregon. As such, I abide by the regulations and ethical guidelines imposed on all social workers by the governing state licensing board. In this book I discuss the theory and underlying principles of the three primary models for change that I have integrated into Dynamic Energetic Healing®—energy psychology, process-oriented psychology, and core shamanism. Each of these models expresses very different views and assumptions of the world from what is considered mainstream or consensus thinking in the field of psychology. Much of energy psychology derives from the underlying principles of traditional Chinese medicine, which are said to be over five thousand years old. Process-oriented psychology incorporates principles of ancient Taoism, Jungian psychology, and modern quantum physics. Core shamanism is said to be at least thirty thousand years old and has always had strong ties to the natural world. The combination and integration of these three distinctive paradigms makes a unique and highly effective model for change that lies at the foundation of my successful clinical practice.

It is important to state that clinicians who apply Dynamic Energetic Healing® in their practice must abide by the regulations governing their area of practice. For example, since I am not a certified Chinese medical doctor, I cannot prescribe medicines to my clients; neither can I use acupuncture needles with them. But I can and do apply various principles derived from Chinese medicine, such as directing my clients in tapping on acupressure points. When issues of deeply held personal values or spiritual orientation come up in a therapy session, I realize I need to be sensitive and open without imposing any of my personal beliefs about what is appropriate for the client.

One definition (from the *Random House Webster's College Dictionary*) of *psychology* is "the science of the mind or of mental states and processes," but psychology is anything but scientific. It is presumptuous for Westerners to impose our beliefs on and try to define reality for others. We have a long and unfortunate history of ethnocentrism—European explorers coming to the Americas, enslaving, and almost wiping out native populations who they considered to be savages is just one example.

Fortunately, ethnocultural awareness is being taught more and more in graduate programs. These programs attempt to counteract the deeply embedded ethnocentrism that devalues people from cultures which are unfamiliar to us. I believe that multicultural awareness must be brought into modern psychology so that the proscriptions of those operating in a biased cultural framework do not limit our repertoire of possible psychotherapeutic solutions.

Individuals perceive their experiences uniquely and construct their own conceptual models for how and why things work in the world, so "mind and mental states" (which are amorphous concepts and slippery to define) defy singular analysis. As a result, each client requires a unique approach to coming back to wholeness within the psychotherapeutic context. For example, because people don't all think the same way, a cognitive behavioral approach is not appropriate for treating every client. Some clients just need someone to listen to them; others need support for difficult feeling states (such as anger or sadness) so these states can be acknowledged and expressed.

Mainstream psychology has often tried to separate itself from religious and spiritual issues. But for some clients, the spiritual dimension of their being needs to be addressed in order to alleviate their pain and suffering. This occurs when their mental processes or states cannot provide the understanding and support they need in order to reconcile the paradox of living in the modern world and feeling the strong stirrings of an ancient soul. The ancient principles of shamanic practices are sometimes effective in these cases. We like to believe we are modern people in the twenty-first century, but we have soul and ancestral memories that go back thousands of years and press upon us in our present-day experience. All of us, regardless of our current religious or spiritual beliefs, have ancestral roots that reach back to a time—it could be a recent time, or a time countless generations ago—when shamanic practices were integrated into the fabric of culture. Like Jung's archetypes, these principles and practices are part of the human psyche and experience.

Many people find it difficult to accept shamanic concepts because they challenge our very identities—identities that are supported by the dominant culture that defines what is "true." Nevertheless, our ethical imperative is to bring forth and offer, with sensitivity and integrity, everything that we have available to assist our clients while honoring the dictum "do no harm." We must always orient to the best interest of and highest good for our clients.

As a seasoned clinician, I know the importance of helping my clients to identify and embrace the internal resources they already possess. The healing that occurs in our sessions helps clients to expand their consideration of what is possible, become empowered, and stay strong in the face of great challenges. Clients' internal resources are things such as a positive memory of winning a race, a mental image of being with their children, a flowing river that becomes a symbol of transformation from the collective unconscious, or the vision of Jesus Christ that results from time in church or at prayer. Whatever these internal resources are, it is the person's subjective experience and personal strengths that are accessed and affirmed to facilitate change at multiple levels of their being. This reflects the Great Mystery and provides the magic that is part of the psychotherapeutic process.

My images or visions of what I call the compassionate spirits are just some of my many internal resources that help me support my clients. I believe it is important to share these images often with clients. By doing so, I help clients trust their own multisensory creativity and uncover and develop their internal resources, which helps to empower them. After many years of practicing Kundalini yoga and meditation, I can now "see" my own and others' chakras. This can be very helpful in a therapy session. Because I have spent many years practicing psychotherapy, I can feel the disowned emotions of clients that they are frequently unaware of. This too is very helpful in a therapy session. I bring all my experience and sensitivity to therapy to be helpful to my clients.

Sensitivity is both an innate quality and something that can be cultivated over time. This is true in many contexts. For example, painters train themselves to notice subtle distinctions of color and shading in order to bring out a dimension often not perceived by the rest of us. My wife, Anita, a professor of music and concert pianist, exemplifies the cultivation of sensitivity in another context. Through many years of practice and training, she has developed an ear for the subtleties of sound that I am completely unaware of. When we go to concerts together, what I find enjoyable may give Anita a headache. You might say that she has developed a nuanced perception of sound that many others do not have. This doesn't mean that I couldn't acquire this ability, but it would probably take a large commitment and a substantial period of time for me to cultivate this heightened ability to discriminate sound. But after many years of training and using spiritual practices, I do perceive energetic phenomena. Feeling the affective states of the disowned parts of my clients, seeing chakras that are congested, having visions of guardian angels—it's really all about sensitivity. Developing and cultivating your second attention in order to become more sensitive to field phenomena when you are working with clients comes up again and again in this book. It is an important and even pervasive theme in Dynamic Energetic Healing®.

For readers who are interested in energy psychology, process-oriented psychology, and core shamanism, I have included some relevant references in the bibliography. I have also listed various resources on my website (*www.DynamicEnergeticHealing.com*) that you may be interested in investigating.

Dynamic Energetic Healing® is many things, but at its essence it is an integrative model for practicing psychotherapy in a psychotherapeutic context. I am delighted to share this new healing model; I hope it will make you feel more comfortable in uncovering and accessing your spiritual resources in order to help others. The truth is, there is great power in the universe. Whether you call it prana or chi, archetypes or compassionate spirits, this power is all an expression of love.

ACKNOWLEDGMENTS

I feel indebted to many people for their support, encouragement, and help. Though I spent a long time compiling the initial manuscript, its culmination into this book could not have happened without the help and sincere interest of a number of people.

First and foremost, I am most grateful to have found my wonderful editor, Linda Jenkins. Her skill and facility with crafting language helped me to more clearly define what I was trying to express. Additionally, I appreciated her challenging me to articulate certain ideas more definitively. Most importantly though, I feel blessed to have found such an expert editor who supported my work without reservations. I felt deeply appreciated as a writer and encouraged to express myself completely, in spite of my initial hesitancy to describe some things that might be considered to fall outside most people's normative experience. As a first-time author, it was affirming to be taken seriously; Linda's patience and reassurance fueled in me the drive I needed to push through my occasional resistance, keep up, and persist through the many months of hard and arduous work. She is a real gem.

I am grateful to my friend and colleague Robin Gress, who took time out of her busy schedule to read through the manuscript and offer many helpful suggestions, particularly on shamanism. I also want to thank other readers who critiqued my manuscript and offered very helpful constructive criticism that resulted in significant tightening of the text. These readers include Geraldine Brooks, Pam Clark, and Brigid O'Hagan.

My dear friend Michelle Stringham first introduced me to the practice of shamanism and was for many years my mentor and teacher. For this and for her heartfelt support in all matters, I am deeply grateful.

I appreciate the energy, enthusiasm, and support of my friend and colleague Mary Hammond-Newman. During the initial development of Dynamic Energetic Healing®, Mary's input and help was invaluable as we put together our initial training manual. Writing various segments of our manual was to some degree a catalyst that inspired me to write more about my own synthesis of Dynamic Energetic Healing®. I also want to acknowledge my friend and colleague Nancy Gordon who, with Mary, contributed her ideas and enthusiasm in our initial study group as Dynamic Energetic Healing® was in its formative stage.

I consider myself a lifelong student. I am always curious to learn more about healing from a variety of theoretical models. I know I will continue to study with new teachers and familiar teachers, for this is my way. I am deeply grateful to all the teachers I have had over the years, the work of many of whom is described in this book. This includes my current living teachers as well as those who have passed on and can be accessed in nonordinary reality. A special note of appreciation goes to Dr. Judith Swack for her innovative ideas. They led to my own creative stirrings to retrieve the behavioral kine-siology applications of manual muscle testing, which I first began using in the 1980s. Her energy psychology model provided much of the stimulus and inspiration for what has emerged as Dynamic Energetic Healing®.

It is important to acknowledge my clients, for without them I would never have discovered the unfolding healing possibilities that Dynamic Energetic Healing® has to offer. I am regularly learning from my clients, and for them I am grateful.

I want to express my deep gratitude to my wife, Anita. She is a model for me of living one's passion. Because of her own commitment to following her passion, she both inspires and enables me to live and pursue mine. She comes from a place of deep integrity and strong convictions. A better partner I could not ask for.

INTRODUCTION

Dynamic Energetic Healing® is a new psychotherapy model that fits under the umbrella of energy psychology. Mary Hammond-Newman and I, the co-founders of Dynamic Energetic Healing®, drew on over forty years of combined clinical experience to develop the initial conception of this new approach. Energy psychology has proliferated over the last ten years, and in its present form Dynamic Energetic Healing® is only eight years old. It was developed after Mary, our colleague Nancy Gordon, and I took initial trainings in innovative energy psychology methods. These methods included Thought Field Therapy, emotional freedom techniques, and healing from the body level up, among others. Mary and I created a series of unique protocols and a comprehensive training program for those interested in applying these methods. After further developing and expanding on some of these ideas in my own clinical practice, I have decided to share my findings and experiences by writing this book.

Dynamic Energetic Healing® has proven successful in addressing depression, post-traumatic stress disorder (PTSD), eating disorders, anxiety and panic disorder, addictions, dissociative disorders, the emotional/mental underpinnings of physical illness, and the spiritual and developmental issues that surface in midlife. Mary and I use this approach successfully with our respective marital and group therapy clients.

Dynamic Energetic Healing® integrates well with established therapies. Consequently, we often incorporate more widely used and accepted therapies such as hypnosis, cognitive-behavioral therapy, neurolinguistic programming (NLP), processwork, and play therapy into our work with clients.

Dynamic Energetic Healing® emerged over a two-year period during which Mary, Nancy, and I met regularly. This was a time of great alchemical change for us, a time of personal, professional, and deep spiritual growth. We were tremendously excited to discover new clinical applications for the energy psychology methods we were learning. Since these energy psychology strategies involved an entirely new paradigm for us, we needed each other's skills and insights. All seasoned clinicians, we formed a study group and worked on each other. We made astounding discoveries, both personally and collectively, during this extremely high-energy time. During some periods we met twice a week, hardly able to contain our excitement and enthusiasm for healing old patterns that had seemed so intransigent and persistent before.

As we studied and learned energy psychology fundamentals, including using manual muscle testing and energetic strategies incorporating the acupuncture meridians, the chakras, and the human biofield (auric field), our creativity sparked and accelerated rapidly. With our combined clinical backgrounds in human development, processwork, transpersonal psychology, play therapy, hypnosis, core shamanism, and treatment of addictions, we shared our insights for how we could integrate and apply energy psychology strategies into the therapy models we were already using.

We also learned that our clients are our greatest teachers in developing new work. We experimented with the energy tools, used our intuition, listened intently to our clients, and Dynamic Energetic Healing® emerged.

Dynamic Energetic Healing® guides people to a place of thorough and complete emotional, mental, and spiritual healing, and of greater clarity regarding their life purpose. Dynamic Energetic Healing® is as effective with couples, families, and communities as it is with individuals.

One characteristic that distinguishes Dynamic Energetic Healing® from many other energy psychology models is the emphasis on *Process*. Throughout this book I differentiate between Process (which is integral to the dreamtime experience and the almost mystical in-the-moment organic flow of unfolding events, whose concept is likened to the Tao of Lao-tzu) and process, an interactional dynamic. Most effective therapists have a sense of Process as they work, but during our initial energy psychology trainings we were directed to follow rigid protocols. This is often useful for new learners, but when protocols become prescriptive and practicing them feels like following a recipe, the creative and magical elements of the therapeutic process are significantly compromised. From my ten years of training in process-oriented psychology and a further ten years' experience facilitating process-oriented therapy groups, I have learned to honor and defer to Process. Process not only guides my therapy sessions—it is the guiding principle for how I live my life.

By following Process, I can truly "not know" anything at all about what I'm to do with my client and yet be absolutely confident that our session will unfold in exactly the way it is meant to. When I defer to Process, I remain curious, expectant, and highly sensitive to whatever is happening in the moment. (See chapter 5, "Integrating the Second Attention into Dynamic

Energetic Healing®: Acknowledging the Dreamingbody" for more about following Process.) Deferring to Process yields many outcomes, one of the most significant being that clients learn to trust and honor their own perceptions. In addition, it makes the therapist's work interesting, creative, always new, and fun. We learned from Fred Gallo that energy psychology is a science, but we experience Dynamic Energetic Healing® as an art.

Deferring to Process is one of the more challenging elements that trainees have to deal with in learning Dynamic Energetic Healing®. For many, it becomes just another piece of the puzzle as an entirely new paradigm starts to fit together.

Our study group also agreed that acknowledging that we work in the realm of the Great Mystery is an integral part of Dynamic Energetic Healing®. In traditional graduate school programs for counseling, social work, and psychology, spiritual issues are rarely if ever explicitly taught. Carl Jung addressed these issues, and there are some transpersonal psychology programs that emphasize the spiritual component, but most developmental psychology textbooks do not discuss spiritual issues as part of the normative human developmental life cycle. I find this interesting (and dismaying), since spiritual issues are a core human value that frequently inform my work with clients. I make no apologies for this. In fact, the acknowledgment and existence of the soul, as evidenced in our work with energetic origins (particularly past-life origins), is absolutely central to the consistently successful therapeutic outcomes of our clients. This is another important distinguishing characteristic of Dynamic Energetic Healing® within the energy psychology community.

This is not to say that other energy psychology models never acknowledge soul—Asha Clinton's seemorg matrix work model and Tapas Fleming's Tapas acupressure technique model are explicit about the existence and importance of soul in healing work. The existence of soul is why we are very careful about creating sacred space whenever we work with clients, either individually or in groups (see chapter 17, "Creating a Sacred Space"). We each maintain our own spiritual practice through which we nurture our respective ongoing relationship with Spirit. This relationship informs, directs, and supports our work with clients (see chapter 7, "Collaborating with the Compassionate Spirits: Embracing a New Paradigm"). In fact, it is from this core value, my relationship with Spirit, that all of the work emerges.

As we worked with the energy psychology paradigm, we all came to agree on one thing—the efficacy and efficiency that manual muscle testing provides on many levels. And though we recognized that using manual muscle testing is a skill cultivated through disciplined practice, it is obviously an art more than a science. For more information on the muscle testing process, see chapter 28, "Preparing to Work on a Specific Intention."

A most important point to articulate is that our recognition of manual muscle testing *as a guide* appeared to consistently corroborate (for both the client and ourselves) the sequence of steps used to address particular therapeutic issues. From beginning to end, the guidance of manual muscle testing corroborated clients' subjective experience while trauma was cleared from their energy field and the best and most effective interventions were selected. Although there are many in the energy psychology community who never use manual muscle testing, we find it to be an incredibly reliable and affirming tool for following the client's process and identifying completion of that process in a way that clients know is true for them. This is in contrast to traditional talk therapy where, at the end of the session, the client and the therapist are often uncertain that a concrete change in a trauma pattern has indeed been effected. In my practice, I have come to realize that if my client or I don't know something, we ask the body. Manual muscle testing is a powerful way to access information stored in the body, a profound way to elicit the client's deepest wisdom, and a wonderful example of the intelligence of the mind/body/spirit holism.

Whether applied kinesiology is an art or science, what matters most to me is how manual muscle testing reliably enables Dynamic Energetic Healing® to sustain consistent healing of old trauma and related patterns for clients with various presenting problems. By asking the proper questions, I am able to retrieve the pertinent information that guides us to the place of positive therapeutic outcomes.

Energy psychology is considered quite new and innovative, even though clinical applications in this field are well into their second decade. Mastering Dynamic Energetic Healing® is a stretch for new trainees who are confronted not just with the cognitive adjustment but a completely new paradigm. A paradigm is an orientation to and a way of explaining how things work in the world. It is a description of our perception of the world or what we see as reality. This encompasses everything for us. For most of us, our paradigm in a generalized sense is consensual—most of us agree about most things and operate from that "consensus reality." Thanks to media-created stereotypes, clients and inexperienced therapists have preconceived ideas about what therapy is supposed to be like and how change is supposed to occur. Part of this paradigm shift is about a completely new and innovative way for creating change within the collective field that psychologists have held sacred for over a hundred years. As explained in the discussion on paradigm shifts (see chapter 1, "Beginnings"), it was very challenging for me to accept that changes can be made so quickly by harnessing the body's essential energy system while maintaining an openness to Spirit. Dynamic Energetic Healing® challenges many of our assumptions about how change occurs. Yet it continues to be my experience that clients recommend that their friends check out this strange and wonderful new therapy. Certainly, educating new clients is an important component for their successful therapeutic outcomes. But it is the consistent and predictable healing responses that excite clients and new trainees alike.

PART 1:
THE STRANDS THAT
WEAVE DYNAMIC ENERGETIC
HEALING® TOGETHER

CHAPTER

1

BEGINNINGS

W hen I was a junior in high school, I was drawn to J. Krishnamurti's *The Flight of the Eagle*. As I read through Krishnamurti's teachings about awareness and how "the observer becomes the observed" and how attention must be an ongoing meditation, I began to wake up. It catalyzed something in me that had lain dormant my entire life.

I was brought up in a Jewish middle-class family in west Los Angeles. We never spoke about things spiritual. My parents only went to temple on the high holy days. The rest of the time there was no religious or spiritual practice in any form in our house. There was no observance of the Sabbath, there were no religious rituals, and there was never any talk about any of that.

I attended the University of Southern California (USC) for my undergraduate years. I never did connect with a spiritual community in college. Even though I was reading *The Doors of Perception* by Aldous Huxley and the early books of Carlos Castaneda, there was not a group of people with whom I could share this growing spiritual awareness. This was the early 1970s when many young people were experimenting with and using drugs. Marijuana and psychedelics were prevalent at this time. I was always mystified by how the "doors of perception" opened up for me when I occasionally smoked marijuana. I related to the experience Aldous Huxley described in that small volume of the same name, as the filters blocking my perception were removed. This was always a very profound awareness-expanding experience for me. Yet for many of my college friends, getting drunk and stoned was just for the sake of the recreational experience of the moment—it was just something to do. Given this cultural milieu, the music of the time, and my curiosity, I wanted to try a psychedelic drug. But I was wary; I had read a great deal about overdoses and bad trips. I had also read about the importance of having the proper set (mental attitude) and setting (context) in order to have a successful experience.

During Christmas vacation of 1971, my good friend Mark (who had already experimented with mescaline a couple of times) agreed to be my support person, my guide, through my first experience with this drug. We listened to some music as I waited for all kinds of hallucinatory and psychedelic experiences to unfold. I was waiting and waiting and nothing happened until all of a sudden, about two and a half hours after ingesting the mescaline, I had an intense upsurge of feeling from my solar plexus all the way up through my upper chakras and out across to Mark, enveloping and enfolding him. It was a very powerful, emotional experience. I told Mark the energy that was enveloping me was also being directed toward him *but I was embarrassed to say what it was!* He responded with the question, "Is it love?" And yes, that is exactly what it was. It was unmitigated, pure, unconditional love directed toward a good friend in a way that was beyond anything I had ever experienced before.

As I sat there suffused with this feeling, radiating pure love with this unbelievable and wonderful rapport, my thinking mind became engaged. My thoughts spun very quickly as I marveled that this could be a *new* emotional experience for me. Why had I never had this experience before with my family or with anyone? This was just unbelievable to me.

I started thinking, "What if everybody had this experience? How might our culture, our world be different?" I suddenly began to understand why so many people who were taking psychedelic drugs at that time (mescaline, LSD, and psilocybin) were strongly advocating that *everybody* experience this. I understood why this shared experience had very rapidly become a proselytizing cultural tsunami with all the zealotry of a mass religious movement. I had just become a convert though my direct experience, which for me was indeed mystical. *What I experienced was the opening of my heart chakra for the very first time!* At twenty years of age I was thinking how wonderful it would be if everybody could have this experience. Thematically, this is the initiatory experience that all the young people have, with the guidance of an older mentor, in Huxley's *Island*. I thought, "What a different world we could have if everybody came from a place of unconditional love."

As thoughts continued to spin out and circulate rapidly in my mind, I just knew that there are *some* people who have had this experience and yet had never taken this drug. I just knew it: to have this experience you did not have to ingest a drug. This was a turning point for me — at that moment my path in life, my path of heart, was determined. I had just been initiated by a powerful spiritual teacher to taste unconditional love. I wanted to be in this state of unconditional love all the time, and I was going to do anything and everything that I could to achieve this.

In subsequent months, I ingested psychedelics only twice more. Each time was a very positive experience. I took mescaline again once and I took some LSD. Though it was a low dose of LSD, I discovered that this was, potentially, a very dangerous experience. I experienced what I called "simul-taneous two minds." Fortunately my ego stayed intact during this experience so I retained my awareness of myself and my relationship to my surroundings while another part of me was hallucinating bizarre experiences that were completely out of my control. It was as though I was holding my mind (my conscious rational mind) in one hand while holding another, out-of-control, hallucinating mind in the other hand. It was a simultaneity of divergent states of consciousness.

I realized that this very powerful experiment in consciousness had the potential to be extremely damaging to the psyche. There was no pre-existing cultural context that could act as a container for me. There was no cultural field with which to hold this, such as the Native American Church and its use of its sacrament, peyote. I thought afterwards, "What if the power of these drugs, of this particular drug experience, was such that I had no conscious relational ego as a reference point?" Ancient and revered spiritual scriptures had described this state in various ways: the One, Nirvana, Suchness, and so on. The traditional dissolution of the ego, which is what many of the age-old spiritual traditions refer to as the merging of the individual consciousness with the unitary cosmic consciousness, prepared the initiate for the leap to a nondualistic experience of reality. *But how would one integrate this?*

After my third experience, and after seeing many of my college friends get-ting very messed up from bad trips, I decided that even though the experience was life-changing, I was never going to use a chemical agent again. I decided to develop, cultivate, and achieve this awareness in an ongoing, natural way that would support all parts of me. But after Krishnamurti, Aldous Huxley, and Carlos Castaneda, the psychedelic drugs were among my first spiritual teachers.

To this day, I am extremely grateful that I happened to live in the time in our cultural history that provided me with the opportunity and the context to experience the personal transformation that opened my heart and my mind.

I developed an intention: to find a way to achieve this expanded state of consciousness and maintain it all the time. One day as I was walking across the outdoor quad at USC, I saw a sign that said "Kundalini Yoga Lessons." I was drawn to find out more, so I went in and started participating in these yoga classes three times a week. Our instructor told us we could maintain a powerful natural high and significantly increase our awareness by practicing Kundalini yoga. However, it was absolutely essential to stop using drugs of all kinds, including marijuana, psychedelics, and even caffeine. We were going to practice this form of intense Kundalini yoga to stimulate the life-force energy called *prana* (described in the Hindu yogic tradition) and to gather and store this intensified, concentrated prana. We would accomplish this through *pranayama* (controlled breathing exercises), yogic postures, movement, and chanting. This was to rewire our nervous system, balance our chakras and endocrine glands, and stimulate dormant brain centers.

I threw myself into it and completely committed myself to this practice. I stopped drinking coffee. I had not been using marijuana or drugs at that time, so it was an easy transition for me. Surprisingly, I ended up with much more energy than I ever anticipated. My thinking was clearer and my energy level was better sustained over longer periods of time so I could study well into the evenings without having to drink coffee. I was very pleased.

Kundalini yoga was brought into the United States by Yogi Bhajan in 1968. He formed 3HO—the Healthy, Happy, Holy Organization—the next year. His mission was to raise consciousness, teach people how to cook and eat vegetarian, and teach Kundalini yoga, meditation, and White Tantric yoga. Yogi Bhajan was a Sikh from northern India. (He died in 2004.) Yogi Bhajan—often referred to as Yogiji by his students—was a spiritual master who was very precocious spiritually from the time he was a child. He studied with many masters in India and became the master of Kundalini yoga. Through the energetic transmission from his teacher, he also emerged as the only living master of White Tantric yoga. He created an eclectic model of spiritual practices by blending some of the basic tenets of the Sikh tradition with the yogic aspects of Kundalini yoga.

I was a very determined student. I did my yoga practice one hour every day after I learned the basics in the on-campus classes, and I felt good physically and mentally. I was on track. Because I felt so good physically the practice was self-reinforcing. After I learned the fundamentals of Kundalini yoga I started meditating on my own. My yoga teacher was not teaching us meditation; he was only teaching the active Kundalini yoga *kriyas* (postures and sets of exercises), breath of fire, and some group chanting. To my later chagrin, I took it upon myself to start meditating without any instruction.

I wanted to know God. I was reading about world-renowned mystics and studying scriptures from a wide variety of spiritual traditions. I decided I knew enough to make up my own mantra and start my own meditation practice. As I focused my energy at my third-eye point (the sixth chakra), the place just above and behind where the eyebrows meet, I mentally affirmed to myself, "I am one with the inner light of God *and I will see.*" I did this for twenty to thirty minutes at a time. After a few weeks of daily meditation, an amazing thing happened. I started experiencing a powerful rush of energy from the base of my spine up into my head. These surges of incredibly powerful energy emerged spontaneously. As I continued to concentrate on my mantra, my whole body went completely rigid. As I became aware of this, try as I might, I could not move my body. Then I would see (my eyes were closed during this time) with my mind's eye an expanding globe of golden radiant light inside my head growing larger and larger as the energy I was bringing up continued to surge more and more powerfully. At a certain point I felt that if I continued to concentrate and focus on this image and affirmation at the third-eye point, the inside of my head was literally going to explode. That was when I cut off the experience and stopped. I realized that my mouth was completely dry and my arms felt like dead fish, heavy and almost lifeless.

From the little that I had read, I realized that I had raised the mighty Kundalini energy. In the yogic tradition, this is called the *Shakti* energy, or the creative life-force energy. It is said to be wrapped around the base of the spine three times, like a serpent. When properly stimulated and unleashed, the serpent uncoils its energy as it travels up and through all the chakras, providing the yogi with enlightenment as this Kundalini energy bathes the brain in its radiance. I had no context for this experience. I asked my yoga teacher about it, but he did not have any personal experience he could reference. After all, he was only twenty-four or twenty-five years old at the most, teaching yoga because he liked it and was getting high from the energy. He did not have enough experience to know anything about the significance of my experience with this Kundalini energy; he just thought I was experiencing a great thing and encouraged me to keep doing it. That was not satisfactory for me, and since nobody else I knew could relate to my energy surges, I started going to bookstores to research my experience.

I went to the Bodhi Tree Bookstore in North Hollywood and looked through all the titles on Kundalini. One author, Gopi Krishna, had written a couple of books on Kundalini. One was simply called *Kundalini*. The other was called *The Biological Basis of Religion and Genius*. Krishna was an Indian civil servant who meditated every day. At the age of thirty-seven, he had quite unexpectedly and suddenly experienced the raising of his Kundalini. Krishna went through months of tortured initiation sickness. This began a very turbulent time for him as he continued raising his Kundalini energy. Eventually, he became transformed into a spiritual genius. His story describes the Indian tradition from which the Kundalini initiatory experience comes and the experiences common to practitioners who start raising the Kundalini energy. I now had a context, and for the next eighteen months I continued this meditation and my Kundalini yoga every day.

There were times when nothing happened except the feeling of pressure at my third-eye point at the forehead. Frequently I would have the surging of Kundalini energy from the base of my spine and often I would have to open my mouth as the pressure in my ears was so intense that it felt like my eardrums were going to explode. I would often hear a roaring sound similar to the sound of a powerful waterfall as this energy surged up. Once I even asked my father (who is an ear specialist, an otologist) about this experience of sound and pressure in my ears. He had never heard of it, nor had he ever had any reports of this phenomenon. This experience of surging energy became increasingly frequent, and I was very excited about this. Every time I elicited the rush of Kundalini up my spine through my chakras, I would experience these incredibly powerful surges of energy. As this continued, I occasionally thought that this was a developmental process. As I continued to strengthen my nervous system through Kundalini yoga, I would be better able to assimilate this increasing voltage as the creative force of Shakti continued to leave its ancient mark on me.

However, about eighteen months after this started, the quality of these experiences began to change. As soon as I put my attention on my third-eye point, I would immediately see vivid apparitions. One particularly scary image was of a very large, dark, threatening manta ray that was coming right at me. As I continued my daily meditation, these apparitions persisted. From the little that I had studied from the Tibetan Buddhist tradition, I first thought that these were simply archetypal images from my own unconscious mind, reflecting personal limitations and fears that I had to overcome. I speculated that this was typical of a spiritual aspirant and that these phenomena were cross-cultural and part of the larger collective unconscious. As I was trying to understand this, these psychic phenomena persisted. They became so disturbing that I finally could not meditate any longer—it was simply too scary.

As I wondered what my next step would be, it dawned on me that Yogi Bhajan was living in the Los Angeles ashram just fifteen miles from my apartment! I called his secretary and made an appointment to meet with him. The year was 1974 and I was twenty-three years old. I had read about spiritual masters but I had never been face-to-face with one. I felt rather overwhelmed and intimidated, but I had no other options.

When I entered the ashram, I was led into a room and there was Yogi Bhajan. He was a very big man, about six-feet-four-inches tall, well over two hundred pounds; he wore a long beard, a large white turban, and many large gemstone rings on his fingers; and he was enfolded by a flowing white robe. He was reclined on a settee. I introduced myself and told him why I was there. I explained that I had been practicing Kundalini yoga and that I had been meditating in a certain way. As I continued to explain, he cut me off in mid-sentence and said, "I know why you are here. I am psychic and I can see and I know exactly what is going on with you. You are no good for anybody right now. You cannot meditate, you cannot do anything." He continued, "Why do you think I came all the way from India to teach Kundalini yoga and meditation? You are dealing with energies that are so powerful they can completely mess up your mind. I will give you a meditation to do. I want you to be sure to cover your head with a natural-fiber cloth when you meditate to insulate your crown chakra. Keep your spine warm by wrapping a blanket around you while you meditate and you will be fine."

In my shock and naïveté, I said, "Are you sure?" My experiences were so strong and so persistent it seemed unbelievable that his just telling me this would make everything OK. I later learned that something always happens on a higher level of healing when you are in the presence of a true spiritual master. This is called *darshan* in the Hindu tradition. What I now know is that at an energetic level, everything was balanced in relationship to this problem simply by being in his energy field. Since that time, I have never had a bad or negative spiritual experience while meditating. I had many other encounters with him over the next ten years, all of which were equally amazing and healing to me.

My interest in the spiritual dimension of life continued to be strong, and upon graduation with a bachelor's degree in humanities, I decided to pursue a master's degree in comparative religions from the graduate program in Social Ethics at the University of Southern California. Between 1973 and 1976, I worked on that degree and went deeper into my understanding of Eastern spiritual traditions. My academic mentor was Dr. Robert Ellwood, an expert in Eastern religions. Consequently, I had the opportunity to do a great deal of independent study in Buddhism, Hinduism, and Taoism, all applicable toward my master's degree. It was a wonderful time for me. My major paper, comparable to a master's thesis for my ethics class, was on the metaethics of Krishnamurti, which gave me an opportunity to deeply explore and immerse myself in Eastern philosophical and spiritual traditions. It was also a way to explore my growing spirituality, since at the time I really did not have any other way than to inquire intellectually and ground myself in a conceptual understanding of what Eastern religions had codified over thousands of years of empirical research.

I intended to teach comparative religions at the college level because I loved the subject matter, but the job market for college instructors is extremely competitive. I ended up being runner-up to a Roman Catholic priest with three master's degrees for the only opening I could find! That was when I realized that with the master's degree I was not going to get a teaching job. Upon inquiry, I learned that it is fairly standard in academia to need a Ph.D. to even be considered for a teaching position.

One of the things I did not like about the Social Ethics Program at USC was that although the professors were very helpful, they had no personal convictions that they were willing to share relating to their own spirituality—*it was all intellectual*. This so turned me off that I decided I would never pursue a Ph.D., at least not in that program. After losing out to the Roman Catholic priest, I reconciled myself to not get a teaching position after all. That being the case, I asked myself, "What else would I enjoy doing?"

I had an organic vegetable garden in my backyard and very much enjoyed that. I was reading the *Mother Earth News, Organic Gardening and Farming*, and many similar books from Rodale Press. It was a pretty romantic time for me, and I had my whole life ahead of me. I had married my college sweetheart, who had earned her RN degree and could get a job almost anywhere.

I started doing research at the University of California at Los Angeles (UCLA) library to find out what kinds of orchard fruits I could grow easily without pesticides. My research revealed that blueberries grow very easily organically and would be a good candidate for starting a U-pick farm. I also discovered that blueberries grow indigenously throughout the Willamette Valley in Oregon. As I was growing weary of the smog and congestion and of having much of my life determined by the traffic patterns of Los Angeles, we decided to move to the Willamette Valley. My wife got a job in Salem, Oregon, and that is where we headed. Because I had a strong romantic vision and we had saved a little bit of money, we were able to acquire a fifteen-acre "farmette" with an old, ramshackle house. The floors were crooked since it did not have much of a foundation, but the property came with its own well, a beautiful pasture, and a gushing creek. It is very close to Falls City, Oregon, a small community about a thirty-five-minute drive from Salem, located up against the Coast Range. I intended to plant and cultivate blueberries after we got settled, but clearly my life was being directed by Spirit. I discovered that at Oregon State University in Corvallis, one of the professors was going on a sabbatical. Because I had extensive academic training in comparative religions and my former mentor, Professor Ellwood, was well known at that time, I replaced the professor on sabbatical. I was to teach undergraduate comparative religions to a class of thirty-three, and I was very excited.

I prepared my lectures and engaged the class with enthusiasm, but it didn't take long for all my romantic visions of university teaching to shatter. My students were taking the class just to get their elective credit. Even though we were using Huston Smith's classic text, *The Religions of Man*, and even though I was presenting the material creatively to make it interesting, only three or four of those thirty-three students showed any real interest. I became disillusioned. By the end of the semester I was quite disinclined to teach any more at the college level. What I did end up doing for the next two years at Oregon State was to teach colloquia, small group seminars in the university's Honor Program. These colloquia were on topics emphasizing human values and the power of love from the viewpoint of different religious and philosophical traditions. They were very intimate, very wonderful. These students chose to take these colloquia, adding them to their regular course load. I discovered that even in these classes, in academia we could only go so deep into the material because the learning context was intellectual. It did not matter whether it was Krishnamurti we were exploring or Erich Fromm, Carlos

Castaneda, Paul Tillich, or the Bhagavad Gita. It all had to be approached intellectually, and I was being impelled to go deeper. At that point I made the decision to pursue another master's degree and leave academia. Within a couple of years, I had set up my private practice in Salem, Oregon.

Once in Oregon, I discovered that Yogi Bhajan was also teaching something called White Tantric yoga. I learned that Yogi Bhajan was the *Mahan Tantric*, the only living master of White Tantric yoga on the planet. His ability had been passed down to him from the previous master (just prior to his death) through spiritual transmission. It was a very secretive, initiatory transfer of power that essentially allowed for only one living master to teach this ancient practice.

The first time I participated in a weekend of White Tantric yoga was in a church hall in Eugene, Oregon. There were close to a hundred people participating. For the first hour to an hour and a half, we did intensive Kundalini yoga as a group to generate a strong flow of pranic energy within each of us. After that, we chanted collectively for an hour to raise the vibrations in the room until Yogi Bhajan discerned (from a distance) that the energy was sufficient for him to enter and conduct the White Tantric yoga. Before actually initiating the process, he lectured for about forty-five minutes about some esoteric aspect of spiritual growth and healing. The topics were always different and quite obtuse. As a consequence, participants ended up in an even deeper altered state than we were already in from the preparatory Kundalini yoga and chanting. I am certain it was intentional on his part as a way to open us all up to greater receptivity to the healing energy that we would soon experience.

The way he organized us spatially was very interesting. He had us seated in long rows of women and men facing each other, one row after another throughout the hall. Each of the same-sex rows ran perpendicular to the dais, and Yogi Bhajan sat above us on the dais facing us. He explained that we were working with the energies of polarity, of yin and yang, the universal female and male energies creating a very large and intense energetic battery. After we all sufficiently raised our energy and our collective vibration through the Kundalini yoga and the chanting, he selected a theme around which the entire weekend was organized. The weekend started on Friday night and ended on Sunday.

Throughout the many years I participated in White Tantric yoga, *every time I went the theme was different*. They included balancing the two hemispheres of the brain, clearing out birth trauma, connecting the heart center to the solar plexus center, and opening up the sixth chakra, or third-eye point. As we faced our partners, Yogi Bhajan directed us to look into our partner's eyes and hold our arms up in a certain position, put both palms against our partner's palms, or assume a variety of different positions. Over the many years that I engaged in this group practice, no single exercise was ever repeated, which always impressed me—it was always new, always unique, and always in the moment. We held these various positions for up to forty-five or sixty minutes. Sometimes we chanted, sometimes we internally meditated, and sometimes we did a certain kind of pranayama, or breathing exercise. While directing us to hold these positions and keep our spines perfectly straight, he would be channeling pranic energy through the field of this energetic battery of male and female polarities, so that the energy moved back and forth— zigzagging, he called it—as it continued to build in intensity. He explained that as this energy field built up (as we were each doing our respective parts in it), he would be filtering our negative karma coming up through our unconscious minds, through the collective field of the group, and then through his *shushumna*, the central subtle energy channel through which the Kundalini energy moves in and out. This way we would never have to consciously experience the release of the trauma that was being lifted up and sifted through the field as the energy kept building until there was that final release. He would verbally direct us to "keep up" until there was a collective release sufficient for him to say stop. When that point came, Yogiji would see a blue aura encompassing the entire collective field that would indicate to him that the energetic clearing we had been working on had released.

There were many times during this group process when the pain was so excruciating from sitting cross-legged and holding my arms up unable to move them that I thought I would collapse. In fact, during the weeklong summer solstice celebrations in the mountains of New Mexico when we practiced White Tantric yoga for five consecutive days with upwards of a thousand participants, the current of collective group healing energy would get so intense by the fifth day that the monitors were literally dragging people off the lines as they were collapsing from the pranic energy overload. Yogiji would exhort us to constantly "keep up," saying that if we moved our spine or let our arms down he would feel pain in *his* spine. It was a very physically stressful and demanding process and, of course, mentally I would go through all kinds of things. And yet, with just a very few exceptions, after each experience I would feel great—completely clear in my consciousness, emotionally very open and physically revitalized. We did not really appreciate or fully understand what was happening energetically at the time. Most of us were twenty-something and just beginning on our path. Yogiji was initiating us and giving us opportunities to personally experience feeling, and sensing tremendous currents of energy through these ancient technologies (as he referred to them).

Psychedelic drugs were still prevalent and immediately accessible in terms of providing instant experiences of altered states of consciousness. However, even as Richard Alpert and Timothy Leary were hoping (during one of their "experiments") to stay high all the time by dosing themselves with LSD on a regular basis for two weeks straight, they and others discovered the disappointment and despair that so-called normal reality provided after the high wore off. Yogiji was providing an alternative with ancient technologies, and though they required some time and effort, they generated more than just powerful altered states of consciousness in the moment. These practices promised ongoing states of heightened awareness that enhanced perception and life experience in general. As a spiritual master, Yogiji provided us with a map and a tradition that had thousands of years of previous experience. I consider myself very fortunate to have shared in this ancient practice.

Yogiji was doing collective energy work as each one of us collaborated in a collective energetic field. What was so wonderful was that we all shared the same intention for being there: to expand our consciousness and become more awake. White Tantric yoga was my favorite experience in the world. I followed Yogiji to Los Angeles, Berkeley, Portland, and Seattle. I even went twice to Espanola, New Mexico, where a thousand mostly young people experienced an entire week of White Tantric yoga in the high desert during summer solstice. It was wild and wonderful as yoga students came from all over the country to share and work in community in addition to participating in the yoga and meditation. On a couple of occasions I experienced absolute bliss, literally crying tears of bliss as energy was moving through me on the last day of the White Tantric yoga. My White Tantric yoga experiences went on well into the late 1980s, at which time Yogi Bhajan developed heart disease.

I remember one weekend in Los Angeles participating in a White Tantric yoga set that was particularly challenging. Afterwards, a small group of men formed a barrier from the rest of us as they escorted Yogiji off the dais to regenerate himself. He looked haggard with dark circles under his eyes, and he almost needed to be dragged off because he was so weak from taking on our toxic energetic residues during the previous energetic clearing. He later told us that we were so "messed up" (in his words) that he felt it was his spiritual obligation to do this ancient practice every single weekend throughout the country to make this healing gift available to as many individuals as possible. He told us the scriptures prescribed that the Mahan Tantric should only do this group healing work once a month at the most, but he said that we were like a patchwork quilt and every time he got together with us he would restitch the pieces that had started to come apart again. In the late 1980s, Yogi Bhajan had to withdraw from actively facilitating White Tantric yoga in person and started doing it from a distance. I had really enjoyed the personal relationship that I had with him, and when he withdrew to facilitating this at the astral level and cut back on his personal appointments, I lost one of the most healing, dynamic, and mysterious ancient practices I would ever participate in.

Throughout the years that I participated in White Tantric yoga I had numerous powerful experiences. I recall sitting in my blue recliner the day following my first White Tantric yoga weekend experience when I spontaneously began having a very clear vision. I saw (internally) a large aluminum culvert pipe with a clog in the very middle of it. As I observed this, quite suddenly the clog blew out one end and I saw energy moving through the pipe in both directions, like heat waves on the beach on a very hot day. I wondered what this had meant, as there was no immediate physical experience that I noticed. However, over the course of the day and into the next, I began to feel different. Soon thereafter, I became inspired to begin writing love poems to all my friends. This was something I had never done before. I soon began to realize that my heart center had opened up in a big way! I was even writing a love poem to my friend Steve. I was somewhat embarrassed to give it to him, but it was agapeic love from the heart. This inspiration went on for many months as I integrated this opening that was unsolicited and unexpected. It was a wonderful gift to have received.

At another White Tantric yoga weekend, I approached Yogiji and asked him for some guidance about dealing with money. It wasn't that I didn't have enough or wanted more of it but that dealing with money seemed complicated. He looked at me intensely and then, as he touched my third-eye point with his index finger, he said, "I want you to grow." Yogiji gave me the experience of *Shaktipat*, a powerful transmission of pranic charge that hit me like a bolt of lightning. I was instantly put into an altered state of consciousness that felt absolutely wonderful! I experienced the feeling of bliss course through my entire body as I floated back to my seat. This was an energetic healing experience of the highest order. The Shaktipat, or Guru's touch, is revered throughout the traditional Eastern guru–disciple relationship. It reassures the student that the teacher has sufficient stores of spiritual power that can be transmitted. Even more so, it is a spiritually transformative experience intended to rewire the subtle energy anatomy of the student to accelerate the student's progress on his or her path. This was the only time Yogiji bestowed this gift upon me, and to this day, I believe it has had profound and lasting healing benefits.

At this time, I also began training in Ericksonian hypnosis. I went to the third international congress in Ericksonian hypnosis in 1983 in Phoenix, Arizona. I trained with Stephen Gilligan, Stephen and Carol Lankton, and Jeffrey Zeig. I spent about three years studying different ways of working with hypnotic language patterns and began integrating this into my private practice. I was very excited about the powerful changes that the unconscious mind was capable of generating. Clients were achieving amazing results in all kinds of problem areas. At a certain point, however, I began to realize that even though I did quite a good job at putting people into trance and helping them achieve a positive therapeutic outcome, I was doing all the work! Of course, clients were using their own unconscious resources and reassociating at the unconscious level to discover their own solutions. In theory, I perfectly understood how the process of hypnotic trance accomplished its astounding results. But the reality was that my clients were lying down with their eyes closed, deeply relaxed in a wonderful altered state of consciousness *enjoying the experience I was facilitating for them*, through very elaborate multiple embedded metaphors and creative storytelling.

It occurred to me that I was actually playing out the "rescuer" role with my clients that was not unlike patterns I had been brought up with, in my family of origin. This may have been different for other therapists with other personality types and personal histories. For me, it did not feel right. In spite of the many therapeutic successes, I realized I needed more interaction. What was missing for me, what felt left out and wanting, was the incorporation of the body in the therapeutic process. I also was reminded just why I became disenchanted with academia—I needed more depth in the therapeutic relationship. I put out an intention to the universe to find another way to celebrate psychotherapy, because hypnosis had become too cerebral, notwithstanding the awareness of replaying old family patterns.

It did not take long for my prayers to be answered. As I was listening to *New Dimensions* on the radio one evening, I heard Dr. Arnold Mindell being interviewed. Mindell was a psychologist, a Jungian analyst, who had been a training analyst at the C. G. Jung Institute in Zurich, Switzerland. He had previously been a physicist who had earned his degree at MIT. Mindell went beyond Jungian psychology and analyzing dreams within the traditional depth psychological model to creating his own methodology that he initially called dreambodywork. It eventually came to be known as process-oriented psychology, or processwork. As he was describing processwork, I became incredibly excited. I absolutely knew that this was the model I needed to learn to take me to the next level. At the end of the interview, however, I became crestfallen when he mentioned that if listeners wanted any further information about processwork he could be contacted in Zurich, Switzerland, where he was living. Unfortunately, my life circumstances at the time did not allow me to take time off and travel to Switzerland to train with him. I did not know what I was going to do, but I just knew that somehow I had to connect with him and his processwork model.

As providence would have it, six weeks later I received a postcard from the Oregon Friends of Jung Society, of which I was a member, letting me know that Mindell and his training staff would soon be arriving at Marylhurst College in Lake Oswego, Oregon. Arny was presenting a weekend introductory workshop followed by a monthlong intensive training, the first such international training ever held in process-oriented psychology. I was ecstatic! By this time I was living in Salem, having moved off the farm. Lake Oswego was only a forty-five-minute drive from my house. I signed up for the weekend introductory workshop, and I loved it. There was authentic movement, people confronting each other in fierce tones, full-body wrestling, and acknowledging both sides of the inner splits that got externalized and acted out. There was excitement and there was Tao. Process was worshipped, and I felt I had arrived at the Promised Land. I signed up for the monthlong intensive training. I put my whole life on hold and jumped into this unknown world of processwork. It turned out to be a major paradigm shift for me, and I never looked back.

For the first two weeks of this intensive residential training experience, I was actually scared. People were doing things that I had never imagined: inner work, relationship work, movement work. People pushed each other, yelled and screamed at each other, moaned and groaned. It was just unbelievable. Yet as terrifying as it was, it was also extremely freeing, as it strongly contrasted with hypnosis, which is basically a very internalized, quiet, in-your-head kind of therapy. Processwork, for the most part, is the opposite. Although it does allow for doing internal work in a very quiet way by visualizing and connecting with your inner parts, most of it is externalized engagement and interaction. I loved it dearly and spent the next ten years of my professional life as a therapist studying with Mindell, attending one-week and two-week-long seminars all over the West Coast. I became a very proficient process worker, integrating Process as the underlying guiding principle for my life in general. I adopted that into my therapeutic practice and for the next ten years facilitated process-oriented therapy groups and established it as the primary model from which I worked with my clients.

It was also in the early 1980s that I began my training in classical shamanism. This happened through a fortuitous meeting with Michelle Stringham, the mother of my son's best friend, Jeremy. As Noah and Jeremy got together after school, Michelle and I would visit. As we talked, she revealed to me that she had been trained as a shaman for many years. Her father was an archaeologist, and from the time when she was very young, she had encountered numerous medicine people and shamans through her father's travels in many different Middle Eastern countries. This was in addition to taking Dr. Michael Harner's core curriculum and becoming a certified teacher for Harner's Foundation for Shamanic Studies. Michelle became my mentor, teaching me the basic journey method, power animal retrievals, soul retrievals, and more. Over the years with Michelle's tutelage, I gained excellent shamanic skills. In fact, it became apparent as I continued my shamanic practice that I had quite a knack for it. My journeys were extremely vivid, and it was easy for me to access the shamanic state of consciousness at will.

As I continued to deepen my experience of shamanic healing techniques, I became curious about energy healing techniques in many different modalities. I was initiated by a Reiki master who enabled me to facilitate Reiki energy channeling. I was using some of the healing meditations taught by Yogi Bhajan to learn how to more effectively connect with the healing energies of Guru Ram Dass to channel healing energy through my hands. It was at this time that I started practicing with friends doing table work. My work was accompanied by an audiotape from the Foundation for Shamanic Studies called "The Women's Chorus for the Singing Journey." I would have that music on while I was going through the different Reiki positions, and what I discovered happening more and more was that I began to have spontaneous visionary experiences of the compassionate spirits working with me while my hands were on somebody. I also discovered that through my ongoing relationship with the spirits, spontaneous extractions of dark energies would occur as I was in this semi-altered state. That was a remarkable and completely surprising experience for me, and I attribute it to the generosity and benevolence of the compassionate spirits themselves—the spirits were doing the healing! It was the compassionate spirits who were removing or extracting the dark energies that I could see with my third eye as I moved from place to place with my hands on the subject's body. I had stayed focused on my intent to learn to channel healing energy for the benefit of my clients. I had no preconceived idea that the healing energy being channeled by me would end up being the compassionate spirits themselves. It was a shocking revelation, and yet it was my undeniable experience.

In shamanism, the compassionate spirits are experienced with as much reality as anything else in our outer world. For the indigenous peoples who embrace this paradigm, everything is imbued with and alive with spirit. The trees, the rocks, and all the animals have their own individual soul and spiritual essence. In fact, the compassionate spirits with whom the shaman connects through the journey method—in the upper world, in this middle world, and in the lower world of nonordinary reality—are conscious beings living in a parallel reality. Usually, the drum or rattle is the percussive vehicle through which we achieve the shamanic state of consciousness. These beings are not regarded as metaphoric creations from our imagination or unconscious mind. They are real, though accessible in nonordinary reality, and we can develop as deep a relationship with them as we feel inclined. The compassionate spirits were very generous to me. They initiated me as a true healer, not simply a therapist, to the continued benefit of my clients. I feel humbled by their generosity and continued interest in helping me to learn more about healing in order to help others heal. To this day my shamanic skills continue to grow and deepen.

During my years studying the great religious traditions, I came to appreciate the richness that different traditions and cultures have to offer. A central theme throughout the many different religions is religious faith, which was always a sticking point for me. It asks the devoted one to believe certain tenets and assumptions as Truth, usually originating from the personal experience of the founder of the religious tradition, be that Jesus or Mohammed or Buddha.

The sticking point for me is not about doubting the originator's experience. But institutionalized religion has become so hierarchical that only the high priests carry sufficient spiritual clout to "know the Truth" from an authoritative position, and others are importuned to trust them as their intermediaries through faith. I always had a problem with this approach to knowing God because it relies on trusting someone else's subjective experience to create a template for your deepest values and guide you spiritually as you navigate through life.

I consider myself lucky to have benefited from the attitudes and ideals of the 1960s and to have direct personal experience as my legacy. My experiences, from raising Kundalini to experiencing bliss in White Tantric yoga to the various times my heart center has opened, have always been deeply personal and undeniable. My rational critical-thinking mind could not doubt or dispute my experience. Faith was a non-issue. Yogiji used to remind us that Kundalini yoga is the yoga of experience. As my knowledge of and experience with shamanic practices deepened, it became my good fortune to be blessed with the gift of direct revelation, a gift that is bestowed upon me by the compassionate spirits. I am very grateful that the compassionate spirits have generously come into my life to serve and assist me so I may help others.

At this point I had incorporated many powerful methodologies into my therapist's tool kit and was enjoying actively working with clients in the process-oriented model. I felt strongly that this was going to be my professional path because I so loved processwork. However, things changed for me dramatically in early 1997, when my colleague Mary Hammond Newman excitedly shared with me what she had learned at a seminar on Thought Field Therapy (TFT).

Thought Field Therapy is the current name for what were initially called the Callahan Techniques. Psychologist Roger Callahan developed these techniques, which involve tapping specific sequences of acupressure points (what he calls algorithms) along the twelve major acupuncture meridians, along with the Governing Vessel and the Central or Conception Vessel, while the client is thinking about or feeling into the specific disturbance that is creating the problem (what is referred to as *attuning*). The disturbance might be anxiety, fear, depression, or a host of other possible disturbances. I was rather skeptical that anything could be as gratifying to me and as fulfilling therapeutically to my clients as processwork. But since Mary and I had been working together at that time and had co-facilitated some process-oriented therapy groups, I decided to take the seminar.

The Thought Field Therapy seminar was given on two weekends, with each weekend covering specific fundamentals and with a one-month period in between for integration. I found the first weekend to be different from anything I had participated in before. I experienced profound changes quickly, as did others. But when that first weekend was over, I was undergoing extreme cognitive dissonance. I was very disturbed. I was grumbling. I was upset. I was angry because there was not yet a place in my paradigm—stretched as it was, I thought—for how people change by simply tapping on acupressure points. In fact, by the time the fourth week rolled around I was not even sure that I was going to participate in the second weekend because it just felt too simple to me.

I do have to qualify this, however, by saying that much of what I had done in terms of my own therapeutic and spiritual development through the years involved the dramatic shifting and restructuring of paradigms. Over the years, my paradigm of what constituted my reality was continually challenged. When I first experienced the opening of my heart center with mescaline, I realized I had undergone a profound paradigm shift. I asked myself how could this incredibly profound experience be happening just from the effects of a chemical? The experience of my heart center opening to unconditional love changed my relationship to life forever. Later, my first experience of the rising of the Kundalini energy was paradigm-shifting for me. I wondered, what the hell was this blasting energy coming up my spine? What exactly did this mean about me as a human being and as a spiritual being?

When I was studying Ericksonian hypnosis I had another period of cognitive dissonance, especially when I learned how Dr. Milton Erickson put people in trance and had them experience profound life-changing healing without their own conscious awareness. How, I wondered, could this man provide such tremendous facilitation to change for individuals who often did not provide him with their personal history or information on their family of origin? The background information was often irrelevant to Erickson—by focusing on presenting symptoms he was able to determine what that person needed. He offered them suggestions in his own ingenious way via their unconscious mind, and people made positive healing changes in their lives immediately. That bothered me for years in terms of the cognitive dissonance that it generated in me. Erickson's approach was in complete contrast to the training that graduate programs provide on the need to conduct a therapeutic interview and obtain a comprehensive history of the family of origin in order to form a clinical assessment.

When I first started learning processwork with Mindell, I went through a life-transforming paradigm shift. I did not fully understand the power of Process, and it was scary to me. I discovered how Process is constantly moving and shifting as the interaction of larger energetic unconscious fields and "dream figures" becomes embodied within individuals and groups. I was learning that there are dreamfields filled with dream figures in every relational context and that archetypes which seek expression reside in the body as a conduit for the living unconscious. These dream figures could be moved, danced, talked to, and drawn. Processwork integrates Taoism, quantum physics, and ancient shamanism. It took years for my paradigm to expand sufficiently to accept and internalize processwork, but it did. Now the same thing was happening again with my introduction to energy psychology methods and Thought Field Therapy. However, I persisted.

I went through the second Thought Field Therapy training session just as Gary Craig, one of Callahan's first students and one of his first trainers, developed his own distillation from TFT, which he calls emotional freedom techniques, or EFT. Craig described EFT as the basic recipe incorporating all twelve major meridian points along with the two midline points. Using EFT means you do not have to muscle test for each of the algorithms as Callahan did for each problem every time. It simplified matters, and I liked that. It smoothed the way and created a much easier relational flow in the therapeutic context. I connected to it right away. When I completed the Thought Field Therapy seminar, I started using EFT with my clients. To my great delight and surprise, *nearly all* of my clients started making significant therapeutic changes very rapidly.

Shortly after the second Thought Field Therapy training session, while I was practicing and integrating this energy psychology paradigm into my professional life, I heard about a new energy psychology model called healing from the body level up (HBLU) that was taught by Dr. Judith Swack. With Mary and some other colleagues, I took that first training in November 1997 from psychologist Helen Tuggy, who had been trained by Swack. In the HBLU model we were introduced to behavioral kinesiology, which is known in the energy psychology world as manual muscle testing. Though I had used muscle testing in the early 1980s with a procedure I developed called the Life Pattern Analysis (which also incorporated the use of Bach flower essences), I eventually moved on to other interests and abandoned the muscle testing. Swack introduced us to the concept of energetic boundaries as well as some energy psychology interventions such as the Tapas acupressure technique (TAT), which was developed by licensed acupuncturist Elizabeth (Tapas) Fleming, frontal occipital holding (F/O holding), which she had learned from Three In One Concepts, and other energy psychology interventions she had learned from other trainers.

Perhaps the most interesting aspect of Swack's trainings was her way of addressing supernatural phenomena, which I had encountered for many years prior through my shamanic work. Swack's assessment of supernatural interference is that it can be absorbed into the energy field. In the shamanic model, supernatural intrusions must be addressed through the journey method and the merging with a helping spirit in the shamanic state of consciousness. This ancient and time-tested method allows the shaman, in partnership with the helping spirits, to identify in nonordinary reality what the entities or intrusions are. The shaman then uses various means, often involving a formal extraction process, to rid the body of these intrusions or possessions. Swack teaches that there are a variety of ways to release supernatural interference using energy psychology strategies. She identifies the interference via manual muscle testing and then uses energy psychology interventions to release much of the supernatural phenomena.

For many years prior when I was doing energy-healing table work, I would often have the experience of "seeing" and then feeling dark energy forms when I had my hands over people as I was channeling healing energy at different places in their body. Often, I would see and perceive these dark energies as a serpent or a large, revolting, slug-like creature. Sometimes these energies would easily lift out and be removed with the assistance of my helping spirits. Other times they would be quite resistant and would actually generate a great deal of bad energetic agitation or intense negative emotional response from the client as the energy that I was channeling would interact with that dark energy form.

Based on my personal experience, I feel strongly that if practitioners are going to be confronting dark energy intrusions, they need to be deeply grounded in a spiritual tradition such as core shamanism. Throughout my shamanic training, it has been impressed upon me that I need to have with me a power animal or a number of guardian spirits that will protect me from these dark energy forms while I work with clients shamanically. This very important principle (an imperative, really) has been established so there is always the support of a protective spiritual ally to ensure safety when encountering dark forces. For me, visualizing healing light or connecting to God in the abstract is not the same as having perceived it in personal experience, which is the case in my shamanic practice.

I believe that perceiving this healing light or connecting to compassionate spirits is a skill that anyone can learn—and that therapists *should* learn. As therapists make these connections, they energetically transform what they learn from the compassionate spirits into internalized spiritual resources and inner reference points. Once a therapist has cultivated these resources—which contain great spiritual power whether they are compassionate spirits, Jesus, or the nurturing light of the Divine Feminine—they are available whenever the therapist needs them to assist a client. The important point is that the practitioner is connected to Spirit in his or her own personal way.

Additionally, I have learned from the compassionate spirits that it is absolutely essential to establish a sacred space prior to starting any kind of group training or seminar session, or even before beginning work with a client in my office (see chapter 17, "Creating a Sacred Space"). I always start a therapy session or a group training process by getting quiet and taking a moment to connect with my spiritual resources. I ask my client or the participants to do the same in their own way. This ensures spiritual support and safety, which are essential when dealing with powerful and opportunistic dark energy forms.

One of the most important things I learned from processwork is that all parts must be honored. If you overlook one part, whether it is within yourself, within a family system, or within a spiritual paradigm, it eventually becomes what Mindell calls a secondary process that can dangerously blindside you when you least expect it. The spiritual energies we are now working with are quite real and very powerful. They must be acknowledged as part of the human equation.

When I was first learning about shamanic practices, I became curious about acquiring new spiritual teachers or helping spirits. It became evident to me that one way to do this was to set an intention and, with the guidance of my power animal or guardian spirit, travel to the upper-world realm where the souls of the great spiritual teachers and masters reside. One day I set an intention to connect with the healing spirit of Jesus. I have read a great deal about the historical Jesus and have read and studied the New Testament. However, since I was brought up Jewish, Jesus was never emphasized as a meaningful teacher for me. I intended to learn about and connect with the healing spirit of

Jesus. My guardian spirit took me to the upper-world realm, which is the place where I discovered Jesus exists in nonordinary reality. This celestial realm is infused with radiant pink, the color of rose quartz.

I first saw an enormous olive tree. It was a very dark, rich brown with a wide girth. Next to it stood this radiant figure of Jesus. I could not see his face. I can never see his face, but I perceive a very clear image of the rest of him in white robes with a rose quartz radiance around him.

He greeted me, telling me that he was happy to see me. He had been expecting me, and we walked off together. As we chatted I told him why I was there and what I wanted to learn as well as what I wanted to learn about him. I asked if there was anything that he could teach me, if he could do any healing work on me, and if he could help me in my healing work and therapy practice with clients. One of the first things he did was have me lie down on my stomach (in nonordinary reality). I remember that with his right thumbnail, he went along my spine as if he were cutting it open, and as he made a cut all along the length of my spine I saw tiny moths fly out and turn to dust. Then he put his hands over my kidneys (which were, at that time, very depleted from a great deal of stress and overwork) and held them there for about one minute. I could feel heat in my real physical body! It was a rather remarkable experience. When we were done with that personal healing to my physical body, he gave me a prayer to recite. Anytime I did healing work with a client or put my hands over a client to call upon spiritual support, I should say this prayer to myself and always remember that it is his energy that is coming through me. He is doing the healing—I should never presume that I am doing the healing. So I have recited this prayer to myself hundreds of times, and it has worked beautifully over the years. In fact, my relationship with this healing spirit of Jesus has deepened substantially as I have continued to call on him. I often get impressions of him, sensing him near me with his loving energy of what he refers to as "fierce compassion" coming through me during therapy sessions.

This interior reference point has become a source of spiritual strength for me. In any challenging healing work that involves dark energy intrusions, I can always rely upon this powerful, healing, benevolent, protective energy in me and around me. I know without a shadow of a doubt that this energy will facilitate the healing work and keep me safe (see case history 16, "Validating Empirically the Existence of Past Lives").

Mary, Nancy, and I continued to meet regularly to integrate principles of energy psychology into our practice. We worked on developing our own model for addressing and integrating energy psychology methods into the models and methodologies that we had already learned. We discovered that something wonderful was beginning to emerge from the wealth of clinical experience that we each brought into our collective alchemical cauldron.

As Mary, Nancy, and I continued collaborating and sharing our insights and experiences, we each began integrating energy psychology methods into our practices. We met once or twice a week from 1997 to 1999, and we soon developed our own adaptation of a more integrated energy psychology methodology. We developed an entirely new model that emerged as Dynamic Energetic Healing®. We synthesized and applied disparate elements from a variety of energy psychology models we studied, including those of Judith Swack, Asha Clinton, Tapas Fleming, and Gary Craig. Onto these, we overlaid many different principles and techniques from our own therapeutic backgrounds. Mary and I have continued to integrate new applications of Dynamic Energetic Healing® methods. Nancy has become more interested in pursuing primal rhythms and the wisdom of indigenous peoples; she is going deeply into learning a model called Ta Ke Ti Na. Mary and I both continue to practice Dynamic Energetic Healing®, but our spiritual emphases are different. Mary now has a strong connection with the Divine Mother as her primary spiritual resource and has started her own ministry by the same name.

So there it is—an abbreviated account of the personal experiences that led me to develop Dynamic Energetic Healing®. As you read through this book, I ask that you consider how Dynamic Energetic Healing® fits with your understanding of how healing occurs. You may be able to incorporate some of these principles and practices into the therapeutic model that you currently work with to complement and accelerate your own healing work.

CHAPTER

2

ANTECEDENTS OF DYNAMIC ENERGETIC HEALING®

P sychotherapy has gone through many transformations since its introduction by Sigmund Freud at the turn of the twentieth century. Freud's
theories recognized—and subsequent developers have acknowledged and
expanded on these theories—that when you experience trauma, something
happens to your psyche or your mind that disrupts normal functioning,
including the processing of thoughts and feelings. Freud identified numerous
defense mechanisms such as dissociation, rationalization, repression, and
others. These he identified as unconscious adaptive strategies that (unknown
to our rational conscious awareness) the psyche creates in order for the individual to better survive and cope with the pain that accompanies a traumatic
experience. He believed that through free association generated through the
psychoanalytic process within the relational field between the psychoanalyst
and the patient, repressed or dissociated memories could be brought to
awareness and healing would result.

It is not my intention to trace the history of psychotherapy in detail, but
it is important to review some of the different therapeutic orientations from
which Dynamic Energetic Healing® has evolved. Some of these theories
and treatment models are incorporated into Dynamic Energetic Healing®;
others are simply not relevant. Dynamic Energetic Healing® has developed
as an alternative to these sometimes helpful, but ultimately imperfect,
approaches.

Cognitive Therapy

I believe that the goal of good psychotherapy is to facilitate healing so clients can experience a state of homeostasis, which is also called a state of balance, of well-being, and of wholeness. Regardless of the term used, therapists understand this state to be different from the state achieved simply by eliminating the symptoms that are often the consequence of a traumatic incident. Cognitive therapy is based on the presupposition that what we are thinking is the cause of our problems. If we can identify the erroneous thinking patterns, then we can correct them through awareness, reeducation, and cognitive modification. The optimal outcome is thus to create a more positive outlook for the client and to reduce and eliminate neuroses, as Freud was fond of saying.

Body-Centered Therapies

These therapies, such as hakomi, presuppose that in inhospitable environments or traumatic situations, individuals armor themselves physically. Again, this is an unconscious process, and the trauma and the closing off of the individual from the traumatic experience creates armoring in the musculature. Thus, trapped and repressed emotions end up in the physical body. Many body-centered models take this a step further by saying that trauma is trapped in the very cells in the body. With different kinds of interventions, ranging from gentle movement and palpation to intense Rolfing and deep-tissue massage, it is claimed that these repressed emotions can be released, allowing the client to be brought back to a state of balance.

Transactional Analysis

The transactional analysis model was developed by psychiatrist Eric Berne. He introduced his model in 1958, identifying what he called the three primary ego states: parent, adult, and child. He discovered that unlike Freud's concepts of id, ego, and superego, his ego states were more readily *experienced* by people and were observable patterns of behavior and feeling (i.e., phenomenological) that became quite apparent in social "transactions," the basic interactions between individuals. Whereas Freud's theories discuss unobservable, theoretical concepts, Berne's three ego states can be confirmed through observable behaviors. His approach to therapy was also radically different from Freud's. While Freud and most other psychotherapists focused primarily on asking patients about themselves through extensive interviews, Berne believed that therapists could learn what a patient's main problem was by carefully observing what the individual communicated. This was not just through words—body language and facial expressions were also part of the unfolding ego states. Instead of just asking questions, Berne's model emphasized the transactions that occurred between the patient and other individuals, particularly in groups.

Through various techniques (such as voice dialoguing and externalizing ego states and acting them out), awareness can emerge with the help and facilitation of the therapist. As transactional analysis increases our awareness, we can consciously integrate what previously were essentially autonomous inner parts that were out of our conscious control.

Gestalt Therapy

The German word *Gestalt* essentially means "whole form." Its principal developer, German-born psychiatrist Fritz Perls, challenged the tenets of psychoanalysis and developed a therapeutic approach that was a radical departure from the traditional psychoanalytic model developed by Freud.

Freud's imperative was to interpret the patient's unconscious processes, which Perls believed would intellectualize the patients. Perls asserted that the intellectualized orientation of the analyst–patient relationship limits the potential of the patient's ability to heal.

In contrast, Perls's interest was in helping patients discover new understanding and meaning by eliciting their experiential awareness. His approach focused on patients' personal experience in the present moment rather than on interpreting recollections and garnering insights mined from personal history. Perls believed that this empowered patients by engaging them much more actively in their own healing and growth and by creating a more equal and collaborative relationship between therapist and patient.

In addition to the importance of here-and-now awareness, the other primary idea of Gestalt theory is that we can only truly know ourselves in relational contexts. This puts the emphasis on what is occurring in the interactive field in the present moment. As a result, the Gestalt approach places a great deal of attention on physical and sensory-based awareness in order to help patients become more real and authentic. This transition also helps patients become more aware of what they are feeling emotionally.

Perls and his wife (also a Gestalt therapist) moved to New York after World War II and began training the first generation of Gestalt therapists in the early 1950s.

Hypnotherapy

Hypnosis, or hypnotherapy, assumes that the unconscious mind holds the key to healing and that the hypnotherapist can assist clients to go into a state of trance by facilitating relaxation. This trance state is one of inner attentional absorption where the conscious, rational, critical mind is temporarily suspended. Through a variety of hypnotic interventions ranging from reframing, storytelling, multiple embedded metaphor, and direct suggestion, the unconscious mind reassociates while the individual is in this state of trance. With the conscious, rational mind partially out of the way and no longer intruding and questioning every new idea offered, the suggestions proffered by the hypnotherapist can facilitate profound change at the unconscious level without the conscious involvement of the client.

Self Psychology

Kohut's model on self psychology is based on the idea of damaged parental relationships. Taking an object-relations position, he believes that an individual needs to be reparented over a period of time so the basic ingredients for wellness and maturity can evolve within the therapist–client relationship. These basic ingredients include positive qualities such as self-confidence, self-esteem, and self-acceptance in the eyes of another. Kohut then includes dealing with the therapist as a positive parent figure with positive transference onto that therapist, so that over time, the therapist becomes the surrogate (and archetypal) good mother and good father figure. Eventually, the client feels sufficiently supported, acknowledged, and affirmed to essentially graduate from the therapy process once the developmental reparenting process has occurred. Wholeness and balance within the personality results when the client has matured to the appropriate developmental level.

Psychodynamic Therapy

Psychodynamic therapy is probably the most widely recognized form of psychotherapy. Family-of-origin influences are paramount, with a great deal of emphasis laid on how we are like our parents in so many ways. While nobody can credibly dispute the impact on children of modeling by their parents, people are more than their families and their history. The discussion of genograms as the depiction of your extended family through time, along with the respective influences of each family member in your family tree, contribute to make you the person you are today. More than anything else, psychodynamic therapy attempts to expand our frame of reference when we ask "Who am I?" and "Why do I behave and react in these ways?" As a foundation for a person's growing self-awareness as they continue to individuate into young adulthood and autonomy from their family of origin, psychodynamic therapy can often be an important starting point on their healing journey. This therapy model helps us to better appreciate how we are similar to our parents and how we are not. Successful outcomes for your journey on the path of personal transformation can be stymied when you blame your mother or father relentlessly for difficult developmental challenges or pattern-clearing impasses. Spending years and years with a psychodynamic therapist may be comforting to some (recall Kohut's model in which the therapist becomes the positive transference object of the good mother or good father). However, this may become a psychological labyrinth as the needy client forever circumambulates overly familiar territory, stuck in their familiar pondering and the regurgitation of their family-of-origin issues.

Process-Oriented Psychology

Mindell's process-oriented psychology, or processwork model, has a more complicated view of how individuals come to a place of wholeness. Processwork integrates a variety of schools of thought, including quantum physics, Jungian psychology, shamanic principles, classical Taoism, and modern communication theory. Primary to the processwork model is that there is always a deeper stream of Process to connect to (which Mindell has integrated from traditional Taoist thought). To allow us to flow with nature rather than resist or control other people and events in our lives, Mindell teaches through experiential process, often in large groups, that spontaneity, integrity, honesty, and presence provide us with awareness of what he calls the dreamingbody.

When you become sufficiently trained to be aware of your thoughts, feelings, bodily sensations, inner pictures, and inner voices, these perceptual channels can be worked with and "unwound" so you become aware of how you are always dreaming. You become aware of how the dreaming process is always inside you (as well as outside you), always unfolding, blocked only by your judgments and illusions that you are in control. When you become aware of your dreamingbody experience, you learn to accept yourself more fully, become more humble, and allow repressed parts of yourself to emerge and develop. As this occurs, you become more aware of yourself in relation to the outer environment and become a multidimensional being.

Much of processwork involves identifying the inner blocks to your personal freedom, such as the perennial inner-critic figure who is often a judgmental parent figure that you have unconsciously internalized. This inner-critic figure is often the symbol for consensus-reality conformity that further limits your personal freedom to be fully living the dreamingbody.

Much of processwork is relationship work, since it is often in the context of the other that we lose ourselves and compromise our deepest values in the name of peace and harmony. The paradox becomes evident as we compromise ourselves in order to preserve outer harmony in our relationships—we end up internally split as the conflict we avoided on the outer level manifests itself as disharmony on the inner level. Various chronic symptoms may then manifest from this internal conflict. These symptoms may be psychological, such as depression and anxiety, or physical, such as ulcers, migraines, cancer, fatigue and exhaustion, and musculoskeletal disorders. Processwork becomes our life's work as we strive with increasing awareness for more personal freedom from both the outer pressures to conform and our psyche's inner programs and dream figures that tyrannize us if we allow them to.

Processwork also teaches process-oriented meditation or inner work. This is a way to work on relationship problems, bothersome symptoms, or disturbing dreams by oneself and, in essence, to unfold the process waiting to happen. Process is always ready to burst forth into life and awareness, so taking the time to do innerwork brings rich rewards. It allows us to bring into the light what was previously unconscious (due to a lack of awareness); it also frees us to challenge our natural tendency to stay stuck at our growing edge.

Energy Psychology

This relatively new and innovative form of psychotherapy is still considered by some to be experimental because it has not been used by professionals long enough to have a solid, well-traveled longitudinal research base. The operating assumptions of energy psychology affirm that change happens at the energetic level and that the interventions used target the client's energy body rather than the thinking process or the unconscious mind.

The techniques used in applied kinesiology, behavioral kinesiology, and Thought Field Therapy evolved to acknowledge that tapping, holding, and lightly pressing specific acupressure points on one of the twelve major acupuncture meridians will stimulate the flow of chi that circulates throughout the body as well as outside of the body. As clients focus their attention on a specific disturbance, whether a thinking pattern or an emotion, they tap on specific acupressure points that have been correlated to specific emotional states or specific emotions. This stimulates the chi and creates the chi field that balances the energy field which was creating and perpetuating the distressing thought or disturbing emotional state. The change happens very quickly—often instantaneously. The therapist witnesses extreme emotional states flattening out to calm, usually in the course of just minutes.

The Chinese have been intentionally working with chi for over five thousand years! They have identified and mapped out these pathways of energy (the meridians) with specific points related to specific organs, diseases, and states of disharmony. It has only been since President Nixon's trip to China in the 1970s that the United States has become open to and interested in exploring and considering this ancient therapy.

The primary operative assumption of energy psychology is that human beings are infused with and circulating a kind of energy often referred to as the vital life force. There have been various names for this vital life force throughout history and within many different spiritual traditions. This energy is called *prana* in the practice of yoga, *chi* in Chinese medicine, *ki* in the Korean martial-arts traditions, *power* in the shamanic tradition, and the Holy Spirit in the Christian tradition. In spiritual literature, cross-culturally and throughout history, this vital life force has different names that are synonyms for the same thing. To date, Western science has not been able to prove the existence of this vital life force using its scientific method. But the fact that Blue Cross insurance now covers acupuncture indicates that even this conservative, Western science-based organization acknowledges that the positive therapeutic outcomes that result from using chi to enhance human functioning are measurable using the traditional Western scientific method.

The Hindu yogic tradition also identifies energy centers called *chakras*, which are defined as spinning wheels of energy found throughout the body—from the top of the head down to the base of the spine. Traditionally, the practice of yoga has been to balance the body and the "monkey mind" by physical *asanas*, mantra, and meditation that will subsequently balance the energy fields of the seven major chakras. This is done by balancing the prana circulating in each of these chakra centers, similar to the Chinese tradition of balancing chi energy flow via the meridian pathways of energy. When the energy shifts, homeostasis in the whole person occurs, thus balancing the energy polarities within the individual. In Chinese medicine this is known as the balance of yin and yang, the feminine and the masculine energies.

What follows is a brief summary of the origins and development of energy psychology.

Applied Kinesiology. In the mid-1960s, Detroit chiropractor George Goodheart Jr. established a new field he called applied kinesiology. This is a method for evaluating various bodily interrelationships using manual muscle testing (MMT). Through work with his patients and his ongoing curiosity, Goodheart developed the applied kinesiology technique of origin and insertion treatment for muscles. He introduced this discipline at the 1964 charter meeting of the American Chiropractic Association. Applied kinesiology was born and given legitimate professional sanction.

As Goodheart continued to develop applied kinesiology, he began making correlations not only between muscles and specific organs but between various muscles and their associated neurolymphatic reflexes in other areas of the body.

In 1966, Goodheart began studying *The Meridians of Acupuncture*, written by British medical researcher Felix Mann.

As a substitute for needles, Goodheart explored and discovered the effectiveness of applying pressure to acupoints as well as percussing or tapping on the points. While the interconnection of glands, organs, and meridians was well known to acupuncture, by bringing his knowledge of muscle testing to the arena, Goodheart and his colleagues discovered a connection between the various muscles and the meridian pathways. (Gallo 1999, 59)

Touch for Health. Numerous derivatives have emerged from Goodheart's applied kinesiology. In the mid-1970s, John Thie, a chiropractor who worked with Goodheart closely, added his own understandings to applied kinesiology and called the result Touch for Health. He developed the Touch for Health approach for a wide audience so practitioners other than licensed doctors could learn procedures to balance and strengthen muscles. Throughout this book, I occasionally refer to an intervention as a balance. This language comes from Thie, as the following quote reveals:

A muscle which tests weak indicates some blockage or constriction in the energy flow. The process we use to unblock the energy and restore balance to the system is called balancing. There is no such thing as a Touch for Health treatment. Instead, no matter what the person has in the way of symptoms, we balance the body energies . . . (Gallo 1999, 62)

Thie disseminated a great deal of information about the meridians and how to use them in relation to MMT. He also identifies and teaches yet another way to strengthen and establish better energetic balance:

The flow of energy through a meridian may be stimulated by using the hands to trace the meridian line in the proper direction on the surface of the body. . . . Using the flat of the hand . . . it is only necessary to come within 2 inches of the meridian, either off to the side or even above the skin and over clothing, for it to be effective. (Gallo 1999, 63)

Behavioral Kinesiology. An important development in the evolution of applied kinesiology that relates to psychological issues is John Diamond's behavioral kinesiology. Diamond, an Australian psychiatrist, began studying applied kinesiology in the 1970s. In 1979, he began to integrate a number of different models. These included aspects of

psychiatry, psychosomatic medicine, kinesiology, preventative medicine, and humanities. . . . Diamond's earlier approach involved the use of affirmations, the thymus thump, homing thoughts, imagery, and elements of the Alexander Method to balance life energy or Chi after a meridian imbalance was detected through kinesiological tests. . . . Diamond's work represents the first attempt to integrate Applied Kinesiology and psychotherapy, especially key elements of psychoanalysis. (Gallo 1999, 68)

Thought Field Therapy. In 1979, clinical psychologist Roger J. Callahan began studying applied kinesiology with John Diamond. As Callahan's interest grew, he attended the 100-hour applied kinesiology course and became certified by the International College of Applied Kinesiology. Soon afterwards, he developed what was perhaps the first widespread energy psychology methodology. This was referred to initially as the Callahan Techniques and has been known more recently as Thought Field Therapy (TFT). Thought Field Therapy uses various diagnostic procedures, including manual muscle testing, to

> determine meridian imbalance combined with percussing at specific acupoints in a prescribed sequence in order to treat an array of psychological problems. Percussing along with affirmations is also used to treat what Callahan refers to as psychological reversal as well as some negative affects such as anger and guilt. (Gallo 1999, 69)

Thus, energy psychology methods have evolved from a specific lineage and are quite recent additions to the current collection of psychotherapy applications. I am tremendously indebted to these pioneers for their paradigm-challenging innovations in the field of energy psychology. Because these constantly changing techniques are less than twenty-five years old, they are frequently referred to as being innovative and experimental. In the context of Western psychotherapy, this judgment reflects our rationalistic and scientistic predilection for establishing an epistemology of mind and psyche. But this is Western bias—much of what forms the foundation of energy psychology has been known for thousands of years. Some scientists are trying to bridge this gap between Western rationalism and Eastern energy-based applications.

Energy psychology theorists explain what happens in energy psychology interventions with references to quantum physics. Drs. Gary Schwartz, Ph.D., and Linda Russek, Ph.D., are doing an excellent job explaining what happens at the energetic level through the language of quantum physics (1999). Thoughts are actually waves of energy, and each thought or wave has its own specific frequency. These frequencies can be measured through electronic instrumentation, specifically an electroencephalograph (EEG). Sensors (electrodes) that are attached to the scalp are sensitive enough to pick up brainwave activity, which falls into four main categories: beta, alpha, theta, and delta. The four categories of brainwave activities have different oscillation frequencies.

Beta waves oscillate between 14 and 30 times per second (Hz). This state is associated with normal, waking consciousness. It is usually externally oriented, taking in information through the senses and engaging the intellect. It is present with stressful emotions such as anger, panic, and worry. Alpha waves oscillate between nine and thirteen times per second. Typically, the alpha state is a more relaxed, calm, and meditative state of consciousness. It is often referred to as inwardly tranquil and associated with mind–body integration. Theta waves are found in deep relaxation and oscillate between four and eight times per second. They are associated with a state of consciousness often found in advanced meditators and are present in bursts of creativity and inspiration, dreams, and vivid mental imagery. Delta waves are the slowest, oscillating between 1 and 3 Hz. A person experiencing delta-wave activity is in a deep dreamless or trance state sometimes referred to as somnambulism (Fuentes 2000).

Every day of your life, your brain-wave activity is constantly changing in response to outer and internal stimulation. As your brain-wave activity shifts, so too does your state of consciousness. Dynamic Energetic Healing® provides a context for psychotherapy that becomes an alchemical cauldron wherein states of consciousness amenable to deep healing occur. As I explain in chapter 13, "Energetic Origins from a Hypnotic Perspective," the variety of stimuli and interactions that occur in a typical session facilitate movement toward the alpha and theta states of consciousness. As the rational mind operating at the beta frequency becomes less dominating, the doorway opens for dramatic and rapid psychotherapeutic change to occur.

Spirit-based and indigenous traditions, including core shamanism, say that everything has a vital energy, or soul, and everything is filled with spirit. So from a religio-spiritual point of view, energy is spirit, and spirit can be equated to life-force energy. But according to physics, energy is an electromagnetic field that takes on different forms or structures—liquid, gaseous, or solid. Schwartz and Russek acknowledge that "Energy is one of the most mundane yet mysterious concepts in modern physics." They elaborate on the nature of energy as follows:

> Though the measurement of energy may be defined precisely, the interpretation of energy is abstract and is difficult to comprehend (even by seasoned physicists). The inherent difficulty in understanding energy cannot be understated. The abstract nature of energy may be one reason why the concept of energy, though appreciated by certain early scholars of psychology and medicine (e.g.,

Freud and Jung), has yet to make its way into the mainstream of modern psychology, neuroscience, and medicine. (Schwartz and Russek 1999, 234–5)

From a psychological point of view, energy is made up of fields of consciousness (i.e., information) that include thoughts and feelings. As we stimulate a particular chakra or meridian point while focusing on a disturbing thought or feeling state, a balancing action takes place. The presupposition is that there is no separation between what we are thinking, what we are feeling, and the basic essence or life force that is part of everything. Once again, Schwartz and Russek are helpful in articulating (and possibly clarifying) these abstract concepts based on their physics research:

> In summary, we can think of information as a form or structure of a system—and energy as the force or function that moves the system and enables it to emerge and evolve. In living systems, information and energy typically go hand-in-hand—energy contains information, and information is expressed through energy. Not only does energy convey information, in a deep sense energy does the work of information. It follows that organized energy both expresses and actualizes information. (Schwartz and Russek 1999, 236)

What strikes me as just fascinating is that even though Western science (to date) has been unable to prove the existence of this vital life force using its scientific method, ongoing research in quantum physics might well be the scientific discipline that bridges this gap.

Clearly, Western psychology has gone through many evolutions since its inception with Freud. Therapists still tend to focus on psychodynamic therapy with an emphasis on the influence of the family of origin, and it is certainly valuable to know how you are perpetuating the patterns of behavior and emotional expression of one or both of your parents. Most of us do carry these familial patterns, albeit unconsciously, which can be empowering or extremely destructive. Individuals who truly desire to grow beyond their family patterns enter some kind of therapy wherein these repetition compulsions, as Freud called them, can be identified and discarded if they are not helpful. What is truly sad is the many people desperately seeking help who fall prey to the consensus-reality trance generated by the dominant culture at large. Many end up becoming addicted to the drugs their well-meaning family doctors prescribe for them, such as the omnipresent antidepressants that continue to grow in popularity among the masses. Every year these powerful brain-chemistry modifiers become more widely prescribed.

In Dynamic Energetic Healing®, we stay focused and intentional with our thoughts and feeling states while applying these ancient healing techniques and integrating them into a Western psychological framework that has always had its limitations. After all, it may be helpful to have awareness of a trauma from years ago, but talking about it does not always effectively release what has been imprinted and absorbed at the various levels of a human being. Energy psychology methods are incredibly effective at quickly, and often permanently, releasing old traumatic symptomatology.

There are many permutations and innovations within the emerging field of energy psychology. Each variation is making its own contribution. As mentioned previously, TFT and EFT use tapping on specific points of the twelve major meridians and the two midline channels while focusing on a problem state. The Tapas acupressure technique (TAT) combines gentle pressure on the bladder meridian points near the bridge of the nose, gentle pressure on the occipital area at the back of the head, and stimulation of the sixth chakra point to effect a change while the client focuses on a problem. Fred Gallo, in his evolving energy diagnostic and treatment methods (EDxTM) model, uses manual muscle testing along with the meridian therapies to effect a positive outcome. Asha Clinton's seemorg matrix work model has the client stimulate the chakras by tapping or holding them while focusing on the matrices of limiting core beliefs. Judith Swack's approach combines neurolinguistic programming, manual muscle testing, Three In One Concepts Inc., and various meridian therapies with her background in rigorous research methodologies. Dynamic Energetic Healing® has synthesized a variety of energy psychology strategies, and it includes the principles of core shamanic and process-oriented psychology. Armed with this awareness, and with my deeply held belief that the body does not lie, I am excited to be on the crest of this sweeping wave of change. Ultimately, Dynamic Energetic Healing® trusts Process as our guide as we navigate the soul's journey within the Great Mystery.

3

MY ROLE WITHIN THE CONTEXT OF DYNAMIC ENERGETIC HEALING®

When clients see me for psychotherapy, their presenting problems run the entire gamut of human experience. It is essential for me to be congruent with my clients about who I am, what my deepest values are, and what role I am to play in the psychotherapeutic context with them.

There are many therapeutic orientations within the field of psychology. Each psychological-change model is based on certain assumptions that form a theory for how positive therapeutic change occurs. It is these presuppositions that determine the role of the therapist. Cognitive-based therapists, for example, are not so interested in helping their clients identify and express deep affective states that have been repressed. Instead, the cognitive-based therapist operates through a lens that focuses on what the client is thinking and how the therapist can help the client to think more constructively.

My training as a psychotherapist includes almost all psychotherapeutic models except the pharmacological model. I also have over twenty years experience practicing and teaching Kundalini yoga, meditation, and core shamanism, and seventeen years practicing process-oriented psychology (processwork). Much of my Dynamic Energetic Healing® grows out of my training in processwork.

Mindell was a physicist before he became a training analyst at the C. G. Jung Institute. From his background in physics and Jungian psychology, I learned about fields of energy (particles and waves) from a physics perspective and the collective unconscious from a Jungian perspective. Mindell's wonderful synthesis of these two disciplines provided me with enormous insight. I learned that individuals are always being affected by larger collective fields of energy and that larger collective fields are always being affected by the individual. I also came to realize that how you express your experience in words is metaphoric at best and solely dependent on your frame of reference within a relational context.

With every client, I emit a positive attitude of healing. My energy field holds a number of core beliefs, including the following:

1. Positive change is possible and likely.
2. Clients will achieve a positive therapeutic outcome.
3. Clients will experience personal healing on many levels.
4. Dynamic Energetic Healing® strategies will awaken the client's soul.
5. I am personifying a new paradigm for healing (for most new clients) that creates a state of internal confusion in clients. This tends to destabilize the limiting approach they previously had for dealing with their problems, which creates new possibilities they had previously not considered.

First and foremost, I am a process-oriented therapist. This has enormous ramifications for *how things occur* within the therapeutic relational context. As a process-oriented therapist, I hold a unified field of attention. This unified field incorporates multilevel awareness. Within this multilevel awareness I occupy multiple roles, constantly switching back and forth. I am an active listener, paying attention to the content of what clients are telling me and to *how* they communicate their message. As a supportive and active listener, I establish and build rapport with my clients. I am aware of their language patterns, and I notice how they perceive their experience as human beings in relationship. I complete the communication feedback loop so clients are reassured that what they are telling me is acknowledged and understood.

There are times when I work with my clients that I feel their energetic release through my own body as a deep, physical exhalation of breath. Because I have trained myself to be sensitive to energy, I often experience this energetic release on a physical level, even when my clients do not notice anything. It is important to verbalize my experience to my clients, as my role in that moment becomes a modeler of energetic and more subtle extrasensory experiences. As balance at the energetic level occurs, the manual muscle testing will confirm for clients that blocked energy was released. It is important for me to go with my experience of the energetic releases each time this happens and to verbalize to clients as a way to help them become more sensitive to their energy body.

I teach and encourage my clients to trust their internal perceptions. As a process-oriented therapist, I am the lead partner in a team that is co-creating experience for change. As I describe and reflect back to my clients my ongoing energetic experiences, they are being taught and encouraged to trust their internal perceptions *within the context of relationship*. Eventually, clients begin to understand how important this is to their personal development, and they come to rely on their internal perceptions to cultivate their own second attention. When clients learn to trust themselves, they start on a path of self-empowerment and begin to develop self-appreciation and self-love. I become the advocate for the part of my clients that has been disavowed through lack of support by their family of origin and the culture at large.

The dominant cultural paradigm of this century has a strong orientation toward valuing external reality. This is true in our workplaces as well as in our entertainment via the media. To a large extent we are observers, watching rather than participating. The art of conversation and the expression of deep feeling states has been supplanted by a cultural imperative to orient to technology and computers as the vehicle for doing our work and communicating in general. Between the possessive hypnotic and addictive pull of television and the computer screen (including the minuscule Game Boy screens), worker drones and our children are being trained to orient outside themselves for meaningful and important information. When a client's feelings are acknowledged and supported, that in itself is extremely healing. When a client's more subtle experiences are acknowledged and supported, the individual becomes self-referential. Like anything else, this requires gentle support and encouragement, since it involves shifting and expanding the paradigm that informs clients about self within the context of a culture that has no apparent interest in them if they are unwilling to conform to the herd mentality of an external orientation to life.

As this process within the client begins to deepen, that person becomes one more cell in the organism of the culture that begins emitting a different frequency signature. As I am a catalyst for change for my clients, my clients become catalysts for change for humanity, moving beyond a limiting identity to a place of greater harmony and love.

As a process-oriented therapist, I become aware of subtle and unusual experiences by accessing what Mindell refers to as the parapsychological channel. Combining this orientation with my experience in core shamanism, I make this realm accessible to my clients. Though most of my clients believe in a spiritual side of life, part of the shift that occurs for them with Dynamic Energetic Healing® is toward recognizing the possibility of accepting that they can access powerful spiritual resources in their daily life. It is important to acknowledge that I am teaching my clients that there is another reality which can be accessed for health and healing.

Because of my heightened ability to feel and see energy fields, I sometimes identify dark energy in clients' chakras, in their physical bodies, and in their auric or biofields (see chapter 15, "Working with Supernatural Energies"). Though some of my clients are surprised when I tell them I perceive dark energy, most of them are fully aware that something dark and negative has become part of them. They know that something is wrong (which is often the result of prior trauma), but previous therapy experiences have done little to ease their anxiety and fear. In dealing with dark energy, the role of a traditional clinician or psychotherapist is rarely useful. Rather, the therapist must be fluid enough to move into the dreamtime experience to assist in releasing the dark energy surrounding the client. Part of this involves embodying the energy of the divine through what Sandra Ingerman (2000, 189–90) describes as shapeshifting into one's divinity. In this process, my connection to Spirit creates a resonance shift in which I vibrate at a significantly higher level than the darkness that has densified into the client's body and energy field.

The Dynamic Energetic Healing® model addresses what some people call supernatural phenomena. My clinical experience continues to affirm that complete psychological and emotional healing often will not occur unless dark energy is identified, addressed, and released. *The important missing link in treating psychological disorders and mental-health issues is the dark energy component.*

Unfortunately, most psychologists, therapists, and doctors are not educated to accept that dark energy exists and that it can affect people emotionally and mentally. This is a major flaw in the conventional treatment of mental and emotional issues and one of the primary reasons for the continuing increase in the use of antidepressants.

Dynamic Energetic Healing® can successfully address the entire spectrum of traumatic residue, including repressed emotions, limiting beliefs, soul loss, and compromised energetic boundaries (which are discussed in chapters 30 and 31). When individuals are in abusive or traumatic situations, their energy fields become compromised by fear and the experience of power-lessness. When this occurs, negative thought forms and other low-density supernatural phenomena can easily penetrate a person's energetic boundaries and cause long-lasting, erosive psychic and emotional injury. In large part, it is the persistent and unrelenting feeling of violation that the still-present dark energy continues to perpetuate. Clients know intuitively that something bad or evil happened at the time of the trauma and that they have never been able to heal. When confirmation of this experience occurs, hopelessness and depression begin to dissipate, and clients begin to believe that recovery is actually possible.

4

THERAPEUTIC PRESENCE

Therapeutic presence is perhaps the most important element in the entire energetic healing process. Clients present all kinds of problems. These may be something current (such as a phobia that has just developed, a difficulty in a relationship, or a parenting problem with an adolescent), something that recurs intermittently (such as a deep and intractable pattern of depression), or something chronic (such as a post-traumatic stress disorder that has persisted over many years). When clients come for help with one of these deeper, long-standing patterns that prior treatment has not resolved (and for which they are on medication), therapeutic presence becomes central to the therapeutic equation. These clients come with a sense of desperation and hopelessness because nothing has worked for them in a curative way. Although the medication is helping to keep them stable enough to maintain a relationship and keep a job, they know in their hearts that they are not well. They know that something has been terribly wrong for a long time.

Often, they have heard about me through a friend who recommended me based on a positive healing experience. This helps a great deal, because already there is a positive expectation based on the experience of someone they trust. This positive expectation becomes the underlying hope that the treatment they will experience with me might resolve their pain. However, some clients schedule an appointment because they have insurance benefits and I am on their insurance list; some come via a referral by another therapist who knows I do this kind of work (or that I address these kinds of problems);

and, more rarely, some clients have found me in the Yellow Pages and don't know anything about me. When any of these more random situations occur, prospective clients have no real expectation that I will do anything better than any other therapist would. Regardless of how clients end up in my office, and regardless of their apparent readiness to address their problem, a great deal depends on my expectations for what is going to happen during the course of treatment and on what is energetically radiating from my presence.

My attitudes and expectations as a therapist have changed dramatically from when I was doing hypnotherapy, focused processwork, or cognitive therapy. I now know that each time I work with a client *we are going to heal and resolve problem states* and that this healing will be confirmed in that session through manual muscle testing and then immediately corroborated by the client's internal experience. Because I know this, and because the energetic strategies I use are so powerful and operate so quickly and efficiently, the energetic field that I now embody as a therapist/healer is completely different from any other therapy model I have used before. *Essentially, my ongoing experience emphasizes and engenders in-the-moment awareness.* In this regard, it is my own mental health and evolving consciousness that directly and energetically affects the clients with whom I am interacting.

When I emphasized processwork in my practice, I knew we were going to have an exciting session, things were going to be interesting, and clients were going to generate a great deal of new awareness associated with their problem. Through the process of generating more and more awareness, *I believed* that over time, things would substantially improve for the clients. Positive change resulted. When I used a lot of hypnotherapy, I knew that clients were extremely open to allow hypnotic trance to work on their unconscious mind and to allow change to happen. Positive change resulted.

There is a substantial amount of literature about therapeutic presence and the impact of the therapist in the psychotherapy setting. But much of this is addressed within the conceptual framework of transference and counter-transference that goes all the way back to Freud. It is a phenomenon that is quite real and very important. Clients typically transfer or project onto the therapist their feelings (either positive or negative) about their mother or father. All of this is going on unconsciously, out of their awareness. As an advocate for the client, the therapist takes on that projected role to address the unconscious projections within the therapeutic context. Ideally the therapist remains emotionally neutral so that even if the client becomes angry with the therapist, there is a larger context for dealing with this projected anger.

The role of the therapist is very different in my Dynamic Energetic Healing® model. I address the information in the energy fields held by the client. I use specific energetic strategies to collapse those energy fields and dissipate or discharge the information that has been generating the symptoms (see part 2). Clients are not invested in transference in the same way as in traditional talk therapy. To some degree, transference and countertransference will always happen—it is virtually impossible not to project onto someone else. But because the dynamics of the therapeutic relationship are different in this model, my role as therapist is different. In Dynamic Energetic Healing®, I have done my personal work to a substantial degree (as required for advanced training and facilitation), so I am more capable of holding a very large spiritual container (i.e., energy field) that can accommodate whatever clients bring in that has not yet healed. In order for clients to *heal* such deep issues as persistent, long-term depression or post-traumatic stress from old trauma, the spiritual component must be integrated into the therapy.

Though transference is always occurring to some degree, the assumptions about what will occur in the Dynamic Energetic Healing® session are completely different than in a traditional therapy model. I will always be projected onto to some degree, but because I am not working and guiding the client to address psychodynamic issues in a cognitive therapeutic context, I am much less prone to be projected onto as the negative father or the negative mother. If per chance I am, then the projection will be quickly dissipated by whatever is coming up *in that moment* through an energetic strategy that will collapse the projection and its underlying cause. For example, a client may be dealing with a current-life energetic origin or a specific event that occurred when they were younger. They may be remembering quite vividly how their parent figure was abusive in a certain way, which will immediately bring up feelings that could be projected onto me—all at the unconscious level.

Dynamic Energetic Healing® targets traumatic memories *as they emerge*. These may be affective components of a trauma (such as the initial shock and fear, or the anger and feelings of helplessness that followed) or the client's interpretations of the event (such as "people can never be trusted"). One of the tasks of psychotherapy is to help clients evoke these repressed components of traumatic events. The dilemma has always been how to resolve and heal the traumatic residue that is often repressed and amnesic. My focus is to have clients stay with that feeling—stay with the thought field of the event (referred to by Callahan as *attuning*)—to bring into their awareness as many associations, feelings, and memory fragments as possible while we engage the energetic strategies *in process*. These strategies may include tapping on meridian points, stimulating or holding a chakra, or applying frontal/occipital holding (to allow the healing energy and deep wisdom of spiritual resources to come through and provide greater healing).

My intentions and presuppositions are different than those of therapists who practice traditional psychotherapy. The intentions I bring and articulate explicitly to my clients are that we are going to identify the information in the energy field (or the thought field specific to an issue or traumatic event) as it is present and that together we will select the best energetic strategy to clear that information from the client's energy field. This information may be held at the unconscious level; it may be held in the body; it may be distortions in the client's auric field. But my goal is very specific—to collapse that specific energy field.

Once an energetic strategy is selected and implemented, I use manual muscle testing to determine if that information, energy field, or thought field has completely dissipated. If there is even a trace of the disturbance left at any level, we use manual muscle testing again to find another energetic strategy to clear it completely.

By the time we are finished, the manual muscle testing confirms that there is nothing left of the energy field which contained the information and that we have *healed* the issue—that issue, that affect, that reaction, that pain has been resolved. *It is no longer in the client's field.* It is gone! This is what makes energetic healing strategies different from traditional psychotherapy. The psychotherapeutic methods (i.e., the energetic strategies) have resolved the client's issue at a more fundamental level than is likely to occur using a more traditional psychotherapy approach. The specific issue worked on is completed and we can now move on to what is next on the client's agenda or what Process reveals as priority.

My intention from the very first time I speak with a client is that we will do healing work within the context of a psychotherapeutic framework. When clients and I use Dynamic Energetic Healing® strategies, I know they are going to leave each session having healed more completely. I hold this intention (this thought field) for my clients, and this consciousness conveys this information to my clients. This happens at a purely energetic level as well as at a subconscious level via direct and indirect suggestions that I continually offer to my clients.

When clients agree to work with me, we establish a therapeutic contract that defines our mutual expectations and obligations. My clients ask for help to resolve certain problems; I agree to use certain strategies, methodologies, and techniques to help them change in a positive and healing way. Implicit in the therapeutic contract is that I will share my experience, my training, and my sincere desire to assist them to achieve their therapeutic goals in all the appropriate professional ways that I can. If my heart is open, I share open-heartedness with my clients. If my consciousness is expanded, I share this expanded consciousness with my clients. How do I share my consciousness with my clients? I convey this information through intention and my energy field.

This is my expectation, and this is what happens based on my experience. I know that when my clients and I work together, they heal a little bit more in every session. They release a bit more trauma; they have access to more of their emotional body; they become progressively less limited and more open to connect with their essential self. That is miraculous to me. I am so grateful every time I have the opportunity to work with a client.

I know from my work with the compassionate spirits that they are present with me and assisting in the healing process. I am certain that my own expectations are going to affect the healing. Researchers Dean I. Radin, Janine M. Rebman, and Maikwe P. Cross (1996, 143–68) address this in their emerging model of the mind, which suggests that "consciousness is an ordering principle. It can insert information into disorganized or random systems and create higher degrees of order." They also refer to coherence as another significant element in the energetic induction process. "Coherence among individuals is important in the ordering power of consciousness. Coherence may be expressed as love, empathy, caring, unity, oneness, and connectedness."

I do not believe that the power of positive thinking by itself is sufficient to accomplish a complete healing for the client. However, many people who follow spiritual teachers claim that the most positive experience they can ever have is darshan—the energetic transmission that occurs when you are in the presence of your spiritual master and receive blessing. It is simply being in the energy field of the master that heals. The degree to which the master is filled with the light of Spirit positively affects the student on an energetic level. The same phenomenon in the therapist's office is called induction. Charismatic figures embody this kind of phenomenon whether they are religious leaders, political candidates, or sports celebrities. There is a certain energy, a certain brightness, a certain enthusiasm that emanates from these individuals. Other people feel it, and they want to be close to it and to feel inspired and uplifted. They want to be in that energy field. They want to be close to that person so they can get some of that healing effervescent energy. I had this experience numerous times with Yogi Bhajan.

There is a long history of this in the traditional Hindu guru–disciple relationship, and the process of energy transmission through presence or touch continues today in charismatic Christianity and with celebrities. When I studied with Starr Fuentes for two weeks in 2000, the teaching of Divine Intervention could only be acquired by being in the continual presence of this teacher. This was acquisition of the teaching through energetic transmission. There is a well-known reference in the New Testament (Luke 8:40–48) to a woman who touched Jesus' cloak from the back—Jesus felt his energy come out of him and the woman was healed.

As in any apprenticeship, trainees in the Dynamic Energetic Healing® model go through their own healing process as they learn how to become excellent facilitators. During the beginning learning stage, they begin to heal old traumas and limiting identities that have kept them bound to the past. As this process progresses by layers, there is less residue and blockage from the past, which enables them to be ever more present with their clients. As therapists become more present, there is less for them to react to, and their essential self progressively opens up. As this occurs, the stronger energetic induction process provides a more dynamic therapist–client healing field. What happens then for clients is more positive healing. Powerful therapeutic change happens faster and is more complete as the healing process is accelerated by the therapist's presence.

5

INTEGRATING THE SECOND ATTENTION INTO DYNAMIC ENERGETIC HEALING®: ACKNOWLEDGING THE DREAMINGBODY

As a model of psychotherapy, Dynamic Energetic Healing® is innovative in the way it integrates ancient healing principles from a variety of traditions. We all have certain assumptions about Western psychology thanks to Freud's seminal theories on the role of the unconscious mind and the many defense mechanisms that adapt to psychic injury. Today, many of these theories are generally agreed upon. This agreement is based on the accumulated psychological literature and research findings that make up the foundation of many of our psychology graduate programs.

In recent years, it has been refreshing to see new emphases emerge in the field, including transpersonal, Gestalt, Ericksonian hypnosis/NLP, and process-oriented psychology. There are many more examples of how Western psychology continues to grow and evolve.

Perhaps there is really nothing new about energy psychology as a discipline of psychology. After all, acupuncture is over three thousand years old. The application of energy for healing purposes predates acupuncture: the ancient Vedas of India refer to energy in spiritual terms, as do many other spiritual wisdom traditions. Therefore, holding and tapping on specific meridian or chakra locations while keeping a problem state in your awareness is not really new. Perhaps we can now bring these paradigms together, since modern physics provides us with acceptable language for describing scientifically what previously could only be explained in "vague spiritual terms."

Energy psychology is not the only recent model of psychotherapy that incorporates the body for healing the psyche. There are many body-centered therapies that have been used for many years, albeit often on the fringe of mainstream practice. Thus, it does not surprise me that working with acupoints and chakras that interpenetrate the body is on the fringe of today's consensus psychological thinking. Though I have been a longtime student and practitioner of Kundalini yoga and more recently qigong (both of which use the physical body to stimulate the body's essential energy system) for over two decades, I like that the physical body is the central vehicle or organizing platform for much of what I do in Dynamic Energetic Healing® now. For example, I manually test the resistance of my clients' arm and shoulder muscles. I also have clients touch or tap their various acupoints or chakras to effect change at multiple levels. It is very affirming to explicitly include the body as the central organizing platform, since one of the primary goals of therapy is to acknowledge and affirm the whole person, including both psyche and soma.

"Mind/body health" has become an increasingly popular catchphrase—even among the medical establishment—of late. But tapping on the body, which activates a cascading series of bioenergetic changes, makes the body's role in healing more explicit and less understated. There truly is something inclusive and refreshing about incorporating the physical body in healing the psyche. Many of us suffer from body-related problems that can have a major impact in undermining our sense of well-being and personal fulfillment throughout our life. I am relieved and excited that the body is now a primary platform for my healing work.

After spending many years training in Ericksonian hypnosis and achieving considerable success with that model, I became painfully aware that I tended to ignore my body while overemphasizing the cerebral imperative to create clever, multiple embedded metaphors to help my clients reassociate and reframe their experiences at the unconscious level. This in no way diminishes all that Dr. Milton Erickson has taught us about how to work with language patterns and the creative unconscious to achieve change. But let us remember that Erickson spent much of his adult life in a wheelchair, with his physical body severely restricted by repeated bouts with polio. He developed what became his healing gifts through many hours of observing micro-movements and the minimal cues of others, together with listening to their unique patterns of using words. He was certainly a sage and perhaps even a wizard. I am indebted to Erickson for helping me better understand and experience trance states. But I needed something more. That something more was process-oriented psychology, which Mindell brought to the United States in 1987 in his first international training course. This one-month residential training at Marylhurst College changed my life and my appreciation for integrating the body into psychotherapy.

As a process-oriented therapist, I have learned to both follow and defer to Process when I am with a client. Happily for me, process-oriented psychology (processwork) enables me to include and integrate everything I have learned under the rubric of psychotherapy. As a result, I am now prepared to address anything that clients bring into a therapy session as presenting a problem. This includes yoga movements, spontaneous and unexpected sounds, inner visions, red swollen hives, piercing headaches, physical exhaustion, and any other presenting symptoms. Classical Taoism might be defined as following the flow of nature. This is an appropriate metaphor for Process, which is both the stream of events that is happening in the conscious moment and the unknown and waiting-to-happen inchoate events that are out of conscious awareness, ready to burst forth into life. The Dynamic Energetic Healing® model incorporates a process-oriented approach to working with clients. Processwork helps the client and the therapist achieve a multilevel awareness sufficient for them both to "live the dreamingbody." This refers to many things, including following your bodily sensations, visions, dreams, feeling states, intuition, and what is occurring in the relational context. What is unique in how Mindell articulates dreaming is that the stream of experiences he calls the dreamingbody (or the dreambody) not only happens at night but is, in fact, an ongoing experience. Process workers become adept at gaining access to the dreaming process at any time, including during the day. The dreambody occurs within us (intrapersonally), with couples and groups (interpersonally), and between and among larger collectives such as states and countries (globally). What makes all this meaningful within the context of Dynamic Energetic Healing® is awareness.

Dreambodywork is all about sensing your bodily sensations and other channels of perception and allowing them to direct the way you live. As Mindell (1993, 23) says,

Following the dreamingbody is a most important task. It is the channel for what some call the "dream maker" and what others refer to as the "spirit," or the unconscious. Native Australians call it "dreamtime."

But *how* to access the dreamingbody remains the important question.

Mindell asserts that the quality of attention determines whether we are in our first or second attention (these are terms he has borrowed from Carlos Castaneda's teacher, Don Juan). Even as you move in and out of dreamtime, as a process worker you need to carry on a normal life and acknowledge *consensus reality*. Mindell calls this orientation the first attention. When you focus your first or normal attention, you perceive the meaning of the content of what someone is saying to you. You need this first attention to accomplish your concrete goals and do your normal daily work.

The second attention is cultivated to notice unusual processes—the dreaming process that normally appears to us in the background (to the extent that we tend to ignore it). When you are in your second attention, you notice things on the periphery of your awareness. These experiences can be either external or internal, and may be subjective or irrational. Mindell believes that for most ordinary folks, these "signals" and intimations of the dreamingbody are rejected and ignored because we often find them disturbing. They appear uninvited and may be strong emotions, painful bodily sensations, provocative fantasies, or strong discordant countertransferential impulses.

Working with energy as an operational principle must include the dreamingbody experience for which the therapist must take personal responsibility in order to keep the therapeutic field clean. All information in the field, both intrapersonal and interpersonal, must be acknowledged and processed when working with a client.

I am not suggesting that a therapist working in the Dynamic Energetic Healing® model act out one or both sides of every polarity or inner split of their client. This might be the modus operandi for a process-oriented Gestalt therapist. I used to do this as one way to facilitate heightened awareness for my clients and keep the relational field clean. If clients started generating a strong internal image that was disturbing, I might have had them draw the image and then personify it and act out the inner dream figure. This would heighten the clients' awareness of the secondary process they were disavowing regarding hidden relationship issues. I no longer do that as a matter of therapeutic course. I do, however, continually move from my first to my second attention throughout the day as a way to sense the magic of the world around me. I try to live the dreamingbody experience so I do not get too stuck in my everyday normal identity, my primary process. In the dreaming-body experience, my "normal" everyday self-identity is constantly shifting and changing as I move from one altered state to another—which makes me wonder what is normal, since we know that consciousness is fluid and we are constantly shifting the focus of our attention. This happens in sessions with clients as well. Mindell (2000b, 511–12) elaborates on this:

> Once you loosen your attachment to your CR (consensus reality) iden-tity and learn to step into dreaming, you realize that your dreaming body is not one fixed thing, not just the opposite of your everyday identity, but a fluid experience, an awareness of whatever catches your attention. . . . Since the beginning of history, people have believed that when we step into dreaming, we experience our body as a dreambody, a non-local, non-temporal form or tendency only weakly attached to our CR bodies. If we learn to follow the body's dreaming, we can develop the shamanic subtle body, the most ancient method to freedom.

So how does one cultivate the second attention as a Dynamic Energetic Healing® therapist? I will share some of the things I do—perhaps you are already living the dreambody experience. When I start a session with a client, I establish sacred space first. I call upon Spirit and pay attention to what I notice. Do I begin to notice a presence, an intuitive or inner auditory commu-nication, or perhaps a shiver down my back or feeling of love or openness? What I have come to recognize is that the presence and power of Spirit makes my head start to twitch. This is my kinesthetic indicator that spiritual power is becoming available to me. Next, I turn my attention to my client, noticing expressions of posture and appearance to determine if I perceive a particular dream figure or archetype sitting across from me. I notice the client's voice and the feeling in the field itself. Is it relaxed, tense, fearful, or something else? I pay attention to *my* energy level. Is it normal, tired, or agitated? Per-haps you already do these things. These things are not necessarily out of the ordinary, but they require intentionality in order to cultivate the second atten-tion as an ongoing way of being.

When we begin muscle testing, I become aware of the interpersonal field and the degree to which clients are comfortable with me moving in close to their body. Do I begin to feel welcome or get the nonverbal communication to keep my distance? In which channel am I getting this information? Is it a sensation on my skin, a feeling of muscle tightness in my shoulders, or a feeling of nausea in my stomach? When we begin the interventions such as tapping on meridian or chakra points, what begins to happen to me? If I feel energetic releases, I will exhale very deeply and let out a sigh. Is this the client's or my own energetic release? Sometimes I will intuitively sense that there is an energetic contraction at one of the client's chakras and I will encourage the client to continue tapping there until it is clear. What is happening here? I say it is the dreamingbody experience. Sometimes I feel tremendously deep emotion as my client taps and releases trapped energy. I comment aloud that I feel this deep sadness or shame or anger, and I ask what the client's experience is. This has always been helpful. Often, it is also the catalyst for clients to claim their disavowed or repressed emotion and experience it then and there, as if finally having permission to access a part of themselves they had denied.

When I do the frontal occipital holding intervention, I immediately move into the dreamingbody experience. I know this because I have visions, intuitions, and peeks into the life and energy field of the client that always astound me. I am just a witness at this point, connected to the dreaming river that flows between us and far into currents and branching streams that need to be acknowledged. Sometimes my client and I have the same internal experience, sometimes not. They share, I share. It is Spirit moving through us, the dreamingbody experience.

Sessions are rich because there is acknowledgment of moving back and forth between first and second attention, into and out of altered states of consciousness where more of the Great Mystery is revealed and experienced. As client and therapist open to these unexpected experiences where Process unfolds, both feel creative and more whole. There is an acknowledgment that remarkable things happen in these sessions. And we are always surprised. It is not just I as the therapist who accesses my second attention—clients learn to develop their own second attention and to trust their own perceptions, however unusual or different. This is essential for clients to become self-empowered and less externally referenced.

I was once working with a man whose goal was to overcome his chronic anxiety. One of the energetic origins interfering on this goal had occurred when he was twenty-six years old (about twenty years before). As we spoke he mentioned how being married with a family seemed to preclude retirement saving. As he said more, I helped him identify some limiting beliefs he had been harboring, one of which was that being married prevented him from maintaining financial integrity and achieving his financial goals. After addressing psychoenergetic reversal and doing some EFT tapping, we next needed to do the frontal occipital holding intervention. As this was occurring, I *saw* his inability to say no to his wife and how he had no energetic boundaries with his future. Then I saw his father not being able to say no to his mother. Then I saw how he had internalized this as a child, and I knew it was a curse. How did I see and know these things? It was the dreamingbody experience, which anyone can cultivate awareness of because dreamtime is always happening right now. When you as the therapist are in your second attention, there is access to information that would otherwise be unavailable.

The field is constantly shifting and changing when I am working with clients. I say I am working with energy, which is not always something easy to define. I have tried to describe and illustrate the concept of the dreamingbody and how, with the cultivation of the second attention, both the therapist and the client can expand the field of possibilities for greater healing to occur. What's more, I believe we can experience life more passionately and with a greater sense of newness when the dreamingbody experience is embraced, in spite of the implicit demands that consensus reality imposes on us to conform.

6

The Compassionate Spirits: Moving into the Dreamtime Experience

I have been a shamanic practitioner for over two decades and I feel I am still a beginner. This is because compassionate spirits are always teaching me new healing techniques when they perceive I am ready to receive them. What follows is some basic information you may find helpful about shamanic healing techniques and their underlying assumptions. This cross-cultural spiritual practice is believed to be over 30,000 years old. As the foundation of this practice, the shaman enters another reality (what Carlos Castaneda has referred to as "nonordinary" reality) and directly interacts with the beings that inhabit this reality. These beings are most often referred to as the *compassionate spirits*. Harner (1982, xxi) refers to these beings as follows:

> When I speak of "spirits," it is because that is the way shamans talk within the system. To practice shamanism, it is unnecessary and even distracting to be preoccupied with achieving scientific understanding of what "spirits" may really represent and why shamanism works.

Though there are shamans known to access this other reality by using psychogenic plants, Harner's research indicates that approximately 95 percent of shamans worldwide use some sort of percussive or sonic drive to enable them to make the shamanic journey. This is usually done with rattles or drums. The shamanic journey enables the shaman (or shamanic practitioner) to enter into the state of nonordinary reality by generating an altered state of consciousness. I suppose this would be characterized as an out-of-body experience; however, in this case it is intentionally generated and under the shaman's full control. The shamanic journey is a vehicle to bridge this world of consensus reality and the world of the spirits in nonordinary reality.

When I am journeying, I am aware of what is going on around me if I choose to be. The experience is of being slightly dissociated and able to access both realities simultaneously. Certainly it is best to set up the context for journeying where the shaman will not be disturbed by the outside world. However, if there were an emergency requiring my immediate attention, I would be able to attend to it without delay.

In indigenous societies, the shaman has many tribal responsibilities and will journey for a variety of reasons. As shamans gain experience, their abilities and skills increase. The unique thing about how shamans work is their *total reliance on obtaining information directly from the spirits*.

It must be understood that for practitioners to embrace shamanism as a healing path of heart, they must first acknowledge that *our consensus reality is a cultural trance*—an unconscious, unspoken agreement that we Westerners choose to believe about how reality is organized. Shamanism has certain presuppositions that are very different from Western consensus reality and that are consistently empirically corroborated by the shamans' journeys, including these:

1. The compassionate spirits are as real as you and I and inhabit a reality that is as real as our everyday outer reality. This other, nonordinary reality can be easily accessed through the shamanic journey. The spirits and this other reality are not imagined or made up; they are just perceived differently from how we usually perceive the outer reality (i.e., through consensus thinking about the way the world should be).

2. Nonordinary reality is made up of three realms—the upper world, the middle world, and the lower world. The upper world and the lower world are purely spiritual and operate out of time. In these two realms, the spirits (in animal and anthropomorphic form) are deeply compassionate and always interested in helping the shaman alleviate pain and suffering in our world. The shaman experiences no pain or suffering in the upper or lower world during the journey. The middle world includes the physical realm where we live. In this realm, there is and always has been pain and suffering. We often refer to the spiritual

beings found in the middle world as ghosts who have become disoriented, trapped, and wandering aimlessly. These disembodied middle-world spirits are of all species, not just human. They have not yet progressed to continue their evolution to the upper and lower worlds. They can become a disturbance, an intrusion, or an attaching spirit causing involuntary possession. They can also be a cause or source of illness. Shamans journey in the middle world with the same ease as journeying in the upper and lower spiritual realms.

3. When shamans call in the spirits for help, they are calling in "power." The healing energy bestowed upon the shaman by the spirits is power, and it is often conveyed to the client or patient. Miraculous healing can occur via this power and via the energy of the universe (which also includes knowledge and healing information provided by the spirits). This can happen through the direct intervention of the compassionate spirits themselves or when the shaman embodies a helping spirit (also referred to as merging) and becomes a direct conduit of its healing power.

4. As shamans become more proficient in their skills, they are able to move back and forth between our consensus reality and nonordinary reality at will. This ability to have access to both the visible and invisible worlds is sometimes referred to as the dreamtime experience. Like any spiritual practice, this requires discipline. Shamans must also have the clear intention to help alleviate the pain and suffering of other humans with the support of their helping spirits. If the personal needs of the shaman's ego violate and supersede this dictum, sorcery—with its emphasis on power and control—is often the result.

5. Helping spirits are typically beings (human or nonhuman) that once lived in ordinary reality. The degree of compassion and personal power that each helping spirit has is a reflection of its own spiritual evolution in either the upper or lower world. The spiritual realms of the upper and lower world occupy the same interior spaces visited by spiritual masters and enlightened beings, and they are described by the sacred scriptures of all of the great religious traditions. Upon their death, these masters and saints transition into the upper or lower world. Millions of devotees pray to them, and shamans visit them and solicit their help in their journeys. There is no correlation at all between the upper world and what is traditionally called heaven;

similarly, there is no correlation between the lower world and what is called hell.

6. When a client is experiencing a challenge, weakness, or illness, power animals are retrieved to augment the client's personal power. During this process, the shaman is guided by his or her own helping spirits to find the helping animal spirit that wants to merge with the client, help empower the client, and infuse its essence into the client's core.

7. Healing processes and interventions of the shamanic practitioner most commonly facilitated through the shamanic journey include
   a. divination, which includes shamanic diagnosis of illness;
   b. soul retrievals, which involve bringing back fragmented parts of a traumatized individual to help restore emotional wholeness, the benefit of which also includes an increase in mental and physical well-being;
   c. extractions, whereby dark energy intrusions are removed from a weakened individual;
   d. psychopomp work, which addresses a deceased's spirit (which may be trapped in the middle world) or the suffering of the dying;
   e. receiving personal healing and specialized teachings from your helping spirits, as the spirits determine your readiness (as a shaman) to receive them.

For individuals with a strong spiritual inclination, the desire for greater closeness or contact with one's soul or essential nature has frequently (and historically) been a cause of great pain. The yearning for greater closeness to God has made individuals do all sorts of things to achieve this closeness. These practices have included fasting to the point of starvation, self-flagellation, celibacy, ingesting psychogenic plants, and self-isolation (including monasticism), all of which enable uninterrupted prayer or meditation for extended periods—even an entire lifetime.

Though this may sound irreverent or blasphemous to adherents of well-established religious traditions, *experienced shamanic practitioners are easily able to establish and maintain a personal relationship with one or more compassionate spirits*. The great souls that millions of devoted adherents pray to every day *exist now* in the realm of nonordinary reality! Shamanic practitioners commune with the great saints through their direct experience—using all their senses through the shamanic journey. Having the love of Jesus come into my heart, or being filled with the power of another helping spirit, is the blessing that the shamanic journey provides.

Historically, shamans were systematically hunted down and murdered throughout the world. Perhaps the main reason for this is that the shamanic journey provides the direct experience of connecting to and merging with Spirit. This technique is easily learned and has been empirically validated repeatedly and consistently over time, and individuals who practice it are often no longer dependent on a traditional religious institution. When traditional religion no longer holds sway over someone who has a reliable methodology for a direct experience of Spirit, the religious institution is threatened. Experiencing the numinous, heretofore reserved for the elite priestly caste (the interpreters of the Holy Scriptures and of the word of God, as revealed through the one chosen prophet), suddenly becomes possible for everyone! The hypocrisy of institutional religions, which claim to serve the people by providing an accurate interpretation of the word of God through their prophets, is revealed and their interests are jeopardized. The shamanic practitioner doesn't need a church, doesn't need Holy Scriptures, doesn't need priests, and doesn't need faith in a God that is described by others. This was true for shamans 30,000 years ago, and it remains true for shamanic practitioners today.

Contemporary Western civilization is set apart from nature by its attempts to dominate and control nature, but the shaman's experience of being in harmony with all things is continually reinforced through the shamanic journey. Consequently, today's shamanic practitioners are not only antithetical to institutional religion but also at odds with the dominant cultural paradigm of the exploitation of nature and unrestrained consumption of natural resources.

Sociologists of religion have said that traditional religious institutions are linked to the dominant cultural paradigm of directing people to think in prescribed ways. After all, if people are told to believe in a certain way or risk their soul suffering the pain of hell, those who choose the latter will likely be labeled as sinners and ostracized by the collective. Shunning and exclusion are merely the first step. Throwing Christians to the lions, as the Roman Empire did when it perceived them as a threat, is just one example of a dominant culture responding to a threat to its worldview.

In *Civilization and Its Discontents* ([1929] 1955), Freud suggested that social chaos will result from the erosion of the church's influence and the increasing number of disbelievers. He recognized that through fear and guilt induction, the church has been able to keep the powerful impulses of what he called the id (primitive animal impulses) in check. Freud claimed that the church has managed the id by conditioning people's minds. When enough people fall away from the church, morality as we know it will dissolve into social chaos.

I would argue very differently for what might occur if enough people were to open up to the shamanic journey experience. After all, since Copernicus revealed that Earth is not the center of the universe, and since the Apollo space missions have brought us pictures of our planet suspended in space, the existential and very human need to feel connected to something greater than ourselves has become stronger than ever.

Recurrent themes borne out of the shamanic journey experience consistently revolve around the individual's connection to all of nature and the universe. Additionally, alleviating pain and suffering by soliciting the compassionate spirits of the upper and lower worlds and the spirits of nature remains central to the shaman's experience. In my practice, the most common presenting complaints of clients involve feelings of depression and anxiety related to abandonment, alienation, and feeling alone. Due to the very nature of life in the middle world, we struggle just as hard now as our ancestors did 30,000 years ago to survive and to ensure that we have food and the other basic necessities of life. Because we must compete in order to survive, it is our shared legacy to be raised in families that are, for the most part, accurately labeled dysfunctional. Unfortunately, the experience of receiving unconditional love and regard within the family, especially as a tender, sensitive child, is rare. Therefore, connecting to and interacting with beings that are dedicated to compassionately and willingly helping us not only comforts our souls but also opens our hearts to another way of being in the world.

It is very humbling to know that each of us can receive this spiritual help and support from these beings of enormous compassion and power. It is not necessary to study for decades at the feet of a master in order to receive the benefits from the compassionate spirits. To learn the shamanic journey method and reap the benefits of being fully human, all that is required is sincerity of heart and the guidance of an experienced shamanic practitioner.

CHAPTER
7

COLLABORATING WITH THE COMPASSIONATE SPIRITS: EMBRACING A NEW PARADIGM

The compassionate spirits are real, but they are normally invisible to the human eye. If you were not born a psychic, learning the shamanic journey method as a way to interact and commune with the compassionate spirits is your first step toward reliably accessing the invisible realm. It is easy enough to learn, particularly if you are supported with the guidance of an experienced teacher. Once you can reliably and easily travel into the realms of the lower world and upper world, where the compassionate spirits are located (see chapter 6), establishing a solid connection with your power animals and your teachers comes naturally. Like most things in life, the more you practice journeying, the easier it becomes and the more confidence you gain in your abilities.

I have found that it takes some time for most people to adjust to the phenomenological fact that there exists another reality populated with compassionate beings that are just waiting and wanting to help us! This adjustment process requires a shift in your orientation about what is true. This catapults you into embracing a new paradigm where your view and belief of reality expands to allow for many other possibilities. Reality slowly becomes redefined; as it does, so does your self-identity.

Because of my own cultural and ethnocentric biases, it took me a number of years to deeply accept the reality of the compassionate spirits. I needed repeated initiatory experiences by them before I was willing to surrender my stubborn insistence about what is true. I have heard that scientists have determined that the vast majority of us use less than 5 percent of our brain. I believe that accessing the nonordinary realm of the compassionate spirits engages much more of the human brain and that it expands our consciousness and creates new beliefs about what we are capable of perceiving in extrasensory ways. As our inner sensing expands and we receive the guidance and the teachings of the compassionate spirits, along with the power (of the universe!) associated with them, we step up our evolution as human beings and as participants in the universe at large.

Over the years, as I have worked more and more with the compassionate spirits, I have discovered that they can be accessed at any time, even if I am not drumming or rattling (the traditional ways to generate the state of consciousness required to access the compassionate spirits). This is similar to what Christians refer to in prayer as the indwelling of the Holy Spirit. This took me a step closer to the new paradigm and challenged, once again, the limitations of my thinking and beliefs about what is possible. At the same time, this discovery expanded my consciousness and my perceptions of what is possible.

Many people react with skepticism and hostility when mention is made of the compassionate spirits. Dr. Michael Harner, a former professor of anthropology and author of numerous books on shamanism, has studied this phenomenon for many years. He has determined that there is a particular kind of prejudice involved:

> It is the counterpart of ethnocentrism between cultures. But in this case it is not the narrowness of someone's *cultural* experience that is the fundamental issue, but the narrowness of someone's conscious experience. The persons most prejudiced against the concept of nonordinary reality are those who have never experienced it. This might be termed *cognicentrism*, the analogue in consciousness of ethnocentrism. (1982, xvii)

The adherents of the great religious traditions believe that Jesus or Krishna or God is with the faithful all the time. The difference between collaborating with the compassionate spirits from within the shamanic paradigm and these traditional religions is that the shamanic paradigm is not a faith-based religion. You are not being asked to believe that anything I am telling you is true. You are not being exhorted to have faith that will, hopefully, bear spiritual fruits for you in the future. Instead, I am asking you to consider direct experience as your evidence that what I am describing is true. This process of discovery is not just for me. It's for anyone who has the desire and willingness to consider the possibility that the angelic and spiritual realms are not merely metaphoric or mythic but a reality (albeit spiritual and nonordinary) that is available to us to interact with all the time.

To the degree that we master the shamanic journey methodology, we can choose to be active, conscious participants in this other reality for the benefit of others as well as for ourselves. The compassionate spirits carry within them great power, unlimited knowledge, and ancient wisdom that, though seemingly magical, is actually as normal and commonplace as the miracle of life itself on our great planet.

Scientists can explain the phenomenon of photosynthesis as an interactive process that enables plant life to flourish on our planet. Yet scientists cannot satisfactorily explain the miracle of life and consciousness itself, any more than scientists can explain the beauty and sweet redolence of a newly opened rose. While it's true that scientists have not been able to prove the existence of the human soul or the compassionate spirits, neither have they been able to disprove the existence of them.

From over twenty-four years of clinical experience, I know that the experience of anomie, existential aloneness, and isolation is a theme that shows up frequently among people of all ages. When I read Aldous Huxley's *Island* and *Brave New World* in college, I was beginning to explore altered states of consciousness and their relationship to spiritual practices and religion. In *Brave New World*, Huxley considered the perfect drug Soma as the solution for alleviating the profound anomie of the human condition. People took Soma because it lulled them into a mood of acceptance of what is; more than that, it provided a heightened sense of well-being without any deleterious side effects. It eliminated anxiety, worry, and depression, providing individuals with a chemicalized solution to the trials and tribulations of being human, which inherently involves suffering. Huxley was very prescient. The use of modern-day pharmaceuticals such as Zoloft, Prozac, Paxil, and other popular antidepressant and anti-anxiety drugs is increasing—these drugs are society's technological and scientific answer to the unsatisfactory solutions that the great religious traditions provide.

In *Island*, the common rite of passage for an adolescent involves a teacher or parent facilitating the experience of the numinous via a psychoactive mushroom called the moksha medicine. This rite provides a structured paradigm shift that enables the adolescents to get out of their rational mind-set and expand their appreciation and consciousness of what's possible beyond the limitations of the intellect. It's a different wrinkle from *Brave New World*, yet the intent is much the same: to find ways to alleviate the pain and suffering inherent in human experience.

In shamanic practices, a link is developed so you always have spiritual helpers available to assist you, regardless of your personal circumstances at the time. Each of your helpers has its own specialization. Some will provide you with personal healing, some will provide you with the ability to divine things, some will help you to restore the lost souls that others have suffered from a trauma in their life, and some will act as your personal bodyguard, accompanying you all the time to ensure your safety and protection. Over time, a relationship is developed with each of your helping spirits that becomes a strong bond. Many of my helping spirits work together, conveying to me a strong sense of family. What is unusual and wonderful about this family is the always-present unconditional love and regard that I feel in their presence.

It is one thing to take the perennial leap to faith in what is described as a loving God. It is quite another thing to know, based on your undeniable personal experience, that you have spiritual helpers which you are bonded to—and in an ongoing relationship with—who are always available in a real and meaningful sense when you need them. Western culture has not provided us with this paradigm, but that doesn't mean the paradigm is not useful. It's simply a cultural phenomenon (a belief system) that hasn't been included in our *Weltanschauung* (worldview). It is another reality. It's up to you to explore this hidden universe and make the discoveries that are there for you if you are ready and curious. The techniques are easy. The learning curve is not too steep. I am reminded of a catchphrase that Jimi Hendrix made popular in the 1960s: "Are you experienced?" Then, it was a veiled invitation to expand your consciousness using psychedelic drugs. Even today, we need to move beyond intellect. If you are open and intrepid in exploring via these shamanic practices, you will discover that Spirit provides for unconditional love and appreciation for all human beings, animals, and the living earth itself. To you, dear reader, I extend this invitation.

8

LIVING LIFE INTENTIONALLY

In a typical psychotherapeutic setting, therapists work collaboratively with clients to develop a treatment plan. They identify presenting problems and come up with treatment goals so they can agree on a therapeutic contract. As discussed in chapter 2, there are myriad therapy models from which the therapist chooses a specific orientation (e.g., cognitive-behavioral) to accomplish the chosen treatment goals.

In Dynamic Energetic Healing®, my departure point is framed much differently. After a comprehensive review and discussion of the client's personal history, I listen intently to what brought this person to see me. Clients tell me their problems, of course, and I then ask them to list their therapeutic goals. After further discussion, I ask them to prioritize what feels most important to address first. When they have done this, I ask them the following questions through manual muscle testing: "From your soul, is this indeed your highest priority goal *at this time*?" and "Is it in your 'highest good' to pursue this goal *at this time*?" When the client's muscle testing answers affirmatively, we proceed on the chosen goal. When the client's muscle testing indicates no, together we test to determine if any of their other therapeutic goals meet the criteria of these two questions. Sometimes their soul chooses a goal they have already identified as a starting point. In other cases, however, the client's starting therapeutic goal is something completely different from what the client initially listed consciously. In either case, we discuss their "chosen" starting point to ensure that the client is in accord with the entire therapeutic process as it is being organized within the Dynamic Energetic Healing® model. There is one caveat to this: When a client is in a crisis, we move into a triage orientation and attend to their immediate need in order to stabilize affect and create emotional homeostasis.

Because Dynamic Energetic Healing® is a psychospiritual methodology, it is appropriate to start the therapeutic process by deferring to the guidance of the client's soul. The soul wisdom of the client holds much more than simply the rational intellect confined by the ego identity. The soul is the repository of all the knowledge and experiences throughout its history. The soul's knowledge includes all of our many lifetimes' experiences, referred to as our karmic history.

At this juncture, I want to make a distinction between a therapeutic goal and an intention as our starting point.

It is fairly common to define *intention* as a strong purpose accompanied by a sharply focused determination to produce a specific result. We understand intention as a consequence of the application of our mind or will fixed on some goal that lets nothing stand in the way of achieving the outcome. While this fierce determination is certainly an admirable trait, it is important to define how intention is recruited and used in the Dynamic Energetic Healing® model. One of the best definitions of the spiritual and energetic underpinnings of intention is from Carlos Castaneda's teacher, Don Juan. He describes intention this way:

> In the universe there is an unmeasurable, indescribable force which sorcerers call *intent*, and that absolutely everything that exists in the entire cosmos is attached to *intent* by a connecting link. They were especially concerned with cleaning it of the numbing effects brought about by the ordinary concerns of their everyday lives. Sorcery at this level could be defined as the procedure of cleaning one's connecting link to *intent*. (Castaneda 1987, 12)

When Don Juan refers to the importance of cleaning our connecting link to intent and the numbing effects of the ordinary concerns of everyday life, he is talking about all our thoughts and actions that reinforce our sense of separateness. Being possessed by the tyrannizing and relentlessly intrusive chatter of an internal critic figure certainly keeps us numb and insulated from conscious awareness of our connection to Source. Dynamic Energetic Healing®

provides us with a way of managing the inner-critic figure. It ensures that we maintain excellent energetic boundaries with that part of ourselves which persists in reminding us that we are, in a variety of ways, not OK.

Don Juan elaborates on the power and nature of intent and our conscious relationship to it:

> Sorcerers beckon *intent* by voicing the word *intent* loud and clear. *Intent* is a force that exists in the universe. When sorcerers beckon intent, it comes to them and sets up the path for attainment, which means that sorcerers always accomplish what they set out to do. (Castaneda 1998, 9–10)

This suggests that intention is much more powerful and vast than the strength of a determined ego or an individual's will. Consider the possibility that intention is not something which you create by your will alone but is instead a force that exists in the universe as an invisible and infinite field of energy, responsive to your every thought. From this starting point, our task becomes clear—to access the power of intention, the field of unlimited possibilities!

I understand this to mean that intention is a force which we all have within us and that every aspect and expression of nature is also connected to this force. Luther Standing Bear describes this in the following way:

> From Wakan Tanka, the Great Spirit, there came a great unifying force that flowed in and through all things—the flowers of the plants, blowing wind, rocks, trees, birds, animals—and was the same force that had been breathed into the first man. Thus all things were kindred, and were brought together by the same Great Mystery. (Buhner 2002, 39)

In February 2004, Sandra Ingerman taught me a shamanic technique called the *transfiguration process*. I learned to journey into a space that is a formless vibrating field of energy. I experience this as pure Spirit, limitless and unbounded. It is an incredibly cosmic experience. I was guided to this place, which is Original Perfection, by one of my teachers who exists in nonordinary reality, Dom Ignacio de Loyola. I learned that this is the field of intent, of Source, which all things emanate from and return to. I realized that this field of intent cannot be described with words or symbols, because they also emanate from this field and separate us from it by constricting us back into our ego identity. For me, this was another empirical validation that the realm of Spirit is nonconceptual and thus *cannot be accessed through our ego*. The *Tao Te Ching* (Bynner 1944, 25) describes this knowledge as follows:

Existence is beyond the power of words
To define:
Terms may be used
But are none of them absolute.
In the beginning of heaven and earth there were no words,
Words came out of the womb of matter;
And whether a man dispassionately
Sees to the core of life
Or passionately
Sees the surface,
The core and the surface
Are essentially the same,
Words making them seem different
Only to express appearance.
If name be needed, wonder names them both:
From wonder into wonder
Existence opens.

Upon reflection, I realized that for most people, how to live life intentionally is a mystery akin to trying to negotiate a stunning paradox. It requires the individual to be in physical form (and the realm of time and space) while at the same time *embodying Spirit*. Being in physical form means that we define ourselves by our physical body and separate egoic self-identity. Spirit is a dimension that is boundless, nonmaterial, and timeless. Yet in spite of being corporeal, we are also Spirit.

Our task is to resolve this paradox by integrating the two aspects of being through our awareness and our unique free will. In order to do this, we must have a self-validating, empirically based, firsthand experience that generates a reliable internal reference point. This reference point becomes an *accessible* inner resource for creating an instant link to Spirit. Unless we are blessed with a spontaneous, archetypal mystical experience, it is typically only through some kind of spiritual practice or discipline that we are able to make this link. Otherwise, our tendency as unique and separate human beings is to shift our thoughts away from Spirit and orient to ego, where conscious connection to the power of intention is lost.

What I experience as the silent mind—one in which all the inner chatter has stopped—is a space where intention is profoundly present. I believe that we are all connected by this all-pervading Source to everything and everyone all the time. We can't *not* be. But if this is so, why do so many people feel disconnected from Source, feel like victims of the universe, and experience ongoing frustration when trying to achieve their goals? The primary reason is ego—it separates us from everyone else, as does our body. Because our ego is the primary filter through which we perceive everything in our experience, we end up out of alignment with our intent. Additionally, we are run by the programs in our unconscious mind that create matrices of beliefs which limit us and, more often than not, sabotage us as we strive toward our desires and aspirations. In *The Soul's Code*, Jungian scholar James Hillman elaborates on this idea. He suggests that many of the influences that limit our ability to live a life fulfilled and to claim our destiny result from a self-created life narrative or myth. In the end, this life narrative reduces us to a victim identity, which the dominant cultural paradigm reinforces.

> At the outset we need to make clear that today's main paradigm for understanding a human life, the interplay of genetics and environment, omits something essential—the particularity you feel to be you. By accepting the idea that I am the effect of a subtle buffeting between hereditary and societal forces, I reduce myself to a result. The more my life is accounted for by what already occurred in my chromosomes, by what my parents did or didn't do, and by my early years now long past, the more my biography is the story of a victim. I am living a plot written by my genetic code, ancestral heredity, traumatic occasions, parental unconsciousness, societal accidents. (Hillman 1996, 6)

We are always creating by virtue of our omnipresent energetic link to the field of intent. The trouble is, most of us are not *awake* while we're doing it! In order to live an intentional life, *we must go through an initiatory process that activates our conscious connection to the power of intention*. In this way, we can realize that we are connected to our natural, organismic self. I have some very specific recommendations for enabling this activation. *Once activated, your life will transform.*

So, how do you disidentify from the tyrannizing influence of your ego? Constructive altered states of consciousness are integral for achieving and maintaining alignment with your intent. Your first reference point must be the single Source of all; that is, the field of intent. To the degree that you can sustain this awareness with the help of a daily spiritual practice, whatever that may be, you will more easily and elegantly achieve your intentions.

Part of any spiritual practice generally includes an element of self-reflection. Whatever your practice, you are training yourself to become comfortable in and adept at navigating through the invisible realms. Our culture does not support these realms. On the contrary, the power and increasing dominance of the many forms of media (video games, DVDs, home theater systems, streaming video newscasts via the Internet, etc.) are becoming more central to and pervasive in all of our lives. This orientation to the external is true even within mainstream psychology. James Hillman (1996, 92) speaks to this tendency:

> Invisibility perplexes American common sense and American psychology, which hold as a major governing principle that whatever exists, exists in some quantity and therefore can be measured.... When the searchers failed to find the soul in the places where they were looking, scientistic psychology also gave up on the idea of the soul.

We must continue to erode the mistaken belief that we are separate—this is the key. The more deeply we recognize, feel, and experience our interconnectedness, the more quickly, even instantly, we will recognize our intentions and confirm that thought is indeed creative. Having said that, constructive altered states of consciousness will help to destabilize the dominance of our ego in directing our daily lives. The more we can move in and out of dreamtime, the more new insights and possibilities become available.

As described in chapter 5, integrating the dreamingbody experience helps to move us out from the dominant cultural trance of consensus-reality thinking. We accomplish this by cultivating our second attention. Maintaining this heightened state of awareness in all of our day-to-day doings, we loosen the grip of the ego and become more available to step into the stream of Process that is always present. Whether you call it Process, Tao, or the field of intent, this moving back and forth between the worlds of ego and Spirit is what dreamtime is all about.

Establishing and maintaining an energetic practice is another fundamental part of becoming more sensitive to subtle energies. This increasing sensitivity to perceptions that are not sensory-based (but that are extrasensory or invisible) is another important component in challenging the dominance of the ego for determining what's true for us. The disciplines of qigong, tai qi quan, yoga, and meditation are all energetic practices that fit into this category.

Prior unconscious conditioning to defer to others first (so we won't be regarded as *selfish*), which often occurs in dysfunctional family systems, also impairs our ability to stay in alignment with our intent. There are several names for this concept, such as external versus internal locus of control and codependency, which derives from many different influences. One of these influences is being brought up in a dysfunctional family where it was never safe to express your true feelings—your personal emotional truth was never supported and validated. Another influence may be your religious background, which may also have supported the belief that it is selfish to think of your own wants or needs. Clearing and releasing core trauma patterns related to the family of origin, along with supportive energetic boundary work, enables codependent personalities to overcome the tendency to defer to others to the detriment of their own valid emotional needs and aspirations.

Having said all that, it is important to clarify that what happens in a Dynamic Energetic Healing® session is really a microcosm of what is possible for an individual—to be in the conscious and intentional act of creation all the time. When I help a client work on a specific intention, a path becomes cleared for that intention to open up and come to fruition. For example, if a person is suffering from insomnia, the therapeutic goal is the intention to overcome insomnia by falling asleep easily and sleeping deeply through the night. We are creating a very narrow and specific context for the power of intention to be activated. We approach this intention step by step, making sure there is no psychoenergetic reversal and no internal conflicts or energetic origins (traumatic events from the past) that contribute in any way to maintaining the problem state. We determine if there are any limiting beliefs, boundary issues, or outside negative influences that might be impinging on the problem. Manual muscle testing is our corroborating tool throughout the process. By the time we are finished, there are no emotional, energetic, psychological, or karmic residues supporting what was previously the problem state. Working to actualize this intention is truly a microcosm of what can be accomplished on a much larger scale in your life if you are committed to changing your self-identification as a separate individual and to doing whatever is required to restore your conscious connection to Source. This is the bottom line.

If you have toyed with this notion of being in alignment with your intent *as an ongoing state of being*, you will find the following protocol very empowering. If you are not experienced with manual muscle testing, I recommend that you read through chapter 28 ("Preparing to Work on a Specific Intention") first so you can develop some confidence in your muscle testing skills before going through this and other protocols I have outlined in the book.

Protocol for Activating Your Conscious Connection to the Power of Intention

Starting Intention: *I want to be in alignment with my intent. I want to live an intentional life. I want to be in harmony with the power of intention. I want to be a free agent of choice in this universe. I want to be on purpose.*

Step 1: Make sure that
- you understand what this intention means—discuss all aspects with your therapist, partner, or spouse to clarify your conceptual understanding;
- you understand consciously that this is about co-creating your ongoing reality;
- you are in accord with this intention; i.e., all aspects of your being are consciously comfortable with this powerfully stated intention.

Step 2: Manual muscle test for psychoenergetic reversal on the intention (see chapter 9, "The Mysterious Phenomenon of Psychoenergetic Reversal"). If any of the following five core psychoenergetic statements are reversed, correct them using Dynamic Energetic Healing® interventions (see part 2).
- I don't want to ... (fill in the blank with the intention statement)
- It is not possible to ...
- It is not safe to ...

- I don't deserve to . . .
- I will not . . .

Step 3: Manual muscle test to determine if there is any inner conflict within you about your willingness to address this intention. If yes, resolve the conflict using the Dynamic Energetic Healing® protocol (see part 3), and then continue with this process. If no, proceed by manual muscle testing these two questions:

- Is your soul connected to Source?
- Are *you* connected to Source at all levels?

Step 4a: If the answer to both of the questions in step 3 is yes, ask if there is anything remaining that interferes with actualizing this starting intention. If yes, follow the Dynamic Energetic Healing® protocol to resolve it. If no, begin the dialogue with your therapist, partner, or spouse that maps out specific therapeutic and life goals which you want to *intend and create* into manifest reality. You have now activated your conscious connection to the power of intention.

Step 4b: If the answer to either of the questions in step 3 is no, muscle test the following statements (Clinton 1999) to determine if there is any remaining psychoenergetic reversal:

1. I am alone and separate in the universe; I am alienated.
2. I am my body.
3. I cannot become one with Intent.
4. I cannot become one with God or the divine.
5. God does not exist.
6. I am unworthy of being connected to God or the divine.
7. I am not connected to God or the divine.
8. I am unsafe with God or the divine.
9. I am separate from God or the divine.
10. God hates me.
11. I am the only being.
12. God abandoned me because I am a mistake.
13. I do not deserve to be in alignment with my intent.

If any of these statements muscle test strong, this is an indication that psychoenergetic reversal is present. Follow the Dynamic Energetic Healing® protocol to correct any reversal statements.

Step 5: Use manual muscle testing to retest the two questions:
- Is your soul connected to Source?
- Are you connected to Source at all levels?

If both of these questions are answered affirmatively, ask once more if there is anything else that interferes with actualizing your starting intention. If yes, follow the Dynamic Energetic Healing® protocol to ferret out and resolve any block. If no, begin the dialogue that maps out specific therapeutic and life goals that you want to *intend and create* into manifest reality.

You have now activated your conscious connection to the power of intention. The purpose of this protocol is to help you understand the underlying principles for how intention works and to ensure you make a solid connection to Source. The rest is up to you.

As you will see in chapter 18, "Living Life Free of Trauma," once a significant trauma or trauma pattern related to a particular intention has been identified, it can be completely and easily cleared with Dynamic Energetic Healing® techniques.

I agree with James Hillman's idea that unresolved traumatic experiences from our past affect our ability to choose freely in the present. Further, it has become evident to me that, for many clients, once they clear and resolve persistent traumatic patterns that kept them stuck in certain areas of their lives, the binding quality of their pasts seems no longer present *in any area* of their lives. I suspect this is because we organize our epistemological experiences in such a way that the effects of trauma and its sequelae (including the places where we get stuck in relationships and with associated pervasive limiting core beliefs) overlap.

For example, if a person is able to clear and release the trauma pattern associated with an abusive parent, a whole series of related matrices of beliefs will concurrently collapse. This is because the Dynamic Energetic Healing® model targets the information fields that perpetuate the behavioral responses to and distorted interpretations of traumatic events (i.e., limiting beliefs). In many cases, once the unresolved trauma-related patterns connected to an abusive parent are resolved, the individual's energetic boundaries with other people are restored to full robustness, limiting self-devaluing beliefs are dissolved, psychosomatic symptoms disappear, and the tendency to perseverate over anticipated fears vanishes. As these changes emerge spontaneously, it is common for clients who became overidentified with their victimization to finally begin asking, "What do I want to do with my life now that I'm no longer 'stuck' because of a horrible event in my past?"

This is not some New Age wishful thinking—it is the natural and predictable result of coming back into harmony with your true self. After you activate the power of intention in a clinical context in order to eliminate the apparently inescapable and completely controlling forces of past trauma, an opening occurs that finally allows you to choose a course that will bring you into alignment with your intent.

It is nobody's business to tell you what you ought to do with your life. By being in alignment with your intent, you open yourself up to the unlimited possibilities for how you can direct and experience your life. For me, the possibilities for a better world—one filled with individuals in alignment with their intent—continue to be reaffirmed through the comprehensive approaches of Dynamic Energetic Healing®.

9

THE MYSTERIOUS PHENOMENON OF PSYCHOENERGETIC REVERSAL

O ne of the most significant contributions to the field of psychology is what Dr. Roger J. Callahan coined *psychological reversal*. This phenomenon is confounding to the intellect, even though everyone has experienced it to varying degrees. *Psychoenergetic reversal* (PR) (a term that I believe more accurately defines the phenomenon) is a form of self-sabotage that can block you from accomplishing your most important dreams. When psychoenergetic reversal is present, you will ultimately fail in your selected pursuit. Regardless of how determined and persistent you are in striving for change, you will be frustrated and ultimately foiled. In the energy psychology community, we believe that psychoenergetic reversal affects both psychological and medical treatments. But psychoenergetic reversal is not limited to healing issues. You can be reversed academically, athletically, socially, or in any other context.

If you always get high grades in school but continually falter in math, it is likely that you are psychoenergetically reversed. If you are a competitive athlete in a team sport such as baseball or a solo sport such as golf, your pattern of choking—not coming through in the clutch—is probably caused by psychoenergetic reversal. If you are never able to connect with that special person and believe you will always be alone, it's likely that you are psychoenergetically reversed. Of course, psychoenergetic reversal is just one piece of the puzzle when dealing with a particular problem. But if you haven't corrected an existing psychoenergetic reversal condition on a particular issue as a first step in treatment, it's likely that the problem will persist, even if you have released all past residual trauma.

So, just what is psychoenergetic reversal?

To say the least, psychoenergetic reversal is paradoxical. Let's look at an example: John has a number of very good reasons for integrating an exercise program into his life. He has backaches from sitting in front of the computer all day; he has gained over twenty pounds in the last four years; his blood cholesterol is way up; and he is too tired to do anything constructive on the weekends. John has medical reasons as well as personal ones for including exercise in his life; he doesn't need convincing from anyone. He recently bought a membership at his local gym and agreed with his wife that he would exercise directly after work four times a week. As is frequently the case, John started off as a ball of fire. He bought new gym shoes, met with the trainer to develop an appropriate routine, and felt quite proud of himself for taking the initiative. Unfortunately for John, three weeks later he lost his burning motivation and had flat out stopped exercising. John started exercising to improve his health and feel better physically. By the end of the third week, not only was John not exercising, but he felt bad about himself for losing his resolve. He had let himself down. John was psychoenergetically reversed about exercising. No matter how hard he tried and no matter how well he prepared, he just couldn't get himself to do it.

The primary paradox about PR is corroborated by manual muscle testing. If I were to muscle test John on the statement "I want to exercise," his arms would go weak! If I were to muscle test John on the statement "I don't want to exercise," his arms would be strong as steel, indicating agreement. Why is this paradoxical? Because there is no logical reason for John to muscle test strong on *not* wanting to exercise — it doesn't make sense. And yet, virtually everyone has struggled with this same experience from time to time.

Psychoenergetic reversal is different from what psychologists call secondary gain. A cognitive therapy–oriented psychologist might interpret John's behavior as secondary gain, with the payoff (possibly unconscious) being either the ability to continue lounging around the house and being lazy or feeling bad about himself ("I'm worthless") for not succeeding in improving his health. These are his payoffs for not exercising. Certainly, for some reason, John is sabotaging his own efforts to be successful. *You are psychoenergetically reversed when your actions are in conflict with your conscious, intentional desires.*

Energy psychologists theorize that at an essential level, this conflict is generated by a reversal of your energy flow. A helpful metaphor is the action of two magnets, especially since we, too, are electromagnetic. Imagine two magnets, each the size and shape of a flashlight battery. If you push together the positive end of one magnet and the negative end of the other magnet, you will have a very solid connection. In a sense, the magnetic energy is coherent, in that the magnets work together to create a balanced flow in and through each other. The two magnets are drawn to each other electromagnetically. But if you try pushing together the two positive ends or the two negative ends, they repel each other because their energy is no longer coherent or in harmony—they are opposing each other.

Energy psychologists theorize that this phenomenon is what occurs with psychoenergetic reversal. The flow of your electromagnetic or chi energy, which is intimately coupled with a particular thought field, will be energetically opposed or reversed. When this happens, there is a disconnect between your chi energy and the energy that generates your thinking (i.e., consciousness). This manifests as action or behavior, and the result is self-sabotage.

How and why does this happen? I believe it is the result of long-term conditioning or negative reinforcement of a specific part of our life that has been perpetuated over time. Consequently, we become habituated to think about ourselves in a certain way. I know from my experience as a hypnotherapist that the unconscious mind is quite literal. If you continue to repeat a belief or a judgment to a child (when the unconscious mind is most impressionable and does not have the necessary ego defenses to reject self statements that are hurtful or diminishing), over time those statements become an embedded belief in the unconscious mind of that child. Many psychologically sophisticated people have come to accept the veracity of this unconscious imprinting and conditioning process. What becomes established at the unconscious level as a child persists into adulthood as an influential and contributing factor that determines motivation and behavior. A good hypnotherapist tries to reassociate the matrix of beliefs that have already been established in the unconscious mind. This is done by helping the client get into a relaxed state of mind (trance) so that the critical, rational mind is temporarily suspended and no longer interfering with the positive suggestions offered by the therapist. Dr. Roger J. Callahan (quoted in Gallo 1999, 103) describes psychoenergetic reversal as follows:

At times we all become aware that we are behaving in a destructive and hurtful way toward people we love, and yet we seem helpless to stop behaving that way. It is almost as if our willpower is suspended and we seem unable to do anything about it. At such times we are what I call psychologically reversed.

When you are psychologically reversed, your actions are contrary to what you say you want to do. You might say that you want to quit eating when you aren't hungry, and in your heart of hearts you really do want to quit overeating. But in reality you are continuing to overeat. You are sabotaging your own efforts, you feel helpless and you don't know why.

If you have generalized or massive psychoenergetic reversal, you will likely be negative about everything in your life. An overarching sense of hopelessness coupled with self-defeatism will be pervasive in your life. A succession of unfulfilling relationships, an unsuccessful career, and alcohol and drug addiction characterize the experience of individuals on a path to self-destruction. It may appear to others that these individuals want to destroy their life when they are, in fact, probably massively psychoenergetically reversed and truly unable to overcome their persistent negativity.

My example of John trying to initiate an exercise program is indicative of a *specific* psychoenergetic reversal. Specific PR is always context- or subject-specific. John may be pleased with his life overall, have a good job he enjoys, and have a family he is proud of. But when it comes to exercising, John is totally stuck. This kind of specific PR is present in a great majority of people. There are often one or two areas in life that continue to be rough patches for us. It might be the fear of commitment in our most intimate relationships, or perhaps the frustration of maintaining a daily meditation practice. In these cases, it is likely that we have specific psychoenergetic reversal.

It should be noted that not all psychoenergetic reversal is a direct result of early childhood conditioning. When PR is an outcome of childhood conditioning, the individual has created habits of thinking that are difficult to modify. But PR may simply be the result of experiencing a single traumatic incident, or a resistance to following through on an intention that defies analysis.

Dr. Fred Gallo has defined other categories of psychoenergetic reversal, such as deep level reversal and criteria related reversal, but these are beyond the scope of this book. There is, however, one more version of psycho-energetic reversal that I want to mention, which Callahan called a mini psychological reversal. Mini PR occasionally shows up when treatment is progressing well until the client's progress suddenly hits a wall and a wave of resistance emerges. I view this as a temporary retreat to or psychological refuge in the old habit that is resisting being changed. Everyone knows the tenacity of an old and familiar habit pattern. Once the mini reversal is identified and treated, progress will continue successfully without interruption.

It is very important to thoroughly understand the various levels of psychoenergetic reversal. If I were to miss the existence of PR at the beginning of treatment, the success of my Dynamic Energetic Healing® interventions would probably be eventually compromised, much to the detriment of my client. I have discovered that with some clients, treating psychoenergetic reversal in my office is not enough. When a client returns for subsequent sessions and there is still PR on a specific issue that we had previously treated, it is sometimes necessary for the client to elicit a daily energetic intervention (at home) over a period of weeks. I believe this reflects how entrenched certain habitual beliefs become at the unconscious level, perpetuating a disruption in the client's energy system. I always make it a point to test whether psychoenergetic reversal that was corrected in a previous session has remained corrected. I am helping my clients achieve whole-system congruence — coherence throughout the entire person — with their conscious intention, their unconscious beliefs, and the unimpeded flow of their essential energy system that reflects a coherence throughout the entire person. Sometimes psychoenergetic reversal can be treated once and it stays corrected. There are other times, however, when it takes very dedicated persistence to permanently correct PR.

So, how do you treat psychoenergetic reversal? Most of the research in the energy psychology community follows Callahan's protocols for treating what he still calls psychological reversal. His protocols derive from his Thought Field Therapy methodology, which targets specific combinations of points on the acupuncture meridians (i.e., algorithms). Originally, he also incorporated affirmations to act on the psychoenergetic reversal, a technique that he learned while studying with Dr. John Diamond. Many energy psychology practitioners who treat psychoenergetic reversal still use these positive affirmations in combination with the tapping of specific acupressure points. Other authors, including Gallo (1999) and Durlacher (1994), have done a fine job detailing the energy psychology community's consensus treatment for correcting PR, much of which derives from Callahan. These treatments include tapping on the side of the hand (known as the karate-chop point, which is the small intestine-3 point) for specific and criteria-related reversals; rubbing the neurolymphatic reflex point on the left side of the chest (known as the sore spot) for massive and recurring reversals; and tapping on the points above or below the lips (Governing Vessel and Central Vessel points) while repeating affirmations (Gallo and Vincenzi 2000). I will not cover in any detail all the permutations of PR and their attendant treatments that Gallo and others have already described, particularly since my approach, based on my successful clinical experience, differs from the consensus treatment of PR.

When I start working on a new intention with a client, *I always test for psychoenergetic reversal*. I want my clients to know that they are absolutely, energetically congruent from the very start. If during treatment I detect that a client resists continuing on our chosen path, I retest for PR. With knowledge and awareness of the phenomenon of psychoenergetic reversal, you can easily circumvent client resistance to successful treatment.

Clinicians who use a cognitive-behavioral approach (talk therapy) with their clients frequently encounter resistant clients. In these cases, a negative countertransferential process frequently emerges, and the client is blamed for being noncompliant. This sabotages any positive therapeutic work that the client has already accomplished. Furthermore, the therapeutic relationship becomes poisoned as the therapist unconsciously projects onto the client a noncompliant child who is not minding the negative, critical parent figure (the therapist). Frequently this goes undiscussed, because the client lacks the sufficient ego strength to challenge the therapist, who ought to know better. If these clinicians were trained to allow for the possibility of PR, the client's resistance to accomplish certain therapeutic objectives would be better understood within a larger psychological framework. Thus, treating the so-called resistant client becomes instead treating the phenomenon of PR, a naturally occurring therapeutic bump on the road to change that is easily corrected. A clinician who is savvy about psychoenergetic reversal contributes tremendously to eliminating negative countertransference between therapist and client. The therapist can stay neutral and be much less inclined to contaminate the therapeutic relationship with projections onto the client.

I treat psychoenergetic reversal the same way that I address everything else in Dynamic Energetic Healing®. I use a full complement of energetic strategies that encompass all of my interventions (see part 2). Through manual muscle testing, it is the clients who select the most efficient intervention to correct their own PR. This can be the negative affect erasing method (NAEM), frontal occipital holding, chiming a Tibetan bowl, or tapping on the chakras. Occasionally, clients select one of Callahan's interventions, such as tapping on the karate-chop point on the side of the hand or rubbing the neurolymphatic drainage point on the left side of the chest. Because a major operating paradigm of my healing model is a process orientation, I am not prescriptive. Rather, I make available to clients *the best intervention that their own inner wisdom selects.*

I don't mean to discount what Callahan-trained clinicians use as their treatment protocols. I believe that what works for clinicians is a reflection of what they hold in their field. Energy psychology methodologies work for almost any clinician. And as indicated in *Energy Psychology in Psychotherapy: A Comprehensive Sourcebook* (Gallo 2002), there are many different models that use the underlying principles of energy psychology successfully.

Working in Process is creative and interesting to me. Cognitive analysis is deemphasized as I orient more from my second attention, making much more information readily accessible to me. I experience intuitive impressions, or simply a broader, unified field of awareness to what is happening in the moment within myself and within the therapeutic relational context. In addition, my disposition to readily connect to the compassionate spirits as I work with clients helps to keep me reverent, humble, and in awe.

Dynamic Energetic Healing® is an outstanding therapeutic healing model that continues to evolve. Psychoenergetic reversal, and its attendant self-sabotage, is just one of the many barriers to successful therapeutic outcomes that Dynamic Energetic Healing® consistently resolves.

10

UNDERSTANDING TRAUMA WITHIN DYNAMIC ENERGETIC HEALING®

I n the Dynamic Energetic Healing® model, the long-term consequences of trauma frequently emerge as the primary feature from which all subsequent disturbance patterns arise. The tentacles of trauma reach into all areas of people's lives. Dynamic Energetic Healing® leads to the recognition and deeper understanding of the complexity of trauma and its sequelae, and it is thus consistently successful in generating positive therapeutic outcomes for treatment of emotional trauma.

Stress is an ongoing part of our lives, and we are frequently told that we need to accommodate it by developing healthy strategies to minimize its impact on us. This popular advice does not diminish the impact of stress on our lives—it acknowledges its existence as something that can affect us adversely. Interestingly, similar attitudes persist in regard to trauma. However, we must be careful to make important distinctions between the two.

Stress has largely been defined as the vague but palpable pressures that weigh on our daily lives and cumulatively wreak their damage upon us. These stressors may include long work hours, demanding children, financial concerns, contentious interpersonal relationships, and the ongoing feeling that there is never enough time to accomplish the day's tasks. Health professionals often recommend meditation, exercise, modification of diet, time management techniques, and hobbies as remedies for more healthily dealing with stress. Yet stress remains a part of our lives and will always be present to varying degrees. Stress can lead to disability when not properly attended to.

Trauma is an entirely different order of experience. To varying degrees, trauma is something with which we are all familiar. Whether it is a developmental trauma (such as a child abandoned by his mother, or the confusion of identity that emerges when a young girl first begins menstruating) or a situational trauma (such as a devastating auto accident or a family's home destroyed by a tornado), traumatic experiences are part of life. This is true across the developmental spectrum, from the time we are in our mother's womb to our last breath of air. Trauma did not become a central focus of mainstream psychotherapy until late in the 1980s. While some traumas are developmental and others are situational in their origins, it is becoming increasingly evident that people are profoundly and often permanently affected by trauma. This has been clinically confirmed by researchers in the psychodynamic and the biological orientations, who discuss the incredible impact of overwhelming life experiences (traumas) on both the body and the mind.

Though Freud and other pioneers of Western psychology began writing about the impact of psychological trauma in the early 1900s, "... the relative neglect by psychiatry of the issue of psychological trauma is almost as intriguing as the impact of trauma itself" (van der Kolk 1987, xi). Considering the challenges posed to the therapist by victims of a horrible life event, this neglect is understandable.

> Relationships with victims require therapists to have a continual awareness of their own subjective reactions and their need to defend themselves against the tidings conveyed by their traumatized fellow men and women who have plumbed the darkest depths of life. (van der Kolk, McFarlane, and Weisaeth 1996, 39)

People who have been wounded by severe trauma end up feeling stuck in very specific areas in their lives. Trauma not only limits what you feel capable of accomplishing, it also creates significant ambivalence and confusion in your efforts to seek help. Trauma victims are often filled with shame, and many believe they are broken or damaged by their utter helplessness to escape from their inner prison. Because of these feelings and the accompanying vulnerability, many individuals are hesitant to seek counseling assistance. When trauma victims do finally seek psychotherapeutic help, it is doubtful whether the clinician is sufficiently emotionally integrated (let alone professionally trained) to support these individuals and see them through to a positive therapeutic outcome. The literature supports these assertions.

> Traumatized patients are frequently very difficult to engage in psychotherapy. This probably is related both to a fear of attachment, which reawakens the fear of abandonment, and to the reluctance to remember the trauma itself. After intense efforts to ward off reliving the trauma, a therapist cannot expect that the resistances to remember will suddenly melt away under his or her empathic efforts. The history of the neglect of the trauma issue of psychiatry is probably as much related to the patient's efforts to forget as to the profession's reluctance to deal with the helplessness that accompanies the treatment of the sequelae of overwhelming life events. Many patients interrupt therapy and attempt not to have to deal with the issues related to the trauma. (van der Kolk 1987, 187)

Post-traumatic stress disorder (PTSD) was not included in psychiatry's classification system (the *Diagnostic and Statistical Manual of Mental Disorders*, or DSM) until 1980 with the DSM-III. Because the psychiatric community lacked clarity and agreement about what eventually came to be described as PTSD, it took years of lobbying, countless committee meetings, and numerous presentations at conferences of the American Psychiatric Association (APA) before PTSD was included in the DSM-III.

> All the different syndromes—the "rape trauma syndrome," the "battered woman syndrome," the "Vietnam veterans syndrome," and the "abused child syndrome"—were subsumed under this new diagnosis. However, all of these different syndromes originally had been described with considerable variations from the eventual definition of PTSD. (van der Kolk, McFarlane, and Weisaeth 1996, 61)

Since the diagnosis of PTSD has finally become accepted within the larger psychological community, its complex symptomatology has become legitimized. What would previously have been regarded simply as "neurotic" behavior is now accepted and understood as the aftermath of experiences that overwhelm the human organism's capacity to cope. PTSD has provided the framework for better understanding how we are affected and shaped by our experience. Initially, mainstream psychiatry regarded the trauma response as an individual experience, characterized essentially as intrapsychic. What seems obvious now is that "psychological trauma invariably occurs in a social context involving either the loss of attachment figures or the destruction of the basic sense of security and continuity that results from accumulated secure experiences with others" (van der Kolk 1987, 153). Though still relatively new in Western psychology, PTSD is no longer being minimized or marginalized as some kind of malingering or hysterical behavior. In fact, researchers and clinicians are discovering how common PTSD actually is. Because of the depth, persistence, and "black hole" nature of PTSD,

> the introduction of the PTSD diagnosis has opened a door to the sci-
> entific investigation of the nature of human suffering. . . . It refocuses
> attention back on the living person instead of our overly concrete defi-
> nitions of mental "disorders" as "things" in and of themselves, bring-
> ing us back to people's own experience and the meaning which they
> assign to it. (van der Kolk, McFarlane, and Weisaeth 1996, 5)

Because the large drug companies have been so successful in promoting their psychoactive drugs, family doctors are too eager to prescribe these power-ful drugs to patients who come in for anxiety or depression, which are very often the manifestations of undiagnosed underlying trauma. These pharma-ceutical drugs often take the edge off acute symptomatology by flattening out the sufferer's affect and mitigating symptoms, including nightmares and flash-backs. But these drugs and many doctors' lack of awareness of underlying trauma simply mask the symptoms of more deeply troubling problems.

As discussed in appendix 1, there is growing concern about the cavalier use and insufficient testing of pharmaceutical drugs prescribed to alleviate depression and anxiety. In an article in *Newsweek* magazine (April 5, 2004), the FDA reported that there is growing evidence that some patients taking antidepressants get worse and even become suicidal during the first few weeks of use. I find it remarkable that a risk of taking these drugs is the "side effect" of suicide in adults and children who are prescribed them! The FDA high-lights its report with the warning that children might be particularly vulnera-ble. Statistics indicate that 30 million Americans, including 10 million children, are currently on the drugs. The same article states that NOP World Health, a research firm that has polled doctors on this issue, reported in a recent study that "72 percent of psychiatrists and 78 percent of child psychiatrists strongly agreed that the benefits of antidepressants outweigh the risks, even after learning that the FDA was questioning the drugs' safety."

David Healy, author of the forthcoming book *Let Them Eat Prozac*, is quoted in the same *Newsweek* article about the willingness of primary care providers (i.e., family doctors) to prescribe these drugs. He says, "Rather than being skeptical, they've been almost more enthusiastic than the drug companies." Similarly, Dr. Bessel van der Kolk (1987, 75) has noted the following:

> Despite the marked recent interest in PTSD, there are no carefully controlled studies on the effects of medications. The sparse literature consists entirely of case reports and small open trials. Clinical reports have claimed success for every class of psychoactive medication.

Fortunately, Dynamic Energetic Healing® provides a viable alternative to the use of the powerful brain-modifying drugs frequently used to treat PTSD. Cultivating your second attention when dealing with severely traumatized clients is absolutely essential in order to successfully navigate the ever present land mines of PTSD. The therapeutic relationship with these clients is incredibly complex. The interpersonal field has to be approached with extreme sensitivity and awareness, because the typical PTSD client is hypervigilant to any comment that may smack of criticism, rejection, betrayal, or blame. These relational issues tend to be reenacted within the psychotherapeutic relationship. Discordant or negative countertransference by you as the therapist is always a risk—you may have your own unresolved issues related to intense emotional experiences, resulting in vicarious traumatization. This is why it is essential for therapists who work with clients with PTSD to have done their own healing work.

Therapists trained in the cognitive-behavioral model (talk therapy) are ill-equipped to help PTSD clients if their primary goal is to explore the trauma in order to generate insight and revive the event. This exploration is often the first step, but it must be followed by helping clients regain control over their emotional responses and see the trauma as a historical event (or events) within the larger context of their life, without any fear of experiencing the trauma (or the memory of it) again while exploring it.

> Treatment needs to address the twin issues of helping patients (1) regain a sense of safety in their bodies and (2) complete the unfinished

past. It is likely, though not proven, that attention to these two elements of treatment will alleviate most traumatic stress sequelae. (van der Kolk, McFarlane, and Weisaeth 1996, 17)

If clients with PTSD do not feel safe in their physical body, I literally see them as being somewhat dissociated—a part of them is hovering above their head. This kind of out-of-body dissociation is one of the common responses to trauma. When I see this, I establish the intention for them to be 100 percent in their physical body. This intention often generates a circuitous route to finding out the energetic origin(s) of the traumatic event(s) that must be uncovered and resolved in order for the intention to be realized. If individuals do not feel safe physically, it is fairly predictable that they will not feel safe in any context. I have found that when a PTSD victim is fully embodied, their ability to remain present in a relationship is enormously enhanced. This often initiates a shift from clients being in their head (often accompanied by the traumatic memories of the past) to being more present in the here and now.

> The aim of therapy with traumatized patients is to help them move from being haunted by the past and interpreting subsequent emotionally arousing stimuli as a return of the trauma, to being fully engaged in the present, and becoming capable of responding to current exigencies.... The key element of psychotherapy of people with PTSD is the integration of the alien, the unacceptable, the terrifying, and the incomprehensible into their self-concepts. (van der Kolk, McFarlane, and Weisaeth 1996, 419–20)

Because traumatic experience is so overwhelming, psychological integration of the self is very difficult for PTSD victims. A great deal has been written about dissociation as a response to trauma, which was first described by Pierre Janet in 1889. In fact, if there has not been a brain injury, then it is predictable that the dissociation is a response to a trauma.

What exactly is dissociation? When specific memories and feeling states associated with a traumatic event are split off from your core personality (i.e., your normal self), they return as various symptoms that seem bizarre and out of your control. Most often, these symptoms become intrusive, persistent, and uninvited. They may include panic attacks (overwhelming anxiety for no apparent reason), which are experienced physically; visual images, which may include flashbacks and nightmares; experiences of depersonalization (perceiving that you are outside your physical body watching yourself go through your day in a robot-like fashion); and an inability to stop thinking about something obsessively. Repeating or reenacting any part of the traumatic event is also an aspect that can become out of your control and therefore intrusive. One of the most perplexing aspects of the dissociation experience is that the parts of you that split off carry the memories with them. This means that the memories and feelings connected with the trauma are frequently forgotten because they can no longer be accessed—they are hidden from conscious awareness, protected by the dissociated parts that harbor them. When people start reenacting aspects of the trauma that are out of their conscious awareness, their relationships suffer terribly because of interpersonal communication patterns that don't make sense. Indeed, the victims of trauma end up feeling tremendous shame for continually acting out behaviors that run counter to their goal of having a mutually respectful, cooperative, loving relationship. This is because traumatized individuals often experience the same emotional intensity of the original trauma but without a proper historical context or understanding of why the emotional eruption occurs. Thus, PTSD victims tend to react to a stimulus in much the same way as they originally did; that is, with a fight-or-flight response completely out of proportion to the current event. The relationship between memory and trauma has been a key issue in the study of trauma for decades.

> Ever since psychiatrists and psychologists have devoted themselves to the study of trauma's impact on consciousness, they have noted that memories are stored in a state-dependent fashion, which may render them inaccessible to verbal recall for prolonged periods of time. (van der Kolk, McFarlane, and Weisaeth 1996, x)

> Researchers conducting longitudinal studies of shell-shocked soldiers noticed that over a period spanning decades, long-forgotten traumatic memories would spontaneously reemerge.

> Archibald and Tuddenham found that reexperiencing of war trauma sometimes did not start until as long as 15 years afterward. (van der Kolk 1987, 185)

Post-traumatic stress disorder is aptly named as a syndrome that includes a variety of responses to trauma that occur after the fact. It is the human organism's adaptive response to an overwhelming traumatic life event that, at the time, is generated to support survival. It is because we have no control over the particular constellation of responses to a traumatic event that PTSD has become so confounding. Kardiner (quoted in van der Kolk 1987, 2) describes the five principal features of the human response to trauma as

1) a persistence of startle response and irritability, 2) proclivity to explosive outbursts of aggression, 3) fixation on the trauma, 4) constriction of the general level of personality functioning, and 5) atypical dream life.

It is now well noted that when a particular trauma is not integrated into the person's overall life experiences, a fixation on the trauma results. A tragic irony is that in spite of all efforts to avoid any aspect of the traumatic event, sufferers of PTSD frequently end up with a lifelong preoccupation with repeating the trauma. Even when they try to push traumatic memories out of their conscious awareness, the memories continue to return as intrusive and dissociated symptoms. The following quote from a Vietnam veteran illustrates the point.

After a certain moment you just keep running the hundred yard dash. You are always ready for it to come back. I spend all my energy on holding it back. I have to isolate myself to keep myself from exploding. It all comes back, all the time. The nightmares come two, three times a week for awhile. Then they let up for a bit. You can never get angry, because there is no way of controlling it. You can never feel just a little bit. It is all or nothing. I am constantly and totally preoccupied with not getting out of control. (van der Kolk 1984, 124)

Krystal (quoted in van der Kolk 1984, 5) points out that the entire personality changes and lists some of the symptoms of what he calls the disaster syndrome:

1) loss of capacity to use community supports, 2) chronic recurrent depression with feelings of despair, 3) psychosomatic symptoms,

4) emotional "anesthesia" or blocked ability to react affectively, and
5) "alexithymia" or inability to recognize and make use of the emotional reactions.

What Krystal refers to as *alexithymia* is a distinctive feature of PTSD. When you find yourself unable to translate somatic sensations into basic feelings such as happiness, anger, or fear, you end up experiencing emotions as physical problems. When you cannot translate and communicate to others your feeling states, your relationships become chaotic. In psychologically healthy people, emotions provide awareness, information, and guidance regarding the nature of subjective experience. For sufferers of PTSD, traumatic residue often leads to loss of affect regulation since their awareness of their emotional experience has been contaminated by the trauma. It is very common for traumatized people to be emotionally reactive and go directly from a stimulus to a strong emotional response without any conscious mediation to first figure out what created the upset. The behavioral consequences of this are typically a strong overreaction that intimidates others or emotional numbing that leads to shutting down and self-isolation. When these responses occur, victims of trauma try very hard to *not feel*, since their inability to modulate affect becomes their dominant experience. Their experiential conclusions confirm their belief that they have no control over regulating any of their internal states. As a consequence, traumatized people have little tolerance for psychological and physiological arousal—physical sensations and emotional reactions become overwhelming. This chronic sense of feeling out of control often leads to psychological and physical numbing, which can result in "psychological constriction, depression, social isolation, anhedonia [the inability to experience pleasure], and a sense of estrangement" (van der Kolk 1987). When the numbing response becomes pervasive, it is common for PTSD victims to withdraw from conscious life and, ultimately, feel dead to their social world. In Dynamic Energetic Healing®, it is common to discover that traumatized clients have a stronger wish to die than will to live. Frequently this is unconscious, ferreted out and corroborated through manual muscle testing. When the wish to die is discovered and released, it is remarkable how quickly the motivation to heal increases.

Many victims of PTSD medicate themselves with alcohol and drugs. This is an understandable response to their hyperarousal when faced with emotional or sensory stimuli. Because PTSD victims often find it difficult to control their anxiety or aggression, they frequently become preoccupied with keeping these feelings at bay. A complication is that "their physiological responses are conditioned to react to reminders of trauma as an emergency.... Any arousing situation may trigger memories of long-ago traumatic experiences and precipitate reactions that are irrelevant to present demands" (van der Kolk, McFarlane, and Weisaeth 1996, 421). Over time, triggers for traumatic memories become less obvious and more generalized, reinforcing the feeling of being out of control no matter what the context or stimulus may be. For example, consider a young child who loses his mother to cancer just before Christmas. Some years later, the now-adolescent experiences a major depressive episode every Thanksgiving. Even though the anniversary of the trauma immediately precedes Christmas, the seasonal cue of the Christmas lights appearing around Thanksgiving subconsciously reminds him of his profound loss and restimulates negative emotional traumatic residue.

Contemporary Western psychiatry is finally addressing the very real and damaging effects of PTSD. Reports of success in treating PTSD are anecdotal because there have been almost no controlled studies done. While the combination of cognitive-behavioral therapy and pharmacological therapy tends to be the mainstay of the psychiatric approach for helping PTSD victims, consistent and predictable positive therapeutic outcomes continue to be elusive.

> Controlled clinical trials, however, are needed to confirm the clinical impression that psychotherapy and other restorative experiences can positively affect post-traumatic hyperarousal and possibly "re-set" the nervous system at premorbid levels. (van der Kolk 1987, 79)

Studies of PTSD victims have demonstrated the degree to which psychological and physiological reactions are interrelated. My experience suggests that trauma also creates memory at the cellular level. I have had many clients who have had the memory of a traumatic event originate in the place in their body where injury or abuse happened previously. It is becoming evident that, due to the lack of affect modulation that frequently causes chronic hyperarousal, many long-term PTSD victims may experience a change in their biochemistry.

The literature on PTSD indicates that successful psychotherapy cannot proceed if clients are unable to tolerate feeling states associated with the trauma without some kind of dissociative experience occurring at the same time. Consequently, modern psychiatry successfully promotes supplementing psychotherapy with psychoactive medication. These powerful drugs quickly affect the brain biochemistry of the PTSD victim. While they can provide quick relief by suppressing and alleviating the severity of dissociative intrusions, further research may show that their benefits are outweighed by their risks.

There seems to be no consensus among practitioners who treat PTSD with respect to what consistently works best. Blake (quoted in van der Kolk, McFarlane, and Weisaeth 1996) says that

> despite the fact that most studies with positive results for ameliorating PTSD symptoms have used a cognitive-behavioral framework, most clinicians treating traumatized patients continue to practice psychodynamic therapy ... in addition, there have been no careful studies comparing manualized cognitive behavioral treatment with a rigorous psychodynamic approach.

Dynamic Energetic Healing® incorporates a variety of powerful interventions from energy psychology and core shamanism for successful treatment of PTSD (see part 2 for detailed explanations). In the energy psychology model, it is understood that traumatic events cause an energy imbalance when specific meridian points or chakras in your energy system are negatively affected. One explanation is that some of the energy in that particular meridian or chakra may become disrupted or depleted, creating an imbalance. Tapping on one or more acupoints or chakras increases the flow of energy through direct percussive stimulation, which enables that acupoint or chakra to come back into energetic balance. Remember, each meridian and each chakra has its own emotional correlates. When your energy system is in proper balance, your vital energy is flowing freely throughout your body so that each meridian and chakra is in optimal energetic balance. Trauma, either physical or emotional, generates an energy imbalance, which leaves you unable to resolve the trauma-induced problem and keeps you vulnerable to similar problems whenever they may recur.

Dynamic Energetic Healing® has also shown that some energy imbalances are, in fact, passed on from one generation to another. Specific unresolved traumas suffered by a deceased relative are called ancestral energetic origins. These can be passed on in the intergenerational energy field and ultimately influence you. You may have negative thinking patterns and a predisposition toward certain negative emotional feeling states, which in turn may make you feel more vulnerable, all of which can have a major impact on your life if not treated.

Dynamic Energetic Healing® is extremely effective at identifying the energetic origin of presenting problems, but there are many energy psychology models that can successfully eliminate fears and phobias—even if the therapist doesn't understand their origins. The detectable electromagnetic-like fields addressed in energy psychology are the counterparts to neuropeptides, the chemical correlates of thought. Energy psychology targets what Dr. Roger Callahan referred to initially as "thought fields" (the energetic presence or manifestation of a thought). When a disturbance occurs within a thought field, it always corresponds to a specific energy point (meridian or chakra) on the body. Interestingly, the cognitive understanding that generates insight and awareness connected to traumatic memories is an epiphenomenon that nearly always emerges spontaneously once the trauma residue is unpacked and released.

Treatment of PTSD is still very much in the research stage. Yet as early as 1887, well-known French neurologist Jean-Martin Charcot (quoted in van der Kolk 1987, 9) described traumatic memories as "parasites of the mind." What I find particularly interesting about this description is how analogous it is to what shamans have been addressing for thousands of years that they refer to collectively as *intrusions*. Though intrusions are often described as negative thought forms, the word is frequently used to describe any kind of negative energy that becomes lodged in the body (physical or energetic) of the victim. This term has also been adopted by modern psychiatry to describe persistent, uncontrollable dissociated memories and experiences. Perhaps this is an example of the morphic resonance that biologist Rupert Sheldrake describes in relation to the treatment of psychological trauma.

With the assistance of a helping spirit, the shaman will often see intrusions in the body of the client as maggot-like insects; obstinate, dark, serpentine creatures; or nail-sharp or dart-like objects embedded in the person. Once the shaman removes the intrusions, the part of the body that harbored the negative energy is replaced by and filled up with positive healing energy. This intervention is called an extraction.

It is understood in the practice of shamanism that people are vulnerable to intrusions when they experience a loss of personal power, which happens when people experience traumatic events that overwhelm their capacity to cope. During these times, people will also likely experience "soul loss." I talk about this in detail in chapter 11. Briefly, you experience soul loss when part of your "vital essence" splits off from your core, often taking traumatic memories with it. People who say that they have never quite felt like themselves after a particularly traumatic event are exhibiting a symptom of soul loss. In contrast to the approach taken by Western psychotherapy, the shaman (with the help of his or her helping spirits) is able to locate and retrieve the part of the patient that separated from the core at the time of the traumatic event.

Shamans in various cultures have been using these healing strategies for thousands of years. They are as effective now as they were five thousand years ago. The underlying principles of energy psychology also go back thousands of years. Admittedly, scientific studies need to be done to validate and thus legitimize these "radical" models for addressing PTSD. In the meantime, clinical reports by credible therapists along with conference presentations and seminars continue to inspire intrepid and dedicated therapists to expand their repertoire by considering these ideas and possibilities.

In Dynamic Energetic Healing® trainings, I stress the importance of clearing both the recent trauma that has brought the client to the therapist's office and what might be the deeper underlying structure of the traumatic pattern. Frequently, the recent trauma is but one star in a larger constellation of linked traumas. In the intermediate training, I share with participants how I use the energetic origins protocol to determine the origin(s) of the present trauma pattern that is interfering with a client's intention. I determine if the origin is in the current lifetime (which can include an event that occurred in the womb) and whether there is more than one energetic origin to be addressed. I test to determine if there are related origins to this recent trauma from ancestral or genealogical roots on either parent's lineage. I have found that with deeper trauma patterns, there are often energetic origins from a past life that must be resolved. These "karmic" past-life origins are often the predecessors of current-life traumas that establish and maintain the energetic attractors which re-create the conditions that allow similar traumas to occur.

As psychology considers new and better ways to successfully treat PTSD, it is important to reflect on the role of learning and memory as an integral part of the human organism's response to overwhelming life experiences. Schwartz and Russek believe that it is important to understand how the response to trauma takes place systemically in all systems at all levels. If the systemic memory process is true, then memory is not limited to the brain. Every cell, and every molecule within every cell, will accumulate a unique story. (Schwartz and Russek, 1999, 150)

It is their contention that we need to develop better strategies in order to help people retrieve their memories, particularly when inaccessible and dissociated memories perpetuate PTSD symptomatology. In their systemic memory hypothesis, they assert that psychologists will have to consider the idea

that "spirits" and "souls" exist as info-energy systems that play a role in what all of us do. Moreover, we will have to become more humble about claiming that "our" thoughts come exclusively from "us." (1999, 150)

Elaborating on their ideas about learning and memory, they go on to list a number of possibilities in response to the question "Where do each of our thoughts come from?" This is an important question since Western psychology maintains a limited range of possibilities for where traumatic residue as information comes from and where it is stored.

- Did we "create" it?
- Did it come from "our" unconscious?
- Was it a "random" event?
- Did we receive it from someone else?
- Did it come from the "present" or the "past" (and if the "past" is actually present, as Sheldrake reminds us and the systemic memory process requires, then is it all "present")?
- Did we receive it from a higher "soul" or "angel"?
- Did we even get it from the Grand Organizing Designer of the universe him/herself?
- Did we get it from the universal living memory?

The truth is, science doesn't know. If memory can be everywhere, including in info-energy systems living in the vacuum, then where is consciousness per se located? Is consciousness primarily a construction of the brain, or is the brain just one magnificent tool for experiencing consciousness? (Schwartz and Russek, 1999, 150)

The current Western psychological approach to treating PTSD does not typically address the origins of trauma patterns that often predate the actual emergence of PTSD. Rather, it favors a cognitive-behavioral approach combined with medication to create emotional "stabilization." I am hopeful that Dynamic Energetic Healing® will stimulate interest in considering these other possibilities within the field of Western psychiatry, much like Dr. Brian Weiss's clinical experiences on past-life therapy support many psychiatrists who have experienced similar revelations with their own patients.

It is important to understand the central role that trauma plays in reducing our choices to live an intentional life (i.e., being in alignment with our intent). If trauma continues to interfere and intrude in our lives, we will continue to focus on and re-create experiences that only confirm our relationship to the trauma and selectively keep out the positive experiences we wish to generate in our lives. Dynamic Energetic Healing® is a comprehensive psychotherapy and healing model that collapses, dissolves, and transforms persistent trauma patterns, leaving restored human beings who are completely free of the trauma. As you experience this, you are able to move into your full potential and embrace and creatively express the unique task that you are here to accomplish.

CHAPTER

11

SOUL LOSS

A predictable consequence of a traumatic event is that part of the individual's vital essence abandons the physical body. This is called *soul loss* in the shamanic tradition, the counterpart to what is called dissociation in the Western psychology tradition. It is important to make distinctions between soul loss and dissociation in order to better appreciate how profoundly soul loss affects traumatized individuals.

At Western psychology's beginnings, Freud identified many defense mechanisms that spontaneously emerge as an adaptive response to traumatic experience. Freud determined that these defense mechanisms become strategies around which individuals organize themselves. They are unconscious, which means that individuals have no awareness that they have generated this response to a particular traumatic experience. Creating defense mechanisms is one way in which people try to protect themselves from anything that is at all similar to the traumatizing incident. Defense mechanisms are a very ingenious, albeit unconscious, adaptation or strategy to survive emotionally and cope with overwhelming fear that results from a specific traumatic experience.

Modern psychologists agree that when an individual experiences shocks or jolts, it is not unusual for part of that person to dissociate. This is described in different ways in contemporary psychological jargon. Essentially, a part of the individual's psyche or consciousness "leaves" the physical body and ends up in some amorphous place in the unconscious mind. The psychotherapist's job is to help clients recover the lost memory of the traumatizing experience and integrate the "part" that left because the experience was so painful and overwhelming.

Psychotherapists use a variety of therapeutic models and interventions to help victims work through their trauma. One common approach is hypnosis, which alters the state of consciousness through relaxation and suggestion and works directly with the client's unconscious mind. A primary therapeutic objective is to help individuals reassociate and retrieve dissociated memories, dream fragments, and any other archetypal imagery they may present. The theory is that by temporarily displacing the individual's conscious, rational, critical mind with an altered state of consciousness through hypnosis, the experience that has been insulated from conscious awareness becomes more accessible for conscious reintegration.

Freud's psychoanalysis attempted to accomplish the same thing via reassociation. He believed that over time and with the help of the psycho-analyst's probing questions, individuals would be able to create deepening associational links to re-create or replace what had been missing. Freud believed that through the therapeutic relationship and what he called "free floating attention," awareness would eventually emerge as the repressed traumatic memories and dissociated experiences slowly began to reappear and become more accessible.

Dream analysis, which might be specific to a depth psychology or Jungian orientation, attempts to do the same thing by teaching clients how to remember their dreams. With the help of the analyst and a dream journal, individuals make connections by interpreting the symbolic imagery presented through their unconscious mind. Gestalt therapy and process-oriented psychology (processwork) attempt to access the hidden or repressed emotional material by focusing on awareness, particularly on feeling states. By encouraging those feeling states to become more present, the therapist supports and assists the individual to accept and even amplify various emotions through different techniques. One well-known model developed by Gendlin is called focusing, a technique that encourages clients to stay with their feeling states to discover how they unfold organically. Another technique involves allowing images of internally generated figures (or what Mindell calls dream figures) to emerge, and then either drawing these figures or acting them out. In this way, clients flesh out the dream figures and interact with them until more awareness emerges from a relationship with the part that had been split off. Ultimately, the aim is the same—to bring to more conscious awareness that which has been repressed and hidden in the so-called unconscious realm.

Dissociation is a very common, even predictable response to trauma. Though it tends to be underemphasized in psychotherapy generally, I have found that helping clients to retrieve those lost memories or gaps in their lives is an integral part of healing their trauma. When this retrieval occurs, they can finally return to that place of wholeness which existed prior to the significant trauma.

Without fully realizing it, many people spend a great deal of time trying to retrieve lost parts of themselves. For example, many people explore different spiritual paths as they try to find greater depth and meaning to their lives. I believe that many of these people are seeking their lost or dissociated parts in an attempt to experience wholeness. In our culture, it is fairly common for children to disavow their "angry part" because their anger is disallowed by a parent. After being yelled at, hit, or shamed for expressing their angry feelings numerous times, children learn that this is not an acceptable way *to be*. These children often make a conscious or unconscious decision (i.e., an agreement with themselves) to act in a way that feels safe. Anger then becomes a threatening experience, and the part of them that carries their anger goes underground into the unconscious.

In the shamanic worldview, soul loss occurs when the threatened part leaves to another realm, which is called nonordinary reality. The consequences are many—not only will these children grow up without access to the experience of their own anger, but they will have difficulty dealing with other people's anger as well. What's more, these individuals will look for the part of themselves that is angry (and that carries that anger) in other people. At an unconscious and energetic level, they are drawn to people who express, experience, and direct anger in all the ways that the individual as a child was not allowed or able to express. Unwary individuals project onto other people the split-off parts of themselves that they are looking for. They are then simultaneously repelled by and drawn to people who express this anger because those people mirror to them the part of themselves that is no longer accessible.

This unconscious seduction process happens all the time. Instead of finding their missing part inside of themselves, individuals look for it outside, in a meaningful relationship. But looking for this lost part of themselves in their relationships ends up being destructive and traumatic. They are re-creating and thus reexperiencing the same kind of parental relationship dynamic that they experienced as children. This reenactment is a way to unconsciously retrace their steps to the time when this experience, which they desperately need in order to become whole again, was lost to them. It is a painful, difficult way to find and discover a lost part of yourself. Yet more people than you would ever suspect do this over and over again. (There is more discussion on the reenactment of trauma in chapter 10, "Understanding Trauma within Dynamic Energetic Healing®.")

Western psychology sees dissociation as the hallmark of trauma. Nearly everyone has heard of multiple personality disorder, which is now called dissociative identity disorder. This occurs when, as a result of very severe trauma (typically early in an individual's life), the personality shatters or fragments into multiple aspects, and each of these fragments takes on an independent, internal identity. Within the Western psychological model of dissociation, this classic example graphically illustrates the consequences of a dissociative separation from the whole of the personality.

Random House Webster's College Dictionary (1992) defines *soul* as "the essential element or part of something; a distinct entity separate from the body." In the shamanic paradigm in indigenous cultures, what Western psychologists call dissociation is something that encompasses much more. It is called soul loss. This "condition" happens when a part of the vital essence separates from the rest of an individual in order to survive a traumatic experience.

Psychologists agree that when individuals dissociate from a sudden trauma (an auto accident, for example), they may leave their body or may be jettisoned out of their body temporarily so they can cope with the intensity of the traumatic incident. It is often assumed that they will later return to their body as they become more calm. Many therapists have had their clients describe prior auto accidents or sexual molestation from the reference point of watching from above the car or from the ceiling looking down. There is a great deal of clinical evidence in Western psychiatric literature of this phenomenon.

In the shamanic paradigm everything is alive with spirit. Every earthly form is infused and animated with its own spirit. Using the journey method with accompanying drumming, the shaman journeys into nonordinary worlds to connect with the soul or spirit of a plant, an animal, a tree, a river, or another individual. You can even connect and communicate with the spirit of an ancestor or a great teacher who passed away thousands of years ago.

Everything is accessible in the realm of nonordinary reality. A loss of soul or the loss of spiritual energy is one of the most serious conditions requiring healing. According to Mircea Eliade (quoted in Ingerman 1991, 28),

> Everything that concerns the soul and its adventure, here on earth and in the beyond, is the exclusive province of the shaman. Through his own pre-initiatory and initiatory experience, he knows the drama of the human soul, its instability, its precariousness; in addition, he knows the forces that threaten it and the regions to which it can be carried away. If shamanic cure involves ecstasy, it is precisely because illness is regarded as a corruption or alienation of the soul.

In the shamanic paradigm, if a person is weak, unhappy, or feeling disharmony, soul loss is likely the problem. If a shaman can find the lost part and retrieve it with the help of his or her own guardian spirits, harmony and wholeness can be restored to the individual.

There are many possible consequences and symptoms of soul loss, and they are similar to the symptoms of dissociation. Individuals experience a lack of physical energy that often results in a feeling of physical depletion and greater vulnerability to infection and viruses. They may also sense a lack of connectedness or a feeling of existential emptiness. Another symptom is difficulty staying present in the physical body—the perception that you are actually outside of your physical body. Psychologists call this disconnect between the body and the self "depersonalization." Some individuals also have difficulty concentrating and remembering things. Clients have reported to me that when studying for an exam, they find themselves reading the same line and the same paragraph repeatedly without retaining the information. Other symptoms of soul loss include feeling light-headed or queasy, physical numbness, flattened affect, lack of emotional feelings, and not feeling alive (feeling kind of dead inside).

I suspect that chronic depression is caused by soul loss. I have learned over the years that chronically depressed clients (those whose depressed mood has persisted over a long period of time, sometimes for years) have usually suffered soul loss—part (or parts) of them have left. Consequently, they report a feeling of not having it all together, of not being all there, or of not being present. People always know there is something wrong; they know that there is a lack of emotional or energetic integrity. People know this but they have not been able to put their finger on it or articulate what it is. In the shamanic tradition, the underlying cause of these feelings is clear and obvious—it is soul loss. Psychologist Jeanne Achterberg (quoted in Ingerman 1991, 22) describes soul loss as follows:

> Soul loss is regarded as the gravest diagnosis in the shamanic nomenclature, being seen as a cause of illness and death. Yet it is not referred to at all in modern Western medical books. Nevertheless, it is becoming increasingly clear that what the shaman refers to as soul loss—that is, injury to the inviolate core that is the essence of the person's being—does manifest in despair, immunological damage, cancer, and a host of other very serious disorders. It seems to follow the demise of relationship with loved ones, career, or other significant attachments.

What is interesting to me is that the Western psychologists who are trying to address dissociation assume that the parts that have dissociated are in the realm of the unconscious mind. It is very difficult to find language that clearly defines just what or where the unconscious is. It is generally accepted among psychologists that it is a part of us (our consciousness or our mind) that we do not have access to and that lies below the level of our everyday conscious awareness. Psychotherapists use a variety of traditional Western psychotherapeutic models or modalities to try to access dissociated parts in the unconscious and then integrate them into the conscious personality construct.

For the shaman, dissociation is a very different orientation and intention. The shaman knows that the lost soul part or parts reside in the nonordinary worlds that comprise the upper-world realm, this middle-world realm of earthly reality, and the lower-world realm. The shaman's charge is not to engage clients in a dialogue or in a hypnotherapeutic process to stimulate and engage their unconscious mind—these are Western strategies. Instead, the shaman's job is to journey into these nonordinary worlds with the help of his or her guardian spirits to find the part or parts that have become lost. In some cases, the lost part left voluntarily and is hiding out in a particular realm because it feels safer there. Sometimes the lost part gets trapped for one reason or another in these nonordinary worlds and is unable to come back, even if it so desires. With the help of the drum or the rattle, shamans enter an altered state of consciousness (what Michael Harner calls the shamanic state

of consciousness) and initiate the traditional journey that allows them to recognize these different interior topographies of the upper-world, middle-world,
and lower-world realms. The lost soul parts are identified by the shaman with
the help of his or her guardian spirits and are coaxed to explain how this situation came about. Often the originating traumatic event is revealed to the
shaman. The lost part is then brought back by the shaman and integrated into
the individual as an energetic aspect that had been missing.

Over the years, I have done many soul retrievals through the traditional
journey method and, with the help of my guardian spirits, always find the
missing parts and always integrate them back successfully. Clients experience profound changes. Sometimes these changes are immediate, occurring
during the journey itself. Sometimes the changes occur over a period of
weeks, as the energy of the "new" part reintegrates and clients become
refamiliarized with a part of themselves that had been lost—often for many
years or even decades.

When I began thinking about how to teach this to students of Dynamic
Energetic Healing®, I wondered if it were possible to incorporate what is
accomplished with soul retrieval without having to introduce an entirely new
paradigm—namely, the shamanic journey method. Not that they are incompatible, but I want Dynamic Energetic Healing® to be more accessible to
Western-trained psychotherapists within the larger umbrella of energy
psychology. While some therapists are open to and interested in learning the
shamanic journey method, I suspect many will find this methodology a bit too
foreign. To find a way to include a component in Dynamic Energetic Healing®
that would elicit positive results comparable to those achieved by soul
retrieval (using shamanic methods), I looked to the body for guidance.

Over time, I had become increasingly aware (through my ability to psychically see) that many of my clients were not fully embodied! With the help
of manual muscle testing I began inquiring, "Are you 100 percent in your
physical body?" To my surprise, virtually everyone I muscle tested was *not*
100 percent embodied. In fact, many (if not most) of my clients muscle tested
in much lower percentages of embodiment than I had imagined would be
probable. This was in spite of previous healing work that we had done
together, in which the clients had cleared many energetic origins and subsequent traumas that had resulted in soul loss. This was a very curious thing to
me. I started asking my clients if it was the right time and in their highest
good to be fully back in their body; most of the time the answer was yes. As

a result, I now ask a series of specific questions through manual muscle testing, test for specific psychoenergetic reversal, and make sure that clients have 100 percent energetic boundaries with their physical body (see chapter 14, "Energetic Boundaries"). When this is completed, I follow the energetic origins protocol to find out if there are any unresolved traumas that need healing on this specific intention, in order for clients to be 100 percent in their physical body.

In the traditional Western psychological model, a dissociated part is somewhere in the unconscious mind or the psyche. In the shamanic paradigm the split-off part that generates soul loss ends up in nonordinary worlds. In Dynamic Energetic Healing®, the split-off part is somewhere in the energy field. This makes sense given that an energetic origin may be in one of a number of energetic time frames. The origin may be in this lifetime, reflecting an event that occurred when we were very young, or it may be an event that occurred in a previous lifetime. In the latter case, it is still in our energy field because, after all, where do we go when we regress back to a past life? We move into a space through an intention to access that information in our energy field, supported by an underlying presupposition that time is not necessarily linear—events from past, present, and future are happening simultaneously within us. And what if the energetic origin is in a place held by an ancestor twelve generations back in our mother's or our father's lineage? As we regress to the ancestral energetic origin to connect with that ancestor, we are going "back" in as much as we are going "in" our energy field. A different paradigm requires different language to conceptualize consciousness in its own unique and useful way.

This is a way for me to teach trainees to retrieve and integrate split-off parts, whether this phenomenon is called psychological dissociation or soul loss. With help from my colleague Mary Hammond-Newman, this was modeled beautifully at our breakout presentation at the Third International Conference on Energy Psychology in San Diego in May 2001. The individual with whom we worked for our demonstration was initially only 60 percent in her physical body. First, we cleared the energetic origin that had occurred over twenty years before in a skiing accident, resolving old trauma that had never been addressed. Then we addressed the anticipatory anxiety connected to a surgery planned for two weeks later that related to the old ski injury—a fortuitous connection we were all surprised by. We next established energetic boundaries with the upcoming surgery. When we were finished, the trauma healed at the origin and her anticipatory anxiety about the surgery was completely resolved. And, to our collective delight, her muscle testing corroborated that she was 100 percent in her physical body with no remaining indication of the soul loss that had occurred in the previous skiing accident.

It is more and more evident to me that by addressing soul loss through my embodiment protocol (to ensure that clients are 100 percent in their physical body), clients begin to heal in a most dramatic way. It is a peculiar thing to think about not being fully embodied, but more people than I ever would have imagined are not fully in their bodies *for all kinds of reasons*! The primary reason appears to be the cumulative residue of old traumas and their attendant beliefs. A particularly common persisting belief from trauma is that it is not safe to be in the body. Over a long period of time, it becomes a habit or a tendency to not be fully embodied. People are then disinclined to be fully in their physical body, not just because it feels unfamiliar but because it feels unsafe. It is not unusual for people to become "dissociators" in a habitual sense.

When there is physical trauma, frequently there is body memory connected to the events that occurred when the individuals experienced the initial soul loss. All aspects of the initial trauma must be resolved in order for them to once again feel safe in their physical body and restore appropriate relationship to their body (i.e., energetic boundaries). Many of the symptoms described earlier that characterize dissociation and soul loss tend to spontaneously resolve when clients are restored to being 100 percent in their body. However, it is very important for individuals who are once again back in their physical body to change their habitual thinking and behavioral patterns in order to stay fully alive and present in their physical bodies. My clinical experience has shown that if the behavioral, emotional, and cognitive patterns (or habits) from before the full embodiment restoration are still present after the restoration has ostensibly been accomplished, these highly familiar tendencies will support the dynamics of not being fully embodied.

Fortunately, Dynamic Energetic Healing® provides a comprehensive trauma-resolution procedure that thoroughly tests and resolves any residual emotionally related pain that is connected to the initial soul loss. Thus, it is unlikely that individuals will regress into the former symptom complex that persisted for so many years before complete embodiment is restored. For many, the old habit is to not be in their body, and for very good reason (from the point of view of the part or parts that split off and left). That is why the follow-up work after the client has experienced the integration of split-off parts is extremely important.

What follows is my embodiment protocol. It explains how I ensure that my clients return to being 100 percent embodied, and stay embodied.

Protocol for Ensuring That
Your Client Is 100 Percent Embodied

Step 1:   Using MMT, ask: "Are you 100 percent in your physical body?" If no, use MMT to determine what is the exact percentage of embodiment.

Step 2:   Ask: "Do you know why you are not fully embodied?" You will often get a lot of information about clients' experience of dissociation. They may even have recollections of when they began dissociating.

Step 3:   Set the intention for the client to be 100 percent in his or her physical body. Make sure there are no objections to attaining full embodiment from any inner parts of the client.

Step 4:   Check for psychoenergetic reversal:
- I want to be 100 percent in my physical body.
- It is safe for me to be 100 percent in my physical body.
- It is possible for me to be 100 percent in my physical body.
- I deserve to be 100 percent in my physical body.
- I will be 100 percent in my physical body.
- It will be in my overall highest good to stay 100% in my physical body.

If you find any psychoenergetic reversal, correct it before moving on to step 5.

Step 5:   Begin inquiring about energetic origins using the Dynamic Energetic Healing® protocol.

It has been my experience that many clients come to therapy not being fully embodied. It is becoming increasingly clear to me that when one is not fully embodied, chronic symptomatology tends to persist.

In the traditional Western psychological model, dissociative identity disorder can result when trauma is extremely severe. From the shamanic/indigenous worldview, soul loss can result when aspects of our inviolate core split off and do not return. My observations and ongoing research indicate that this consequence of trauma is pervasive. It is important for me to get a complete description of presenting symptoms from the client once I have identified this problem. Common complaints include the inability to concentrate or stay mentally focused, uncharacteristically forgetting things, a tendency to daydream or space out, queasiness or occasional dizziness, watching oneself perform tasks, not feeling fully present, and reports of the "astral body" trying to leave the physical body, particularly in the middle of the night when spontaneously awakened. Some of these symptoms can also be descriptions of depression. More and more, I see these symptoms related to both soul loss and depression, with soul loss often being a large (and often causal) component of depression.

Dynamic Energetic Healing® strategies are usually sufficient to correct dissociation. I continue to rely upon MMT as my guide for the best intervention to integrate the split-off part. Since soul loss usually has an energetic origin, retrieving and integrating a lost part may take more than one session to complete.

Occasionally, it is necessary for me to do a formal soul retrieval through the shamanic journey method. The client's body and soul wisdom make that determination. That is why I have chosen to describe the unique consequences of trauma as soul loss instead of as dissociation. Soul loss for me holds a much broader definition of the problem. I have learned from my clients that when a part of the soul is retrieved, accompanied by the gift that part possesses, it is easy to understand why these individuals have not been able to experience more complete healing or resolution of the problem until now. My research indicates that when people are not fully embodied due to soul loss, a weak or compromised immune system and the proclivity to become ill frequently can be a common and persistent problem.

When I have completed my interventions, I use MMT to determine if clients are now completely in their physical body ("Are you now 100 percent in your physical body?"). If not, I continue asking to determine what the percentage of embodiment is—it should be 100 percent. I continue asking using MMT to determine what else may be interfering. Sometimes it is necessary to establish energetic boundaries with the client's physical body in order to ensure that the newly integrated part(s) feel safe in the physical body. I always ask using MMT if energetic boundaries are required. Sometimes it is also necessary to teach the client some grounding visualizations to establish a firm connection to the earth to prevent the reoccurrence of the problem.

It is important to keep in touch with clients after they have been newly embodied. It is not unusual to require some additional integration work over the following two to three weeks. The degree of integration seems to depend upon how long they were out of body and to what degree there was psycho-energetic reversal. If the soul loss was from a traumatic incident in their child-hood, you can expect a longer integration time than if the incident occurred four weeks ago. I continue to inquire in follow-up sessions about any prior symptoms returning, and I use MMT to determine whether clients continue to have 100 percent energetic boundaries with their physical body and to recheck for psychoenergetic reversal. When clients have had chronic physi-cal symptoms or illnesses, a part of them might be disinclined to be in their physical body. It is important to stay with them on this. When all of our energy is fully integrated in our physical body, healing of various problems accelerates dramatically.

CHAPTER

12

ENERGETIC PRACTICE

W hether it is called *chi, prana,* or *mana*, there has always been consensus among spiritual traditions that a universal life-force energy permeates all things. When I began my training in Kundalini yoga and meditation, I had no context for what this universal life-force energy was all about. An intuitive or internally driven experience motivated me and propelled me forward.

At the time, I was reading a great deal of Krishnamurti's teachings—he was, essentially, my first spiritual teacher. He was an iconoclast and a Jnana yogi, and he dismissed any kind of formal spiritual practice. Jnana yoga is the yoga of intellectual discrimination, not a path for most people and certainly not an easy path. Krishnamurti emphasized attentional absorption leading to expanded awareness. I resonated with this intellectually and intuitively—it reminded me of the wisdom I had studied from the Vedas, the ancient Indian scriptures on nondualism. A particular passage I recalled says, "Not this, not that," meaning that our conceptual identification with all external reality keeps us from the experience of the silent mind of unified consciousness. What Krishnamurti tried so hard to describe and explain to people is that *if through your attention, you have sufficient mental energy* to focus on each experience, in and of itself, moment by moment, breath by breath, then you as the observer become the observed. If you become totally focused on and absorbed in the object of your attention, then the separation of the observer observing the observed dissolves. What results is only that which Krishnamurti describes as the observer merging with the observed such that there is no sense of the separate egoic self. I understood this intellectually. I spent years studying this and even practicing to the extent I could by paying attention to my thinking patterns.

Krishnamurti describes how our sense of separateness derives from our own separate identity. This sense of separateness creates fear because we become identified with experiences from the past and anticipate past fears being repeated in the future. I began to really understand the role of the mind in creating realities that are disharmonious. Krishnamurti would not have described himself as a monotheist or an atheist because those are descriptions about a belief. Krishnamurti embodied and personified this state of being-in-the-moment awareness.

I was tremendously challenged and inspired by Krishnamurti—his epistemological approach created a foundation for me that helped train my mind to think about things in a different way. It created my awareness of a meta-communicator, which Buddhism refers to as the fair witness. I became aware of how I think about things unintentionally and unconsciously as part of the constant inner chatter. This internal critiquer, who provides constant feedback, keeps me from being present. This Jnana yoga of intellectual discrimination became the underlying foundation for all my spiritual work that followed.

I understood that my practice of reflective self-awareness would be ongoing and persistent. Krishnamurti referred to this process of ongoing awareness as meditation *all the time*, in contrast to sitting down and focusing on a mantra or image and then forgetting about the mantra and going about your life. This practice of reflective self-awareness is something I access and use all the time as my own fair witness has become ever more evolved and developed over the years. I came to realize that for this ongoing and rigorous practice to be sustained, a great deal of mental energy and stamina would be required. It was through the energetic practice of Kundalini yoga that I was able to access the energy I needed.

Ah, Kundalini yoga—how I loved that powerful natural high. The practice of Kundalini yoga involves stretching and a lot of movement along with the breath of fire, a very rapid, powerful breathing through the nostrils that is incorporated in many of the exercises throughout each yoga set or kriya (a completed action). I did a different kriya every day—for the heart center, for the endocrine glands, or for the lower chakras, or to balance the energy at the third-eye point. I did them on a rotating basis to stimulate the chakras, which I later found out are central to the body's essential energy system.

What I did not realize at the time, because I did not have the words, was that I was engaging in an energetic spiritual practice. I was manipulating my essential energy system in a very intentional and self-directed way (of course, with the direction and assistance of a teacher). By using the breath of fire, I was drawing in the prana—the life-force energy.

I did not appreciate until much later that when Yogi Bhajan arrived in the United States in 1969 to teach Kundalini yoga, he was teaching us a very advanced, accelerated form of energetic spiritual practice! He claimed that because of the times (the Aquarian age) and because of the shift in the earth's energies and our collective consciousness, Americans were ready to integrate this into our lives and that it was absolutely essential that we do so. This Kundalini yoga would stimulate and balance our chakras and endocrine system, strengthen our nervous system, expand our consciousness, and allow us to grow spiritually, thus preparing us to help bring in this new age. He was adamant that the changes in the energies coming into and onto the earth were going to be so intense that people would go crazy from the stress. He claimed that many people were not prepared to handle the upcoming changes very well. In retrospect, if he was referring to the increasing pace of life brought on by the information revolution and its pervasive influence in our lives, he was very prescient indeed.

Yogi Bhajan did not need to convince me how powerful Kundalini yoga was—Kundalini yoga convinced me on its own. I experienced a change in my awareness that was very quick and very profound. As mentioned earlier, I stopped using coffee, I never smoked marijuana, and I did not drink alcohol— there were no longer any drugs in my system. I was committed to infusing my nervous system with concentrated prana through the intense exercises and breath of fire of Kundalini yoga. I intended to raise my consciousness, and that is exactly what happened. I practiced Kundalini yoga and meditation for twenty years, including the ten years of the energetic group practice of White Tantric yoga. This energetic practice gave me tremendous energy. It opened up my intuitive awareness and stimulated my internal Kundalini energy. I was raising this energy to the point that it was purifying and stimulating my chakras as well as expanding my consciousness in ways that I was not yet aware of.

I regularly practiced a meditation that Yogi Bhajan had taught me. He said that one who does this meditation daily would "know the unknowable and see the unseeable." It is called the Kirtan Kriya, a complex meditation that involves chanting the mantra SA TA NA MA. Yogi Bhajan explained that this mantra is the primal or nuclear form of *Sat Nam*, which loosely translates as "Truth is my essence, Truth is God's name." (For more information, see chapter 25, "Sound As Vibrational Healing.")

I did this meditation for thirty-one minutes in the morning and thirty-one minutes in the evening every day in addition to the Kundalini yoga kriyas. I was determined to permanently change my consciousness, and over the years my intuitive capacity began to flower and a very subtle balancing of my chakras began that continues to unfold to this day. From practicing that meditation along with the Kundalini yoga, my psychic abilities have continued to develop and open up. That was a side benefit of doing the meditation and the yoga—it had not been my intention in and of itself. This added benefit has helped me in being able to know and intuit certain things about my clients' processes and defenses so that I can say things more incisively and guide clients more compassionately into the space that needs to be addressed. Though I would not have used these terms back then, I had powerfully plunged into my first energetic practice, which continues to benefit me today.

As I recognize now when I look back at the time when I was doing daily Kundalini yoga and meditation practice, I was systematically working with the life-force energy (prana) in very intentional ways. In a similar way to my current qigong practice, I was visualizing where the pranic energy was being directed (which was to one or more chakras) and augmenting this with specific breathing practices. Little did I know that all this would be the precursor to my current professional orientation as an energetic-based psychotherapist.

In the energy psychology model, I am working within the human vibrational matrix, which is made up of three components. The first component is the chakras, which are often referred to as the focal points or collection centers for the life-force energy that is constantly being circulated throughout our bodies. The second component, the primary Chinese meridians, is characterized as the rivers or the pathways through which that energy is distributed throughout our bodies. And the third component is the human biofield (or aura), which envelopes and surrounds the human physical body. Throughout my first twenty years of energetic practice (i.e., Kundalini yoga), my approach was specifically oriented to stimulating the chakras, channeling the prana (along with its directed visualization) accompanied by the vehicles of *pranayama* (conscious breath control), and using sound current or mantra.

Yogi Bhajan also taught Naad yoga, the science of sound current or vibration. Yogi Bhajan often told us that before there were medicines there were sound and mantra as healing agents. People were given different mantras to cure particular illnesses and resolve specific problems. He asserted that there are different mantras for different issues and different intentions. Over the years I worked with a variety of different mantras, but I found myself drawn to one mantra in particular, which I have previously described as the Kirtan Kriya. I incorporated this into my daily meditation practice. In my daily yoga practice I incorporated different mantras into specific yoga kriyas, which we also did when we were practicing the larger group energetic healing process of White Tantric yoga.

Vibration and sound have always been an important component in my energetic healing practice. That is why I have incorporated use of a Tibetan bell, Tibetan bowl, Tibetan cymbals, and the healing drum along with mantra as important interventions in my Dynamic Energetic Healing® model. My research indicates that few people in the energy psychology community incorporate the interventions of sound and vibration. However, because it has been such an integral part of my own energetic practice for so many years, it is very easy for my clients to experience positive healing changes using sound current and vibration when working with me. These principles are often found in various applications of processwork as another example of an energetic practice.

As discussed in greater detail in chapter 5, "Integrating the Second Attention into Dynamic Energetic Healing®," following Process means incorporating anything that is emerging in the moment. In contrast to the prescriptive kriyas of Kundalini yoga and the established algorithms of acupressure points delineated by Callahan's Thought Field Therapy, following Process is an organic unfolding. It is completely inclusive of the larger collective field that we are always immersed in. It often involves spontaneous yoga postures and chanting as the path to healing becomes revealed. Because it is not prescriptive, the energetics of following Process are less easily understood. For example, when a client's process reveals a tightening at their solar plexus requiring direct physical pressure on that area of their body, the moaning or screaming that emerges is the release of the vital life force that had been trapped as repressed emotional energy. Whether you refer to the release as emanating from the third chakra or the stomach meridian, the resulting balance of the client's essential energy system is the same. But the path to achieving the energetic balance (i.e., the operational principles that support the process-oriented paradigm) is different from that of Kundalini yoga or tapping on acupressure points.

Going deep into processwork helped me tremendously in healing old trauma and personal wounding. Process-oriented psychology opened me up to be in the moment with whatever feelings, thoughts, perceptions, and experiences I was having rather than suppressing them out of a sense of social decorum. I started to integrate process-oriented meditation into my life. The basis of this meditation is what Mindell refers to as the perceptual channels: internal and external auditory; internal and external visual; kinesthetic (movement); and proprioception (feeling and sensation). I learned to be sensitive to how information is processed internally through these different channels and trained myself to recognize when these info-energy perceptual channels switch back and forth.

As I became more fluid at working with Process both for clients and for myself, I started moving away from my energetic practice of Kundalini yoga and the Kirtan Kriya meditation. I began to practice process-oriented meditation because I felt it was important to adopt and completely integrate that paradigm into my life. I practiced process-oriented meditation for a number of years. In retrospect, I realize that my process-oriented work was more a practice for healing and awareness, an essential predecessor for what would soon become Dynamic Energetic Healing®.

Five years ago I started feeling the need for another energetic spiritual practice, since I had not been inclined to rekindle my Kundalini yoga. I was looking for something different. I was led to qigong.

In my search, I happened on a book by Master Hong Liu, an allopathic medical doctor trained in China. I read his book *The Healing Art of Qi Gong*, which is initially the story of how he became curious about the phenomenal, miraculous healings of qigong masters in China. His mother always had traditional Chinese healers in her house while he was growing up, and during his medical training in China he started studying with qigong masters. He eventually became a qigong practitioner and a qigong master himself. He is now living in southern California and has established a holistic clinic teaching qigong and using traditional Chinese chi-related healing techniques along with Chinese herbs and Western allopathic medicine. His story is very inspiring.

Master Hong Liu features eight exercises he calls the Golden Eight. I began incorporating these into a daily practice. However, I felt a need to have a personal connection with a qigong master and there were none in the Salem area. I decided to start praying to connect with a qigong master who could teach me more.

Synchronistically, it was only a couple of months later that my colleague Mary told me that her friend Julie Porter was teaching Soaring Crane qigong at Mary's office. I was greatly disappointed to learn that Julie's class was on the same night that I was facilitating therapy groups. I called Julie to talk to her about other possibilities. She told me that she was trained by a Chinese qigong master residing forty-five minutes north of Salem, in Portland. The qigong master turned out to be a woman, Professor Chen, Hui-xian, who had recently retired from her teaching position at the Oregon College of Oriental Medicine. I contacted the college, was put on the waiting list, and eventually took the beginning training (and the intermediate training six months later) from Professor Chen.

I have been doing Soaring Crane qigong nearly every day since. It is a forty-five-minute routine that leaves me feeling tremendously expanded and mentally crystal clear, just as I felt after doing Kundalini yoga. It is a focused, intense, meditative practice that involves slow movements to exercise the entire body. It also includes focused visualization on specific acupuncture channels. Additionally, specific emphasis is directed to particular acupuncture points including tian mu (sixth chakra), lower dan tian (just below the navel), bai hui (crown chakra), and a number of others. While doing Soaring Crane qigong, not only am I focusing on my own meridians in and around my body, I am also focusing through visualization and intention to access the universal chi field, which is an integral part of qigong practice. Professor Chen emphasizes that chi, the universal life-force energy, is in all things. Qigong trains us to access chi any time from anywhere because it is the very stuff from which the universe is made.

Before Professor Chen came to the United States, she was diagnosed with breast cancer and suffered surgery, radiation, and chemotherapy. She shared with us that as she was in the waiting room to tell her doctor she could not tolerate any more chemotherapy (which she did stop against his recommendations), she struck up a conversation with a man who had had pervasive lung cancer. He assured her that if she did Soaring Crane qigong as he had done, she would completely cure herself of cancer. She was desperate and decided to learn qigong. She cured herself of the very aggressive form of breast cancer that had invaded her body. Years later when she visited her former doctor, he showed her chart to her on which he had given her only a 25 percent chance of survival. This healing was life-transforming for her. As she continued to practice and study qigong with various masters, she decided to dedicate her life to sharing and teaching Soaring Crane qigong.

Professor Chen learned that by focusing on the universal chi field, bringing in that chi with very specific movements and mental focus that stimulate the major acupuncture meridians of the body, we are able to open and keep open our acupuncture channels so that the flow of chi in the body is unblocked where before it had been stuck or stagnant. An underlying principle of traditional Chinese medicine is that disease is caused by the flow of chi in the body being blocked. As chi flows through organs, tissues, and muscles, the flow of chi is blocked where there is tension and the muscles are tight. If organs are diseased, it is because the flow of chi has been restricted through stress or injury in a way that prevents the flow of chi and blood through that area.

Qigong is a self-healing practice, and it is my insurance for maintaining good physical health and overall well-being. Professor Chen cured herself of cancer. There are thousands of accounts of people curing themselves of mental, emotional and physical diseases through the intentional practice of qigong. This energetic practice is designed to keep your vital energy flowing. Much of energy psychology's successes are a result of integrating these principles into a psychotherapeutic context.

There is an underlying presupposition that Professor Chen states explicitly: "The chi knows where to go." In the intermediate training, we learned the standing meditation that allows for spontaneous physical movements as the student feels into the flow of chi. This process requires becoming physically relaxed while focusing on the lower dan tian. The chi has its own intelligence and its own knowing for which parts of the body need to be healed so that movement becomes spontaneous. A process-oriented qigong practice is alternated with the very structured five routines within the Soaring Crane qigong discipline. The chi knows where to go, Professor Chen tells us, because it has the intelligence that is the universe—and at its very center, its very core, the universe is whole. It is balanced with yin and yang, with positive and negative polarity. If we allow the chi to move us, the chi will generate spontaneous movements. By deferring to the chi and allowing it to move us, we can expect all parts of ourselves—physical, mental, and emotional—to heal through time. Soaring Crane qigong is a profound energetic practice.

One of the things I have learned from qigong practice is that it is absolutely essential for the body to be relaxed so that the chi is not restricted. The more the body is physically relaxed, the more the chi will flow without obstruction. This is not just an intellectual awareness; this has become my experience. I now know that when I am getting tense and my muscles are getting tight from sitting or overuse, the best and most healing thing I can do is lie down for fifteen minutes and allow my body to go into a deep relaxation trance. My body has become trained to let go of its cumulative stress when I do this. The chi has its own intelligence, and it brings me back to physical balance quickly so it can once again circulate freely and without obstruction. A question I sometimes ponder is what qigong and shamanism have in common.

My shamanic practice began in 1981 and continues to deepen. Is shamanism an energetic practice? Indeed it is, for the compassionate spirits embody the universal life force as compassion in its essence. Certainly shamanism does not fit within the definition of energy psychology, but the compassionate spirits as defined in core shamanism are energetic by their very nature. They are a particular formulation of energy and a part of the invisible realm. Clearly, core shamanism and qigong are different practices that enable me to tap into the power of the universe and discover that I am an energetic being.

The emphasis of Dynamic Energetic Healing® is, of course, quite different from that of qigong. The practice of qigong involves opening the channels (i.e., meridians) of circulating chi (qi) throughout the body while magnetizing and visualizing the outer, universal chi to be directed into the lower dan tian just below the navel. The channels are opened to store and accumulate the vital life force that animates us and pervades all things in the universe. Qigong is considered an energetic practice, much as Kundalini yoga is, with its emphasis on collecting prana.

Since chi and prana are considered subtle energies that scientists still cannot identify and measure to their satisfaction, it is prudent to ask if this is an energetic issue or a spiritual issue. I say it is both. In core shamanism, everything is infused with and alive with spirit. Each tree, plant, river, and animal has its own spirit. We can communicate with these spirits through various shamanic means. The compassionate spirits often take on an anthropomorphized form and identity, and sometimes they appear simply as emanations of energy while communicating.

There are documented accounts on film of qigong masters hurling an attacker across a room simply by emanating chi from their hands. Similarly, there are accounts of qigong masters shrinking cancerous tumors in less than three minutes. This is commonplace in China. In fact, there are "medicineless" hospitals in China where patients who have a variety of maladies and who have lost hope of being cured work intensely and successfully with qigong masters, supported with specialized diet, herbs, and daily qigong practice. The major emphasis of the qigong masters is the proper use of chi to effect their cures. Core shamanism and qigong are traditions whose approaches are completely different, yet in both it is a subtle energy that produces the healing results for the recipient. Whether it is chi being channeled by the qigong master or the spirit of the wind that I see as a whirling vortex reweaving someone's torn auric field, the experience is energetic for both the healer and the client or recipient.

Why have an energetic practice? If you are working with energy in a conscious, intentional way, it is of utmost importance to develop sensitivity to the flow of chi within yourself and between you and others. The more you participate in and discipline yourself to have a daily energetic practice, the more sensitive you will become to your life-force energy. What continues to unfold for me is an ongoing discovery of more experiential awareness of subtle energies in all kinds of different ways. For you, this awareness may come through sensing via your hands. It may come through becoming more clairvoyant, by being able to look at people, see things about them, and just "know." Or it may come through clairaudience—hearing truth from your own inner voice that lets you know about another person. It will come in a variety of ways, but qigong practitioners know that after a number of years of disciplined practice, it is quite common to become aware of subtle energy in yourself and other people. This occurs spontaneously as a consequence of unblocking your own channels and allowing your chi to flow freely. In *The Seat of the Soul*, Gary Zukav (1989, 13–14) discusses the development of the multisensory human as an important next step in the evolution of our species. I believe that whether you are doing Kundalini yoga, qigong, or any other regular energetic practice, you will inevitably become healthier, more intuitive, and consequently, more multisensory.

As your channels begin to open more, and as your chakras come more into balance and alignment, your ability to perceive subtle energies will grow. As I continue to clear trauma through Dynamic Energetic Healing® methods and do regular Soaring Crane qigong energetic practice, I notice more and more what I call the experience of the silent mind. In past years I noticed this for perhaps twenty to forty seconds at a time, and it was especially noticeable while taking my daily morning walk in the park. For a very brief snatch of a moment, everything would get quiet internally and I would be seeing the outside world without any interrupting thoughts. In this quietude is a state of intense beingness. The next moment it would be gone. I had no understanding for why this was happening. I always looked forward to it, but it came only fleetingly.

Lately, this phenomenon has become more and more persistent—it may last for minutes or for the better part of a day. But now I notice that I am able to shift my attention at will from my constant inner chatter to the silent-mind space. There are times during my morning walks when I intentionally choose to think through a problem or consider different alternatives for a creative project I am working on. Then, when I want to shift out of that internal thinking space to move into the silent-mind space of heightened awareness, I just say "shift" and my awareness expands as I feel incredibly, intensely present. I have the energetic awareness of perceiving all around me, including from my back! It is as though my awareness of the outside world is coming from receptors all around and throughout my body. I am looking out from my eyes without a sense of myself being separate. It is very different from my normal thinking-mind awareness, which tends to be very self-absorbing and internal. In this expanded state, I particularly notice and enjoy that the colors of flowers are much brighter. Trees stand out in their structural form for what they are, clear of my imposing interpretation and internal static, which tend to obscure their majesty. Plants, bushes, and grass are all much more vivid, and my presence and interpersonal experience with people is also more intense. Sometimes I find myself having to stand a bit farther back because there is just so much presence!

That is the best way in which I can describe this experience, but I believe it still sounds awkward, particularly if you have no familiar experiential reference point to this silent-mind space. My sense of presence has become so intense recently that I have had to establish energetic boundaries with what I call "outer reality" to avoid feeling overwhelmed. Yet experiencing the silent mind is a wonderful, wonderful experience that I believe is a direct consequence of my energetic practices over many years. I know that if I can be more present without the habitual inner chatter trying to support a preconceived conceptual reality, I can be more available and more in that state of love that I experienced years ago the first time my heart center spontaneously opened. What I thought of initially as enlightenment has changed for me. I no longer aspire to be "enlightened" because my understanding and appreciation of what enlightenment represents experientially is now very different. Instead, as my awareness expands I have an appreciation that life is a series of ongoing enlightenments that come with increasing clarity, ongoing awareness, and a sense of a larger interconnectedness to all things. With my expanding awareness continuing to grow, I have spontaneous "enlightenment experiences" (i.e., the silent-mind experience) that now occur when I am driving, when I am walking, and when I am just sitting in a cafe and being present. I realize this is another paradigm shift.

Each time I have another enlightenment experience or another "ah-ha," it is experiential. It is not just an intellectual ah-ha; it is more about my energetic experience in relation to everything else. Consequently, my understanding of what reality is changes and shifts, and thus my paradigm also shifts. As mentioned earlier, paradigm shifts have always been astounding and life-changing for me. Starting to raise the Kundalini energy was an incredible paradigm shift that catapulted me out of my old reality and into new possibilities. Finally accepting the reality of the compassionate spirits and that they are the agents through which healing frequently occurs when I am working with clients was a life-changing paradigm shift for me that I still reel from. Tapping on acupuncture points and discovering that I could often create instantaneous emotional balance for my clients and myself was another paradigm shift. These new awarenesses happen when we least expect them. I do not believe that they are invited. Instead, I believe that they are spontaneous awakenings or enlightenment experiences that change us forever and throw us into new areas and new realms—mind-expanding possibilities for the newly evolving human.

When you engage in a regular energetic practice, inevitably you will experience shifts in your experience of reality. Working with the universal life-force energy, the energy that animates all things, is working with the miracle of life and the Great Mystery. You can be sure that as you work with your own essential energy system, whether it is working with your chakras, your meridians, or your own biofield in any kind of energetic way, you are plugging into the universal chi field. You then become very intentional and judicious in your practice in order to keep your energy moving and balanced. As you strengthen your connection to the collective level and then to the universal level, huge shifts occur. Enormous changes that you can only imagine (from the seemingly fictional stories of the spiritual masters), or perhaps not even imagine, become your reality.

Yogi Bhajan often told us that freedom isn't free. In order to experience the freedom that we all want in our soul and in our heart of hearts, we must exercise discipline. That has always stuck with me. I also believe that disciplined practice supported by a strong underpinning of passionate interest and curiosity begets success. Many people work hard at their job for money, acknowledgment, and recognition. Yogi Bhajan once chided a lecture audience by saying, essentially, "You people take better care of your cars than you do of yourselves. Why is it that when your car needs service you always take it in so that it won't rust and won't fall apart? You get oil, you get lubrication, you get tune-ups, you do this on a regular basis, but you won't spend one hour a day praying to God, doing your Kundalini yoga and meditation to keep yourself in optimal health and optimal connection to spirit."

It does take discipline and commitment. Even more, it requires making a decision about something that your heart tells you is important and then staying with it. It is often hard to talk about, and we have all kinds of reasons why we should not or cannot do this practice that we know is valuable for us. Perhaps by addressing psychoenergetic reversal and uncovering some hidden sabotage patterns you will find a way to choose an energetic practice to help you to achieve expanded awareness, self-healing, and spiritual well-being. Or, maybe your passion alone will be sufficient for you to make the commitment to begin an energetic practice that speaks to your heart. Know that the universe is filled with a vital force that is compassion. I invite you to celebrate in its abundance.

13

ENERGETIC ORIGINS FROM A HYPNOTIC PERSPECTIVE

Throughout the years that I have been using energy psychology methods, I have noticed that an important aspect of the therapeutic relationship needs greater attention. Most therapists tend to ignore what continually occurs hypnotically between the therapist and the client. Since spending many years early in my career studying the complexities of traditional and Ericksonian hypnosis, I have been keenly aware of how verbal and nonverbal communication creates hypnotic impact within the therapy session. Conscious awareness of the underlying dynamics of hypnosis is the foundation for establishing and maintaining rapport—and thus for engendering openness to new healing possibilities. As Dr. Milton H. Erickson said, sufficient rapport allows the unconscious mind of the client to accept new ideas and possibilities.

I have integrated my knowledge of how hypnosis accelerates clients' healing outcomes into Dynamic Energetic Healing®. Establishing rapport in the very first session (or even before, when talking on the telephone with a prospective client) is absolutely paramount. Being in rapport means energetic harmony has been established. In rapport, there is mutual understanding and support, resistance is minimized, and a collaborative ethos prevails. Simple rapport-building techniques include matching and mirroring clients' movement and expressions, both verbal and nonverbal. This evolves into pacing and leading clients into a deepening internal orientation within the relational context of the therapy.

What exactly do I mean by "deepening internal orientation?" Rapport creates an unconscious agreement with my client to work together on specific objectives without any mental or emotional resistance. There is agreement about our roles. I am the therapist with a certain amount of knowledge of and experience with the things that the client wants help with. When there is rapport, this agreement provides me with explicit and implicit permission to assist and lead my client to interior places that may be either known or unknown. A deepening internal orientation is the beginning of a therapeutic trance process, one in which clients are able to remain easily focused on certain inner states of awareness that they might otherwise move away from or avoid altogether. Once rapport is established, Process begins to emerge in the therapeutic relationship so that seemingly miraculous events can happen.

Another pacing technique or "intervention" I use is reporting my subjective experience of the energetic releases that I perceive and "feel." I do this by expressively exhaling in a way that clients can obviously hear. I provide this feedback to my clients to help them create an ever-deepening response potential to their own internal experience. This feedback also teaches clients to become sensitive to another, more subtle aspect of their experience of bio-energy on multiple levels. If I can feel, experience, and express their energetic releasing, I expect that with minimal modeling on my part, my clients will soon become sensitive to their own energy body and begin to own it.

Part of this hypnotic aspect of the therapeutic relationship allows me as the therapist to report descriptively my interior experience. This includes images, feelings, sensations, and *energetic releases* that relate to and are relevant to the specific Dynamic Energetic Healing® intervention I am using at the time. This is different from the countertransference experience first described by Freud, which occurs within the analyst as he or she opens to his or her "free-floating attention." The major difference between countertransference and the hypnotic aspect of the therapeutic relationship that I am describing is the therapeutic model from which each derives. My healing approach includes Mindell's processwork model, from which I integrate what he calls the second attention (described in chapter 5). This is a much larger framework for what is happening in the therapeutic relationship.

As a process-oriented therapist, I am extremely open to the richness of the dynamic field within the client–therapist relationship. As a result, I know that what happens in the relationship is meaningful and ought to be *acknowledged by processing it in some way.* In other words, whatever is happening in this relational context is a field of information shared by the client and the therapist. There are no secrets! The accessibility of the information is totally dependent upon the therapist's and client's level of awareness and ability to be present.

It is also therapeutically useful to acknowledge to clients what is happening in the field, since the therapist takes responsibility for keeping the field clean. However, there are times when it is important to choose to contain and withhold certain awarenesses if you as the therapist ascertain it is in the best interest of the client and the therapeutic outcome to do so. This is all about the ecology of the field. The therapist either allows the field to stay polluted or chooses to make strategic interventions in order to keep the field clean. To disclose your awareness is to keep the field clean.

Language is inherently hypnotic, and using words such as *energy, fields, chi,* and *soul* to describe subtle experiences necessitates that the client experience what is called transderivational search (TDS) in the neurolinguistic programming (NLP) nomenclature. TDS induces deepening hypnotic states. Essentially, the TDS experience is what occurs when I go inside myself (albeit very quickly) to find a place of reference for whatever the client is saying. If he says the word *field,* I have to go inside and decide if the reference point is farming, physics, or spirituality. This goes on constantly, and it reflects how we are always to some degree in an internalized state of being when we are verbally interacting with (or even just listening to) someone. We go inside for the reference point, and then we come outside to reconnect and communicate an interpretation of our own. This is always going on interpersonally.

I recognize that the TDS experience generates varying degrees of ongoing trance states of confusion (i.e., altered states of consciousness) and deepens the client's internal orientation. I also know that transformative change occurs more readily when the individual is in an altered state of consciousness. With this awareness of what is occurring hypnotically, I can more gently guide clients to experience greater openness and perceive more information—information that they would otherwise be unaware of or tend to deny.

Therefore, as the therapist you must use language judiciously and intentionally because your direct and indirect suggestions are always being communicated to your clients. They are more open to suggestion than they would normally be because altered states are more accessible in this therapy model and because you and the client are maintaining an ongoing rapport. It is important to remember that the therapist's suggestions may be interpreted as being positive or negative, while the sharing of my personal experience is often perceived as metaphoric because clients interpret reality subjectively.

Another interesting interpersonal communication phenomenon is what the NLP community calls representational systems. People describe their experience colored by a certain bias that reflects the way they primarily engage the world. Take the preceding sentence, for example. I used the words *colored* and *reflects*, both of which describe a visual representation of the world through my language bias. If someone talks back to me using visual representational terms, they are talking my language! At an unconscious level, we are in a beautiful rapport. If *on the other hand*, you tell me that you cannot *get a handle* on the computer program you are trying to learn and that this makes you *uptight* and *feels* like trying to *grab hold* of sand that keeps *slipping through your fingers*, you are coming from a completely different representational system— a kinesthetic and/or proprioceptive one. One of the reasons couples frequently have "communication difficulties" is because they are speaking in different representational systems. In addition to visual and kinesthetic/proprioceptive, there is also auditory, olfactory/gustatory, and extrasensory biases. Being aware of representational systems allows me to establish even deeper rapport with clients (by matching and pacing their language patterns and overlapping representational systems) and thereby to further deepen and guide their experience. It should be noted that the more conscious the therapist is of these hypnotic phenomena, the more respectfully and responsibly the therapist will manage the healing process within the therapeutic relationship.

Manual muscle testing (MMT) itself is a very hypnotic interaction. Though it may not seem so, I am often using commands and being very directive. Clients agree to comply with me by holding their arms out for various lengths of time, and consequently they experience bilateral arm catalepsy or relative degrees of arms-extended rigidity. In the jargon of process-oriented psychology, I am eliciting what for most Western people are the most unoccupied of all of the perceptual channels, namely kinesthesia and proprioception. This combination of authoritative commands (i.e., "Hold your arms out please"), bilateral arm catalepsy, and stimulation of the two least-occupied perceptual channels creates an immediate hypnotic trance characterized by great receptivity to positive suggestions for constructive therapeutic change. In the therapeutic interaction, as the client's trance deepens, I simply state "arms," or even just hold my arms out in front of me, and the client's arms rise up to meet my own as if magnetized to my hands. Directives are hypnotic communications whose goal is to motivate the client to achieve a positive therapeutic outcome. Watzlawick (1978) describes the use of those "linguistic structures which have a virtually hypnotic effect without the use of trance" as hypnotherapy without trance. He points out that all of hypnosis is characterized by the words "Do this."

Additionally, the face-to-face positioning that occurs during MMT directs clients inward as I speak and look into their eyes, creating another unconscious, relational agreement to comply. Since respectful hypnosis is always consensual, clients agree by their actions to go into an internal orientation and, therefore, into a state of heightened hypnotic suggestibility. This is largely because my directions and interventions in a new paradigm are constantly disrupting clients' normal cognitive processes.

Another dimension of the muscle testing relational context is how often clients volunteer to close their eyes when I preface questions with "From your inner wisdom" or "From your soul." These phrases create a mild confusion state as clients use TDS to search for their personal meaning of inner wisdom or soul. Also, clinical hypnotherapists know that eyes closed, eyes opened, eyes closed, and so forth create a deepening hypnotic state of openness to positive suggestion. As a footnote to this, when clients tap on their own meridian points or chakra centers, I frequently observe them spontaneously closing and opening their eyes, going into deep hypnotic trance.

Asking clients who are being muscle tested if they have cleared all "negative emotional charge" at all six levels (conscious, unconscious, body, soul, auric field, and chakras) is another confusion technique. This is because most clients do not have reliable internal reference points for the words *unconscious*, *soul*, *auric field*, and *chakra* that they *consciously understand*. Thus, I am placing onto clients' other "nonreference points" yet another layer of experience that their conscious minds will probably have trouble fitting into their worldview of everyday experience. This adds to clients' deepening internal orientation, creating greater openness to new possibilities outside of their normal conscious, conceptual framework of the world. This is helpful because searching within the same familiar framework where the problem first originated often is not the most expeditious road to change. As clients continue to wonder what is happening in their experience and continue to inquire internally, their response potential for deeper healing continues to grow. *This is because the therapeutic interpersonal context is being both supported and facilitated by the process of waking hypnosis.* Altered states of consciousness are consistently being generated within this larger context of waking hypnosis (i.e., hypnotic trance), and it is within the experience of these altered states that profound, transformative energetic healing occurs.

CHAPTER
14

ENERGETIC BOUNDARIES

From the outset, I want to make it clear that having solid energetic boundaries is not about isolating yourself from something or someone else; it is using energetic strategies to establish harmony with another context. Most people are familiar with the phrase "establishing firm boundaries" from the popular literature on codependency. We have been told that the codependent enables the other, often an alcoholic/addict who requires everyone else to adjust to their needs. The codependent is the one identified as having insufficient boundaries, whether she is living with someone who is an alcoholic or someone who has a proclivity to fits of irrational rage. In this more traditional psychotherapeutic conceptualization of boundaries, the codependent is the one who tends to reference to the other's needs first, not having sufficient personal resources to advocate for her own needs in the relational context. The codependent often personifies the caretaker or rescuer personality. Their self-esteem is wrapped up with pleasing and serving the other, often as a compensatory strategy to avoid conflict and anger. This creates an internal polarization or split whereby the anger and controlling influence (internally disowned) is typically "dreamed up" as the partner from hell.

In Dynamic Energetic Healing®, the interpersonal relational context remains central for the establishment of healthy boundaries (since personal relationships are a core issue of psychotherapy), but establishing boundaries is substantially expanded (from the codependent model described earlier) to include other related or linked contexts as well. These additional linked contexts organically emerge when I begin to inquire about how and where clients feel disempowered in their lives. For example, if the diagnostic phase of the initial muscle testing determines that you (the client) have no energetic boundaries with your family of origin, this would likely become our subsequent focus. I would inquire in detail about all aspects of your relationship to your family: What are the particular disturbance factors you experience? How are you being affected right this moment when you talk about or think about your family? What are your thoughts, your feeling states, and your overall relationship to them? The more information we can bring into the field, the more the relational context is defined and expanded and the more you will have to focus on during the subsequent interventions to create the balance.

Our goal in this scenario is to restore 100 percent of your energetic boundaries with your family. We will select the appropriate interventions and muscle test afterwards to determine if you are now at 100 percent (at all levels). If we have succeeded, it means that you have made a frequency shift *at an energetic level* to create a harmonic resonance in relation to your family. This is yet another demonstration reflecting the power of focused intention in relation to a specific context and specific outcome. There may still be unresolved and residual trauma with your family that remains to be dealt with. However, since doing this boundary balance to "reset" the energetic relationship between you and your family, you have now built in an insulating layer of energetic protection that creates a safety zone in which to address the dreaded trauma. You will now be able to think about your family without getting into an extreme emotional state. If need be, you will be able to talk to family members over the telephone without PTSD symptoms being triggered.

Once your energetic boundaries have been established, we will continue to inquire with manual muscle testing about any other family-related boundary issues. These could include unfinished business with particular individuals, particular incidents that occurred within the family, a particular time during your life with your family, and so on. Our goal is to map out the entire matrix of disturbances that, in one way or another, have created weak links in your energetic field (which normally keeps you in a state of homeostatic balance) vis-à-vis your family. The more we identify and define specific relational contexts that are pertinent to our working intention or goal, the easier the work becomes. Energetic boundaries essentially reframe *how we are related* to something that is creating a disturbance in our life. Our ultimate goal is an optimal, appropriate relationship between you and the disturbance.

Let's look at a more specific example. Let us say that one of your parents treated you abusively when you were younger. As an adult, you still find yourself uncomfortable and vigilant any time you encounter that parent. In fact, it's common for you to experience some tension and anxiety whenever you are in the same room with that parent. Establishing 100 percent energetic boundaries with that parent allows you to maintain your own power whenever you encounter him or her. Your parent may continue to be as controlling or verbally disrespectful as in the past, but being more empowered gives you more choices for how to respond. Having solid energetic boundaries does not suggest you will like this individual any more than you ever have, but it will enable you to sustain an optimal, appropriate relationship with the abusive parent as a way to maintain your emotional homeostasis in that relational context.

Contexts for establishing energetic boundaries are many and varied. If an individual has been negatively influenced by his religious upbringing, he may now carry a great deal of fear about dealing with supernatural phenomena. It is not uncommon for me to encounter clients who are very apprehensive about dealing with spiritual matters, particularly spirits or the concept of evil. In these cases, it is important to establish 100 percent energetic boundaries with supernatural phenomena. Once this is accomplished, a bridge has been built supporting the client to consider possibilities that otherwise would have simply generated fear. Dealing with supernatural phenomena becomes the targeted context for establishing optimal appropriate relationship.

The truth is that driving automobiles is usually more frightening than dealing with the supernatural. During one of my trainings, a trainee exclaimed that she continued to be anxious and hypervigilant while driving her car in traffic. This was the result of an earlier collision she had been in. It had been months since the accident, but her anxiety had not improved. We established the intention to eliminate all her anxiety and hypervigilance while she is driving her car. Our first order of business was to establish 100 percent energetic boundaries with her experience of driving her car in traffic. This was the context in which she needed to restore optimal appropriate relationship. We selected frontal occipital holding as the intervention. As I gently made contact with her, I could see that she still carried traumatic shock in her energy field and in her body. With the help of spiritual resources, all traumatic residue was released—no more trauma-elimination work was needed. When we next muscle tested, she was at 100 percent energetic boundaries with driving her car in traffic. A couple of weeks later, she reported that she was driving normally once again without any anxiety or hypervigilance. She had reclaimed her power and confidence as her energetic boundaries were restored.

Boundary work is one of the most important focal points of Dynamic Energetic Healing®. As you may have gathered by now, any problematic context can be addressed from this conceptualization of energetic boundaries. Common client issues resolved by establishing or restoring energetic boundaries include the following: sleeping difficulties, compulsive overeating, dealing with particular emotions such as anger or sadness, specific individuals, work environments, air travel and airports, weather (such as the continuous cold, gray, wet weather during our winter in Oregon), and psychic phenomena (such as being too psychically open and being overwhelmed with information that is unsolicited).

A brief case example illustrates the creativity that can be generated by addressing energetic boundaries. Sarah, a client of mine, is a licensed massage therapist. One of the issues she wanted help with was feeling more empowered and at ease around men. Because of a significant amount of early trauma in her life, it had been challenging for Sarah to maintain 100 percent energetic boundaries *with men in general*. Though she was comfortable with many individual men one-on-one, when she referred to or encountered men as a collective she began to feel intimidated and disempowered. As Sarah now continues to work on releasing old and residual trauma from her early life events, she is able to maintain her energetic boundaries with men in general for longer periods of time before they begin to erode.

In one particular session, I started out by testing Sarah's energetic boundaries with women in general and men in general. She was at 100 percent with women in general, but her energetic boundaries with men in general were once again compromised. I then started thinking about contexts. I asked Sarah if her energetic boundaries were compromised with all of her male clients— they were not. I next asked her (through manual muscle testing) if they were compromised with just one client—no. It turned out that her energetic boundaries were compromised with two of her current male clients. When I asked Sarah to talk about it, she told me that each of these two clients has a particular health issue that made her uncomfortable.

The first client she described had hepatitis B from a hospital blood transfusion. After she tapped on her heart chakra for two minutes, she had restored her energetic boundaries to 100 percent with this man. I next asked her to describe the other client with whom she had no energetic boundaries.

She told me that there was a general unhealthy quality about him. She just never felt comfortable around him and always sensed darkness around him. His body smelled and he had herpes sores on his buttocks. Following up on her description, I asked if there was any dark energy associated with this client—there was. The manual muscle testing indicated there was an earth-bound spirit attached to this man. Her intuitive sensing had recognized this! Sarah had already called a dermatologist to inquire about the contagion factor for both hepatitis B and herpes. When we completed the interventions and restored her boundaries to 100 percent, she was reminded how important it is to energetically clean her work space as well as her own energy field after working with each client.

Sarah's next appointment was four weeks later. In the interim, her attitude toward the client with hepatitis B completely changed from feeling threatened by him to feeling compassion toward him. As to the client with herpes, at the end of his next appointment he announced that he was not going to schedule any other massages. He did not elaborate and Sarah didn't ask. Sarah had never had a client who terminated their massage treatments so abruptly or spontaneously. We wondered about this together. All we could surmise is that when Sarah established 100 percent energetic boundaries with this man, she came into an energetic resonance with him so that she was in optimal appropriate relationship. When this occurred, everything energetically shifted within their relational field. Sarah had talked to me about considering asking this man to leave because of her own health concerns; he got the message energetically and took the initiative on his own.

Sarah's harmony was restored by establishing energetic boundaries. Though Sarah's story may seem amazing, it is not unique. Working on the energetic level is working at a more essential level than most cognitive-oriented therapists do, which enables changes to occur rapidly and consistently. One might say that Sarah effected a change in the relationship with her client at the quantum level. As she shifted energetically, the entire field shifted in accordance! This is an example of why I love Dynamic Energetic Healing®.

15

WORKING WITH
SUPERNATURAL ENERGIES

D oes psychology fit into the sciences or the arts? My studies indicate
both. Researchers continue to probe what motivates humans to
behave in the ways they do. This aspect of experimental research psychology
is based on the scientific method conducted within double-blind parameters.
Research emphases range from cognitive-behavioral to nutritional to pharmacological. Research is even being done into parapsychological phenomena;
this research attempts to verify aspects of the human experience that traditional science, with its emphasis on quantifiable measures and structured
methodologies, finds difficult to study.

Clinicians in the energy psychology community and quantum physicists
are conducting research to scientifically validate the subtle energies upon
which the consistent, positive therapeutic outcomes of Dynamic Energetic
Healing® are based. Many in the energy psychology community recognize the
importance of conducting research experiments that will support the field's
underlying presuppositions

In Dynamic Energetic Healing®, I am working with the various aspects
of the energy body. These include the pathways of energy called meridians
that the Chinese have used for thousands of years. Imagery is also thousands of years old as a tool for healing the psyche. Carl Jung and Joseph
Campbell researched and developed the healing power of images, symbols,
and dreams in their respective fields, depth psychology and mythology.
Today, Western medical schools include courses in "complementary medicine"

and "alternative healing" methodologies in many of their curricula. In *Quantum Mind*, Mindell (2000b, 24–5) refers to the two realities that often seem to collide:

> For millennia, shamans have tied the sciences of physics and psychology together by working in the real world and the dream world at the same time. Today's scientific thinking splits these worlds apart. Physicists call everyday reality the "classical" reality and use terms such as space, time, matter, and observer, which by consent are used by most people. Psychology calls the second world the realm of direct, personal experience, dreaming, deep feeling, psyche, and personal growth. This world consists of such subjective experiences as emotions, telepathy, and so forth.

The supernatural realm is part of the subjective, personal experience of an individual. The *Cambridge International Dictionary* (1999) defines *supernatural* as "caused by forces that are not able to be explained by science." Albert Einstein, on the first page of *The Meaning of Relativity* (1955), makes a distinction between these two worlds:

> By the aid of language different individuals can, to a certain extent, compare their experiences. Then it turns out that certain sense perceptions of different individuals correspond to each other, while for other sense perceptions no such correspondence can be established. We are accustomed to regard as real those sense perceptions which are common to different individuals.

The world's oldest cross-cultural healing system is collectively referred to as shamanism. In this worldview, everything is seen as being alive with spirit and it is through interacting with compassionate spirits that we can often be guided to discover the source of a person's illness. This ancient wisdom is also found in nearly all of the great religious traditions, Christianity notwithstanding. From an energetic perspective, thoughts have the power (as a focused form of undifferentiated consciousness) to heal us or hurt us. The notion of the self-fulfilling prophecy is a familiar theme throughout well-known literature. The field of clinical hypnosis is based on the premise of the power of suggestion and belief.

Dark Energy Intrusions

Supernatural or "dark energy" intrusions have historically been left to the priests, medicine men, and shamans. These intrusions can now be addressed via the Dynamic Energetic Healing® model, which recognizes supernatural or parapsychological influence as an element that may block clients from resolving the problems that bring them to the therapist's office. One does not have to believe in the veracity of curses or demons in order to release these negative energies. I do, however, respect the power of these forces, because I have witnessed the significant negative impact they can have on clients' ability to return to wholeness. To ignore the power and influence of the shadow side of human nature or supernatural influences, however you define them, would be as naïve as it would be irresponsible. Dynamic Energetic Healing® provides a therapeutic context in which issues that Western culture usually considers to be outside the consensus-reality agreement can be addressed effectively and free of religious overtones.

What I have found to be true, and what has been carefully researched by William J. Baldwin in *Spirit Releasement Therapy* (1992) and by psychiatrist Shakuntala Modi in *Remarkable Healings* (1997), is that there are supernatural forces at play in our world. Traditional psychology has largely ignored these forces, but the field of parapsychology continues to inquire into them. Even Freud, in *Civilization and Its Discontents* ([1929] 1955), was aware of how our traditional religious institutions have been slowly losing their influence over society as a whole and over the primitive impulses of the id. Freud discusses collective acts of evil and how the powerful forces of the psyche, if left uncontrolled or ungoverned by religious belief systems, would eventually create social chaos.

Whether we call this phenomenon the psyche, the id, or supernatural forces, it is essential to acknowledge how much it can influence every individual to perpetrate evil. We know it is important to recognize that certain groups of people are often the targets, the scapegoats, of violence that arises from the unacknowledged needs of their persecutors. What is even more important to realize is that all actions—including violent ones—originate within individuals who I believe are largely influenced by these powerful supernatural forces.

In the Dynamic Energetic Healing® model, there are times when it is important to name the particular form or expression of dark energy influence for what it is and how it is interfering in the client's life. When we name it, we acknowledge the larger collective energy field or archetype that is being accessed. C. G. Jung's (1961) concept of the archetype is "...derived from the repeated observation that, for instance, the myths and fairy-tales of world literature contain definite motifs which crop up everywhere. We meet these same motifs in the fantasies, dreams, deliria, and delusions of individuals living today." Naming the dark energy influence gives meaning to the particular problem, puts it into a larger context that makes it less personal, and allows clients to put the problem into a frame of reference that is meaningful to their own belief system. More comprehensive healing occurs as a result.

For example, imagine a contentious divorce. While trying to sue for everything in their joint estate, John overtly curses Susan. It is meaningful to Susan to discover later (months after the trauma of the separation and the legal divorce) that she is still carrying the corrosive energy of the curse. And "curse" is the apt term here—it clearly captures the depth of pain and suffering that Susan has endured and still suffers. With energetic strategies and the recruitment of spiritual resources, the energy of the damning sentiment can be released easily.

In cases such as these, clients often reach a deep understanding of the power inherent in a curse whose aim is to hurt another person. Clients like Susan who release the curse that they discover was placed on them by another person learn something about their own capacity to do harm to another. They learn that cursing another person keeps the two of them energetically connected—an irony, since their conscious intention at that time is to stay as separate as possible from the person they cursed.

Curses

Before we begin examining curses in detail, it is important to differentiate between a limiting belief and a curse. A *limiting belief* is a conclusion you come to—essentially, your interpretation of something—that limits your life in various ways. For example, consider the driver who is stopped at a red light and suddenly experiences the severe jolt and impact of being rear-ended. Not everyone who is rear-ended experiences the same outcomes, but this individual ends up with whiplash, soul loss, and the attendant limiting belief, "It is not safe to drive my car any longer." The conclusion that this individual draws from his experience may significantly compromise and limit his life. Limiting beliefs, which can be conscious or unconscious, are easily corrected once they are identified. A *curse* limits you at the conscious and unconscious levels too, but it also creates a psycho-toxic energy field that is either generated inter-personally or intrapersonally.

It is important to distinguish the different types of curses.

Intentional Curses

An intentional curse is one that is generated by someone else and intended to harm you in some way. These curses are traditionally thought of as being created by black magicians or sorcerers, but I find that this type of curse is more likely generated by an angry person carrying a grudge against you. This may be an ex-spouse or partner who harbors a great deal of intense negative emotional energy (for example, a scorned lover or spouse who wants to punish you). Or, you may be cursed by someone in a position of authority who feels challenged by you, particularly if the person has strong narcissistic tendencies.

When doing past-life work with some of the archetypal patterns, I often find that a curse has been intentionally generated and directed to an individual by an entire community. Finding yourself in the role of a scapegoat (i.e., identified with the Scapegoat archetype) often elicits this type of a curse. In a case such as this, the curse carries lots of cumulative, collective toxic energy; this energy is karmic, and it will affect you at the soul level. You may experience the consequences of this type of curse in your relationships, in your soul purpose, or even in your relationship to your physical body (i.e., as problematic physical symptoms). These curses are very dark and must be cleared carefully and completely.

Most people believe that if they are cursed it must come from someone else. Not so! When you set an intentional curse on someone else out of anger, frustration, or hurt, you are part of the energetic loop of that curse. MMT will indicate that there is a curse interfering on your intention. This type of curse must be cleared to prevent any future karmic relationship from persisting that keeps this toxic energy alive in your field.

Inherited Curses

An inherited curse is present when no matter what you have done to try to move beyond a certain situation, the frustration, feelings of hopelessness, and feelings of being stuck persist. For example, a client of mine intended to be in control of his financial destiny. We discovered that his father (a passive person) worked hard all his life, and his mother spent all of the discretionary money his father earned. His father merely complained that they never had any extra money or savings. My client's MMT indicated that he was financially cursed by the family field in which he grew up (and which he energetically absorbed). He had already acquired limiting beliefs in his internal matrix (reinforced over many years), and since his marriage his feeling of never being able to save enough—no matter how much he earned—felt like a curse to him. This was just as toxic to him as if it were an intentional curse coming from someone else.

These curses tend to be problematic because they can be difficult to identify. Listening attentively to your clients as they describe how frustrated or even cursed they feel about a particular situation or pattern may provide clues.

Unintentional Curses

Unintentional curses, which occur when a person in authority proclaims a "truth" about you, are also toxic. Examples include a parent who says to a child, "I can see you're trying at school, but you'll never be smart enough to go to a good university"; an endocrinologist who says, "It's obvious that you have the same endocrine makeup as your mother, so it's just a matter of time before you start having similar autoimmune disease problems"; and the iridologist who says, "I can see by looking at your iris that you'll have problems with your digestion." The latter two examples were, in fact, experienced by clients of mine. These clients suffered greatly until these curses were cleared and released. These authority figures may have been well-intentioned, but the path to hell is paved with good intentions.

Unintentional Self-Generated Curses

Tom, a client, provides an example of an unintentional self-generated curse. Tom grew up in a family where perfectionism was the gold standard. Tom's parents continually communicated (although not always explicitly) their belief that he was unacceptable in their eyes if he didn't score 100 percent on every exam. Tom internalized the belief that he was stupid; it became his internal mantra. This belief became a self-generated curse—Tom's internalization of the negative attributions made by his parents became a powerful self-sabotaging program. This is in contrast to the example given earlier of an inherited curse; in that case, the client had absorbed the curse from the collective field of his parents' dysfunctional relationship.

Some might argue that this is simply a subconscious belief ("I am stupid") that generates psychic momentum and eventually becomes a self-fulfilling prophecy. In fact, calling this a self-fulfilling prophecy is just another way of describing a self-generated curse that sabotages Tom persistently throughout his life. Though the distinction may seem subtle, self-generated curses tend to be more penetrating and corrosive than simple limiting beliefs. These negative self-statements are often accompanied by guilt or shame, and this emotional component adds the element of feeling responsible for how our actions (or decisions not to act) affect others. A self-generated curse creates major self-sabotage that is usually running continuously unconsciously. Once this type of curse is identified and released, significant healing occurs.

Words have tremendous power, and we add further vital force to our thoughts because (as my qigong teacher told me) chi follows thought. As we become more aware of this connection it is important to be judicious with our thoughts and words. This is true in all of our interpersonal encounters as well as intrapersonally. In that way, we can create positive realities for ourselves. This is explained in greater detail in chapter 8, "Living Life Intentionally."

Soul Stealing

Soul loss and the shamanic soul-retrieval technique were discussed in chapter 11. This shamanic technique is also used in cases of soul stealing, which often involve dark energy forces.

This phenomenon of soul stealing (and the process to correct it) may sound like sorcery, but it is much more common than you might think. Humans have a need and great desire to be whole again in a spiritual sense (i.e., to overcome the subconscious pain of our separation from the Source of all being), and it is a common human experience to emotionally cling to the object of our love. This attachment and bonding is a normative part of the human experience in childhood and in our adult relationships with an intimate other. If the object of your love abandons you (perhaps for someone else), you will go through various stages of grieving that loss, depending on your level of emotional attachment. Most therapists are familiar with the steps of the grieving process outlined by Elisabeth Kübler-Ross. Grieving a loss is a necessary part of the human condition. But if a person decides they are *unwilling* to let go of the other, there are many possible emotional consequences; one of these is soul stealing.

The person (the possessor or soul stealer) who is unwilling to let go of the other is, essentially, laying claim to that other energetically. Possessors may not start out as so-called evil persons, but their actions become evil because they cause ongoing disruption to the other. No matter how psychologists would diagnose soul stealers, it is my assertion that for as long as they claim possession of the other—even over a period of many years—the degree of evil that they perpetrate increases.

Possessors may not consciously intend to steal souls. They may be narcissistic personalities, or they may have inadequate emotional resources to process their loss in a healthy way. Either way, their continual obsessing about their unwillingness to let go of the other will be reflected in an increase in psychic and energetic disturbance within the person who is directly affected. You may be surprised to learn that this frequently occurs between parents and their children and between lovers and married partners. For instance, if a parent's love for their child or a lover's love for their partner is unrequited, a relational dynamic is generated where the object of the unrequited love becomes romanticized. When this occurs, an obsessional preoccupation is generated that becomes controlling and unhealthy. If the dynamic does not change over a period of time, soul stealing is often the result.

In our codependent culture, having healthy interpersonal energetic boundaries is not the norm. This creates the conditions for aggressive and controlling individuals with unresolved trauma and insufficient personal resources to become tormentors in a relationship that was initially loving. Sometimes I see this as a past-life karmic residue from a relationship that has not been resolved. In other cases I encounter it as a present-day problem, when a client who is overidentified with the Victim archetype is trying to get away from a destructive and dysfunctional relationship.

Sometimes when I work with energetic origins—especially past-life origins—clients describe that a part of their soul has been stolen by an evil person. This phenomenon is well known in the shamanic tradition, and it is important for psychotherapists to be aware of it.

When clients report that someone evil has tried to take or has taken a part of their soul, you must proceed very carefully. Although the stolen soul part is usually very willing to return to the client, it often harbors fear that the client will not be able to protect it from the evil one who stole it. There is often (but not always) something akin to a psychic alarm system that alerts the evil person through an energetic linkage that someone is intruding on his or her possession (the stolen soul part). When this alarm is sounded, the evil one will often appear in order to challenge you on retrieving the stolen soul part.

If you are using Dynamic Energetic Healing® strategies rather than shamanic practices, proceed as you would when dealing with dark energy or supernatural interference (as discussed earlier in this chapter). When it becomes evident that soul stealing has occurred (especially in the Bardo or after-life realm of a past-life origin), you will be working at the soul level. It is important to call on all of your and your client's spiritual resources to protect you and help you persuade the evil person to release his/her claim on the soul part and the individual. You will often use an array of interventions described in part 2 (such as Tibetan bell, TAT, F/O holding, calling on Christ, and so on) while you help your client talk with the evil one from a place of Light to persuade it to leave the client and the stolen soul part forever.

This soul rescue is something you cannot force; the evil one must agree to leave the client and release any claims he/she has on the soul of the client. When the dialogue between the client and the evil one is completed, the evil one will either leave and go to the Light or go back to the Dark. Although you may have an altruistic desire to heal the evil one (and you can encourage the client to communicate this to it), it is not your primary agenda to do so. Your priority is to help heal your client and retrieve any stolen soul parts. When the client has completed the dialogue and the evil one has departed, it is essential to confirm via MMT that the stolen soul part has been 100 percent reintegrated into the client and that you and your client are 100 percent free of any residual supernatural contamination.

In the shamanic tradition, there are times when trickery or insistence is employed to overcome a refusal to relinquish the stolen soul part. (For a good example of this, see case history 16, "Validating Empirically the Existence of Past Lives.") This should never be attempted without sufficient supervised experience and adequate spiritual protection such as compassionate spirit helpers and power animals.

Here is an abbreviated outline of how I proceed when I suspect that soul stealing has occurred.

Protocol for Recovering a Stolen Soul Part

Step 1: Use MMT to determine if part of the client's soul has been stolen by someone (as opposed to splitting off or dissociating as a result of a trauma) by asking: "Is this soul loss the result of someone stealing this soul part?" If yes, proceed to step 2. If no, MMT to determine the source of the soul loss and the best intervention to reintegrate the split-off part. Follow the Dynamic Energetic Healing® protocol.

Step 2: Use MMT to find the energetic origin. Then ask if the client needs to go there to do the healing—the answer is usually yes.

Step 3: Ask at the correct energetic origin: "Is there anything more that needs to be done before integrating this soul part back into the client?" If yes, continue to dialogue with your client until the MMT determines that the client has sufficient awareness at the conscious level to proceed.

Step 4: Ask: "Can we go ahead and select the best intervention to reintegrate this stolen soul part?" If yes, ask for the best intervention to reintegrate this stolen part. Often more awareness of the soul stealing will occur during the interventions. If no, and if there is a karmic energetic origin, ask: "Does the client need to meet with and identify the evil one who stole this soul part in the Bardo state?" If yes, go on to step 5.

Throughout steps 1 through 4, be sure to regularly ask, "Are the responses we are getting from your muscle testing false or in any way deceptive?" If you get an affirmative response to this question, this indicates that supernatural phenomena are causing mistaken or confusing muscle testing signals. If this is the case, suggest to the client that the evil one is attempting to deceive the client by hiding the identity of the soul stealer. It is important to be highly vigilant at this point.

Step 5: Tell the client to go to the Bardo state (the after-life realm) of this karmic energetic origin (where the evil one is waiting) and dialogue at the soul level with the evil one. Your task is to support the client and encourage him or her to be firm and courageous. The client's task is to secure an agreement with the soul stealer to never bother the client again and to release all claims on his or her soul through all time. You must be creative and compassionate when assisting your client in this dialogue process.

Step 6:   When this is completed, use MMT to determine if any other specific interventions are necessary to further integrate the stolen soul part. When this is finished, ask: "Are there any additional interventions necessary in the Bardo state to complete this healing process?" If yes, do them. If no, ask if any internal resource states need to be elicited either here at the Bardo state or after integrating the healing from the energetic origin through time to the present.

Step 7:   Upon return to the present, ask the client these questions using MMT:

- Are you now 100 percent back in your physical body and 100 percent back in the present time?
- Have you integrated the healing of this stolen soul part 100 percent at all levels from the energetic origin through all time to the present?
- Is your soul 100 percent free of any karmic claims or attachments from the evil one who stole part of your soul?
- Are you and I both 100 percent free of any and all supernatural contamination from this work we have done?

With respect to the last question, if there is any residual contamination, ask via MMT for the best interventions to clear all supernatural contaminants. When these issues are resolved, ask if you and your client need to work together any further to facilitate conscious integration.

This is an abbreviated guide to give you an idea of just what is involved. Like most things in life, as you open yourself up to more of what is possible, you will encounter this more often and your clients will be the beneficiaries of your work.

If the client has a current-life situation and the soul stealer is still alive, the process to follow is very different. In these cases, energetic boundary work, relationship work, or shamanic interventions are frequently required.

As we continue to explore our capacity to cause injury to other life forms on our garden planet, it seems more important now than ever before (as our population continues to inexorably increase) to be mindful of our shadow side. If we can learn to recognize and acknowledge how powerful and damaging our proclivity to hurt others is, I believe we can, through the power of our collective intention, turn the tide from a growing trend of worldwide violence and overcome these powerful forces of darkness to create a true haven for all living beings. We have the means. We just need the will and sufficient understanding about these forces in order to know that these forces can be overcome.

CHAPTER
16

INTRUSIONS

D ynamic Energetic Healing® recognizes that supernatural phenomena
are inherent in the unusual energies and occurrences that interfere
with your life. In fact, a fundamental feature of the Dynamic Energetic Heal-
ing® approach is counteracting these phenomena effectively.

When a client is depressed after suffering a significant personal loss, part
of my job is to help them come to terms with what they are really feeling.
Depression classically presents a flattened affective state that often borders on
inertia. When a depressed person comes into my office, I feel the entire room
hang with a solemn quietude of resignation and withdrawal, devoid of any joy
and aliveness. Who would guess that within this quiet despair often lies
tremendous anger bordering on rage? This anger is unseen and often unknown
even to the client. The individual knows something is wrong because there is
evidence of something detracting from their normal activities. This evidence
may be a loss of appetite, a strong desire to stay in bed all day, and a seeming
inability to connect with other human beings. The individual feels these
things, and therefore they are *subjectively determined to be real*. With the help
of a good therapist, the client can return to a state of emotional wholeness and
well-being. And yet, many individuals remain chronically depressed, anxious,
or unhappy.

Even though many aspects of clinical psychology are subjective and
"unseen," the medical community vehemently denies and dismisses that which
is called supernatural. Instead, they embrace the paradigm that subjective

states are often the result of biochemical imbalance. Their intervention of choice is prescribing powerful pharmaceutical drugs that significantly alter the brain biochemistry and thereby modify your mood. Cognitive-behavioral therapists embrace a model in which individuals must change their thinking in order to positively affect their behavior.

Hypnotherapists try to bypass the conscious, rational thinking processes of the personality and direct their interventions to the subconscious mind. Hypnosis has become a legitimate and acceptable therapeutic intervention, even among the conservative medical community. What exactly is the subconscious mind? I do not know, nor do I believe that any ten therapists and/or medical doctors who work with the subconscious would agree on any consistent definition of the term. This is because we are dealing with something subjective. The *Random House Webster's College Dictionary* (1992) defines *subjective* as

> 1. existing in the mind; belonging to the thinking subject rather than to the object of thought (opposed to *objective*). 2. pertaining to or characteristic of an individual; personal: *a subjective evaluation*. . . . 4. *Philos.* relating to or of the nature of an object as it is known in the mind as distinct from a thing in itself.

My point is that if something is felt, sensed, or somehow just known intuitively, it is a subjective experience and therefore cannot be proven to anyone else. If I am in a restaurant and suddenly become aware of a tingling sensation around my scalp or an alarming image that persists in my awareness, these are subjective experiences that ought not be dismissed. As a process-oriented psychotherapist, I have trained myself to become exquisitely sensitive to perceive an ongoing, all-inclusive field of awareness. This includes all that is my own experience, my clients' experience, and what is going on in the expanded interpersonal field when I am working with clients.

Whether I call these seemingly unexplained phenomena dark energy, the paranormal, or the supernatural, they can act on us at any time. For this discussion I will use *intrusion* to describe something generic that fits in this category. Various shamanic traditions of indigenous peoples describe an intrusion as an outside or external negative energy that is often regarded as a source or cause of illness. When such an intrusion has been identified through the assistance of the shaman's helping spirits, the shaman uses specific techniques to extract or remove the intrusion in an effort to restore the health of the patient. These shamanic traditions are cross-cultural, and their awareness of the profound negative influence of intrusions is widely known.

Based on my many years of training and practice in shamanic healing techniques, I can vouch for the veracity of intrusions. What I "see" as an intrusion when I am working with a client is from my own internal sensing or perception—it is subjective. After having an intrusion extracted, many of my clients experience a progressively increasing sense of calm and peace, in contrast to their previous agitation or anxiety.

I believe the best way I can explain the strong negative impact that intrusions can have on us is by sharing a personal experience. A few years ago, one of my sisters-in-law was getting married in Denver, Colorado. My family and I flew to the Mile High City, rented a car at the airport, and drove to our hotel (affiliated with a popular national chain) in downtown Denver. We were to stay there for two days, after which we were heading to Estes Park in the Rockies for a week of hiking. When I made the reservation, I specifically requested a nonsmoking room; I was told that although the hotel's policy forbade them to guarantee it, there would not be a problem.

As soon as we got to the front desk to check in, things became very strange. We had to wait about ten minutes before talking to a desk clerk because ahead of us was an irate man and his family complaining that when they had opened the door to their room, there was already a family in there. The gentleman behind the front desk appeared very flustered, unable to comprehend how this could have happened. While we waited, he worked frantically at his computer to resolve the mix-up. Then it was my turn. When the agent looked up my name and reservation number on his computer, he gave me two keys and the room number and told me we were all set. Just to double-check, I asked him if the room was nonsmoking—it wasn't. I told him I had been assured that it would be no problem, and it seemed unbelievable to me that there would not be a nonsmoking room available in this enormous hotel. Suddenly, for reasons I could only explain later, I was in this poor man's face angrily yelling at him, demanding that he get us a nonsmoking room. (My wife said later that she stood by speechless as I angrily cursed this man out!) As the clerk once again began frantically consulting his computer, I noticed that there was a third problem at the reception desk—an older couple was having words with another agent. After what seemed like another ten minutes, our poor, very put-upon agent told me he had rearranged some other reservations (of people who had not yet arrived) so we could have our non-smoking room.

As we made our way up to our room, my wife asked me what had got into me. I grinned sheepishly; I didn't know. I had never yelled at a desk clerk before, and it is not my temperament to become irascible. I was happy that I had represented my need for a smoke-free room (since I can't stand that stale, squalid smell of old cigarettes), but I mused about my "irrational" reaction.

Little did I know that the entire hotel was contaminated by dark energy. This initial incident was a prelude to other intrusions that came as a result of our stay at this hotel. Over the next couple of days, strange things happened to us that might easily (but erroneously) be explained as mere coincidences. Shortly after settling into our room, my then nine-year-old son's nose began to bleed. This wasn't particularly alarming because he had had nosebleeds in the past, but his nose continued to bleed on and off throughout our stay at the hotel, which was unusual. When we got to Estes Park at an even higher elevation, the nosebleeds stopped. To me, this eliminated the argument that the recurrent bleeding was simply due to the high elevation.

Another strange incident occurred in the hotel restaurant. At about 9:30 P.M. we decided to eat a late dinner at the hotel. The restaurant closed at 10 P.M., and we were the last people being served. The waitress took our orders, and our meals arrived about twenty minutes later, except for one. The waitress didn't say anything as she left, so we assumed that Sandi's meal would be coming right up. After another ten minutes, we sought out the waitress to inquire about Sandi's meal. She had totally forgotten the order. She apologized and went to speak to the cook. A minute later she returned, somewhat perplexed—the cook had just left! She did not understand this highly unusual behavior, because the cook always stayed past ten o'clock to make preparations for the next day. The waitress finally got hold of the manager, who cooked Sandi's meal himself. Needless to say, we were all very upset. I thought this was very strange, but I still had not connected all the dots.

It wasn't until the next night, at our lodging in Estes Park, that an experience finally pulled it all together for me. Our modest cabin had old knotty-pine paneling and basic amenities. It was clean and comfortable, certainly adequate as a base camp for five days of hiking. I never have problems sleeping, but that night at about 3 A.M. I was awakened by a very frightening nightmare. I am not prone to nightmares and frequently do not even remember my dreams in the morning. But this was more of a night vision of demonic intrusion. I remember seeing a malevolent or demonic entity coming toward me with the intent to kill me. I felt outright terror. I woke up with a start, sweating and physically adrenalized. My heart was pounding, I was disoriented in the dark, and I feared for my life.

I took a couple of deep breaths and regained my bearings, after which I immediately began tapping on EFT meridian points (see chapter 20, "Emotional Freedom Techniques") to calm myself. After a few repetitions, I muscle tested myself to inquire about what had happened. To my surprise, I had picked up an intrusion that fit the category of demonic possession or angry ghost—it was probably a disoriented, angry earthbound spirit.

It has been my experience that malevolent intrusions are few and far between. Most intrusions are some kind of outside negative energy that, although annoying and troublesome, is not malevolent or dangerous. This was an exception. After reflecting on this new information, I determined to locate the intrusion's origin. I first thought this might be something I picked up from the cabin—this was not the case. I continued to inquire with the help of my own muscle testing and found out that this angry ghost had attached itself to me during our stay at the Denver hotel. I suddenly had the ah-ha experience of awareness. Our hotel was contaminated with something that was affecting everyone in the collective field, something that I might call dark energy! All the pieces fit together: my uncharacteristically angry response at the front desk, my son's persistent nosebleeds, and the debacle in the restaurant. I suddenly realized and knew for an empirical fact that *physical locations retain and emit their own energy field, which we are always open to absorb and be affected by*. This can happen in a hotel room, a doctor's office, an ashram or church, even a beautiful place in nature.

All at once, a great deal of what I had experienced made sense to me. I realized that I was experiencing my dreaming body, or what Mindell also calls the dreambody. My unusual perceptions were the result of training my second attention to become sensitive to the sensations of my physical body and of my expanded awareness of whatever in the field might catch my attention and disturb my normal identity.

The dreambody experience supports a nondualistic orientation to life that enables shapeshifting into fluid identities. This orientation challenges the consensus-reality paradigm that we are simply static, consistent, and predictable personalities. Actively embracing the dreambody experience supports a fluid identity that provides the flexibility to move into the dreaming experience of whatever moods, feelings, visions, or perceptions disturb or intrude into an individual's awareness.

Increasing awareness is an outcome of the dreambody experience, but even more importantly, the experience speaks to the deeper issue of who we believe ourselves to be. Culturally determined expectations ensure that we conform to the collective trance. "According to Buddha, suffering is due to attachment to identity, to consensus reality" (Mindell 2000b, 539). Mindell (2000b, 509–11) explains that

> The dreambody is to your ordinary experience of the body as the anti-matter particle is to the ordinary particle. The dreambody is your bodily sense of another world. Most people pay attention to this sense only when it has become a strong symptom they fear will annihilate them. The dreambody is the body experience shamans use to travel between the worlds.... The dreambody has been thought of as a subtle substance not directly apparent to our ordinary senses. Sometimes it is seen as a ghost or an angel, images that indicate our sense of the dreambody as a piece of human-like intelligence and communication ability inherent in all of nature. In all these cases, the dreambody was a second body, universally thought of as an intelligent source of life, part of the river or the continuum of existence in death.

I have always been sensitive to the energetic influence in the interpersonal context. But this Colorado experience created a paradigm shift for me, and it is why I create a sacred space wherever I work. It is also why I smudge myself and my entire office with sage after a session—I clean my personal field of any negative energy that I may have unwittingly picked up or absorbed from my clients. By doing this, I prevent myself from picking up outside negative energies, and I protect my clients from absorbing the negative energy released from clients in prior sessions. I also internally visualize my chakras to determine if I am still energetically linked to my previous client at any of these energy centers. It is often the case that I am—I perceive congested areas in one or more of my chakras. I then visualize hollow tubes attached to the affected energy centers and watch the congested energy that I absorbed from the client drain into the center of the earth. When this process is completed, my chakras come back into balance with a soft glow of radiant energy. Then I know I am no longer merged energetically with my previous client.

It took me fifteen or twenty minutes to completely release every trace of that earthbound spirit attachment so I could sleep peacefully through the rest of the night. Though I was disturbed from the shock and terror of the experience, I had successfully detraumatized myself so that I could reflect on the experience objectively. As I was drifting off to sleep, I felt excited by my new discovery.

Since then, I always muscle test when I am traveling to be certain that my hotel room or sleeping space is free of dark energy. Since I always take a non-smoking room and I don't want to set off the alarm by burning sage, I have found that my Tibetan bell works just as well in clearing the space of any outside negative energies that may linger from prior occupants (see part 2). What I now know to be true is that *people leave their energy behind, even as they take it with them. This energy is information that can sometimes be picked up by the dreamingbody like different radio frequencies if a person's reception is sensitive enough.* With good energetic boundaries, this information can be accessed and found to be useful. With poor energetic boundaries, this information can be intrusive and even harmful. Since that profound experience in Colorado, I have never experienced another intrusion while traveling. I have, however, encountered other contexts in which I have been contaminated by intrusions. These include my acupuncturist's office and my dentist's office.

In each of these contexts, I came in for some medical treatment. My normal experience after receiving treatment from each practitioner is symptom resolution and increasing physical well-being. However, on a few rare occasions, I felt progressively worse after one of these treatments. Initially, I attributed my ongoing physical distress to tight or sore muscles (or, in the case of the dentist, residual soreness from the pressure and the vibration of drilling). But when the experience continued to worsen over a period of days, it finally occurred to me to muscle test myself in an effort to discover what else might be contributing to my malaise. In each of these rare cases, an intrusion was responsible for the persisting pain. Each time, I picked up the intrusion at the practitioner's office; no doubt it was the lingering negative residue left by a traumatized or fearful patient.

I have worked with many clients over the last few years who have picked up intrusions at their doctor's office, particularly cancer patients who were being treated with chemotherapy or radiation. In many cases, it seems that intrusions feed on fear, anger, and general states of vulnerability. We are more prone to attack by intrusions when we are in a general state of energetic weakness. This would be comparable to the conditions that lead to an individual getting physically sick from becoming run-down. What this suggests is that we have to be extra vigilant whenever we enter a healthcare practitioner's office.

My dentist recently put a crown on one of my teeth. I had the standard lidocaine shot followed by the drilling to make sure that all remnants of the old filling were gone. It was uncomfortable but not particularly traumatic. At the end of the procedure, he fashioned a temporary crown to place on my tooth. My tooth ached for the next couple of days. I had expected this might be the case and wasn't overly concerned. But the achiness increased until finally, five days after the office visit, I had to take an Advil to suppress the pain. The pain seemed way out of proportion to the straightforward procedure that I had experienced. I played phone tag with the dentist's assistant the next day while my pain continued to increase.

It occurred to me to muscle test myself and inquire if there was a dark energy intrusion connected with this. To my surprise, I had picked up an intrusion during my visit to the dentist. It took just a few minutes to release this intrusion by using my Tibetan bell and tapping on specific chakras. I then inquired if it would be in my highest good to continue taking Advil for the pain. My muscle testing answer was no and that the pain would be gone within twenty-four hours. I have a great deal of trust in my muscle testing responses, and the next morning the pain was completely gone!

So how do I now protect myself whenever I go to a healthcare practitioner's office? I ensure that I am consciously connected to Spirit and that all my spiritual resources are present with me to protect me from any intrusions that might be present in the field. In fact, I reaffirm my connection to Spirit every morning. For myself and my family, I give thanks for that accompanying presence that protects and guides us throughout the day *wherever we are*. I take extra care to emphasize my need for added protection whenever I visit a doctor's office.

After picking up an intrusion at my acupuncturist's office, I shared my experience with her at my next appointment and recommended that she do something to keep her offices energetically clean. Unlike my dentist, she understood what I was talking about. In Chinese medicine, this is called bad chi. She was looking for a new building to buy, and one of her criteria would be windows in each office, which would allow for the natural circulation of spent or bad chi.

I want to add why it is so important to make every effort to surround your-self with positive, loving people and to regularly visit places of power, whether they be human-built or in nature. We are all energetic beings. We give off or emit energy, and we pick up or absorb energy. It is the nature of our beingness. If we have knowledge and awareness of this fact, we can use it to our own advantage and for the benefit of others. I have worked with numer-ous clients over the years who have suffered tremendously from staying in toxic relationships, either personal or professional. Due to the sensitivity and temperament of these individuals, their energetic boundaries tended to be weak. Consequently, their regular interactions with these toxic individuals generated a host of chronic deleterious symptoms, including regular intrusion by the negative energy of the other. Because these clients were vulnerable to occupation by intrusions, they experienced an unfortunate by-product—per-sistent anxiety and agitation. Once the intrusions were identified and released, all of their symptoms abated immediately. But for all kinds of reasons, it fre-quently took a long time for these clients to terminate their toxic relationships. As a result, they were constantly exposing themselves to an energy field (of the toxic individual) that became like an energetic worm, constantly and per-niciously energetically eroding their personal health and sense of well-being.

It is important to cultivate your second attention so you can begin to trust the feelings, sensations, and intuitions that inform you of what's going on energetically around you. I never would have thought that an entire hotel complex would be saturated and contaminated by dark or negative energy. I now know better. The existence of this negative energy is why it is so important to make time to be out in nature, so the energies of the earth, the sun, and the nature spirits can feed you, nurture you, and support your ener-getic integrity. It is also very important to cultivate a daily energetic practice such as yoga, meditation, or qigong. These energetic practices will fortify you so your energy field remains robust and radiant. The more consistently strong your energy field is, the less chance you have of being a victim to unwarranted intrusions.

CHAPTER
17

CREATING A SACRED SPACE

Throughout the world, many traditions revere specific sites as "power spots," which are regarded as places of power. These locations, some of which are sites connected to important events in the life of a spiritual master or saint, are a locus or confluence of healing or spiritual energy. The Bodhi tree in India is reputed to be the place where the Buddha attained his enlightenment. Christians from all over the world make pilgrimages to Bethlehem to honor the birth of their savior. One of the five pillars of Islam urges Muslims to make a pilgrimage to Mecca at least once during their lifetime, and pilgrims from all over the world come to fulfill this commitment to their faith. Mecca is where Mohammed first received his revelation from God. Mecca is a mental and internal energetic focus for Muslims throughout their lives—one that sets the intention for the eventual pilgrimage.

Anthropologists have discovered that indigenous peoples commonly revere specific areas or geographic locations, such as a particular mountain, that are considered to be "holy" places. Some people believe that these places of power are where the earth's meridians or chakras coalesce and intersect, thus creating vortexes of the vital life-force energy that permeates all things. It is believed that these specific locations significantly affect the human vital life-force energy system by enhancing and facilitating greater openness to spiritual and healing capabilities.

Many churches in Europe were built on what had previously been regarded as pagan power spots. Throughout the world, the faithful in all religious traditions construct altars in their homes as a way to honor the Divine. The sacred, whether it is one's home altar, one's community church, or the presumed remains of Mohammed in Mecca, is honored and revered. I can assert with absolute certainty that specially designated locations become sacralized through repetitive, ongoing mental focus and devotional practices. People are drawn to the great cathedrals of Europe because over centuries of devotion, these places have become imbued with spiritual energy. This also occurs in an altar in a home.

In Dynamic Energetic Healing®, we recognize the power inherent in devotional prayer (Dossey 1996), a directing of consciousness that is focused for a healing outcome. Consequently, creating a sacred space where we (you and I as therapists) work is built into the Dynamic Energetic Healing® model. This includes a number of components. At the beginning of each working day, I go into my treatment room, stay quiet for a moment, and affirm that all of my spiritual resources be present throughout the day. When I do this, I know and trust that I am being watched over, protected, and guided. I know that I am not alone in the room with my client. I am being supported spiritually in every session, and my treatment room has been transformed into sacred space, imbued with spiritual power by virtue of my renewed personal connection to Spirit.

To augment this, I ask my clients at the beginning of their sessions if they would like to ask for help from their own connection to God or Spirit and invite that spiritual energy (for example, Jesus) to be in the room with us for their session. This adds to the healing power of the space itself, which accumulates more spiritual power over time. It also affirms the clients' own higher power, which can help them heal more rapidly by reinforcing that part of themselves which, to varying degrees, they may have disowned. By creating a sacred space, I affirm to my clients how important I believe it is to draw upon the strength and healing power of Spirit.

But many clients are either agnostic or dispirited. Due to the seriousness of their persistent problem, be it depression, anxiety, or post-traumatic stress disorder, clients may have no connection to or even believe in God. It is not necessary for them to have any belief in God in order for our work to be successful. *I know that my healing space is sacred and radiating spiritual power*. I know I have created and maintain a sacred space for my work with clients. Thus, I am aware and respectful of the possibility that the need for a spiritual container may be greater than what my client is initially aware of. The creation of a sacred work space provides this spiritual container.

I regularly integrate other components into my Dynamic Energetic Healing® sessions in order to maintain the sacred space as well. After each client leaves, I either burn sage (which is called smudging the space) or chime my Tibetan bell to ensure that the space remains free of any residual negativity, dark energy, or stagnant emotional energy. Either modality is effective for cleansing.

It is also very important to follow my second attention, which is discussed in more detail in chapter 5, "Integrating the Second Attention into Dynamic Energetic Healing®." How does this relate to creating a sacred space? To ensure that I do my part to keep the space clean within the therapeutic relational context, it is absolutely essential that I not withhold any of my internal experience or awareness when I am with a client. For example, if I am feeling sadness, anger, or spaciness when with a client, it is incumbent upon me to bring that awareness into the shared relational field in order to keep the energetic field clean. It is also my responsibility, to the degree that I am perceptually capable, to bring to my clients' awareness what I am feeling or perceiving about their experience. Other models of psychotherapy may take issue with this stance, particularly with severely abused clients who are feeling extremely vulnerable. Certainly, sensitivity to timing is important. However, my professional experience is that my being able to stay current with the flow of information both intrapersonally and interpersonally means that any stagnant energy or marginalized affective responses are kept to a bare minimum. Following your second attention is a very important part of the therapist's responsibility to keep the work space clean, thereby maintaining the sanctity of sacred space.

There are many elements that go into making a space sacred. When the psychotherapeutic work space is indeed a *sacred space*, all manner of healing becomes possible. It is simply foolish to presume that because of a therapist's cleverness or technique, positive therapeutic outcomes can be counted on. At the end of the day, deep healing always occurs via the power of the numinous—the power of love. This power is always present in a sacred space.

CHAPTER

18

LIVING LIFE FREE OF TRAUMA

As my immersion in Dynamic Energetic Healing® has deepened, it has become increasingly evident to me that this is a powerful and transformative therapy model. It is clear to me that people who have suffered from anxiety, persistent depression, or intractable trauma now have a way to rapidly and permanently heal from the devastating effects of these experiences. Dynamic Energetic Healing® is a teachable and replicable methodology that guides you to identify the origins of complex trauma patterns that have tyrannized clients for years.

Dynamic Energetic Healing® is in stark contrast to the approach HMOs dictate to clinicians to address problem states. In the HMO medical model, clinicians are only reimbursed for treatments that address what is "medically necessary" in order to alleviate disruptive symptoms and "stabilize" clients. The therapeutic goal is for individuals to maintain "normal functioning" and return back to their work and home environments without debilitating traumatic symptoms. This model usually precludes resolving the underlying cause of the problem, but it does tend to achieve symptom resolution, albeit often via the use of ongoing medication (brain-modifying drugs). The politics of this situation are well known: while the HMOs reduce their costs, therapeutic outcomes are compromised.

As an integrative energy psychology model, Dynamic Energetic Healing® lets the clinician identify and go to the client's energetic origin, the seminal event that first created the pattern—the one to which other events or origins are related. By using various energetic strategies, I can identify the components of a client's original traumatic incident. If a pattern of single but related traumatic incidents has occurred over a period of time, one by one, very methodically, the entire network of interrelated symptomatic trauma phenomena can be cleared.

As I became more proficient at this approach, I realized that Dynamic Energetic Healing® might also be a model for the personal transformation and liberation from suffering that spiritual practices promise. Traditional spiritual models use prayer, faith, meditation, and specific spiritual practices that work with the energy body to clear the traumatic material which is in the way of achieving self-actualization. Examples are numerous: Vipassana meditation encourages students to observe their thoughts nonjudgmentally while orienting to their breathing; Hindu and Buddhist traditions involve repeated chanting of a mantra that encourages one-pointedness of mind and shifting energy to the vibration generated by the mantra; many religious traditions advocate praying to a deity or god/goddess figure to internalize the spiritual qualities personified by the deified figure. These traditional spiritual models, particularly the Eastern models (which are increasingly being adopted by Westerners), require a great deal of discipline. What's more, it takes a great deal of time before you reach a so-called state of self-mastery.

Dynamic Energetic Healing® is a model that allows anyone with the help of a well-trained facilitator to experience profound healing. You can begin to identify the underlying historical events and patterns that are responsible for persistent symptoms easily and quickly, which has always been the goal of traditional psychotherapy. Even more importantly, the traumas and related patterns can be vanquished in ways that do not retraumatize clients or return to haunt them. Once the information contained in the energy fields of these trauma patterns is cleared away like clouds after a storm, clients finally have choices over their own lives and can begin creating a constructive and self-determining reality. To realize your intentions in your own life is to become truly self-realized!

Myths about enlightenment and the perpetual bliss that accompanies this spiritual state reserved for the elite saints and sages can be seen for what they have always been—the inspiration to strive for the "more," which God has always been represented as giving us. The Western counterpart of enlightenment, self-actualization, is not a state of being that occurs as the result of years of a spiritual practice—*it is an ongoing process* that Dynamic Energetic Healing® opens individuals up to creating and providing for themselves.

In effect, I am describing the remaking or reinventing of an individual. Am I referring to some kind of twenty-first-century postmodern shortcut to enlightenment? Hardly. The beneficiaries of Dynamic Energetic Healing® don't have to be the stereotypical seekers of enlightenment who spend years with a guru in relative isolation—the beneficiaries are your clients. These seekers have a job and often a family and are fully engaged in the world, often to the point of being chronically overwhelmed. Imagine them being no longer determined by the conditioning influences from their past. I am not suggesting that we can be completely free from past conditioning influences, only that we can now be free from the commanding insistence of their rule over us.

The subject of freeing the individual from the tyranny of past conditioning influences has been discussed for decades and even centuries. Various psychological-change models, from Skinner's behavior modification to current neurolinguistic programming techniques, purport to achieve just this. Contemporary pharmacological models now maintain that positive change and perpetual optimism can be created through biochemistry. In *Listening to Prozac* (1993, xv–xix), Peter Kramer makes this claim:

> Prozac—the new antidepressant—was the main agent of change. There has always been the occasional patient who seems remarkably restored by one medicine or another, but with Prozac I had seen patient after patient become, like Sam, "better than well." Prozac seemed to give social confidence to the habitually timid, to make the sensitive brash, to lend the introvert the social skills of a salesman. Prozac was transformative for patients in the way an inspirational minister or high-pressure group therapy can be—it made them want to talk about their experience. And what my patients generally said was that they had learned something about themselves from Prozac. Like Sam, they believed Prozac revealed what in them was biologically determined and what [was] merely (experience being "mere" compared to cellular physiology) experiential.... By now, not yet five years after it was introduced, eight million people have taken Prozac, over half in the United States. My concern has been with a subset of these millions: fairly healthy people who show dramatic good responses to Prozac, people who are not so much cured of illness as transformed.

My assertion is that for most individuals, living a life free from the damaging and debilitating influence of past trauma is now a reality. Though therapies have made this claim before, few if any that have practical and accessible energy psychology techniques have been readily available to the public. The jury will be out for some time before delivering their verdict on Dynamic Energetic Healing®. This is to be expected—the world is slow to embrace new paradigms.

Dynamic Energetic Healing® has become a model for personal transformation. It started as a psychotherapy model, transitioned into a model for healing, and is now moving into the next step: a model for personal transformation at the core level involving a spiritual awakening as an organic unfolding of personal healing. Once we are no longer subject to the negative, constricting traumatic patterns and influences from our past, we can be clear about why we are here. There need be no limitations for how we make our contribution and achieve our life mission.

My own life is becoming progressively free of trauma, and my consciousness itself is changing. I experience less and less internal clutter, and my experience of the silent mind continues to evolve and grow more persistent. As this occurs, I am becoming effortlessly more present with everything and everyone. My self-consciousness and inner critiquing are diminishing, and I am occasionally shocked by the presentness of that which is in my awareness. Where this will lead I do not know. My belief, however, is that this change in consciousness is possible and available for anyone who is interested and willing to do their personal work.

My next book will describe advanced protocols that address collective fields of energy, including the archetypal, ancestral, and current global fields that are always influencing us. Identifying the information in these larger collective and global fields, which we carry within ourselves from this lifetime and previous lifetimes, has become an important component of Dynamic Energetic Healing®. For most of us our primary reference point is our physical body, but we are never separate energetically. By starting with the platform of our physical body as the access portal to our connection with the One, we can use energetic healing strategies to identify and collapse traumas and trauma patterns. This allows us to return to a state of innocence, but without childlike ignorance. This is now possible through Dynamic Energetic Healing®.

But first things first. Take some time to assimilate these ideas and energetic strategies and share them with your clients. Discover the wonder and delight that emerges using Dynamic Energetic Healing®. Be intrepid and discover how easy it is to let go of old, persistent, binding trauma.

PART 2:
THE DYNAMIC
ENERGETIC HEALING®
INTERVENTIONS

THE DYNAMIC ENERGETIC HEALING® INTERVENTIONS

The word *interventions* is used throughout Dynamic Energetic Healing®. Interventions are specific actions that intervene on the client's behalf in response to information learned via MMT. As interventions are implemented during the therapy session, multilevel shifts occur in the client's experience.

To a large extent, the structure of the Dynamic Energetic Healing® interventions and the contexts in which they are used emerged from the energy psychology trainings I took. As in the energy psychology paradigm, many of the interventions are designed to directly affect the client's essential energy system. This system includes the channels or meridians from the Chinese medicine model, the chakras, and the human biofield or aura.

Stimulating the client's chi field while the client is attuning to the problem state or disturbance responsible for creating the symptoms causes immediate shifts in the client's experience.

The Resonance Factor

I have over twenty-four years of clinical experience, and among the many therapy models I have been trained in is a large collection of energy psychology interventions. Over the years, I have drawn from my cumulative repertoire to use the therapeutic interventions that are indicated for each client's unique needs. As positive therapeutic outcomes became more consistent through my use of Dynamic Energetic Healing®, I found that for the most part the same small group of interventions are effective in treating the vast majority of my clients. These are the interventions that I have included in the Dynamic Energetic Healing® model. Why is this, and how is this possible?

I believe that different practitioners resonate with particular interventions; I also believe that the practitioner's personal propensities and personality play a role in this process. In working with the human vibrational matrix, we are working with the life-force energy, the very essence that creates and perpetuates all life and existence in the universe. Different individuals are more strongly and naturally attracted to different aspects of various energetic interventions, largely due to the predispositions of their particular soul and the gifts that are brought with it.

For example, Gary Craig is an incredibly effective practitioner and teacher of what he calls emotional freedom techniques (EFT). While other therapists (myself included) use a variety of interventions, Gary Craig uses EFT exclusively to help his clients, and he is extremely effective using this simple energy psychology intervention with nearly everyone he treats. My theory is that he resonates at a very strong frequency with this particular methodology of tapping on acupressure points. This is evident to me by how much passion he generates when lecturing, teaching, and working with clients. For Gary Craig, EFT isn't just a technique; it is a path to healing, and thus it takes on a spiritual dimension for him. I believe this is why he resonates so strongly with EFT and why this intervention works so well for him. Perhaps he is channeling a very special healing energy through this vehicle he calls EFT; of this I am not sure. But I believe he holds a very large "container" that encompasses much more than the eye can see when he uses this intervention with his clients.

Another example is Asha Clinton (developer of the seemorg matrix work model), whose intervention of choice is chakra tapping. Clinton's background includes training in clinical social work and teaching anthropology at the university level. She has meditated for many years, and she has integrated her experiential knowledge of the chakras into her energy psychology model. Though she has incorporated MMT into her work, working with the chakras in various combinations nearly always serves as her primary intervention.

I believe that Elizabeth Fleming's Tapas acupressure technique (TAT) is a third example of this. Fleming is an acupuncturist and has meditated for many years. Stimulating a particular acupuncture point (UB1) for comprehensive healing came to her after taking a nap. A few months later, a patient told her that his T'ai Chi master had directed him to use this point along with another that Fleming incorporated to alleviate headaches.

In the energy psychology community, Clinton, Craig, and Fleming are highly regarded for their unique approaches for creating positive shifts and eliminating persistent emotional problems by accessing an individual's essential energy system. It is interesting to note that these three prominent members of the energy psychology community come from very diverse backgrounds, not all of which include psychology. Yet each of them accepts the same underlying principles and presuppositions for initiating change at the energetic level, even though their interventions are very different and unique to their specific models.

If my theory about resonance is correct, each of us—with our unique vibrational signature—is already connected to Source in a very special way. Through our passion, we can easily recruit this special aspect of Source, which will naturally lead us to the right energetic solutions. There are stories in the healing literature of masters who are able to heal with a single word, a touch, or even simply by being present with someone. Science has not yet been able to decipher or explain how these seemingly miraculous healings occur. But my experiences in Brazil with Joao Teixeira da Faria (Joao de Deus, or John of God) and with other healers corroborate the anecdotal literature of miraculous healings. We each have a unique genius that applies to spiritual and energetic healing. The remarkable healing experiences I had with John of God in Brazil are beyond the scope of this book. If you are curious about them, you can find out more by reading my detailed story posted on my website.

The interventions that I regularly work with are the ones that I strongly resonate with. Unlike the practitioners discussed above, I haven't found any single intervention that is always effective. That is why I selected these to be in my Dynamic Energetic Healing® therapeutic repertoire. These selected interventions are enormously effective when used in combination throughout the steps of the Dynamic Energetic Healing® methodology.

Even though I use only a handful of interventions, there is quite a lot going on. One of the most profound things I discovered in Brazil during my healing experiences with Joao de Deus is that love accomplishes the healing regardless of the specific intervention used. Carl Rogers called the love that enables healers to facilitate seemingly miraculous healings *unconditional personal regard*; Eric Fromm called it *agapeic love*. Mother Teresa powerfully embodied and modeled this quality of the heart during her ministry to the least fortunate and the destitute.

The Dreaming Body

When I step into Process with a client, I am 100 percent present, with all of my sensing receptors open, on multiple levels internally and in the therapeutic relational context. I pay exquisite attention to my client's story, feeling tone behind the words and nonverbal signals. I also stay connected to my second attention and to what Mindell calls the dreaming body—that place of heightened awareness in which I am open to the energetic communication between the client and me—and any additional extrasensory information I become aware of, particularly when I move in and out of the dreamtime experience. You might call this experience of heightened awareness being open to intuition. Interestingly, even Freud was aware of the unconscious communication in the interpersonal field, paying attention to what he called the analyst's free-floating attention.

Psychotherapy has gone through many transmutations since its origins in the early twentieth century. Yet too many psychotherapists are still seduced by the client's words, which obfuscate the pain of the trauma in the background. Very often, clients cannot consciously access this pain because the traumatic residue they still carry prevents them from opening up and being vulnerable with this pain. When this is the case, therapists often support the client's story or narrative, which simply perpetuates a sense of hopelessness and of being stuck. Content is always important, but the unspoken intimations and energetic component occurring within the therapeutic relationship provide the greatest possibility for positive transformative change.

The Dynamic Energetic Healing® Interventions

I want to share with you the interventions that I use. This work is the culmination of over twenty-four years of clinical experience and over thirty years of experience with various spiritual practices.

These interventions are best appreciated within the larger therapeutic context, even though many of them stand on their own merits as energy psychology and shamanic healing methods that anyone can learn successfully.

The Dynamic Energetic Healing® model includes these interventions:

1. Tapas acupressure technique (TAT)
2. Emotional freedom techniques (EFT), including directive tapping
3. Tapping the temporal curve
4. Negative affect erasing method (NAEM)

5. Frontal occipital (F/O) holding
6. Chakra tapping
7. Vibrational healing using sound, which includes
    • mantra
    • toning
    • Kirtan Kriya meditation
    • Tibetan bell
    • Tibetan bowls
    • Tibetan cymbals
    • healing drum
8. Focused prayer
9. Core shamanic methods

Some of these interventions are self-administered, meaning that clients perform the action themselves. The interventions in this category are TAT, EFT, tapping the temporal curve, NAEM, chakra tapping, mantra, and focused prayer. The therapist performs the remaining interventions on behalf of the client.

The Importance of Manual Muscle Testing

In the Dynamic Energetic Healing® model, feedback from the client is constantly solicited via manual muscle testing. The client chooses the intervention to be used at each point in the therapeutic process. I ask the client a series of yes/no questions and muscle test to get the answers. For example, I might begin with, "From your soul or inner wisdom, is EFT the best intervention to use at this time?" If the answer is yes, we proceed with the EFT intervention. If the answer is no, I repeat the question, this time naming a different intervention. We proceed with the questions until MMT identifies the intervention we need to use.

Frequently, I have a strong intuitive awareness about which intervention is the most appropriate when I muscle test. In these instances, I test on this intervention first, though occasionally another intervention is more appropriate. Clients are sometimes guided by their own intuition to suggest which intervention is needed. I always double-check their choice with MMT.

I like this method of selecting interventions because I am simply a facilitator, following and honoring my client's process. Our energy fields are overlapping, so clients can communicate to me via accurate muscle testing which of the core interventions that I hold in my field is the most appropriate and efficient to use at any given time. Applied kinesiology methods are sometimes viewed skeptically because there are those who believe they are not scientific. Gary Schwartz and Linda Russek (1999, 251) discuss this in the context of their systemic memory hypothesis:

> Kinesiology involves diagnoses and treatments that presume that the muscles and organ tissues store information and energy, for example, about traumas. Since traditional models presume that memories are stored only in the central nervous system, the observations and interpretations of kinesiologists are interpreted as being in error. However, the systemic memory hypothesis suggests that all cells may indeed store information, and therefore this information can be potentially retrieved from muscles and organ systems. Having a patient "tune into memory stored in specific bodily regions" may be more than just a metaphor—organs may store patterns of information that are unique and can be added to information stored in the brain.

Whether applied kinesiology is an art or a science, what matters most to me is how manual muscle testing reliably enables Dynamic Energetic Healing® to sustain consistent healing of old trauma and related patterns for clients with various presenting problems. By asking the proper questions, I am able to elicit the pertinent information that guides us to the place of positive therapeutic outcomes.

The remaining chapters in part 2 describe how each of the Dynamic Energetic Healing® interventions is used.

19

TAPAS ACUPRESSURE TECHNIQUE

The Tapas acupressure technique (TAT) was developed by Elizabeth Tapas Fleming. Like Gary Craig, who uses only the EFT intervention, Fleming uses her TAT intervention exclusively. Much like Gary Craig's incredible success using EFT, Fleming claims remarkable healing success teaching and using TAT.

The Pose

With the tips of your ring finger and thumb of the same hand, press gently but firmly on either side of where the bridge of your nose meets your face. While you are doing this, press your middle finger gently but firmly into the center of your forehead. At the same time, cup the occipital area at the back of your head with your other hand (see figure 1).

Your middle finger is stimulating the sixth-chakra location, which stimulates and heightens your intuitive capacity, putting you in touch with your inner knowing. Your ring finger and thumb are stimulating the bladder meridian, which corresponds to emotional trauma. Cupping your occipital area with your other hand completes the circuit by stimulating the Governing Vessel and the part of the brain that accesses information visually.

The TAT Protocol

The four-point protocol developed by Fleming (1998, 8–13) is very easy to implement. Each segment of the protocol is done for as long as you are guided to do it. Typically, three to four minutes for each step is sufficient.

Figure 1

Step 1: Put your attention on the problem as you originally experienced it and mentally review that experience while you do the TAT pose. Hold the pose for up to four minutes or until any change occurs. During this time, pay attention to whether any aspect of the issue or incident remains stuck. If there is an aspect that is persisting, repeat the TAT procedure until there is nothing left of the original disturbance.

Step 2: Put your attention on the opposite condition while you do the TAT pose. (Fleming believes that since most traumas involve a significant amount of denial, it is difficult to get beyond the denial. She suggests that once you have dissolved the negative emotional charge by completing step 1, it is sometimes helpful to do TAT while holding an opposite or positive thought about the situation. I appreciate this honoring of both sides of an issue, particularly when a client feels hopelessly stuck at the negative extreme of the polarity.)

Step 3: Put your attention on either "All the origins of this problem are healing now" or "God (Higher Power), thank you for healing all the origins of this problem" while you do the TAT pose again. Hold the pose for about one minute or until you feel a shift occur. (In this step, Fleming addresses what Dynamic Energetic Healing® calls the energetic origin. This step heals the origin of the problem whether you are consciously aware of it or not; it is also effective for both karmic memory and what Fleming calls cellular memory—the traumatic memories are stored in the cells of specific parts of the body.)

Step 4: Put your attention on either "All the places in my mind, body, and life where this has been held (or stuck) are healing now" or "God (Higher Power), thank you for healing all the places in my mind, body, and life where this has been held (or stuck)" while you do the TAT pose again. Hold the pose for about one minute or until you feel a shift occur. (In this step, Fleming addresses what she calls the resonances or storage space where the trauma or negative thoughts may become stuck. She says it is not necessary to be aware of the exact place(s) where the problem or disturbance has been stored, because this step also heals traumatic residue that is out of conscious awareness.)

Fleming has published a comprehensive manual in which she presents some steps that can be added to the TAT protocol if some element of the trauma or issue remains unresolved. These additional steps specifically address residual anger, resentment, and the need for forgiveness. This manual is listed in the bibliography of this book.

CHAPTER
20

EMOTIONAL FREEDOM
TECHNIQUES, MODIFIED

This Dynamic Energetic Healing® intervention is a modification of Gary Craig's emotional freedom techniques (EFT), which, in turn, is Craig's derivative of Roger Callahan's Thought Field Therapy (TFT). EFT easily fits into the category of what are generically called meridian therapies. This catchall term is used in the energy psychology community for models that have the client tap on various points of the acupuncture meridians.

The Foundation: Thought Field Therapy

To put EFT into context, it's important first to look briefly at Callahan's Thought Field Therapy. TFT is a compilation of various tapping sequences that are prescribed for psychological issues such as particular phobias, traumatic memories, anxiety, and mood disorders. The practitioner must memorize the many algorithms (specific combinations of acupoints) that Dr. Callahan developed to correspond to various psychological and emotional conditions.

Dr. Callahan deserves tremendous credit for his discovery that percussing or gently tapping on the twelve major and two midline Chinese acupuncture meridians will rapidly and often permanently eliminate emotional problems, even those that are severe. Chiropractor George Goodheart Jr. did the initial research integrating Chinese medical concepts into Western chiropractic medicine.

The Development of EFT

Gary Craig is an engineer who became interested in psychology and motivational change strategies, and he was fortunate enough to be one of Dr. Roger Callahan's original students.

Craig found that it was much easier and just as effective to have the client tap on the acupoints of the ten major meridians, the Governing Vessel, and the Central or Conception Vessel as a way to streamline the procedures he learned from Dr. Callahan. In my clinical experience, I have found that adding the liver meridian point under the breast and the triple heater point on the back of the hand provides a more comprehensive treatment approach when working with the acupuncture meridians. Therefore, I have modified Craig's EFT intervention to include all twelve of the major meridians and the two midline points on the Central and Governing Vessels (see figures 2a and 2b).

Craig discovered through his practical experience with countless clients that tapping on all the twelve EFT points, *regardless of the client's problem*,

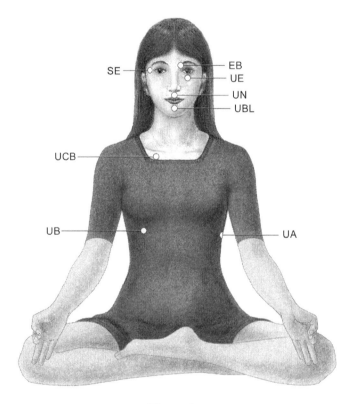

Figure 2a

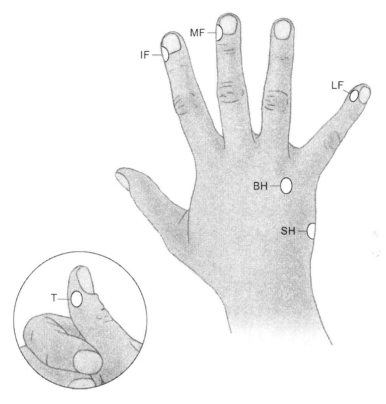

Figure 2b

is sufficient to recruit the client's chi field and thereby generate a change that relieves most presenting symptoms. As the client attunes to his or her disturbance while tapping on all the points in sequence (starting on the face, then to the trunk of the body, and finally the hands), the flow of chi within all the meridians being tapped is mobilized, which affects the client's disturbance pattern and change process at multiple levels. It is theorized that when this happens, the thought fields that carry the information responsible for creating and perpetuating the disturbance or the problem collapse. When these thought fields (which are energy fields of specific information) have collapsed, the information is no longer available to negatively affect the client. The client's system instantly reorganizes itself so homeostasis can return, even if the released information had been carried from trauma many years ago.

EFT is an energy psychology intervention that anyone can use safely and effectively to immediately let go of negative emotional charge. It can be used to dissipate anger and frustration that you are holding on to from an argument you had an hour ago or traumatic residue that you have been carrying from an event that occurred twenty years ago.

Energy psychology is relatively new (just over twenty years old), so many of its therapeutic interventions are considered experimental and innovative. There is an ongoing debate in the energy psychology community about whether EFT is as effective as TFT. Callahan and his adherents press the argument that it is not only the combination of acupoints used but the order in which they are used that is responsible for the effectiveness of the intervention. Craig and his supporters, on the other hand, insist that ordering has very little to do with the successful use and stimulation of the client's chi field.

The points used for EFT tapping are on the face, the front of the torso, and hands because they are easy to access and close to the endpoints of many of the meridians. For example, tapping on the bladder meridian points on the inner edge of the eyebrow is much easier than trying to find points on the bladder meridians that run along either side of the spine. Similarly, it's much easier to tap on the kidney meridian points just below the collarbones than it is to tap on the kidney-1 points at the very bottom of the feet.

Nobody knows definitively why stimulating the chi field while attuning to a problem state dissipates negative emotional charge. There are many theories presently circulating, including speculations about hormones and brain biochemistry as well as more spiritual and energetic explanations.

Meridians

The meridians or channels have been called the pathways that circulate chi into, through, and out of your physical body. They are accessible along the surface of the skin, and they are easily stimulated with acupuncture needles or gentle physical pressure to release or balance the chi. Though the acupuncture points are accessible along the surface of the skin, the meridians that they connect to circulate deeply through the body, traveling through each of the organs and muscle groups. Each of the twelve major meridians is named for the primary organ or physiological system that it is connected to.

The twelve major meridians circulate through particular organ systems, whereas the Central and the Governing Vessels open more directly to your outer environment. But energy psychology meridian treatments include these two midline points (also called central channels) as significant meridians. It has been observed that the energies you encounter in your outer environment can actually move in and out of you through these two central channels (Eden 1998, 97).

Energy psychology practitioners who use EFT direct their client to tap on the designated points while the client attunes to the particular emotional disturbance that has been disrupting their life. The tapping or percussing of the acupuncture points on the meridians stimulates and balances the chi by unblocking stagnant or stuck chi in specific meridians. Although it is somewhat mysterious exactly how this balancing occurs (since Western scientists have been unable to clearly define the nature of chi), clients experience immediate cognitive and emotional shifts.

Chinese doctors and acupuncturists are trained to look for disturbances in meridian energies that are often directly related to health problems and disease. Traditional Chinese medicine has identified the emotional correlates to each of the major meridians that connect to each of the organ systems (see figure 3). Thus, it is well known in traditional Chinese medicine that the lung meridian is related to sadness and grief, while the kidney meridian is related to fear. As the acupuncturist treats the kidney on the physiological level, the emotion of fear is indirectly being addressed as well.

Summary of EFT Treatment Points

Meridian Point	Body	Addresses These Emotions
Eyebrow (EB)	Bladder	Trauma, frustration
Side of Eye (SE)	Gallbladder	Rage, resentment
Under Eye (UE)	Stomach	Disgust, anxiety, nervousness
Under Nose (UN)	Governing vessel	Fear of failure, embarrassment
Under Bottom Lip (UBL)	Conception vessel	Shame
Under Collarbone (UCB)	Kidney	Fear, insecurity
Under Arm (UA)	Spleen	Low self-esteem, insecurity
Under Breast (UB)	Liver	Anger, unhappiness
Thumb (T)	Lung	Grief, arrogance
Index Finger (IF)	Large intestine	Guilt, dogmatism
Middle Finger (MF)	Pericardium	Jealousy, regret, cravings
Little Finger (LF)	Heart	Anger
Side of Hand (SH)	Small intestine	Loss, sadness, vulnerability
Back of Hand (BH)	Triple warmer	Depression, cognitive confusion

Figure 3

Applying EFT to Dynamic Energetic Healing®

Dynamic Energetic Healing® is an integrative model that uses different interventions as they are called forth; EFT is one of these interventions. Gary Craig uses EFT as a stand-alone intervention, but in my model it is often used in combination with other interventions that work synergistically to create an energetic balance for a particular problem.

Using EFT is very straightforward. The client begins by tapping at the points at the base of the eyebrows (EB), and then continues down the face, down the trunk of the body, and finally to the points on either hand. Generally, the tapping is done with the fingertips of the index and middle fingers together, and each acupoint is tapped six or seven times before moving on to the next point.

While tapping, it is important for the client to stay attuned to the problematic feeling or disturbing thought that is the source of discomfort or upset. It is not necessary for the client to associate into the feelings of any memory or traumatic experience—only to mentally refer to it via what is called attunement.

The following step-by-step guide uses the example of a client who wants to relieve the anxiety experienced before giving a public presentation.

Step 1: When EFT is selected as the intervention of choice, ask the client through muscle testing how many minutes of tapping are required. The client's chi field knows precisely how long is needed.

Step 2: Ask the client to subjectively rate the intensity of their problem state on a scale from zero to ten, with ten being the most intense and zero reflecting a complete alleviation of the disturbance. In this example, the client may rate their starting level of intensity at nine.

Step 3: Direct the client to go through the entire fourteen-point sequence of tapping while attuned to their apprehension.

Step 4: Have the client pause and reflect on their anxiety as they imagine giving a public presentation. Then ask if the level of intensity remained at nine or was reduced to reflect the diminution in anxiety. If the client is now at five, ask them to describe any other associations that came up for them while they were tapping.

Step 5a: If no other associations arose, direct the client to continue thinking about and imagining giving a public presentation as they go through the fourteen-point tapping sequence again.

Step 5b: If the client had an additional association connected to the fear of giving a public presentation, ask them to describe it in detail. For example, if during the first tapping sequence the client spontaneously recalled being laughed at in the fourth grade when they misspoke a sentence in front of the class, use this as the client's new mental focus for the next sequence of tapping.

Craig refers to the situation described in step 5b as the emergence of an "aspect" of the presenting problem. Through the experiential process of tapping on the assigned acupoints (while attuning to the problem or newly emerged aspect), you can sometimes identify a matrix of associations that collectively contribute to creating the fear and the consequent symptoms.

The goal of using the EFT tapping sequence is to completely eliminate and release *all* the negative emotional charge, all the fear and residual trauma, and all the stress that was creating the problematic state, so that the intensity level falls to zero. Like all of the interventions used in the energy psychology paradigm, EFT frequently alleviates symptoms and resolves the problem very rapidly.

Directive Tapping

Another useful application of EFT is in situations where a client describes an event that elicits a very strong abreaction, or negative affective response. Whether the traumatic event occurred many years in the past or was an argument that happened the night before, these clients frequently become very upset, often to the point of tears, as they describe their story. Since an element of traumatic residue is generating the abreaction, EFT is well suited for depotentiating an escalating and potentially out-of-control emotional response.

In a situation such as this, I become very directive — hence the designation directive tapping. (It is important to note that I do not use directive tapping with clients until we have established good rapport. It would be inappropriate to direct clients in this way when they are in the middle of an emotional crisis or before I have established a positive relationship with them.) I begin tapping on the EFT points on my face while I tell them to immediately start tapping the same points on their own face. I stay in direct eye contact with the client and continue tapping with them for as long as it takes for their abreaction to deescalate and for them to come to a place of emotional calm.

Two sequences of EFT tapping are usually sufficient for the client to come back to a state of emotional equanimity. In this way, EFT is a powerful and easy-to-apply crisis-intervention tool that can be used in any situation in any context with someone in a state of traumatic shock or severe emotional upset.

I am indebted to Dr. Roger Callahan for his development of Thought Field Therapy and to Gary Craig for streamlining TFT in his development of EFT for greater ease and accessibility. By adding the two meridian points to Craig's basic EFT approach, the Dynamic Energetic Healing® version of emotional freedom techniques recruits all twelve of the major meridians to support the client's energetic change process.

21

TAPPING THE TEMPORAL CURVE

Tapping the temporal curve bilaterally is another energy psychology intervention. It derives from ancient Chinese origins, where it was conceived to alleviate pain.

George Goodheart Jr., D.C., discovered in the 1970s that tapping along the temporal curve from the beginning of the temples back toward the side of the ear creates two distinct phenomena: it stimulates the brain to become more open to learning, and it creates a temporary buffer to other sensory information (see figure 4).

In *Energy Medicine*, Donna Eden reported that tapping on the temporal curve sedates the triple warmer meridian because the tapping is done in the opposite direction of the meridian's normal flow. Since the triple warmer is often responsible for habit formation, this intervention soothes the part of the autonomic nervous system that perpetuates our habits. It allows the client to challenge more easily the habit patterns and the emotional internal conflicts that war with each other by fighting for and against the habit.

Judith Swack introduced me to this technique, and I have since discovered that numerous permutations have been developed by members of the energy psychology community.

Step 1:   When this intervention is selected by my clients, I ask them what statement they need to incorporate with the temporal curve tapping. The statement usually reflects an internal conflict or frustration that

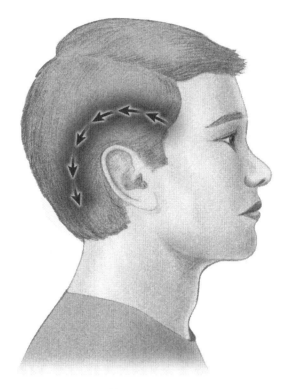

Figure 4

the client has been having difficulty overcoming. An example is, "I want to forgive Susan but I just can't because I am still very angry with her." We verify the statement via MMT before the client begins tapping.

Step 2: Muscle test to determine how many minutes the client needs for the procedure.

Step 3: The client repeats the entire statement over and over while tapping on their temporal curve.

A fourth step is sometimes added to this procedure; it involves associated eye movement.

Moving the eyes in various positions can be very helpful in correcting neurological disorganization associated with the client's presenting problem. Roger Callahan's thought field therapy sometimes uses the Nine Gamut procedure, which involves moving the eyes to the right in wide circles and then to the left in wide circles. In Francine Shapiro's eye movement desensitization and reprocessing technique (EMDR), which is a stand-alone treatment model, clients move their eyes from side to side while watching the practitioner's fingers or wand move back and forth.

Eden and Swack move their hands in a sideways figure-eight while clients follow the movement with their eyes. I find it very helpful to include this while the client is tapping their temporal curve and repeating their internal conflict statement. However, I always ask using MMT if this is to be included in the intervention because different clients require different combinations of this tapping intervention.

Tapping the temporal curve always yields very powerful results. This intervention also affects the brain directly by stimulating the neurovascular points on the side of the head.

22

THE CHAKRA INTERVENTIONS

J ust as the acupuncture meridians are sometimes called the pathways of the body's essential energy system, the chakras are often regarded as the collection centers or power stations of the body's vital life-force energy. *Chakra* is a Sanskrit word meaning "spinning wheel."

I first learned about the chakras when I took up Kundalini yoga. Yoga is an ancient energetic practice, and many of the yoga sets (kriyas) are carefully designed to bring the energy of the seven major chakras into proper balance. These exercises include traditional yoga postures (asanas) and a combination of movement, breath, and sound. The combination of these elements with focused concentration creates a synergy in which the prana (life-force energy) is systematically distributed throughout all of the chakras.

There are various systems that describe the chakras (often differently), but most of today's charts show the seven major chakras. They are shown positioned in the body in a straight line.

Figure 5 and the chart that follows show the name(s) and location of each of the seven chakras.

As the chart indicates, the third chakra is unique in that it has two names and two possible locations. It is in the abdominal region, but it is sometimes depicted right over the belly and sometimes a bit higher, over the solar plexus. In my clinical practice, I see some clients whose third-chakra energy is over their navel center, and others whose third-chakra energy is over their solar plexus. For this reason, I think of the third chakras as having two components: 3a and 3b.

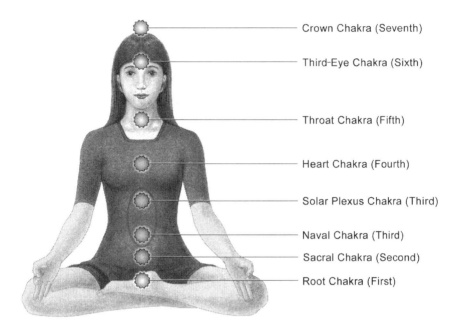

Crown Chakra (Seventh)

Third-Eye Chakra (Sixth)

Throat Chakra (Fifth)

Heart Chakra (Fourth)

Solar Plexus Chakra (Third)

Naval Chakra (Third)

Sacral Chakra (Second)

Root Chakra (First)

Figure 5

Chakra	Name	Location	Associated Gland(s)
First	Root chakra	Base of the spine	Adrenal
Second	Sacral chakra	Lower pelvis	Ovaries, testes
Third	Navel chakra *or* solar plexus chakra	Belly or solar plexus	Pancreas
Fourth	Heart chakra	Center of the upper chest	Thymus
Fifth	Throat chakra	Throat area and base of neck	Thyroid and parathyroid
Sixth	Brow point, the third eye	At the brow of the forehead	Pituitary
Seventh	Crown chakra	Top of the head	Pineal

Each chakra is related to specific aspects of our being, which is made up of physical, endocrinologic, emotional, cognitive, and spiritual components. When Yogi Bhajan was my Kundalini yoga teacher, he frequently reminded us how important it is to keep your chakras balanced so the corresponding endocrine glands secrete the appropriate hormones throughout your body in just the right amounts. We all had lofty spiritual aspirations, but this was a reminder of how practical Kundalini yoga is. Yogi Bhajan stressed the importance of the energy at our brow point chakra being in proper balance, because the pituitary is the endocrine gland directly affected by that chakra. He often referred to the pituitary as the master gland—to a large extent, it regulates many if not most of the other endocrine glands.

Yogi Bhajan described Kundalini yoga and meditation as a science, albeit an ancient one. Interestingly, the cover story of *Time* magazine (August 4, 2003) was on the science of meditation. Researchers are now able to measure the brain waves of meditators as well as the physiological changes that occur with alterations in consciousness. Kundalini yoga and qigong are both energetic practices. While qigong emphasizes the collection and circulation of chi through the acupuncture meridian system, Kundalini yoga stimulates the prana to circulate into and through the chakra system.

The Chakras in Dynamic Energetic Healing®

As an energy psychology intervention, having the client tap on one or more of the chakras while attuning to the problem state or the disturbance is an intervention that I use frequently. This incredibly powerful intervention generates remarkable results in many Dynamic Energetic Healing® sessions. Just as tapping on an acupuncture meridian point stimulates and unblocks the flow of chi throughout that meridian, tapping on chakras tends to generate rapid energetic balance as the prana opens up and brings into balance chakras that have been contracted or shut down.

First Chakra: The Root Chakra

Located at the base of the spine, the first chakra is related to the adrenal glands. Energetically, we connect to the grounding energies of the earth through the root chakra. It gives us the feeling of being supported, and the feeling of stability as we deal with the challenges of day-to-day life. The root chakra is associated with our primal, more primitive drives that deal with survival and the other essentials for keeping the physical body alive. These include issues relating to money, food, and sufficient shelter to keep us protected from the elements.

Because our emotional and psychological stability derive, to a large extent, from our first experiences in our family of origin and early social environment, issues relating to the so-called tribal mind are first-chakra concerns. Group identity issues such as loyalty to our extended family and the rise in nationalistic fervor (such as what occurred after the attacks on 9/11) can affect our first chakra.

When our first-chakra energy is balanced, all of our basic needs are met and we feel safe and connected in the physical world. When this energy is out of balance, individuals likely have problems providing themselves with the necessities of life—they may be unable to maintain consistent employment, and they may experience dissociation, feeling spaced out, and feeling generally fearful. Possible limiting core beliefs linked to the first chakra that generate ongoing unconscious sabotage may include these:

- I was abandoned and left.
- I was hungry and deprived.
- I never feel safe.
- I am all alone.
- I don't belong.
- I don't have enough.

If these limiting beliefs arising from early childhood trauma or neglect persist into adulthood, they can become unconscious sabotage programs that are likely to compromise the person's success in personal relationships and in their career. In these cases, I see a contraction in the energy of the client's first chakra, and I feel their pervasive fear and great sadness. I also hear their hopelessness expressed through these limiting core beliefs; this hopelessness often supports an overidentification with the Victim archetype.

Once my client has identified and acknowledged the specific issue to be addressed (i.e., the early trauma and its consequent limiting beliefs), I direct the client to gently tap at the base of their spine for as many minutes as the MMT indicates is appropriate. It is important for the client to attune to the specific disturbance (limiting belief) or problem state while tapping on the first chakra; this intervention expands the contracted energy and brings it into energetic balance. As this occurs, the negative emotional charge associated with the disturbance dissipates, which makes it more likely that the client will be brought to emotional homeostasis. When the energy fields that carry the traumatic information collapse, the energy of the first chakra quickly realigns itself and positive change begins to occur.

Second Chakra: The Sacral Chakra

The second chakra, which is often called the sexual chakra, is located between the external genitals and the belly button. It influences creativity and pleasure, but it affects much more. The endocrine glands associated with the second chakra are the ovaries and the testes.

This chakra is intimately related to creativity, since it is through the sexual organs that the creativity of the universal life-force energy coalesces to establish a new life form. Within the second chakra, the energy of creativity and generativity come together. This is true both literally (babies grow inside the protective female womb) and figuratively (new ideas take root here and inspiration flowers). The second chakra nurtures the creative impulse and fosters the imagination.

The first chakra is driven toward collective group consciousness; the energy of the second chakra concerns itself more with establishing mutually beneficial partnerships. At the physical level, we are drawn to others by a primitive drive to procreate and perpetuate the species. Thus, sexuality and its expression is a dominating element of the second chakra. But because of its emphasis on the energetic drive toward relationships, the yearning for emotional support and attention to feeling states is equally important. The second-chakra energy also engenders an openness to "healthy pleasures" such as enjoyable and satisfying companionship, life-enhancing tasty food, and the enjoyment of art in all its media.

Individuals whose second-chakra energy is out of balance may be beset by lust, which manifests itself as a compulsive need for more of the sensory-based pleasures—more food, more sex, more wine—which can lead to out-of-control addictive behaviors. Creativity is blocked and sexuality can become perverted.

When a client has been sexually abused or raped, I see the energy at the second chakra condensed and contracted, and I hear expressions of guilt and shame. I also perceive aspects from traumatic residue that reflect a sense of powerlessness, as well as difficulty in or inability to commit in relationships. Behaviorally, I hear descriptions of sexual difficulties or dysfunction along with overindulgence in or lust for sex or food.

Because generative power is stored in the second chakra, many spiritual practices include exercises and meditations specifically designed to transform the essence of these "lower" energies into energy forms that the higher-brain centers can use for creative endeavors. Many of these teachings are explicit in their prohibition of any kind of masturbation, to prevent the squandering of the vital force that is primarily contained in the second chakra.

Yogi Bhajan was a proponent of this view. He included a practice called the Sat Kriya in his vast repertoire of Kundalini yoga exercises. This kriya is designed to transmute the second-chakra energies to the higher centers. You sit on your heels with your arms raised high above your head, palms together with fingertips pointing up to the sky. After inhaling deeply, you squeeze the mulbandh (anal sphincter muscle) as you pull in and up while chanting *Sat*. On the exhale, you chant *Nam*. Meanwhile, you either visualize the energy moving up to your third-eye point or your crown chakra, where it is absorbed and circulated to blend with the higher-chakra energies via transmutation.

Sat Nam is a seed mantra that generates many results. Its literal translation is "Truth is my essence, Truth is God's name." After doing the Sat Kriya vigorously for three minutes, most participants are drenched with sweat and physically spent. You complete the kriya by lying down, allowing the prana to circulate as it brings you into energetic balance.

Third Chakra: The Navel (or Solar Plexus) Chakra

The third chakra is variously positioned between the navel and the base of the sternum. As mentioned earlier, it is sometimes depicted at the navel center and sometimes above this at the solar plexus. In my work with clients, I see the concentration of energy in one or the other of these locations.

In my experience, the primary issues related to the third chakra are self-worth and personal power. When working with clients who have been disempowered by past trauma or abuse, I often see an empty hole or cylinder from front to back throughout the solar plexus area. This is a strong message to me that the energy in the client's third chakra has been profoundly compromised.

Frequently in these cases, the client is not fully embodied and has a strong aversion to speaking their own truth in relationships. This often manifests as a pattern of conflict avoidance and the resulting codependency, in which the client's first reference point is to the other rather than themselves. Clients have even said that it feels as though there is a hole inside them that they cannot fill.

Some of these clients are painfully aware of trying to fill this hole with food, which becomes compulsive overeating.

This feeling of emptiness may manifest itself as other forms of addiction, either process or substance. My colleague Mary identified a dark energy formulation that she labeled the black hole. This is frequently manifested as an insatiable desire for something that becomes an addiction. I believe this phenomenon is frequently a consequence not only of past trauma but also of an imbalance in the third chakra.

In contrast to the second chakra's realm of partnership, giving and receiving, and working in harmony with others, the third chakra is largely about authority issues (inner and outer) and ego strength. The emphasis of the third chakra is on individuation, differentiation, and personal power. As a result, it is through the energy of the third chakra that you are constantly negotiating issues of control and influence in relationships. When you feel that flash of anger or surge of heat in your solar plexus, you are likely in a power struggle. In this energy center your struggles of individuation and differentiation become known in the arena of your developing and evolving selfhood. The "shoulds" from your parents and family, as well as the expectations from the culture at large, are internalized within this chakra. The inner conflicts between who you really are and the expectations put upon you for who you should be are generally felt in the gut.

As a junior in college, I had to confront my parents to inform them that I had decided not to go to law school; instead, I was going to pursue a master's degree in religious studies and social ethics. I had already been accepted to a reputable law school and prior to this meeting had given my parents no clues about this change in my career path. I vividly remember how tied up in knots my churning stomach was just before our meeting. I knew I was disappointing them and failing to live up to the expectations they had for me. But I also knew that my path of heart was honoring the Great Spirit, not law books. This was a classic example of the energy in my third chakra trying to come into balance by defying my parents' powerful expectations. The discussion was painful for all of us, but it was absolutely the right decision.

Performers who describe having butterflies in their stomach prior to going onstage are experiencing a conflict in their third-chakra energy—their desire to win the audience's approval is in conflict with their fear of being rejected or criticized. This conflict is manifested in their gut. By trying to minimize or deny their fears, they are essentially defending themselves against the antici-pated criticism by pushing forward and performing.

The thematic descriptions I often hear from clients who suffer from third-chakra disruptions include statements such as "My parents controlled me my whole life" and "I was constantly intruded upon and victimized." Whether these core limiting beliefs are derived from the client's ongoing experience with their family of origin or from a single-incident assault, the result is nearly always the same: an imbalance in the energy of the third chakra. When these limiting core beliefs reflect an imbalance in the energy of the third chakra, tal-ented and ambitious individuals continually encounter a wall of resistance that defeats their best efforts to succeed. The inner self is at odds with the world, and this is often experienced unconsciously. Outwardly, individuals whose third chakras are out of balance may be rejecting, critical, and controlling. Somatically, they frequently complain of chronic digestive and intestinal prob-lems, eating disorders, allergies, and various types of chronic fatigue.

Having the client tap on their solar plexus while attuning to these issues often generates immediate relief. Newly mobilized energy that was blocked and contracted at the third chakra will initiate change throughout the entire chakra system. This is sometimes sufficient as a stand-alone intervention. But more often than not, I use an entire complement of interventions to alleviate the disruptions caused by a third-chakra imbalance, particularly when the dis-ruptions have been present over many years.

Fourth Chakra: The Heart Chakra

Those who seek a heart connection with others are orienting from their fourth chakra, better known as the heart center. When I encounter someone with an "open heart," I experience a person who is calm within themselves and whose essence emanates authentic loving presence. Generally, these individuals are comfortable with themselves, and their very beingness fosters connection.

A person who is heart-centered is guided more by feeling than by logic or reason. In some of the ancient scriptures, the heart is regarded as the seat of soul. Perhaps this is because an intellectual orientation to life is based on dis-criminating differences that separate. In contrast, the nonjudging heart accepts diversity joyfully and perceives it as a whole.

When the fourth chakra is in proper energetic balance, the individual most likely experiences greater oneness with life. With this oneness comes the experience of unconditional love, which naturally leads to connection with God or the Divine. Associated qualities that characterize this open-heartedness include deep compassion, the ability to forgive easily, and an open empathy to connect easily to the feelings of others. When the heart chakra is balanced, the tyrannizing influence of shame spontaneously dissolves, for it can only exist where there is fear. As fear is a separating feeling state, it is incompatible with an open heart.

There is, however, an important caveat to what often sounds like the spiritual imperative to have an open heart. I believe that contemporary Western culture dangerously overemphasizes the development and cultivation of the intellect and the individual. As a result, the heart center of most people is overridden by the consumerism of the market economy that panders to the materialistic excess of superfluous lower second- and third-chakra ego needs. But an insidious polarization has occurred within the New Age mythos that tends to overvalue and ultimately misrepresent the importance of having an expansive heart chakra. This is problematic because if your fourth chakra is energetically much larger than any of your other chakras, an overall energetic imbalance throughout your chakra system can be created.

The Enneagram of Personality Types is a modern synthesis of a number of ancient wisdom traditions, but Oscar Ichazo is most often credited with bringing Enneagram to the West in the early 1970s. The Enneagram has evolved from its mystical Eastern roots into a practical and accessible model for better understanding personality. I often use this inventory as a way to give clients another reference point, one that contradicts the fallacious notion that all of our problems derive from our family of origin and our upbringing. The Enneagram asserts that there are nine personality types or points and that we each have within us all nine points and all of the points' associated aspects. But the Enneagram of Personality Types teaches us that within our soul, one point of personality predominates.

For example, a point Four, who is sometimes called the tragic romantic or the artist, feels deeply and passionately into their experience. A point Two, the caretaker or the rescuer, likely empathizes with others more deeply than does any other point on the Enneagram spectrum. Caretakers are often the emotional overfunctioner in relationships—they are so overinvolved with the experience of the other that they tend to lose themselves in the relationship. Caretakers typically have a heart chakra that's so open to the needs and pain of others that their own needs are not sufficiently met or even acknowledged. These individuals are outer-referential to an extreme, wondering why their needs are so rarely recognized and met. Their heart chakra can be profoundly out of balance, creating an energetic misalignment throughout the chakras. This misalignment often becomes a habit pattern (both cognitive and behavioral) that is very challenging to change.

The compassion that emerges from a heart chakra that is in healthy energetic balance demonstrates love without conditions and a true delight in simply being with the other. When you come upon these individuals, you instinctively know that the loving presence which emanates from them is something you want to stay associated with. It is a felt knowing, and it is always a gift.

The Institute of HeartMath has done some wonderful research on how powerfully the physical heart influences all the other organs, including the brain. New research is revealing that the heart has a nervous system which contains at least forty thousand neurons and which is independent of the brain; this is called the brain in the heart. What's more, this research suggests that because the nervous system of the heart is so strong (and intelligent), the rest of the body comes into synch with the heart's rhythm and with the actual consciousness that the heart infuses physically, emotionally, mentally, and spiritually throughout the rest of our being.

Because the heart is the strongest biological oscillator in the human system, the rest of the body's systems are pulled into entrainment with the heart's rhythms. When subjects in research studies achieve entrainment of the brain with the heart, they report heightened intuitive clarity and a greater sense of well-being. Positive feelings such as appreciation create increased order and balance in the autonomic nervous system, resulting in enhanced immunity, improved hormonal balance, and more efficient brain function. (Childre and Martin 1999, 46)

The implications of this are profound, and it gives me a feeling of déjà vu—I have heard this so many times before. Only before, it was from the reported experiences of enlightened masters who insisted, based on their empirical fieldwork, that love is known through the heart. I deeply appreciate the Institute of HeartMath's scientific validation that there is a direct energetic interaction between the electromagnetic field produced by the heart and our thoughts, physical well-being, and what occurs in our inter-actions with others.

As an energy center, the fourth chakra is enormously powerful and influential:

As many doctors know, the pattern and quality of the energy emitted by the heart is transmitted throughout the body via the heart's electro-magnetic field. The heart's electromagnetic field is by far the most powerful produced by the body; it's approximately five thousand times greater in strength than the field produced by the brain, for example. The heart's field not only permeates every cell in the body but also radiates outside of us; it can be measured up to 8 to 10 feet away with sensitive detectors called magnetometers. (Childre and Martin 1999, 33)

The endocrine gland associated with the heart chakra is the thymus, which is located under the sternum. The thymus has a central role in main-taining our healthy immune function, so it is even more important to keep the heart center in optimal energetic balance as new microbes and viruses (such as SARS) proliferate and cross international boundaries at alarming speed.

But tapping on the heart center is not only useful for supporting the immune system. As a stand-alone intervention, it is most helpful for rapid self-calming when situations or environments feel chaotic. Additionally, tap-ping on your heart center during an episode of growing anger and resentment creates a strong intention to activate the extraordinary intelligence and ener-getic calming influence of the heart center. As this occurs, the cascade effect of out-of-control emotions can be brought into entrainment quickly by the power of the heart center.

When a client expresses either explicitly or implicitly that they were not loved, it is likely that they have long-standing contraction of the energy in their heart center. This is sometimes expressed through posture—being bent over with a caved-in chest is often a nonverbal way of trying to shield or pro-tect the heart center from the verbal and energetic assaults of others. This is a sad thing to bear witness to and yet, if love is the agency of healing, a wounded heart can be transformed and blossom once again.

Fifth Chakra: The Throat Chakra

The fifth chakra, located at the throat, is the energetic center of communication. Integrity is key for the throat chakra. When a person can be honest and speak the truth as they know it, they are coming from that place of deep integrity. As with the fourth chakra, when the energy at your fifth chakra is either too big or too expansive—if your throat chakra is not in proper energetic balance—you either never seem to have anything to say or you appear to be so omniscient that your presentation borders on self-aggrandizement.

But the power of the spoken word is not necessarily the defining element of the fifth chakra. What is meaningful is not only what we communicate as truth but how we communicate what that truth is. When the throat chakra is open and in energetic balance, we have a solid and receptive connection with our creative muse. Whether we choose dancing, sculpting, writing, or singing, our willingness to surrender to the Divine will and open ourselves to the inspiration from Spirit as the creative muse becomes the expression of who we are and what we are feeling. The challenges of this expression are many, including facing the criticisms and sanctions of the collective, the consensus thinking on the popular wisdom of the day.

When the fifth chakra is open, a person is much more inclined to speak up for their personal needs and take greater personal responsibility, rather than remaining the silent victim. When clients communicate that they have never been heard, they are conveying to me that there have been problems connected to their fifth chakra. But frequently these individuals have problems identifying what their true path of heart is in the world. Because they haven't felt heard, they don't have sufficient trust in their inner knowing to believe that God will respond to their pleas for help by confirming their own deep convictions and desires. When individuals believe they have not been heard, they feel unsupported, and many overidentify with the Victim archetype.

There are many consequences for a person whose throat chakra is contracted. The thyroid and parathyroid glands are connected to the throat chakra. When the energy at the throat chakra is balanced, these glands and their related physical functions are also balanced at the physical level. However, when this energy center is contracted, persistent physical problems such as sore throats, tonsillitis, and thyroid cancer are not uncommon.

Just as the thyroid gland is responsible for so many metabolic functions throughout the physical body, the throat chakra is responsible for issues relating to whether you are able to create the reality or the life for yourself that is based on your deepest desires. When I think about all the people I know who are not doing jobs that they really love, it makes me wonder how difficult it is for most people to keep their throat chakras open, to make a conscious choice to live an intentional life.

I believe that when we feel heard and acknowledged, it is an easy step to trust that God is responsive to our wishes. Implicit in this is our need to surrender our will so that we work collaboratively with Divine will, trusting that in the subtle exchanges between us and Source we will be reliably supported and never ignored.

Sixth Chakra: The Brow Point, the Third Eye

The sixth chakra is our intuitive center. Often referred to as the third eye, it is just above and between the eyebrows. In many spiritual traditions, this chakra is associated with psychic abilities that can be refined through various spiritual practices. The energetic connection of the sixth chakra to the physical body is primarily through the pituitary gland, although the brain and nervous system are also intimately connected to this energy center.

We can transcend our egoic sense of self and tap into different dimensions of reality through specific practices that access the sixth chakra. For me, this is clearly evident when I engage the shamanic journey methodology to connect with the compassionate spirits that inhabit other realms.

During the twenty years that I practiced Kundalini yoga and meditation, I was committed to a specific meditation called Kirtan Kriya, which I practiced daily. (This meditation in described in detail in chapter 25.) There are many different aspects that work together synergistically while practicing this meditation, but it is anchored in the sixth chakra. I am certain that my many years of practicing this meditation are largely responsible for opening my third eye and developing my psychic abilities.

Intuitive reasoning may sound like an oxymoron, but I believe intuitive reasoning is often known as discernment or visionary thinking, qualities best exemplified by the sixth chakra. The sixth chakra is our energetic connection to spiritual vision, extrasensory perception, and what is generally regarded as intuition. When our sixth chakra is not in proper energetic balance, we find ourselves misusing our intellect so that it dominates us.

We become tyrannized by the thinking mind when our advanced human cortex cannot find balance with more subtle ways of apprehending or knowing the world. Precognition of future events, seeing energetic blocks, and hearing inner guidance from a spiritual adviser in nonordinary reality are all examples of a natural capability we have for sensing the world around us. The sixth chakra enables us to transcend what our ordinary senses can perceive.

People who have a strong, innate spiritual drive are sometimes seduced by the allure of power and influence that the manifestation of impressive psychic abilities generates. This can become problematic, even addictive, to the spiritual aspirant who has not spent enough time dealing with and resolving issues related to the lower-triangle chakras (the first, second, and third).

When I first became affiliated with the American Sikh community (during the time when I was introduced to Kundalini yoga and meditation), it placed little emphasis on dealing with emotional issues within a psychological framework. Instead, it was assumed that if you were sufficiently dedicated to your practice of yoga and meditation, all the issues related to the lower three chakras would spontaneously dissolve and resolve. This naïveté about psychology was a result of two things: Yogi Bhajan's insistent encouragement to dedicate your life to spiritual practices, and the allure and power that would be yours if you developed the sixth chakra sufficiently.

I was caught up in this for a short time, until I realized that over-emphasizing the development of the sixth chakra at the expense of the chakras which precede it (i.e., the first through the fifth chakras) was developmentally unsound and misguided. The issues connected to the heart center and the throat chakra had to be addressed as part of the human developmental process. I came to recognize that many spiritually hungry people were seeking guidance for how to practice a time-tested methodology that was directed and led by a powerful, charismatic spiritual teacher. Yogi Bhajan repeatedly exclaimed that Kundalini yoga was the "yoga of experience." This was true; the practices he taught were extremely powerful. In many ways, they were so powerful that individuals who were neither psychologically nor emotionally integrated were having the experiences that often emerge from opening the sixth chakra. This often resulted in the unconscious reenactment of old family-of-origin dynamics and a hierarchical power structure within the ashram community. Perhaps this was because we were all fairly young during a time of great cultural turmoil and change. There were many dynamics operating simultaneously, and it was difficult for many to maintain the personal balance that Yogiji's teachings were attempting to provide. The rapid and powerful opening of the sixth chakra was a large part of this. Perhaps this is a cautionary tale for those of us in the twenty-first century whose yearning for the experience of sacred union remains strong.

Seventh Chakra: The Crown Chakra

The seventh chakra is located at the top of the head. Its Sanskrit name is *sahasara*, and it is frequently depicted as a thousand-petaled lotus. While the sixth chakra enables us to perceive varied aspects of extrasensory phenomena that are not part of our normal sensory-based reality, we experience a merging or an intimate relationship with the Divine through the seventh or crown chakra. Poets, mystics, yogis, and saints refer to this as sacred union, but there are never adequate words to describe it. This union is experienced through the mediation of the crown chakra.

When our seventh chakras are sufficiently developed and in harmony with the other chakras, we are frequently drawn to spiritual practices in an effort to forge a stronger connection to God. Whether we use meditation, reading sacred scripture, or devotional prayer, the intent is the same—to satisfy our yearning to have spirituality become our primary organizing value, the one from which all things are directed in our lives.

It is my perception that when people become disconnected from their physical body, it is because their crown chakra is not in proper energetic alignment. When I am in session with clients, I can psychically see when a part of them has dissociated and is hovering just above their head. Their fear has generated a separation from their physical body in an effort to avoid an uncomfortable traumatic experience. By creating this dissociation, the individual generates the unconscious belief that they will be protected from having to endure the anticipated pain. In this state, individuals feel isolated and vulnerable.

The irony is that when the crown chakra is open to the constant infusion of the spiritual energy (through our connection to the Divine) that nourishes us on all levels, we are fully embodied and able to remain completely present, which enables us to better address any threat to our beingness. Through our connection to Spirit via our crown chakra we are able to transcend our egoic sense of separateness and to experience merging with a part of something greater than ourselves. When open to the Divine, we are never alone and the feelings of separateness dissolve; our natural predisposition is to be fully present and 100 percent in our physical body.

One of the things that is particularly helpful about my qigong practice is the emphasis on energetic balance. The point at the top of the head is called the *bai hui*. From this point, I extend chi up into the heavens. From the yong quan points at the center of the balls of my feet, I extend chi down to the center of the earth. In this way, I am reminded to stay firmly rooted to the earth, fully embodied, as I open up energetically to connect with the Divine.

More and more, my clients are directed through their own process to select a chakra tapping intervention. In some cases, muscle testing solicits an intervention that requires tapping on a single chakra for a prescribed length of time (usually from one to four minutes). Often, the chosen intervention is tapping on a number of individual chakras one after another. For example, a client may select two minutes of tapping on the crown chakra, followed by one minute of tapping on the throat chakra, two minutes of tapping on the heart chakra, and one minute of tapping on the crown chakra again to complete the balance. Occasionally, a client selects tapping on all seven chakras, either from top to bottom or bottom to top, for a predetermined number of minutes. I follow the client's process, simply feeding back to them what they are requesting through their own energy field.

The exception to this is when I use directive tapping, which is similar to a client tapping on EFT points (see chapter 19 for more information). In these cases, I usually sit opposite my client, who is tapping on one or more of their prescribed chakras. When the pre-selected time limit is nearly reached, I often get strong intuitive impressions of specific chakras that need more tapping because their energy remains blocked. When this occurs, I direct the client to tap on these chakras that are still contracted.

I believe that this perceptual skill—whether you call it psychic or intuitive—is an acquired one that anyone can pick up by learning to cultivate their second attention. Having this skill is very helpful because it accelerates the balancing and healing process for the client. When the energy of all your chakras is flowing freely, it is much easier to be consciously connected to the power of intent.

CHAPTER

23

NEGATIVE AFFECT
ERASING METHOD

N egative affect erasing method (NAEM) is a simple but powerful energy-based intervention developed by Fred Gallo. It is used primarily when the client's disturbance is a strong negative affect, such as fear or anger, or a recurring intrusive memory or thought.

There are only four points to be tapped while the client mentally attunes to the specific disturbance (see figure 6). For as long as MMT indicates is required, the client taps on each of the points five or six times in the following sequence:

1. The third-eye point
2. The Governing Vessel point, which is just above the upper lip
3. The Central Vessel point, which is just below the lower lip
4. The heart chakra

Although there are two chakra points included in the tapping sequence, all four of these points are midline points. (Another name for this intervention is midline energy treatment.) The upper two points align with the Governing Vessel while the lower two points align with the Central or Conception Vessel.

The remarkable effectiveness of the NAEM cannot be ascribed to a specific theoretical position that is any different from those presented by various energy theories or quantum theory. I have my own theories on why tapping on this specific combination of points (these two chakra points and these two midline points) is so consistently efficacious. But to me the

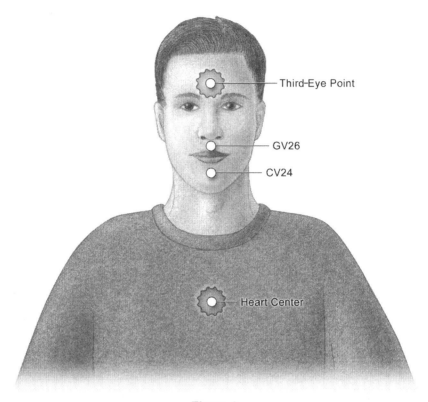

Figure 6

important point is the consistent positive therapeutic outcomes generated when this intervention is applied.

I am reminded of what Callahan described as the apex problem when he first began using Thought Field Therapy treatments with clients. Essentially, clients would deny that the TFT treatment was responsible for their problems dissolving so quickly. Callahan borrowed the term from Arthur Koestler (1967); his implication was that his clients were far from the apex of their perceptual abilities at the time.

Traditional talk therapy (modeled after psychoanalysis) has a reputation for taking a long time to completely resolve a problem, particularly when it is trauma-based. As a result, clients treated with energy psychology therapies such as NAEM often experience a form of cognitive dissonance because they are not prepared for the incredibly rapid alleviation of their troublesome symptoms. They search for other explanations for the results, such as being distracted by tapping on their body.

This is one example of the need for a paradigm shift, which was discussed earlier. I have found that the best way to address this issue is to bring it into the therapeutic relationship from the very beginning. Properly educating clients about what to expect is a way to seed the unconscious with the prospect of new ideas and possibilities. The rapid therapeutic results that clients experience are corroborating experiential evidence that confirms what I told them to expect. As the therapeutic process unfolds, clients start to cultivate a greater perceptual acuity to their own experience and thus begin to develop a more sensitized second attention.

To experience the power of the NAEM for yourself, focus your attention on whatever is bothering you—anxiety about something you are anticipating, for example, or a specific frustration you cannot shake. Using the methodology described earlier, tap on the four NAEM points for three to four minutes while keeping your mind on your problem. Notice how your experience begins to shift.

When the time has elapsed, reevaluate and reflect on how you are feeling and the current status of your problem. If all negative emotional charge has flattened out, then you are done. If anything remains of the original problem or if any new "aspects" emerged as a consequence of the tapping, repeat the procedure while keeping your mind on what remains. When you have completed this second sequence of tapping, reflect carefully again on how you are feeling and notice what you are thinking. I suspect you will be very surprised and delighted at the changes that have occurred.

24

FRONTAL OCCIPITAL (F/O) HOLDING

O f all the interventions I use, frontal occipital holding is the center-piece of Dynamic Energetic Healing® because it has given me such profound experiences in moving in and out of dreamtime in the therapeutic context. This intervention integrates energy psychology methods with the awareness created by core shamanism and processwork to create a wonderful synergy.

The frontal occipital (F/O) holding intervention was originally developed by Three In One Concepts (an educational corporation developed by Gordon Stokes and Daniel Whiteside in 1983) for reducing stress-related tension. Their version of the method requires the therapist to gently place the palm of one hand on the client's forehead while placing the other hand on the occipital bone at the back of the client's head (see figure 7). While the therapist's hands are held in place, the client focuses attention on the problem. In a relatively short time, the negative emotional energy that was keeping the problem in place shifts, often dissipating completely.

As I became more comfortable using this intervention as another energetic strategy, I began to realize there was far more for me here than I was led to believe.

How does F/O holding work? There is some speculation that the palm of the hand stimulates neurovascular reflex points (located on the frontal eminence of the forehead), thereby increasing vascular flow throughout the body and inducing a state of relaxation. Others believe that practitioners become

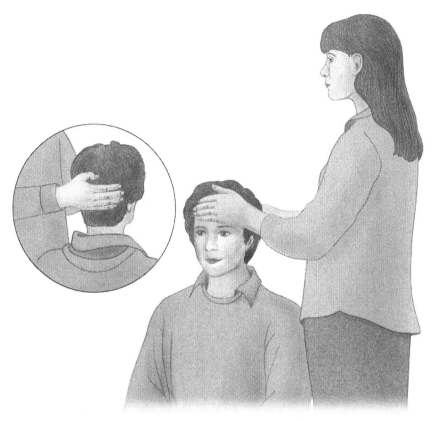

Figure 7

tactilely sensitive to the pulses in these reflex points and that the therapist waits until the pulses synchronize. In either case, clients are supposed to stay in the process until they are aware of a *positive shift* of the internal problem state, such as images changing from negative to positive, a depressed mood balancing to neutral, or a deep sense of overall physical relaxation occurring.

I have discovered that F/O holding can enable a much richer healing experience for both the client and the therapist. In fact, I use this technique as a springboard for training therapists how to read their client's energy field. This deepening awareness has come about through my shamanic and energy channeling experiences. By establishing light physical contact with the therapist's hands, the client immediately goes into an altered state. This increases the client's response potential for transformative change to occur. With minimal training, proper mental focus, and openness to an expanded and more inclusive field of awareness, the therapist can elicit information from the client's auric or biofield. This includes information about stagnant emotional energy, dark energy forms (supernatural energetic intrusions), contracted chakras, meridian points that need to be physically and mentally stimulated, and karmic past-life information.

Many therapists want greater psychic abilities but they distrust their perceptions. I help trainees identify and depotentiate their limiting beliefs, and I provide dyadic practice so that trainees learn to use this powerful healing tool in ways which benefit both client and therapist. Trainees who previously had a tendency to dismiss their internal perceptions soon learn to trust and rely upon them. Many therapists already have training in Reiki, therapeutic touch, and other methods for channeling healing energy. Frontal occipital holding capitalizes on the empathy and sensitivity that these therapists already possess and helps them to expand into new healing realms.

F/O holding is one of the many Dynamic Energetic Healing® methods I use to effect positive therapeutic outcomes. My experience using this intervention continues to deepen and expand into what has become a transpersonal healing modality.

Years ago, when I had already had a number of years of shamanic training, I began doing energy channeling work by working within the structure of the Reiki model. I developed the capacity to "see" into the client's energetic field. By putting my hands lightly on a person's physical body (be it their face, stomach, or back), I immediately got very strong visual and intuitive impressions of what was blocking the energy flow. At the time, I was practicing with friends—I had my subjects lie on a table while I went through the various Reiki positions to channel Reiki or "universal healing energy" for their general well-being. When these strong, unexpected impressions spontaneously emerged, I realized that I was experiencing spontaneous, compressed-time shamanic healing journeys with the help of my power animal. During other Reiki sessions, I saw into my friends' auric field, chakras, and physical organs. I also saw ugly, revolting energetic and entity intrusions. With the help of my spiritual allies, I effected spontaneous extractions or dissolutions of these intrusions.

I continued to train shamanically, but I abandoned the table work when I began my training in processwork. Soon after being introduced to F/O holding, it became clear that this intervention allowed me to use the abilities I had uncovered years before (while doing the Reiki table work) in more powerful ways. I discovered that I can see aspects of my clients' chakra and meridian energy fields and into their karmic past lives. I can also feel into their affective state and, as a result, find the source of their cognitive confusion. I discover much more about my clients in this healing context, and I can even discern and release energetic intrusions using this intervention.

Frontal occipital holding is the Dynamic Energetic Healing® intervention that generates the brightest sparkle in my clients' eyes. For me, it is a wonderful application of moving in and out of the dreamtime experience. As I contact my client by gently resting my hands around their head, I always recite the following invocation to center myself and humble myself before the Great Spirit:

I call on the Great Spirit. I call on the Creator for help. As I ground deep into the earth [visualizing the bottoms of my feet and my root chakra going deep into the earth], centered at lower and middle dan tian [visualizing the lower dan tian point and then the heartmind center aglow], and my crown chakra open to the love that infuses and informs all things in the universe, I ask for the most loving, healing, powerful, benevolent spiritual energies to come through me or in me to help [client's name] achieve their healing results.

As I recite this, I open myself to receive help from the universe and the forces of light, love, and compassion. I am praying for my client and asking for mercy for my client to be healed. I visualize my feet and my root chakra going deep into the earth, so even as I open myself up to the energies of the spirits, I remain fully embodied with all my life-force energy centered at my lower dan tian and my heart chakra. I keep my eyes open, soften my gaze, and wait. Within seconds images and impressions emerge and the healing unfolds.

The only time this does not happen is in cases where the client has somehow picked up an energetic intrusion or a negative supernatural influence (such as an earthbound spirit). In these cases, my inner vision is blocked and I see nothing. If this persists for more than thirty seconds or so, I stop the process and muscle test my client to check whether there is a dark energy influence. Invariably, this is the case. We then reorient to address whatever the supernatural influence is that is obscuring my vision and impeding the client's healing.

We then muscle test again to identify exactly what this outside negative influence is and what energetic strategies we must use to release it. Sometimes the client selects F/O holding, the Tibetan bell, or even mantra or prayer. I respond accordingly—Dynamic Energetic Healing® truly is dynamic, and my task is to follow the client's process closely in order to effect a healing outcome as rapidly and completely as possible.

Teaching Frontal Occipital Holding

In my F/O holding training program, trainees learn how to better attune themselves to their clients so they will discover deeper levels of healing while using this intervention. The protocol I use to teach F/O holding takes an entire day of training to complete.

One of the therapeutic issues covered in the training is psychoenergetic reversal. I warn trainees of the danger of becoming psychoenergetically reversed when they move in so close to the client. Some clinicians are very uncomfortable with this; they believe that they are intruding into their client's personal space and that they should attend to the client in a somewhat distant, detached way. I also make sure that trainees are not psychoenergetically reversed with respect to completely trusting their own intuitive perceptions and abilities. We expand from this point by ensuring that trainees have 100 percent energetic boundaries with a variety of contexts. Some of these include supernatural energies, emotional pain, trauma, strong emotions held in a client's energy field, and being in close proximity to clients.

Learning to use the F/O holding intervention requires trainees to be very clear channels that allow intuitive awareness and additional information to come through. Clinicians must learn that they are healers, but without the hubris that sometimes accompanies this acknowledgment.

The negative self-statements and doubts that many clinicians have about trusting their own perceptions often surprise me. By participating in this group training context and listening to each other's inner perceptions, trainees learn to trust their own inner perceptions. Once they are boundaried with all the categories that we go through in the training, we discuss *optimal therapeutic presence*, concordant countertransference, and discordant countertransference.

There are many things involved in optimal therapeutic presence. What is your attitude and your intention while you are with your clients? Are you thinking about what you will be preparing for dinner, or are you aware of being in your second attention, noticing what is happening with an all-inclusive awareness (both inside and outside of yourself)? Are you in your head, or is your heart open to your clients without any judgment of who they are? Do you intend to be a channel of Spirit through energetic induction, or are you stuck in your arrogance that you will heal your clients? The force of intention is so powerful that if you intend to convey healing energy to your client, your client will receive it. Are you aware that you and your clients are engaged in a holy covenant, or is your practice simply a way to earn your paycheck? These considerations play a central role in the entire therapeutic relationship, and they are very important when implementing the frontal occipital holding intervention.

As to transference and countertransference issues, it is imperative that you (as a clinician) continue to do your personal healing work. This is the only way to maintain therapeutic neutrality, especially when clients describe horribly traumatic events that resonate with your personal experience.

Countertransference can be helpful as long as it is *concordant*. When this is the case, you are able to be empathic and helpful from your own experience because you are not carrying any trauma of your own that would otherwise get in the away. Countertransference becomes *discordant* when your traumatic residue creates within you shudders and resistances that get in the way of you helping clients to go deep into their wounding so they can heal. The only way to deal constructively with countertransference as an ongoing therapeutic issue is to continually update your own personal work. This must be a lifelong commitment. Optimal therapeutic presence naturally emerges as a result of this continuing work.

As your skill with the F/O holding intervention increases, allowing you to go deeper and deeper into the client's energy field, countertransference concerns come to the fore. Boundary issues may arise as well—you may become overwhelmed by the information you are receiving. It is important for trainees to be aware of these potential obstacles and prepared to deal with them effectively.

Trainees are directed to maintain a very specific but broad internal focus of attention while using frontal occipital holding. Practitioners need this focus of attention in order to maintain solid energetic boundaries while learning to attune to the client's chakras, their own spiritual resources, the client's spiritual resources, impressions of the client's past lives, dark energy forms, and many other elements of the client's experience that generate important information. As mentioned elsewhere, clinicians who wish to increase the ease with which they negotiate constructive altered states of consciousness and deepen and expand their personal connection to Source should practice spiritual disciplines such as meditation, qigong, and shamanic journeywork on an ongoing basis. These energetic and spiritual practices help to sensitize practitioners to the things I have described. Practicing these disciplines is also very important for practitioners of F/O holding because this intervention requires them to be fully embodied and, at the same time, completely open to "extrasensory" information in the interpersonal field.

The synergy created by integrating energy psychology methods with the awareness created by core shamanism and processwork is a very powerful one. As a result, the frontal occipital holding intervention generates consistent positive therapeutic outcomes by merging the energy generated by the client's and the practitioner's spiritual resources. This causes the spontaneous collapse of entire matrices of traumatic residue in the client. When clients acknowledge and open themselves to the healing power of Spirit, the psychotherapeutic context becomes the archetypal alchemical cauldron. Within this context clients experience profound psychotherapeutic change, and they leave with a golden glow, transformed.

25

SOUND AS
VIBRATIONAL HEALING

In Dynamic Energetic Healing®, sound is used judiciously and regularly to create energetic balancing. I have incorporated a number of interventions that fit into this category of "vibrational medicine." They are just as effective and rapid in generating positive shifts at the energetic level as any of the other Dynamic Energetic Healing® interventions.

Dynamic Energetic Healing® uses four vibrational healing techniques:

1. Mantra
2. Toning
3. Tibetan bell, bowls, and cymbals
4. The healing drum

Mantra

Mantra is a short, powerful spiritual formula that has traditionally been chanted out loud, although silent *japa* (repetition of a mantra) is also practiced. Mantra has appeared in every major spiritual tradition, Eastern and Western, from time immemorial. In each spiritual tradition, it evokes the holy name of God. Some traditions refer to the specific name of a great saint such as Rama, Buddha, Jesus, or Mary. Naming practices reflect our belief that name and identity are linked. People from all cultures seem to believe and feel that uttering a name can evoke the thing named. The word of the gods—and of God—in myth and scripture is very often the instrument of Divine creativity.

This is best known to most Westerners through the opening verses of the New Testament's Gospel of John (1:1–4):

Before the world was created, the Word already existed; he was with God, and he was the same as God. From the very beginning, the Word was with God. Through him God made all things; not one thing in all creation was made without him. The Word was a source of life, and this life brought light to men. (*Good News for Modern Man* 1972)

At the very beginning God expressed himself. That personal expression (Word) was God himself. This belief is quite similar to that of the Orthodox Hindus, who believe that the name is not just a symbol for God; the name is God.

Naad yoga is the science of sound and how specific vibrations affect us at multiple levels by stimulating certain endocrine glands and their attendant chakras and thereby healing certain physical imbalances. The tradition of Naad yoga also asserts that chanting certain mantras connects us vibrationally to the Universal vibration called God. Quantum physics claims that at an essential level, the phenomenal world consists of vibrations. Thus, ancient spiritual techniques and modern science agree that everything is composed of energy vibrating in different patterns.

In Hinduism, the perfect symbol of the impersonal aspect of the Godhead is the syllable *Om*. The ancient Hindu sages wrote that the subtlest of all vibrations is the cosmic sound or creative Word of God, out of which everything in the universe has evolved. Even the most ancient Hindu scripture, the Rik Veda, speaks of the unmanifested Godhead called Brahman: "In the beginning was Brahman, with whom was the Word, and the Word was truly the supreme Brahman." (Prabhavananda and Isherwood 1953, 39)

Some people who use mantra refer to the impersonal, more abstract aspect of God using a mantra like Om. Others refer to a more devotional, personified incarnation of God, such as Christ, Krishna, or the Buddha. In both cases, the intention is the same: to connect with and stay connected to God.

Kirtan Kriya Meditation

If you are already familiar with and use a mantra from a religious or spiritual tradition, you can probably include that mantra in your repertoire of interventions. I have used this very powerful intervention, which I learned while studying with Yogi Bhajan, for twenty years. This meditation uses a specific mantra called *Sat Nam*.

Do this meditation in a sitting position with your spine straight (see figure 8). Yogi Bhajan has said that when you break Sat Nam (Truth is

Each syllable
of the mantra

Figure 8

my essence, Truth is God's name) down into its constituent parts, you are chanting the five primal sounds—*S, T, N, M, A*—in the original word form of the mantra. Yogi Bhajan divides the mantra into four segments:

- SA = infinity, cosmos, beginning
- TA = life, existence
- NA = death
- MA = rebirth

This is the cycle of creation. From the infinite comes life and individual existence. From life comes death or change. From death comes the rebirth of consciousness to the joy of the infinite through which compassion leads back to life. (Bhajan 1972, 95–6)

This sound current is represented musically with these four notes:

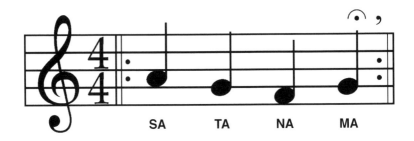

Each repetition of the mantra takes three to four seconds. Keep your arms extended in front of you with your elbows straight while chanting, and touch each fingertip in sequence to the tip of your thumb using firm pressure.

- On SA, touch your index finger to your thumb.
- On TA, touch your middle finger to your thumb.
- On NA, touch your ring finger to your thumb.
- On MA, touch your little finger to your thumb.

The fingertips of both your hands should move simultaneously. After completing one cycle, take a deep breath and begin the sequence again.

Chant the mantra alternately in the three languages of consciousness: human (relating to the material world, in a normal or loud voice), lover (relating to longing to belong, in a strong whisper), and divine (relating to infinity, silently). Use your normal voice for the first five minutes, followed by a strong whisper for five minutes, and then deeply, internally merge with the essence of the mantra while chanting silently. Do the silent meditation for ten minutes, then return to the strong whisper for five minutes, and finish out loud for the last five minutes.

To emerge from the meditation, stretch your arms and hands up as far as possible, stretching your spine and taking several deep inhales and exhales. The total time for this meditation is thirty-one minutes.

An additional component of this kriya requires you to visualize the flow of cosmic energy following the energy pathway Yogi Bhajan calls the golden cord—the connection between the pineal and pituitary glands. Doing this properly ensures proper circulation of prana (life-force energy) in your brain and through your seventh and sixth chakras. Meditate on the primal sounds in this "L" form. As you meditate, visualize a constant flow of cosmic energy entering your crown chakra with each repetition of the four sounds. For example, as you chant SA, visualize the *S* coming into the top of your head as the *A* sweeps around the "L" and out your brow point (sixth chakra) into infinity.

Yogi Bhajan (1972, 96) has said the following about the application of the Kirtan Kriya meditation:

> Practicing this chant brings a total mental balance to the individual psyche. As you vibrate on each fingertip, you alternate your electrical polarities. The index and ring fingers are electrically negative, relative to the other fingers. This causes a balance in the electromagnetic projection of the aura.

Some people have reported experiencing headaches when they do this meditation incorrectly, so it's very important to maintain good mental focus. (In all the years that I have practiced this meditation, I have never developed a headache, so don't worry—just keep coming back to the mantra if your mind wanders.) The Kirtan Kriya meditation is a powerful example of the application of sacred sound current (i.e., mantra) or vibration to directly, immediately, and positively affect your essential energy system. For an account of how one of my clients received immediate, verifiable positive feedback energetically after repeating this mantra for just a short time, see case study 2. This mantra fits perfectly under the umbrella of energy psychology interventions even though its origins are thousands of years old.

Soothing words and sounds have a healing effect—just listen to a loving mother comforting her baby with the sacred words of tender devotion. The instinct and ability to use words and sound for healing is within each of us. All you need to do is to make the connection to your heart.

Toning

A great deal of research is currently being done to identify the healing qualities of vibration and sound. One book I can recommend on this subject is oncologist Dr. Mitchell Gaynor's *The Healing Power of Sound* (2002). Dr. Gaynor uses toning (the natural production of sound) and crystal singing bowls with his cancer patients to augment the conventional chemotherapy and radiation therapies. In his book, he discusses how toning can be used to relieve chronic pain and free deeply held repressed emotions.

When used in healing and spiritual practices, sound and tone have a powerful effect on the body, mind, and energy field. Mantra and collective or group chanting are well-known, cross-cultural examples of sound and vibrational techniques being used to create constructive altered states of consciousness. Examples include the powerful chants of Tibetan monks and the Gregorian chants of Christian monks.

In my practice, I use vocal toning as an energetic intervention. This intervention is sometimes called for just after a client regresses into the energy field of the energetic origin; it helps to soften the traumatic charge before they begin associating into the past-life story. Other times, clients have a strong impulse to make a sound; when I encourage this, their sounds become vocal toning.

In my experience, toning is not used as frequently as the Tibetan instruments. I suspect there is some cultural bias against this for most people. But it is important to be aware that the human voice has just as much vibrational power for balancing blocked energy in the physical body and throughout the chakras as do the other interventions discussed in this chapter.

Tibetan Bell, Bowls, and Cymbals

The sounds of the Tibetan bell, bowls, and cymbals consistently raise smiles among my clients. There is something almost magical that permeates our room whenever any of these Tibetan instruments are sounded.

For years, I experienced the healing power of sound and vibration through my practice of the Kirtan Kriya and the other chanting I did in large group settings. Vibrational healing is an integral part of Kundalini yoga, and I was well steeped in this tradition.

When I began learning energy psychology, there was never any mention of using sound as an intervention for balancing disrupted energies. When I first started working with curses, it occurred to me one day that the Tibetan bell I had sitting on a shelf might be useful. I dusted it off, and to my surprise and great delight I discovered that it was effective in alleviating the clinging energetic residue of curses! After some experimenting, I became very curious about how the Tibetan bell was able to accomplish this.

In November 1998, I decided to do a shamanic journey to find out whatever I could from the spirit of the bell. At first my journey was strictly auditory—I heard a spirit tell me that it is ancient. It told me it is an earth spirit, like an earth elemental that heals through vibration. It aligns itself with the earth's energies, the vibration of love, and the heart center. It collects these energies in a focused form so they become highly concentrated. When the bell is rung, it emits these collected, focused, healing energies, and they radiate to clear out and dissolve any dark or negative energies.

Then I began to get visual impressions. I saw large groups of Tibetan monks praying to elicit a specific healing vibration through which this spirit could somehow come through the bell. The bell spirit told me it is very happy and honored to serve me for I am a righteous man, doing healing work that it approves of. It said it serves only those with pure intent. It then advised me to soften my enthusiastic physical presence when I am with clients and to intend that my *energetic presence* be expanded so clients will experience healing via my connection to Spirit, through my field. Finally, it said it is glad to be acknowledged, much like the genie in the bottle who is often trapped for aeons before being released.

What a journey! I could never have imagined all this information about a Tibetan bell. I now have a personal relationship with the energy behind the sound of this bell. And clients love the sound of it.

Gongs and bells have been used for centuries to facilitate spiritual awakening and as a call to prayer and meditation. Production of Tibetan bells is shrouded in mystery. However, the bells with the sweetest, most resonant sounds

were produced from a 7-metal alloy composed of gold, silver, nickel, copper, zinc, antimony and a particular meteoric iron, found on the high Tibetan Plateau. Because it fell from the heavens, this "sky metal" was associated with the sacred *Dorje*, or thunderbolt of the gods (vajra in Sanskrit) and was held in high esteem by traditional Tibetan metallurgists. The exact method of the bells' construction seems to have been lost sometime during the 20th-century, perhaps due to the displacement of so many Tibetan craftsmen and monks during the recent diaspora. (Classic Yoga for the Antelope Valley 2003)

The bell's vibrations induce deep relaxation, enable more complete circulation of the clients' vital energy (chi or prana), and promote the synchronization of the left- and right-brain hemispheres. They take people into a deep, meditative trance where the sound of inner silence supersedes any thoughts from the rational "monkey mind." When I taught Kundalini yoga and meditation, I often chimed my Tibetan bell at the end of a vigorous session. Participants lay on their back with their eyes closed as I chimed the bell for nearly ten minutes. Participants told me time and again how difficult it was to find words for the delicious feeling of profound peace that resulted from ending the sessions with the Tibetan bell.

In Dynamic Energetic Healing®, I also use three Tibetan singing bowls and a pair of tingshas (a small cymbal-like instrument held together by a cord) to provide vibrational healing and balancing. Each instrument has a unique vibrational signature, and each has a unique spiritual character that has been revealed to me through shamanic journeys. In some mysterious way, the vibrations from these instruments clear and balance stagnant emotional energy and dark energy. They are also powerful focusing agents for heightened awareness.

I notice a great deal when I chime any of the Tibetan instruments with clients. I direct them to attune to the issue or problem that we are attempting to balance. As soon as the sound begins to vibrate through the room, I am immediately brought into my center and feel myself completely drawn into the sound. I soften my gaze and expand my awareness, being open to anything that comes into my perception.

Frequently, I notice immediately that one of my client's chakras is contracted or dark. In these cases, each chiming of the bell, bowl, or tingshas sharpens my perception of that chakra. I am always amazed when the client's muscle testing corroborates that the energetic block is in that particular chakra.

In other cases, I perceive an intuitive, instant "knowing" about some aspect of the problem that was hidden from my client's and my awareness. When this occurs, I share this with my client, and this newly uncovered aspect becomes our point of departure for the next step in the balancing process.

When an energetic release occurs, I experience a deep, spontaneous exhalation. This often happens two or three times in a row. This confirms for me experientially that my client is throwing off stagnant emotional energy which was embedded in their energy field.

I feel very lucky to have discovered an ancient and accessible vibrational healing tool that fits perfectly within the paradigm of energy psychology. I suspect that it was my many years of working with sound in my yoga and meditation practice that allowed the Tibetan bell to reveal itself to me as a powerful energetic intervention. I feel very grateful and humbled to have received this gift.

The Healing Drum

In November 2004, I discovered a new energetic intervention that I have since integrated into my Dynamic Energetic Healing® repertoire.

I was working with Courtney to help her establish energetic boundaries with a particular individual. As she extended her arms out in preparation to be muscle tested, I asked her, "Is the best intervention to establish these energetic boundaries [name of an intervention]?" Typically, the correct intervention slides into my awareness, so I only have to ask once. In other words, rather than having to verbally review an entire menu of possibilities and then choose via muscle testing the most appropriate one, my multilevel rapport with clients is so sensitively attuned that the one best intervention generally just presents itself to me. This makes muscle testing much more efficient and moves the process along more expeditiously. In this particular case, when I asked about the best intervention to establish energetic boundaries, "the healing drum" slid into my awareness.

I wouldn't say that I was stunned, but I was completely surprised and feeling a bit awkward. I had never used my drum (called a fire drum or a hoop drum) in the therapy context as a specific intervention with clients before. Prior to that time, I had used it only to facilitate shamanic journeys. Now this drum was presenting itself to me as an energetic intervention in and of itself.

I explained what had just occurred to Courtney and asked her to stand in front of me. I asked her to attune to the particular individual with whom she was lacking solid energetic boundaries as I beat the drum. I stood about three feet away from her and began a steady rhythmic beating. I looked away from Courtney and opened my awareness to whatever came to my attention. Immediately, my attention was drawn to her solar plexus chakra.

As I beat the drum, I directed the vibrations from the drum into that chakra. After about fifteen seconds, I saw Courtney's essential energy system reorganizing itself as I was drawn to her crown chakra. Soon, I was seeing her chakra system shifting from one chakra to another, and I followed this constantly changing energetic kaleidoscope. I found myself directing the vibrations from the drum to each of Courtney's chakras in turn, as each required energetic balance.

I realized that this was the same thing that happens when a client's muscle testing chooses a chakra tapping intervention. In that intervention, I sit opposite clients as they begin tapping on a selected chakra, and I direct them to tap on various chakras as I see their chakra system reorganizing itself. With the directed chakra tapping, the energetic balance is completed when I see a line of energy from their crown chakra to their root chakra expand vertically and open up.

With the drumming intervention, I perceive the completion of the energetic balance differently. It has become my consistent perception that after all the chakras have gone through all their alternating sequencing, the energy at the client's heart chakra opens up as I see a bright luminescence expanding outward. At that point I stop drumming and muscle test my client to determine the effectiveness of the healing drum. To my delight and amazement, it most often generates a complete balance.

The second time the healing drum was called as an intervention with Courtney, I went through the same sequence of steps as I described above. This time, however, I perceived something that astounded me. As the energy at her solar plexus chakra contracted and called my attention to it, I directed the vibrations from the drum into that chakra. A few seconds later, I saw what I can only describe as shards of light directing themselves into the core of Courtney's solar plexus. I was taken aback by what I was seeing. I continued to drum until I saw the energy shift to her heart center and became aware of that bright luminescence opening up and expanding outward again. I stopped drumming and muscle tested—Courtney's body corroborated that she was 100 percent balanced on the intention.

Courtney shared with me that her experience was profoundly proprioceptive and left her entire body vibrating. She said she felt warm and emotionally moved by the experience.

I was very curious about what was going on. I concluded that there were larger forces at play, and later that day I journeyed to the spirits of the healing drum to consult with them directly in order to receive guidance about what was actually occurring.

After setting the intention to connect with the spirits of the healing drum, I began my rattling. Within seconds, I found myself on my eagle as he flew up to the upper-world realm. After what seemed like a couple of minutes, I saw a large, swirling mass of pink radiant energy that we were drawn into. Soon thereafter, we were moving quickly down into a swirling vortex of this radiant energy and were eventually deposited onto a large platform suspended in space. I sat down and patiently waited, all the while focusing on my intention.

Soon, I became aware of a swirling wind around me. I perceived it as cylindrical with a great deal of kinetic energy. Though I didn't see anything else, I began to receive telepathic communication which informed me that this wind embodied the spirits of the healing drum. They told me they liked what I was doing and wanted to support me in my work. They told me they would teach me "drum medicine." The next thing I knew, the swirling wind came into my body through my solar plexus. I felt very enlivened and sensed my entire body vibrating. I intuitively knew that this merging with the drum spirits was some kind of initiation to create a link to their healing energies. Shortly afterwards, this energy withdrew from me and once again swirled around me. The drum spirits informed me that more will be revealed as I continue to work with the drum. I was told to trust the drum and that the drum will be teaching me. Then the wind around me withdrew and I knew that it was time to return.

Since that journey, I have been using the drum regularly as one of my energetic interventions. As I track the changing and shifting chakra energies, I know that I am being guided as I use the drum. This is but another example of how something seemingly as ordinary as a drum is transformed into a power object. The same has become true for my Tibetan bell and any of the Tibetan bowls that I use.

What makes these objects "power-filled" and enables such rapid balancing and deep healing to occur? With each and every one of these objects, I have made a personal connection with the spiritual aspect that imbues the object with its power. Each of my incursions into nonordinary reality has created an internal reference point that is my active link to the spiritual power connected to a specific object. That is why the results I get using my Tibetan bell are different from those obtained by others who use a comparable bell. In essence, I am describing a way to sacralize the psychotherapeutic process in such a way that my clients and I experience the magic and wonder of dancing in the universe together. This is something that anyone can learn to do.

26

Shamanic Healing Approaches

As explained in chapter 7, "Collaborating with the Compassionate Spirits: Embracing a New Paradigm," a major component of the shamans' skill set is using intentional effort to enter what Dr. Michael Harner calls the *shamanic state of consciousness* in order to experience the shamanic journey. Shamans send their soul or spirit (i.e., their consciousness) into the non-ordinary reality of the invisible world of Spirit so they can interact directly with spiritual beings (often called the compassionate spirits). Over time, the shaman forges a relationship with these compassionate spirits, who become her spiritual mentors, guides, guardians, and allies throughout the realm of the invisible worlds. This growing family of the shamanic practitioner's helping spirits might include different spirits of nature, animals, the elements, ancestors, and teachers from various religious and spiritual traditions.

The most widely recognized method that practitioners use to alter their consciousness for the shamanic journey is a monotonous, persistent, percussive drive generated by the beat of the drum or the sound of the rattle.

Shamanic practitioners use the shamanic journey for a variety of purposes, including these:

1. *Divination.* Shamans use this technique to diagnose and assess clients (among other things).
2. *Power animal retrieval.* This procedure allows shamans to spiritually fortify clients who have become emotionally and physically vulnerable

due to a loss of personal power. This vulnerability is frequently the result of a traumatic experience.

3. *Soul retrieval.* This approach involves recovering fragmented and dissociated parts of a traumatized person to help restore the individual to emotional wholeness.

4. *Extraction.* The shaman removes dark energy intrusions (toxic energy frequently generated through trauma or acrimonious interpersonal encounters) from a weakened individual.

5. *Psychopomp work.* This procedure addresses a deceased's spirit (which may be trapped in the middle world) or the suffering of the dying. Occasionally, a client's problems are the result of an attached earthbound spirit (a deceased person's spirit). Freeing the attached spirit from the client's energy field is an example of this type of shamanic intervention.

As described in a number of the case histories, many of these shamanic interventions happen spontaneously as I am implementing the frontal occipital holding intervention. In these cases, the compassionate spirits are spiritual resources of mine that respond to my pleas for help for my client. Occasionally, clients' MMT directs me to initiate a formal journey process in order to employ one of these five shamanic procedures.

As with all Dynamic Energetic Healing® interventions, I always thoroughly explain the procedure to the client in advance and ask for permission to proceed. Upon completion of the shamanic journey, I use the client's MMT to corroborate the resulting energetic shift.

Divination

When a psychotherapist meets with a new client, it is common procedure to do a thorough evaluation before deciding on a treatment plan. This evaluation typically includes a formal interview during which the therapist elicits a description of the client's presenting problem (including various disturbances and symptoms), a complete medical history, and past and current family history. In this phase of gathering information, the therapist establishes a provisional diagnosis and treatment objectives that support the client's desire for symptom alleviation and restoration to health. All of this is referred to as the assessment phase of therapy. For shamans, the divination journey provides the spiritual counterpart to the clinical assessment.

In traditional societies, divination is understood to be a way of receiving guidance on how to proceed. This guidance comes from accessing the Divine will or receiving important messages from the Divine. Examples of divination include waiting for an omen or reading certain signs in nature. Other methods that are still used in the West include interpreting tarot cards and consulting the I Ching.

For shamanic practitioners who are connected to spiritual allies, the journey method itself is the way to divine guidance on various topics. For example, for Native American tribes that lived on the plains and depended on the buffalo for sustenance, staying connected to the herds was essential to survival. When food became scarce, the shaman's role was to journey into the realm of nonordinary reality and, with the help of her guardian spirit, determine where the great herds of buffalo were grazing so the tribe would be assured of its food source. This is an example of a classic divination journey.

When I work with clients in a psychotherapeutic context, divination journeys are occasionally called for. This is not a substitute for what I have described above as a comprehensive clinical assessment but rather a helpful way to augment and support the client's process if additional information is needed. When I am working in the Dynamic Energetic Healing® model, I rarely need to use shamanic divination. Consistently being in my second attention means that I continually move in and out of dreamtime. Consequently, I am connecting to extrasensory modes of information through my dreamingbody, and they inform and guide me as to what to do next when working with my clients. There are times, however, when a divination journey has been extremely helpful.

In case history 13, "Restoring Healthy Immune Function: Establishing Energetic Boundaries with an Ancestral Earthbound Spirit," the positive therapeutic outcome achieved by my client emerged from the information I received during a brief divination journey. During this journey my guardian spirit pointed out to me that my client was being affected by an attached earthbound spirit. My spiritual ally would not give me any additional information, but it told me that I needed to pursue this with my client in ordinary reality. When I asked my client if he had any awareness of an attached spirit, he immediately identified this spirit as his deceased sister! From that point forward, we mobilized Dynamic Energetic Healing® strategies to effect the positive therapeutic outcome.

The degree to which the shaman is reliably connected to her helping spirits determines the veracity and reliability of the guidance the practitioner receives with respect to the client's issue. In case history 13, the information I received initiated a sequence of events that led to my client restoring his healthy immune function and redefining his disempowering and dysfunctional relationship with his deceased sister.

I believe that we all have spiritual resources that we can call upon to help us and to support others in times of need. Anyone can easily learn shamanic divination by using the shamanic journey method. Though only rarely used in Dynamic Energetic Healing®, I am glad to know it is available when my clients and I need it.

Power Animal Retrieval

In the shamanic worldview, robust physical health and a positive mental attitude are the result of being power-filled. Shamans believe that when individuals are energetically connected to their animal or guardian spirit, they possess natural resistance to disease and emotional disorders such as depression and anxiety.

In today's post-industrial world (especially in the West), the growing popularity of domestic pets reflects the deep relationships we have always had with animals. We continue to perpetuate and nurture our bond with animals, particularly cats and dogs. We love our animal friends and bring them into our lives, embracing them as members of our family. Our ancestors depended on their animals for a great deal of their material life and even survival. Today, as extended families are more scattered and people are more isolated from one another, our devoted pets remain loyal sources of nurture and unconditional love.

At the spiritual level, animal spirits are more than just unconditionally loving—they provide us with power. We Westerners like to talk about things spiritual in terms of energy, and power animals certainly do provide spiritual energy for us. But in the shamanic worldview, power is more than just spiritual energy—it also includes the knowledge, wisdom, and unconditional love that the power animal as a compassionate spirit embodies.

When the shaman determines through a divination journey that the client is dispirited and suffering from a loss of power, the first intervention done is often a power animal retrieval. While the client maintains an open and receptive attitude, the practitioner journeys to the lower world with the intention of finding the particular power animal spirit that is waiting to be joined to the client with the shaman's help. As the shaman journeys into the lower world, the power animal makes itself available by revealing to the shaman its presence and its interest in the particular client. Frequently, the power animal communicates to the shaman (in nonordinary reality) the specific virtues and qualities it has that will help to reempower the client. Sometimes a brief dialogue ensues, during which the shaman receives a great deal of information to share later with the client. When the power animal has made it clear to the shaman that it is ready to merge with the client, the shaman embraces the power animal close to her heart.

The shaman then ascends back into the room, holding a clear image of the power animal to be infused into the client. When the shaman realizes that she has returned to ordinary reality, she cups her hands together and, with the power of her breath, energetically blows the held image of the power animal into the client's heart center. The shaman then helps the client to sit upright; while maintaining the image of the power animal, the practitioner cups her hands again and energetically blows the held image of the power animal into the crown chakra at the top of the client's head. The shaman then briefly rattles around the client to seal in the infusion of power that has been retrieved from the lower world.

From the shamanic point of view, the client is now power-filled. Her physical energy and her ability to resist contagious diseases are enhanced. In a manner of speaking, the client's energy field is more robust—she has become spiritually fortified and much more resistant to outside negative energies.

In my clinical experience, this is just one piece in the much larger mosaic of the client's complex life. For clients who have no further interest in the shamanic journey, they are now the beneficiary of an unconditionally loving power animal. Like a guardian angel, this power animal is dedicated to their protection and well-being. Clients who choose to learn the shamanic journey method will develop a personal relationship with their guardian spirit—one of mutual respect, support on all levels, and ongoing friendship. It is the kind of relationship that we all wish to have in our lives in ordinary reality. It is truly a great gift to receive.

Soul Retrieval

Chapter 11, "Soul Loss," explains in detail that soul loss is perhaps the most significant consequence of trauma. In the shamanic worldview, soul loss is often the primary reason for illness. Trauma is so much a part of our lives, but we tend to diminish the prevalence and pervasiveness of soul loss in our lives because we lack awareness and understanding of its significance.

A person who has experienced soul loss has lost an important part of their vital essence. Soul loss can be the result of growing up feeling unloved or abandoned, just as it can result from the trauma of physical or sexual abuse, loss of a loved one, major illness, or even surgery. Every time we experience soul loss, we become less complete and feel more empty. Soul is vital essence, so significant traumas rob us of our vitality and our joie de vivre.

Because soul loss is so poorly understood by Western medical and health-care practitioners, far too many people suffer from chronic depression, addictions (including to food and alcohol), and autoimmune disorders. The propensity to be too externally referenced, in an effort to fill up the emptiness that the loss of essence has generated, is also common. Every time a part of you gets split off due to trauma, the lost soul part carries away with it critical personal resources and inner gifts that define you as the unique and beautiful person that you are.

Soul loss is a serious matter, and it is the charge of the shaman to help injured clients to restore their wholeness through a soul retrieval.

The shaman discovers (with the help of her guardian spirit) in a divination journey that soul loss has occurred. The beginning stages of a soul retrieval are similar to what occurs during a power animal retrieval—the shamanic practitioner lies down next to the client with the strong intention of finding and retrieving the particular soul part(s) that will best support the client at the time. When the drumming or rattling music starts, the shaman journeys to connect with her spiritual helper. She explains to this guardian spirit what she needs help with and who the client is. In the realm of nonordinary reality, the shaman's guardian spirit is the guide; it leads her to the lost soul part(s) that must be recovered in order for the client to achieve wholeness with respect to the specific problem being addressed. Sometimes the split-off part is represented symbolically and sometimes it is seen in human form. In some cases the shaman can see the event that precipitated the soul loss and identify when in the client's life the soul loss occurred.

When the split-off part has been identified, the shaman communicates to the part the importance of it returning to its current, older self. The shaman does everything in her power (short of forcing or capturing the split-off part) to encourage it to return. Sometimes the split-off part has been waiting for what seems like an eternity to be returned to the core of the person who is suffering; in other cases, the split-off part is reluctant to return for fear of the same kind of trauma recurring. It is important to remember that if the trauma occurred thirty years ago when the client was a young child and powerless to protect herself, the split-off part has the memories and feelings of a child. It sometimes requires some gentle coaxing and lots of reassurance that it will be safe and protected by its current, adult self.

Once the negotiations are completed, the split-off soul part allows the shaman to carry it back with her; the returning part is often encased in an etheric crystal. With the help of her power animal or guardian spirit, the shaman returns to the room where the client is lying down in ordinary reality. Similar to the process used in a power animal retrieval, the shaman holds the image of the part that was discovered in nonordinary reality while she holds a crystal and, through the power of her breath, blows the newly returned soul part through the crystal into the client's heart chakra. She then helps the client to sit upright and repeats the procedure by blowing the held image of the returned soul part through the crystal into the client's crown chakra.

This completes the soul-retrieval procedure. Integration of the part that had been lost—sometimes for decades—is the next step in the client's healing. It becomes part of the ongoing therapeutic process that the practitioner carefully monitors and supports. This process enables the client to integrate the gifts and strengths that have been brought back by the missing part.

Extractions

What you experience as physical and emotional illnesses have spiritual counterparts that the shaman can see in nonordinary reality. Frequently, these intrusions appear in nonordinary reality as invasive and aggressive insects, reptiles, fish, or serpents with large fangs. Chapter 16, "Intrusions," describes some of the things that can happen to individuals as a result of dark energy intrusions. Essentially, intrusions are various forms of outside negative energetic influences that you absorb when you are in a vulnerable or weakened state. Rather than being power-filled, you are in a state of power loss. You can absorb these intrusions via trauma (when your energetic boundaries are compromised), via contentious interactions with others, or simply by being in a particular place (such as a doctor's office or a surgery room).

Traditionally, shamans remove or extract harmful intrusions with the support of their helping and guardian spirits. Different shamans use a variety of techniques (sucking them out, for example) to do their extraction work. In Dynamic Energetic Healing®, extractions are primarily achieved using the frontal occipital holding intervention. As described in a number of the case histories, extraction of dark energy forms is nearly always accomplished through the agency of a spiritual ally.

I have witnessed time and again how clients become completely transformed after an extraction of a dark energy form. My clients always comment to me that they experience a remarkable and dramatic difference in how they feel after dark energy is removed. Once a dark energy intrusion related to the client's particular intention has been identified and cleared, all the blocks that muscle testing had identified as interference to achieving the intention usually resolve spontaneously.

The removal or extraction of dark energy is fundamental to the consistent success generated by Dynamic Energetic Healing®. Fortunately, Dynamic Energetic Healing® trainees and practitioners do not need to be shamanic practitioners in order to remove dark energy forms successfully. Competent MMT combined with the cultivation of second-attention awareness is generally sufficient for the successful extraction of harmful dark energy forms. As long as you (the practitioner) acknowledge and call forth your spiritual resources to be present and supportive during your work with clients, you will be protected from being contaminated by the dark energy forms that are being released.

Psychopomp Work

Traditionally, a *psychopomp* is a person who conducts souls to the next world. In my experience, this term is generally met with raised eyebrows or a furrowed brow by those who haven't had shamanic training. Since traditional Western medicine dismisses the influence of spiritual beings as causative agents for illness, psychopomp work tends to be disregarded. But psychopomp work is a significant component of the shaman's role, and it is an important means of addressing medical, emotional and psychiatric problems.

Part of the paradigm shift that occurs with Dynamic Energetic Healing® is acknowledging the role of spirit intrusions or attachments in mental and emotional problems. In case history 16, "Validating Empirically the Existence of Past Lives: Recovering Power and Terminating Therapy," the positive therapeutic outcome occurred with the help of my guardian spirits. With their support, I helped a resentful spirit that was carrying a karmic grudge against my client let go of his attachment to my client and move on in his own spiritual and soul development. In Dynamic Energetic Healing®, this facilitation sometimes happens through the intervention of shamanic journey-work. More often, however, psychopomp work is required when I am assisting a client in a regressed state in a past-life energetic origin. In case history 4, "Neutralizing Present-Day Allergy Symptoms: Learning Psychopomp Work in a Past-Life Origin," my client had a dialogue with a spirit that was trapped in the past lifetime and was partly responsible for her present-day allergy symptoms. The client became the psychopomp as she facilitated moving the trapped spirit or soul to the next stage in its evolution. She had never done this before, but with just a bit of assistance from me she actively participated in her own healing.

Because Dynamic Energetic Healing® addresses mind, body, *and* spirit, psychopomp work is an important intervention that is occasionally required to actualize the client's intention and complete the healing. To date, none of my clients have balked when psychopomp work has emerged as the intervention of choice. Perhaps this is because by closely following the client's process I am not imposing my own beliefs. Instead, as I honor the client's unfolding wisdom through their body, no internal resistance is generated from within the client. When good client rapport is maintained, all things become possible.

27

FOCUSED PRAYER

Occasionally, manual muscle testing indicates that none of the previously mentioned Dynamic Energetic Healing® interventions is appropriate in a particular situation. When this occurs, I ask if prayer is the best intervention to use.

In 90 percent of the cases in which the client's muscle testing selects prayer as the best intervention, the prayer is to be done jointly. I take this as an indication that the client and I both have powerful spiritual resources to draw upon—when we pray collaboratively, the power of the prayer is amplified. It has also been my experience that joint focused prayer is typically done silently. I suspect this is so that our petition and focused concentration on soliciting help from our respective higher powers is undistracted.

I believe that joint prayer reinforces the therapeutic alliance and the spiritual connection that I have with my clients. When we are praying together for the benefit of my client, I believe that the client is empowered to feel more comfortable to petition his or her higher power for healing. It's not necessary for me know anything about what or whom my clients pray to, regardless of their spiritual orientation.

Interestingly, when prayer has been called for in my practice (via the client's own process through muscle testing), no one has ever balked at embracing the intervention.

Focused prayer in the context of Dynamic Energetic Healing® has always been efficacious. Dr. Larry Dossey has written about the effectiveness of focused prayer, and people from all religious and spiritual traditions have experienced this power for themselves.

I feel strongly that spiritual values and spirituality can and should be integrated into the therapeutic relationship. Because Dynamic Energetic Healing® supports and incorporates the spiritual component of each client's value system, using focused prayer as an intervention is really no different than including any aspect of a client's subjective experience in the treatment process. Using focused prayer implicitly affirms to clients that they can create positive therapeutic outcomes by consciously aligning with the power of their intent while acknowledging their connection to their higher power.

CONCLUSION TO PART 2

Thanks to many years spent cultivating relationships with compassionate spirits, meditating, and practicing qigong, I feel that I am never alone when I am working with clients. My subjective experience confirms for me that I have compassionate spiritual allies that are always doing everything in their power to assist me in helping my clients to heal. This isn't much different from Christians feeling the presence of Jesus or Mary guiding and protecting them throughout the day or from therapists feeling their presence assisting and guiding them in their work with clients.

I believe that because of my strong connection to Spirit, miraculous healings occur regularly when I am working in the psychotherapeutic context using Dynamic Energetic Healing®. For this I am very grateful. But we all have spiritual resources available to us that are always willing and waiting to support us.

I don't require trainees and practitioners of Dynamic Energetic Healing® to learn or practice core shamanism because they can be successful practitioners without it. I do, however, expect clinicians who are learning this model from me to open up to their connection to Spirit. This gives them access to the power of unconditional love which, in the end, is always the agency that heals.

PART 3:
THE DYNAMIC
ENERGETIC HEALING®
PROTOCOL

THE DYNAMIC
ENERGETIC HEALING®
PROTOCOL

Part 1 describes how the Dynamic Energetic Healing® model was developed, the principles upon which it is based, and how it relates to (and grew out of) other models. It also highlights a number of themes that distinguish Dynamic Energetic Healing® from other psychological approaches aimed at helping people come back into wholeness. One of these themes is the emphasis Dynamic Energetic Healing® places on understanding the pervasive and damaging effects of trauma; another is the unique application of a truly holistic complement of synergistic strategies to resolve what often emerges as PTSD. These strategies include energy psychology techniques, adaptations of Mindell's process-oriented psychology model, and core shamanism.

In part 2, I reviewed and detailed each intervention that is used in Dynamic Energetic Healing®. These interventions include working with the body's essential energy system (the acupuncture meridians and major chakras), frontal occipital holding, vibration and sound (which includes working with mantra and the Tibetan bell), and core shamanic principles.

In this section, you will discover the methodology used to apply these interventions in the psychotherapeutic context. Since Dynamic Energetic Healing® treats the energetic origins of presenting problems, there is a certain amount of complexity inherent in addressing the whole person. This section provides step-by-step guidance to help you better appreciate and understand how this complex approach is made more accessible by the

Dynamic Energetic Healing® protocol. I have divided the protocol into sub-sections—starting with the very beginning of your work with a client and ending with the completion of treatment—so you can get a sense of the sequencing of steps.

The major subsections are as follows:

1. Prepare the groundwork for working on a specific intention.
2. Identify and establish a clear and pertinent intention.
3. Identify and treat the energetic origin(s).
4. Unpack and resolve all aspects of the trauma package from the energetic origin.
5. Completion and integration.

Grouping the steps of the Dynamic Energetic Healing® protocol into these subsections should allow you to become more easily acquainted with the methodology. I believe this will also help you to more easily conceptualize the protocol as a map. There are various stopping-off points where you can temporarily throw your anchor—this should reduce the complexity of what at first glance may appear to be too much information to integrate at once.

Optimal learning of Dynamic Energetic Healing® emerges through super-vised training and regular follow-up with a qualified practitioner. This is particularly true given the process-oriented nature of this model. If you are new to this material, I recommend that you refer to the checklist (see appendix 3) until you have internalized the steps and no longer need to refer to anything to remember them.

CHAPTER

28

PREPARING TO WORK ON A
SPECIFIC INTENTION

A great deal must be done before beginning work on a specific intention with a client.

As every good therapist knows, you must build rapport with your client in order to smooth the way for anything productive to follow. During the initial intake session, it takes some time to get to know each other. Though clients come to me for help, I take it for granted that they are curious about me. They want to know about me so they can feel comfortable disclosing aspects of their vulnerability and needs, which is not always easy to do. They need to know that they can count on me as their therapeutic ally and that they can trust me to support them when they most need that support.

During the first two or three sessions with a new client, I always take some time to educate them about Dynamic Energetic Healing®. As I explain how Dynamic Energetic Healing® works, I inquire about their religious and spiritual orientation so I can be sensitive to their relationship to God or their higher power. I explicitly state that I would never intentionally offend them, particularly in regard to their religious and spiritual values. I explain that the acknowledgment and support of Spirit is integral to the work I do. As we come to a mutual understanding of our respective spiritual orientations, I discuss the importance of creating a sacred space that will help to hold or contain the work that follows.

After further discussion that helps me get a handle on what the client needs help with, I explain how we are going to move into establishing an intention (i.e., a therapeutic goal) and that the intention must be very specific.

Working together to narrow down what feels like the most important issue to address first is a very helpful step for clients.

Once clients have a clear idea of where they want to go, I explain that there is some preparatory work that must be done at the beginning of every session. This preparatory work is needed to ensure the accuracy of the manual muscle testing that will follow. This chapter describes the steps my clients and I follow to prepare to develop the intention statement.

Create a Sacred Space

Healing work is sacred, and I solicit clients' help in enlarging the therapeutic context by creating a sacred space. By sacralizing the therapeutic work space, we acknowledge the sacred and allow for the therapy to go beyond just cognitive-behavioral talk therapy. We open the door to connecting to the numinous in our healing work.

I ask clients to take a moment to ask for help from the invisible realm, which encourages them to go inside. This immediately shifts their consciousness from an outer-directed orientation to a more inner-directed one, which helps clients reflect on their issue and better organize themselves for the work that is to follow. Psychologically, it mobilizes their unconscious processes so that inner parts are more accessible and present in their experience. Spiritually, it ignites the flame that will bring in whatever spiritual resources the client has at his/her disposal.

The importance of going inside to connect with Spirit, in whatever way your client does that, cannot be overemphasized. No matter how despairing the client is at that moment, collaborating in establishing a sacred space affirms for them that they are not alone, no matter how perceptive they are or are not to the subtle experience of the numinous. Even if they haven't defined for themselves their connection to Source, their soul is being awakened. In the process of their work with me, they will come to know of their awakening.

Occasionally, clients have no experiential reference point for being a part of something greater than themselves in a spiritual way. When this occurs, I suggest that they remember a time when they were connected and, to the best of their ability, associate into that memory and that feeling to restimulate the part of them that has been shut down. I remind clients that their subconscious mind remembers that time, even if they do not. Even clients who do not affirm the transformative power of their relationship to Spirit in any other aspect of their life have an opportunity to affirm that possibility, that reality, with me at the beginning of every session.

Creating a sacred space also creates a protective field during our therapy session (see chapter 17, "Creating a Sacred Space"). Before I start my sessions each day, I go into my treatment room, stay quiet for a moment, and ask that spiritual guidance be available to me, so I can assist in the client's healing process and to provide spiritual protection from any outside negative influences that might intrude during the day's sessions.

I tell my clients that when they are taking their moment at the beginning of each session to ask for help from the invisible realm, I am also asking for spiritual help for them. I want them to know that their soul knows how to access spiritual resources in this work with me. I want them to know that even as they are affirming that undying part in themselves, I am collaborating with them to affirm their connection to true power. This is how a sacred space is created.

Calibrate Manual Muscle Testing

After we create a sacred space, I talk with clients about what they want to change or accomplish. Dynamic Energetic Healing® is very much a results-oriented psychotherapy model. As we have seen, talk therapy is a very small portion of this healing model. You have heard the expression "Talk is cheap," but in traditional cognitive-behavioral psychotherapy, talk is actually quite expensive. This is especially true when concrete positive therapeutic outcomes are difficult to validate empirically. Of course, there are people with strong auditory predispositions who need to hear themselves think out loud in order to "work it out" with a therapist—this is helpful and therapeutically supportive in many cases. However, my basic orientation in Dynamic Energetic Healing® is quite different. I follow the clients' process, but I also direct my clients to stay focused on the outcome they want. To a large extent, manual muscle testing (MMT) helps to keep us focused on the client's goal and facilitates and guides the therapy process.

Unless the client has a physical limitation, the muscle testing is done standing face-to-face with the client's arms outstretched in front of them (see figure 9). The first thing I must do is calibrate (measure) the relative strength or weakness of the client's resistance when I push gently but firmly on their forearms. I ask clients to think or say "yes," and I then immediately push down gently on their forearms. Normally, their arms remain firm. As a way of double-checking that the client has no negative associations to the word *yes*, I

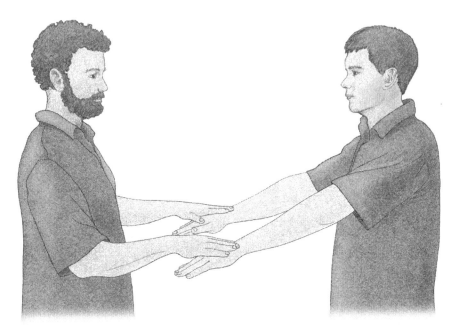

Figure 9

next ask them to think about a positive, enjoyable, or pleasurable experience. I say "hold" and immediately push down gently on their arms. Normally their arms remain firm against my gentle pressure. Next I ask my client to think or say "no," and then I gently push down on their arms. Normally, even as clients try to keep their arms firm and straight, their arms weaken and become mushy. Following this, I ask them to think of something that is stressful to them, say "hold," and immediately push down their arms gently again. If the client is not neurologically disorganized, their arms weaken once again.

This calibration process provides me with the kinesthetic and tactile information I need when working with this client, because MMT is my diagnostic guide. The calibration process also educates clients, providing them with phenomenological verification that the relative strength or weakness of their muscles is directly linked to what they are thinking and how they are feeling. If clients seem incredulous at first, I provide them with additional muscle testing examples. This reassures them that it is their own thoughts and feelings that generate the responses, not any hidden agenda that I may have.

Countless clients have told me how much they appreciate using MMT to facilitate their therapy. They can acknowledge that no matter how clever they are intellectually, their body doesn't lie—they cannot defend their vulnerability by pulling the wool over my eyes. Many clients have said how easy it was for them to con their previous therapists and how grateful they are to know that with MMT, they can finally let go and be honest about what they are really trying to accomplish.

One of the curious things about psychotherapy is that people who seek help with their problems are frequently disinclined to openly trust another person. Because their experiences have been so traumatic, they have difficulty baring their soul to a therapist. We are indebted to Sigmund Freud for his discovery and elaboration of what he called defense mechanisms. These are the coping strategies that each of us has unconsciously developed in an effort to avoid more pain as a consequence of trauma. Three of the common defense mechanisms are dissociation, rationalization, and denial.

Using MMT is one way to help clients reconcile with their own defense mechanisms. Many clients have told me that during the manual muscle testing of a particular issue, they tried extra hard to keep their arms firm so they wouldn't have to acknowledge the truth. But no matter how strong clients are physically, they are unable to resist the gentlest pressure on their forearms if the answer to the question is false.

For example, assume I have been discussing a particularly traumatic situation with Leslie, who knows that the trauma has left lingering scars. Intellectually, Leslie knows that this trauma needs to be healed, but emotionally, Leslie may feel a tremendous fear of having to reassociate with the trauma at a conscious level. In this case, Leslie might be using minimization as a coping strategy or defense mechanism. But if I ask Leslie to state, "I am no longer affected by any remaining residual trauma pertaining to the event you just described," Leslie's arms will be substantially weak when I muscle test them. No matter how much clients like Leslie may be minimizing the traumatic effects of an event, the MMT process helps them to be more honest with themselves.

Test for Hydration

Once I have a good kinesthetic sense of how much pressure I need to use when pushing on my client's forearms, I then test my client for hydration. This is also a common test administered among practitioners trained in applied kinesiology.

I have learned that when clients are dehydrated, I get inconsistent muscle testing responses at best. I do not have a scientific explanation for why this is so, but I know from experience that after dehydrated clients drink one or more cups of water, their muscle testing responses become consistent and reliable.

The test for dehydration is for clients to gently tug on their hair with one hand while I muscle test their other arm. If they are sufficiently hydrated, their muscle testing response is firm. If they are dehydrated, their other arm is very weak and they are not able to resist as I gently push down on it. Some clients have required over three cups of water before we could even begin manual muscle testing. I always have a large jug of purified water nearby, so my clients and I can drink water continuously throughout our sessions. Since there is a circuit of energy that connects me to my clients, it is just as important for me to remain hydrated as it is for my clients. If I become dehydrated, then my portion of the circuit affects the overall accuracy of my client's muscle testing.

Check the Client's Energy Field

The next step is to make sure that the client's energy field is circulating normally; that is, moving normally up the front of the body.

Interestingly, different traditions and schools of thought have different names for this phenomenon. In Chinese medicine, this is called the proper flow of the chi field—the flow of energy of the Central or Conception Vessel, which normally moves up from just below the pubic bone to the lower lip. In applied kinesiology, a chi field that is moving in reverse of what is normal is referred to as a polarity switch or being switched (a term that implies the involvement of body polarities). It is also called neurologic disorganization.

For muscle testing to be accurate and reliable, the direction of the flow of the Conception Vessel must be in proper balance.

In Applied Kinesiology, switching is assumed to entail left-brain/right-brain disorganization, among other features. Some of the signs that are frequently indicative of switching include reversals of letters and numbers, confusing left and right, saying the opposite of what one means, etc. Neurologic disorganization is also evident when an individual is significantly awkward or clumsy. When this condition exists, the client's psychological problem is generally slow to respond or recalcitrant to treatment sequences that should otherwise work to alleviate the problem. (Gallo 1999, 161–62)

There are a number of simple tests to determine if clients are switched. I like to use the "zip up, zip down" technique. As I hold my hand three to six inches from their body, I quickly "zip up" their energy field by moving my hand from just below their pubic bone to their lower lip. Immediately following this upward motion, I ask them to hold their arms out in front and I muscle test them. If their energy field is flowing normally (meaning the energy is moving up the front of their body), their arms remain strong. I then "zip down" their energy field by moving my hand from their lower lip down to just below their pubic bone. Immediately following this downward motion, I muscle test their outstretched arms again. If their energy is running normally, their arms weaken in response to this downward movement of my hand—I have temporarily disrupted the flow of their energy field, which weakens them. A useful analogy is what happens when you move your hand against the current in a river—for a few seconds, the current's flow is disrupted. When a client's energy field is moving normally, their arms go weak from the temporary disruption (i.e., downward motion of my hand). As a final step, I zip up the client's energy field one last time to support its normal energetic flow.

If MMT determines that my client is switched, there are a number of energetic corrections that can be implemented to restore normal energetic flow easily. The intervention that works most consistently for the majority of my clients is having them rub or otherwise stimulate three areas of their body where sensitive acupoints are located. Rubbing the sacrum at the bottom of the spine is done first, followed by rubbing the kidney points (K-27) just below the collarbones. The final step is squeezing the acupoints in the middle of the upper lip and lower lip (the Governing Vessel and the Central or Conception Vessel points). Each part of the sequence is done for thirty seconds. Ninety-eight percent of the time, this corrects the imbalance of the client's switched or overenergized energetic flow.

We can now proceed with our session, fully confident that our muscle testing will be accurate and reliable. Occasionally, even after doing all these preliminary tests for assuring accurate MMT, the muscle testing signals are confusing or inconsistent. When this happens, I troubleshoot to assess whether the client is being affected by an energy toxin (etoxin), which might be some kind of allergic response.

In rare cases, the client–therapist relationship itself is the source of the client's muscle testing problems. It is important for therapists to be aware that this can be caused by negative transference onto the therapist by the client. In these situations, it is important to talk openly with the client about the client–therapist fit. When the client confirms the desire to proceed with the therapist, an intention for the client to achieve 100 percent energetic boundaries with the therapist should be set. Another possibility is that the client may be subject to unknown field phenomena such as supernatural interference.

If I find evidence of an etoxin or some kind of supernatural interference, I troubleshoot to resolve the difficulty before proceeding with treatment (see case history 14 as an example of supernatural interference).

CHAPTER

29

ESTABLISHING A
CLEAR INTENTION

A s described in chapter 8, "Living Life Intentionally," Dynamic Energetic Healing® works from the premise that you can get to where you want to go provided you know where your destination is. By establishing a clear intention, clients begin their mapping process. Following the client's process is nonlinear, so *the route* to actualize the client's intention is never clear at the outset. But the positive therapeutic outcome that clients want from the work we do together—as articulated in the statement of intention—must be clear.

To ensure that clients are congruent about moving forward on their intention, there are a number of steps in the Dynamic Energetic Healing® protocol that must be followed. This chapter outlines these steps.

Test for Psychoenergetic Reversal

Before I address the specific intention for healing that the client and I have discussed, I test for psychoenergetic reversal, both general and specific. As discussed in chapter 9, this phenomenon can be an underlying and significant cause of self-sabotage that interferes with the success of treatment.

To test for generalized (or "massive") psychoenergetic reversal, I have my client repeat these five statements while I muscle test each statement:

1. I want to heal.
2. I deserve to heal.

3. It is possible to heal.
4. It is safe to heal.
5. I will heal.

If my client muscle tests strong for all five of these statements, the client probably does not have massive or generalized psychoenergetic reversal. Typically, clients who are massively reversed exhibit a tone of overall pessimism and self-defeatism. Although many clients come in feeling discouraged by the intransigence of their problems, that does not necessarily indicate a massive psychoenergetic reversal.

I next test for specific psychoenergetic reversal by adding a few words to the five statements and having the client say the expanded statements. As before, I muscle test following each statement:

1. I want to heal and resolve *this specific issue*.
2. I deserve to heal and resolve *this specific issue*.
3. It is possible to heal and resolve *this specific issue*.
4. It is safe to heal and resolve *this specific issue*.
5. I will heal and resolve *this specific issue*.

It is fairly common for a client's muscle testing to reflect a psychoenergetic reversal on one or more of the specific statements.

I want to emphasize how important it is not to overlook or bypass this important step in a client's healing process. A great deal of work and confusion down the line can be avoided by remedying this very important barrier to healing at the start of the therapy process. What's more, I have found that resolving psychoenergetic reversal early on spontaneously resolves many related problems.

Determine the Client's Most Highly Valued Intention First

Next, you must make sure that the client's intention statement is absolutely congruent with what is therapeutically most important for them to address. It is fairly common for clients to have a host of related problems that they want help with. This step in the protocol helps clients to better define what they want resolution with and, with the help of manual muscle testing, helps them to prioritize their issues and decide where to start.

For example, if a client presents conflicting feelings about their job along with intrusive anxious thoughts, at this point I can't know for certain whether the anxious thoughts are related to the job problem. If the problems are independent of each other, I don't know which preceded the other. Rather than making an assumption, I defer to the inner wisdom of my client and ask through muscle testing which issue is the more important one to address first.

Once we have identified the priority issue, we can define more specifically the proper wording for the client's intention for their healing outcome. I continue to work with the client to refine their intention until they receive corroboration from muscle testing that their wording most accurately articulates their intention. We are then ready to proceed.

Ensure No Inner Parts Have Objections

The client may have "inner parts" that object to the specific intention being realized. These parts might create barriers or blocks that try to prevent successful treatment.

What is loosely called the "parts model" has been used in various psychotherapeutic schools of thought for many years. Virginia Satir is well known for her "parts party," and transactional analysis uses the technique of establishing a dialogue among different aspects or parts of our "inner family." Gestalt therapy externalizes these inner parts with its well-known empty-chair technique, which is another way to create more awareness of disowned aspects of the self. Neurolinguistic programming (NLP) has developed various strategies for helping individuals come to terms with disavowed inner parts. Mindell's processwork emphasizes psycho-dramatizing inner parts as a way to establish a dialogue with traumatized aspects of the self.

It is important to note that all of these therapeutic change models work toward the integration of split-off and devalued inner parts of the psyche, which tend to take on a life of their own. When inner parts become autonomous, they act outside of the active personality with intrusive thoughts and feeling states that generate disturbing and often chronic mind–body conflicts. This is known as dissociation.

Checking to make sure that no parts carry objections to the intention is a responsible way to acknowledge and support all inner parts connected to the intention. Usually, an inner part that generates an objection is a part that has been traumatized and has made an adaptation (i.e., a certain behavioral strategy) to help the individual survive or better cope with what the autonomous part perceives as a threat to the main personality. Because of the dynamics that occur during a traumatic event, a traumatized part often becomes repressed and, in a sense, amnesic to the active personality. When this occurs, there is no two-way communication between the traumatized part and the active personality. Problems arise because the traumatized part is essentially frozen in time relative to the specific traumatic event. If an eight-year-old traumatized part adapted by dissociating, thirty years later the adult man will find himself dissociating every time he is confronted by a threat similar to the one that occurred when he was eight years old. Because this traumatized part resides in the unconscious part of the active personality, it's quite likely that the dissociating adult client has become extremely frustrated by trying to integrate the traumatized part. Without competent therapeutic help, there is virtually no way to reliably communicate with a split-off part that has been repressed into the unconscious realm.

There are many techniques for establishing contact with a disowned or autonomous inner part. When the proper precautions have been addressed to ensure the accuracy and reliability of MMT, establishing a communication link with a repressed inner part can be easily accomplished. Once I have accessed an inner part by asking, "Are there any objections?" I work carefully with clients to identify specifically how many objections there are and exactly what they are. I ask my clients if they know what the objection(s) may be. Sometimes clients know exactly what the objection is and we can address it directly. But frequently, because this part has been repressed into the unconscious realm, clients need some help.

Common objections by inner parts include the fear that if the part heals and integrates into the main personality,

1. it will no longer be able to protect the person, as it believes it has been doing ever since the traumatic event;
2. it will die and cease to exist (inner parts are aware that they are autonomous);
3. it will overwhelm and retraumatize the active personality, flooding it (and possibly other parts) with too much emotional pain from the traumatized memories that it has kept at bay;
4. more inner conflicts will be created.

These are just a few examples of common objections that must be addressed and resolved so that the inner part will not sabotage the client's healing process down the road. Most of the objections fall into the category of limiting beliefs that are treated with the same energetic strategies that are used throughout Dynamic Energetic Healing®.

Sometimes it is sufficient to simply identify the objections and balance the energy of each one using energetic strategies. But in other cases the autonomous part can only be addressed by identifying the energetic origin of the traumatic event and clearing the trauma in a more comprehensive fashion.

It is important to realize that when working with traumatized or repressed inner parts, the therapeutic goal is to release the pain of the memories carried by the parts (i.e., the trauma) so that the inner parts will integrate into the rest of the active personality and no longer act autonomously (see chapter 10, "Understanding Trauma within Dynamic Energetic Healing®," for elaboration on this). When all objections generated by concerned inner parts are identified and resolved, all inner parts are in accord with moving forward on the specific articulated intention.

WORKING AT THE
ENERGETIC ORIGIN

E nergetic origins are pivotal events that are frequently traumatic in nature. They hold and carry a great deal of emotional energy that can still negatively affect the individual years later. These key or central events are often directly responsible for the disturbance or problem state that clients seek help for. This chapter

- examines how multiple origins or traumatic events are often linked to make up an interconnected and enlarged trauma field that influences you to continue to "dream up" events that fulfill the underlying traumatic matrices;
- discusses how you can avoid retraumatization (a hazard inherent in psychological regression work) by establishing energetic boundaries with an energetic origin;
- reviews a number of simple regression techniques;
- describes how to map out and determine specific components of the traumatic event once the energetic origin has been found;
- identifies how to track and follow the client's process as you get into the traumatic material in earnest.

Identify and Treat the Energetic Origin(s)

To begin this stage in the Dynamic Energetic Healing® process, you must find out if there is an energetic origin that is directly responsible for the client's presenting disturbance or problem state. An energetic origin is a point in time to which the client is energetically linked. As a result of this linkage, the origin continues to cause problems in the client's present life.

There are four types of energetic origins: current lifetime, ancestral, past lifetime (karmic), and divine separation. We will examine each of these types of origins separately.

The energetic origin that is *an event from the current lifetime* may be responsible for the problems the client is experiencing in the present. Childhood, adolescent, and adult traumatic events are those that therapists have worked with for decades using other models of therapy. This type of energetic origin can be an event anywhere on the timeline of the client's sentient experience, going all the way back to the first trimester in the womb. Pre-birth trauma and birth trauma, which may be a sense of separation, can affect individuals just as significantly as a more recent event that they can consciously recall. In addition, Mary Hammond-Newman and I have facilitated the healing of many pre-birth traumas that clients have energetically absorbed from their mother *or their father*.

With the help of accurate muscle testing, it is very easy to identify exactly when a specific energetic origin (one that generates interference on actualizing the specific intention) occurred. In Dynamic Energetic Healing®, the womb-birth issues are identified with MMT by trimester. Using hypnotic language, the therapist guides the client to experience the physical and sensory qualities of the womb as well as the associated thoughts, intrauterine perceptions, and emotions. The work of Sondra Ray (1983) and Joseph Chilton Pearce (1992) offers some of the theoretical underpinnings for this aspect of the Dynamic Energetic Healing® model. The fetus often carries toxins from alcohol, drugs, or medication used during pregnancy, or toxins resulting from an overproduction of adrenaline during a stressful pregnancy. When I direct clients to focus on the physical and emotional feelings and thoughts (e.g., I feel sick, I feel nauseated, I feel scared, I feel like I'm starving, I think I'm going to die) while simultaneously using various energetic strategies, these origins of traumatic residue are cleared. Clients may also carry parental messages of being unwanted or causing stress in the parents' lives. They may carry emotions such as fear of leaving the womb; they may have internalized their parents' fears about their ability or desire to parent. It is important to be aware that energetic vulnerability in the prenatal stage can imprint the slightest physical or emotional disturbance as trauma in the fetus.

Clearing birth material often clears related karmic (past-life) and ancestral issues. *Ancestral origins* are the genetic energy lineages passed on through our families. Depression, addictions, and schizophrenia seem to have an energetic link as well as a genetic link. Genetic depression is carried energetically as generation after generation of children grow up in the energy fields of their depressed parents. Attitudes about stress, work, fear, love, relationships, money, and food adhere to the energy field of the family as a whole as well as to the fields of the individuals in the family. When working with ancestral origins, I determine if the lineage is maternal or paternal and whether the lineage is in the individual's biological family or adoptive family, where applicable. For example, if the child of a Vietnam War veteran carries trauma in her energy field, I need to determine whether that parent is a biological or adoptive one. I must also find out if the child's trauma started with that parent or whether it goes back further down the ancestral or generational lineage.

Karmic origins are passed on with the soul from incarnation to incarnation. The validity of past lives has been assiduously researched for fifty years by Ian Stevenson and reported in many books, including *Twenty Cases Suggestive of Reincarnation* (Stevenson 1974) and *Where Reincarnation and Biology Intersect* (Stevenson 1997). These origins may be internally perceived as literal truth or, as some authors have suggested, as metaphors. Karma is a Buddhist and Hindu belief that defines consequences for our actions at a spiritual level. This concept is described and explained in *The Tibetan Book of Living and Dying* (Rinpoche 1994). Buddhists and Hindus assert that energetic material from previous lives shows up in subsequent lives in order to be healed.

Whatever you believe about karma and karmic or past-life energetic origins, these origins are often the key to unlocking and healing major illness and trauma with the Dynamic Energetic Healing® model. I use MMT to determine how many karmic lifetimes we need to traverse to reach the origin of the client's issue and then proceed with the simple regression induction and healing using the various energetic strategies.

Entering the karmic realm is much like remembering a dream; some of it appears clear, some of it is unclear. Psychiatrist Brian Weiss's *Through Time into Healing* (1992), which is based on his private clinical practice using hypnosis, details how past-life regression therapy cured many of his patients of intractable mental illness. As a well-respected professor at Yale University, Dr. Weiss described himself as a very traditional if not conservative psychiatrist.

He explains that in a particular case, he was working with a patient whose issues they had been unable to resolve using anything in Weiss's therapeutic repertoire. During one session, his patient went into a spontaneous past-life regression while under hypnosis, vividly describing in remarkable detail an Egyptian lifetime of some three thousand years ago. As a consequence, this patient experienced a complete resolution of her symptoms. In a state of hypnotic trance, the patient also referred to personal information about Dr. Weiss's father—information that he had revealed to no one. Though Dr. Weiss was petrified of the likely derisive responses of his professional peers to his work with past-life regression therapy, he nevertheless went ahead and published his findings. To his great surprise, he began receiving letters from psychiatrists all over the country who had experienced similar clinical incidents over the years. Like him, they were too intimidated to come out in public for fear of professional condemnation.

The root word of *imagination* is *image*. There is abundant evidence of the healing power of imagery among cancer patients. Dr. Carl Simonton and Dr. Bernie Siegel have legitimized the healing power of creative visualization in their work with cancer patients. I have determined with MMT that some karmic material appears to be "factual," while some seems to be metaphorical. Even when the karmic material is determined to be metaphorical or "imaginal," the healing power of the imagery of past lives consistently creates positive therapeutic outcomes for clients.

I have been a believer in past lives for many years, but as with many things spiritual, there is a big difference between believing (and thus "having faith") and experiencing firsthand. In case history 16, I describe how I came to discover the reality of past lives while working in a shamanic state of consciousness. For me, the karmic experience I was privy to in my shamanic healing journeys when treating Denise was literal rather than metaphoric. This is my interpretation based on my subjective experience. Denise experienced healing on multiple levels as a result, but the nub of the matter is that this is all based on my subjective experience. This is the platform which supports all of this work. Attempting to convince others of one's subjective experience is neither productive nor useful. Healing results are what is important.

In addition to current life, ancestral, and karmic origins, Mary and I have discovered the energetic origin that occurs at the point just prior to reincarnating into human form; we call this the *divine separation*. I have encountered many individuals who have a significant emotional block that originates between lifetimes. Frequently, the reluctance to incarnate into another form is due to a persistent limiting belief derived from the previous lifetime's physical trauma. It is not unusual for an individual to carry the belief at the soul or karmic level that life in the body will simply be too painful to endure. This can be the cause of persistent anxiety or panic attacks, which often seem spontaneous and which confound conventional therapy methods. Though mainstream practitioners rarely acknowledge divine-separation blocks as a cause of present-day problems, I have found that chronic problems often dissipate completely once these blocks are identified and healed.

Many energy psychology practitioners use the term "root cause" in the same way that we refer to energetic origins. This may seem to be nothing more than a semantic distinction, but we discovered after muscle testing over fifty clients that the phrase *energetic origin* often elicits significantly more energetic material that can be cleared more comprehensively than the phrase *root cause*. So before going further, it is important to discuss the similarities and distinctions that I make between root cause and energetic origin.

A root-cause disturbance may be the energetic origin of a problem the client is experiencing in present time. The root-cause disturbance is usually some kind of traumatic event from which a constellation or syndrome of symptoms emerge. These symptoms are often energetic patterns that individuals carry at multiple levels (six that I know of at this time) and that frequently permeate through time (even lifetimes).

An energetic origin may have even more energetic influence on a present problem than its root-cause cousin, even in those cases where the root-cause disturbance and the energetic origin are the same energetic phenomenon (i.e., the same event). An energetic origin can be anything—it is not limited to a traumatic event. An energetic origin is a very large, expansive energetic field *that is the primary influential factor* (even if it originates outside of the client's personal experience, such as someone else's traumatic event or an ancestral curse) directly responsible for the client's current problem state. It can be known or remain unknown and unidentified by the client. We have found that the energetic origin consistently holds a larger energy field than the root cause.

If the energetic origin occurred long ago in time, it may no longer be actively affecting the client even though they remain energetically linked to it. Like a distant star, the energetic origin may be radiating light that isn't as warm as the sun but still conveys discernible energy. Its influence on the individual may be waning, unless it is part of a larger energetic field of linked origins.

We began using MMT to determine *which and how many* origins require healing in order to actualize the client's intention. We also used MMT to ascertain that the word *origins* will generally hold a larger energetic field than *root cause*.

To refer to one of the foundational principles of Dynamic Energetic Healing®, I am always respectful of working in the Great Mystery. Whether clients are directed by their own muscle testing to regress through fifteen karmic lifetimes to get the story, or whether they have a spontaneous past-life regression experience by amplifying a strong emotional feeling located in a certain part of their body, the imagery and the attendant story that emerges are personally meaningful to them. I know from years of professional practice how powerful a healing agent a symbol or an image can be. However difficult it is for some clients to accept or grasp the notion of karma and past lives, their healing results are the persuading factor. In my experience, *karmic work combined with the application of Dynamic Energetic Healing® interventions is a significant component of healing major mental and emotional disturbances.* Recognition of this component is missing in mainstream medical and psychological approaches. It is my hope that you will consider these possibilities.

Identify Linkages between Origins; Dream Up the Past

The linkages between origins are essential to my work. For example, in order to heal the impact of abuse experienced in childhood, the client may have to return to an ancestral origin to clear the abuse of a paternal great-grandmother by her spouse, the energy of which has carried forward to future generations. Clients and I may also clear fear from birth trauma, or we may be guided by manual muscle testing to a karmic event when a current-life victim unravels a story indicating he/she was a victim or perpetrator in a past lifetime. I often need to clear the first or the worst energetic origin in the client's current life, but MMT routinely indicates that many more energetic origins linked with the initial intention clear spontaneously because they overlap with the origin that held the most concentrated negative or traumatic emotional energy.

Mary and I began asking clients how many current-life, ancestral, karmic, and divine-separation origins require healing with each intention. For the most part, we have found that we only need to address between 30 and 60 percent of the energetic origins initially indicated to clear the intention, since energetic origins tend to cluster. At each origin, I use various energetic strategies to resolve all aspects of the associated trauma, including unresolved loss, fragmented or dissociated inner parts, post-traumatic stress symptomatology (including all negative affect states, limiting beliefs, and identities), and any associated dark energy formulations, all of which frequently keep us energetically linked to the time and space of past trauma.

Consider an example. John Doe comes in because he's been having relationship problems. He establishes his intention to achieve a mutually respectful, cooperative, adult relationship within which he feels comfortable making a commitment. When we get to the part of the protocol asking about energetic origins, John's muscle testing determines that there are two current-life origins, one past-life origin, and one ancestral origin. Because all four of these energetic origins, are interconnected as one energetic field relating to John's particular intention, they are in effect energetically clustered.

Occasionally, it is necessary to address the energetic origins one at a time. However, I have found that because of the penetrating pervasiveness of the energetic material that is elicited *from an energetic origin*, often I only need to address one or two of the origins before the entire matrix of that vast interconnected energy field collapses. By asking the right questions initially (which often directs us to the "first and worst" traumatic event that is still blocking the intention), I can significantly reduce the time required to clear all interference on the intention. This makes the therapy process more time-efficient, and more importantly, it accelerates clients' healing process, moving them closer to balance and inner harmony more rapidly. On a larger scale, this opens the way for more individuals to experience more rapid and complete alleviation of their pain and suffering. When all aspects of the energetic origin have been resolved and healed, clients realize this not just through the corroborating evidence of their MMT but also in a lightness of being and increasing joyfulness that comes with innate mind/body/spirit wholeness.

At this point it is important to talk about what Mindell calls the dreaming-up process, because the constellation of symptoms becomes a tyrannizing factor in the present when the individual is being actively affected by the traumatic event of the past. This "dreaming up" can be experienced in different perceptual channels (see chapter 5, "Integrating the Second Attention into Dynamic Energetic Healing®"), including but not limited to the individual's relationships (such as repetitive abuse patterns), physical body (such as a chronic symptom or a disease process), relationship to the world at large, and relationship to the parapsychological or supernatural realm. I always muscle test in advance to determine in which of these channels the dreaming-up process is occurring.

How is this useful? Once the energetic origin is identified (time and place of what is usually a significant traumatic event), I ask if there is an active dreaming-up process emanating from that energetic origin. If MMT determines yes, I inquire in which perceptual channel (as described above) the active dreaming-up process is occurring. If, for example, the dreaming-up process is in the relationship channel, the client and I are cued in advance to be sensitive to issues at the energetic origin that are specifically related to relationships. As well, I am alerted to stop and talk with my client to learn everything I can about the difficulties they are having in their current relationships. When there is an active dreaming-up process that relates to an energetic origin, *we will discover an energetic field of influence within a specific perceptual channel that is negatively affecting my client in a very specific way.* In addition, *my client is energetically eliciting and thus reproducing and perpetuating the same process that was initiated at the time of the energetic origin.*

This dreaming-up process is analogous to what Dr. Bessel van der Kolk calls reenacting a trauma, except that in the Dynamic Energetic Healing® conceptual map the reenactment can persist over lifetimes and is perpetuated energetically (see chapter 10, "Understanding Trauma within Dynamic Energetic Healing®"). If the energetic origin was associated with a relationship in which the client felt persecuted, that same process will be actively dreamed up by the client in present time. If there was a physiological issue, physical injury, or disease process at the time of the energetic origin, this has likely been brought forward into present time too, creating the conditions for the same debilitating physical process to influence the client's present reality.

If more than one energetic origin within a larger trauma pattern is blocking my client from actualizing an intention, the dreaming-up process can carry more energetic momentum. For example, if MMT indicates that there are three energetic origins that need healing, all related to the particular intention, two of them may be current-life origins while one of them may be a past-life energetic origin. If this is the case, I ask, "Of the three origins, which one carries the strongest negative energetic charge that needs to be healed first?" Frequently, it is the energetic origin that is furthest back in time (in this case, the karmic origin). However, all three of these energetic origins are linked, gathering energetic momentum as a collective field, as it were, through time to the present. In a sense, this can be likened to a comet hurtling through outer space on a targeted collision course with my client—it is only a matter of time before impact. As the client dreams up this hurtling ball of negative energy, it is as though his dreaming-up process is guiding this increasingly powerful negative energy right into his personal field.

Individuals who carry unresolved trauma from the past are often diagnosed with post-traumatic stress disorder. But as we have seen, this phenomenon is much more complex. It is almost as though the individual is caught in a repetitive time loop like the ones frequently portrayed in science-fiction movies. Because we are dealing with quantum principles, there is more at stake than what is referred to in the cautionary phrase, "He who forgets the past is bound to repeat the mistakes of the past." Ignorance of how deeply and pervasively trauma impacts our lives, especially when it remains unhealed from the past, leaves us in the peculiar position of creating a very dangerous future for ourselves. I want to emphasize that this is not just true for individuals—it is also true collectively, for families as well as nation states.

An interesting wrinkle in Mindell's metaphor of the dreaming-up process is what automatically happens when an individual or group establishes an affirmation for a positive future. For example, some people believe that by repeating something positive long enough they will begin to manifest in their life that which they are focusing on. But these individuals are quite misguided, and the law of opposites (eloquently explained in the I Ching as yin and yang) ensures they are in for a big surprise. For example, consider an individual who conscientiously affirms the phrase, "I am now popular and gregarious." At the unconscious and energetic level, this person is initiating an active dreaming-up process that will link past events in her personal history to present time. The irony is that the dreaming-up process will elicit historical material and experiences that are the very opposite to being popular and gregarious. Initially, this material is stimulated by the thoughts that oppose the affirmation because the affirmation becomes a statement of intention. Any unresolved trauma that is blocking this person's ability to actualize the intention will be evoked or restimulated through persistent focus on the affirmation.

This irony is part of the "divine conspiracy" that drives us all to bring up unresolved matters from the past that relate to our desires in the present. I call this the divine conspiracy because this rehashing of the past seems to be the universe's mechanism for helping individuals come into wholeness to heal.

Those who strive to be positive often face the dilemma of eliciting unfinished business from their past (unwittingly, of course) in order to be more in harmony in the present.

There is increasing research evidence supporting the value of a positive general orientation to life in promoting longevity and well-being. But at an energetic level it is best to first clear the debris generated from the storms of your past in order to open the way for smoother sailing into your future. Even the ancient wisdom of the I Ching counsels caution when yang energy builds up too strongly, acknowledging that the universal law of polarity (opposites) eventually requires you to come back to the energy of yin.

A process orientation that includes Mindell's dreaming-up metaphor and acknowledges the universal law of polarity is built into the methodology of Dynamic Energetic Healing®. Increasingly higher states of evolving consciousness are always preferable to ignorance based on old habits and belief structures that typify anachronistic paradigms. These anachronistic belief structures include such things as naïveté about the power of positive thinking, denial of the need to identify and clear old traumatic residue, and stubborn adherence to one-sidedness by ignoring the law of polarity and the existence of constantly changing fluid identities. At the individual and planetary levels, the Dynamic Energetic Healing® model consistently and empirically affirms that positive transformative change is possible. Once we stop dreaming up past trauma and pain, we can work together proactively to bring about new and constructive ways of being, free from the energetically tyrannizing influences from our pasts.

Establish Energetic Boundaries

Next you must determine if your client needs to establish energetic boundaries with the priority or lead energetic origin. If an individual has a great deal of residual, unhealed trauma connected to an event in the past, it is asking quite a lot of that individual to revisit the event, let alone associate into it. But this is exactly what many therapeutic models (including psychoanalysis, Gestalt therapy, hypnosis (including past-life regression), and most forms of counseling and psychotherapy) have been doing for decades. The themes underlying these approaches are insight and catharsis.

Many in the larger psychological community believe that present-day symptoms will abate if an individual can only discover the causative events and associated beliefs responsible for them. Many also believe that an even more complete problem resolution will occur if the individual experiences an emotional catharsis to rid him/herself of the repressed emotional trauma. But these well-intentioned ideas often fail to allow for the depth of the vulnerability created by the traumatic event(s) and for the important, life-sustaining defense mechanisms that have helped to keep the client functional in the interim. Common problems with these approaches include abreaction (an overwhelming emotional reaction) and emotional flooding (a feeling of sinking into a seething maelstrom of repressed emotional trauma). A consequence of abreaction and emotional flooding is that *clients are frequently retraumatized with the encouragement of their trusted therapist*. Even in a therapeutic context, women don't want to reexperience rape any more than men want to relive killing other soldiers on the battlefield. And yet, many experienced therapists lead their clients directly into a retraumatization experience. They claim that the catharsis of reexperiencing a repressed trauma is healing. It can be for some, but for many others it restimulates PTSD symptoms and creates emotional destabilization (i.e., decompensation) of what had been a compensatory yet functional ego-state. What a terrible irony, especially given the difficulty in getting individuals into therapy, particularly when there has been a great deal of violence, loss, or abuse.

In Dynamic Energetic Healing®, clients are *always* protected from retraumatization. Muscle testing is done in advance to determine if they have sufficient energetic boundaries to safely revisit the selected energetic origin. Origins are frequently events in the client's past that were deeply traumatic and injurious at the time, and fear, anguish, and pain remain in the client's interior world. It is a delicate matter to sensitively facilitate the careful unpacking of an old trauma. By establishing energetic boundaries with the entire matrix of the trauma before entering its energy field, clients are assured that retraumatization will not occur.

However, it must be emphasized that even with energetic boundaries established, clearing the components of complex trauma is hazardous and challenging for clients. Even after energetic boundaries are established, trauma work is often arduous and painful. But *it will not be retraumatizing*. This can make all the difference in the world. Moreover, my clients are reassured that I have taken great care and caution in preparing them for confronting their greatest fears. When MMT corroborates that their energetic boundaries with the energetic origin are at 100 percent, clients are intellectually reassured. They also feel an emotional calm and strength to face the event that is profoundly empowering. They have shifted their vibrational frequency to be in greater energetic resonance with what previously felt like a jagged, ominous field of energy.

Regress to the Energetic Origin

Clients have different styles and varying abilities when it comes to accessing or regressing into an energetic origin, which is often traumatic. Some clients need only minimal prompting to spontaneously regress into the scene of the past event. The easiest direction to a client who acknowledges a fairly good sense or memory of the past event is to simply say, "Go there." Some people can easily access energetic origins in this way, even if the origin is an event from a past lifetime. (I can often do this myself. Once the origin is determined, I simply close my eyes and wait for an image and a feeling to spontaneously emerge. I suddenly become aware of an interior scenario that unfolds before my inner eye. I suspect that my many years of meditation and journeying in realms of nonordinary reality enable me to access past origins easily.)

Other clients have a strong emotional reaction as soon as the energetic origin has been identified. When this occurs, I support their experience by encouraging them to stay with the feeling and even to feel it more. In essence, I am encouraging them to amplify their spontaneous experience. If clients are able to stay with the feeling as it intensifies, the feeling will expand right into the experience of the energetic origin that they had already begun to emotionally access. This induction or regression technique is called the *affect bridge*. The strong emotional state that the client has already begun to access and the origin become linked by the strong affect—the bridge—that leads the client directly into the origin. This method supports the client's process in a completely spontaneous, organic manner.

But some clients orient more to their body than their emotional feelings as a point of departure. These clients often have a strong sensation in their physical body that they might describe as pressure, tightness, tingling, cold, or heat. They may also experience affect and proprioception simultaneously (called synesthesia) as a strong emotion located and felt in a specific location of their body (for example, feeling deep sadness or grief in the middle of their chest). When this occurs, I encourage clients to stay with the sensations of their physical body and allow the experience to intensify. This is called the *somatic bridge*. Similar to the affect bridge, the somatic bridge expands internally into the experience of the energetic origin. Sometimes, entering into the energy fields of the origins using these two inductions can be very smooth and easy. Other times, since there is an amplification of an already intense experience, I direct clients to do some EFT tapping so they experience a soft landing into an event laden with trauma. (This assumes, of course, that MMT has already determined that the client has sufficient energetic boundaries with the origin.)

It must be said, however, that many clients have no idea, let alone feelings or sensations, related to the energetic origin that they are trying to heal via regression. In these cases, there are two easy induction or regression methods that I use frequently.

NLP Timeline Regression

The neurolinguistic programming (NLP) timeline regression technique was developed by Tad James. This technique is based on the assumption that chronological time is linear. This is the way in which most Westerners think of time—it starts at a certain point in the past and proceeds forward into the future. Once the energetic origin is selected, I ask the client to relax, close their eyes, and imagine that they are floating out from the top of their head, thousands and thousands of feet above where we normally reside (on the timeline of active experience). When the client has a sense or a visual impression of floating high above the building and high above the clouds in the upper atmosphere, they have, essentially, intentionally created a therapeutic dissociation. I then direct the client to float in the direction of their past. It is important for the client to remain very high above the timeline while they sense and see themselves floating over their experience of this lifetime and through a membrane or barrier that leads them into the realm of their past lives (if the energetic origin is a past-life origin). By remaining high above the timeline, the client doesn't get pulled down by the so-called emotional gravitational effects of a specific experience before they get to their destination. Since we have created an intentional therapeutic dissociation, my goal is to keep the individual separated from any emotional experience during their regression to the energetic origin.

I was once regressing a client who had significant trauma from her early childhood. The particular energetic origin she was regressing to was a past-life origin. We used the timeline regression technique, and even though I reminded her to stay high above the timeline, she was somehow pulled down into a current-life origin that created a great deal of anxiety and panic. At the time, neither of us knew what was happening. I helped her to calm down by directing her to tap on specified EFT points. When she was calm, I muscle tested her and determined that she had "landed" at a place during early adolescence that was a particularly dark time in her life. This was one of the origins already identified within a larger complex trauma pattern that we were clearing, but it was not the lead origin that MMT had designated to be addressed first. I then realized that she needed to establish energetic boundaries with all the origins which were part of the larger complex energy field that enveloped the entire trauma pattern she was trying to clear. Once this was accomplished, she had no more stopovers on the way to her intended past-life origin. The energy field she was working in was a highly charged field of interconnected complex traumas. Though this is not unusual, this client's particular relationship to some of these energetic origins created a great deal of vulnerability within her. Once energetic boundaries were established, she could safely traverse the area within this larger collective field of associated energetic origins without further incident.

The Tunnel of Light

This highly effective visualization technique was developed by Mary Hammond-Newman. I ask clients to imagine a tunnel of light that winds infinitely into their future and infinitely into their past. I ask them to peek into the tunnel, but not to enter it, and tell me what color they see in the direction of their future. Interestingly, most of my clients see bright, positive-feeling colors in the direction of their future. By this point, most clients are comfortable with their visualization capabilities and ready to take a look in the direction of their past. I remind them not to enter the tunnel but simply to look and tell me what color they see in the direction of their past. Clients usually report muted colors, and occasionally gray or black. If the color is gray or black, it is likely that some kind of dark energy formulation emanating from the energetic origin has contaminated the tunnel. I use MMT to verify this, and I have confirmed the existence of these emanations in approximately 85 percent of these cases. I have also found that clients who see gray or black are experiencing a strong component of anxiety.

The next step is muscle testing to determine exactly what the dark energy formulation is. Once identified, we select the best interventions to clear the dark energy from the tunnel. What we are actually doing is making the energy field of the origin safer for the client to enter by decontaminating some of the "bleed-through" of the dark energy from a traumatic event. Once this is accomplished,

I muscle test to be certain that my client has 100 percent energetic boundaries with the origin, the dark energy specific to the origin, and evil in general.

At this point, I ask my client to look into the tunnel again to see what colors are in the direction of the past. The color is always lighter and no longer feels ominous. I then direct my client to visualize entering the tunnel and either sensing or seeing themselves being swept into their past through the tunnel, toward and into the energy field of the origin. Sometimes clients sense themselves just stopping at a certain point or just knowing that they have arrived at the origin. Most clients get it right on the first pass, but I always muscle test to corroborate that they are exactly where they need to be in terms of the specific energetic origin. Occasionally clients don't go back in time far enough, so we have to continue their regression further back until they are exactly where they need to be. The opposite can also happen—clients occasionally overshoot the mark and have to come forward a little bit into the specific energy field of the designated origin.

When regression is required, I always direct the client to orient internally by saying, "Go into the energy field of the origin while remaining suspended above the actual event where the trauma resides." There are a number of reasons for doing this. Preventing the client from directly associating into the event immediately gives me another opportunity to ask if there are any specific precautionary interventions that need to be executed while the client is in the suspended position above. Sometimes muscle testing directs clients to visualize and direct a specific healing color of light or auditory tone down into the scene. When this intervention (which is essentially done from the soul orientation) is selected, a significant amount of negative emotional charge from the traumatic event is usually dissipated.

Amazingly, many of these interventions that I have facilitated from the soul position have completely cleared and resolved all trauma from the energetic origin. In these cases, the healing process is accomplished *completely out of conscious awareness*. When this happens, I ask clients whether they have collected any insights or new awarenesses and then direct them to return forward into present time. Once they are fully back in their physical body, I muscle test to double-check that the origin has been completely resolved and that the healing experienced at the energetic origin has integrated completely from the internal point of the origin to the present. Though this out-of-conscious-awareness method is not particularly satisfying to the client's intellect, it allows clients to substantially bypass having to deal with an old and painful trauma. It also has a positive effect on the larger energy field, which is usually composed of additional traumas that have all been contributing to blocking the achievement of the particular intention.

When clients associate directly into the story of an energetic origin using either the affect or somatic bridge regression technique, usually there is not an opportunity for channeling healing light or sound into the origin. But I trust that the client's soul has guided them directly into the story with a strong affective response, and I realize this might reflect this individual's personality and preference for resolving a traumatic event from their past.

Given this handful of easy and straightforward regression techniques, elaborate deep trance hypnosis is not required to access a traumatic event from the past. All of my clients are successful in connecting with an energetic origin that must be healed, even if it means cobbling together fragments of an event that their muscle testing has helped us to configure.

Some people see and experience an origin as a detailed story that unfolds image by image, scene by scene. Others simply experience strong affects and occasional images or impressions, requiring more involvement by me with frequent muscle testing and ongoing questions. Having been directed by me to narrate their experience in the first person, *clients essentially relive the story fully identified with the persona that is their past.* When an aspect of the trauma emerges, be it an overwhelming feeling of fear or a self-sabotaging limiting belief, I immediately direct clients to tap on specified EFT or chakra points, or I ask them to stand up while I muscle test to determine the best intervention to balance the emotional or traumatic disruption. There is an astounding array of possible traumatic residue that requires delicate unpacking and healing at the origin. Unpacking traumatic residue is discussed in detail in chapter 10, "Understanding Trauma within Dynamic Energetic Healing®."

Trauma is significant due to its "permanent" effect and the degree to which it shatters our wholeness. Essentially, trauma is extreme stress frozen in the body; it is experienced energetically as a powerful disturbance that can fracture or shatter the energy field, which results in all kinds of disrupting symptoms. Traumas are developmental or situational in their origins; both forms can affect us in destructive ways. Francine Shapiro (1995, 30), developer of the eye movement desensitization and reprocessing (EMDR) technique, provides this definition of the type of trauma that generates post-traumatic stress disorder:

When someone experiences a severe psychological trauma, it appears that an imbalance may occur in the nervous system, caused perhaps by changes in neurotransmitters, adrenaline, and so forth. Due to this imbalance, the system is unable to function and the information acquired at the time of the event, including images, sounds, affect, and physical sensations, is maintained neurologically in its disturbing state. Therefore, the original material, which is held in this distressing, excitatory state-specific form, continues to be triggered by a variety of internal and external stimuli and is expressed in the form of nightmares, flashbacks, and intrusive thoughts—the so-called positive symptoms of PTSD.

Trauma is a multilevel experience. At the physical level, the autonomic nervous system is stimulated to set off the fight-or-flight mechanism in the brain's neurochemistry, which floods the body with epinephrine. People with chronic traumatic responses fight with and/or flee from situations that don't necessarily warrant either response. At the energetic level, trauma manifests itself as fatigue, feeling drained, or feeling down. Furthermore, trauma disrupts the core structure of the individual's biofield (the aura or energy body), which dissolves, collapses, or fragments energetic boundaries. As Donna Eden (1998, 176) explains,

if the energy imbalances within your body become excessive, the aura can't protect you, and it can become thin and disorganized. It may get in the habit of being chronically collapsed, trapping your energies and preventing your life force from connecting with the world.

When my clients and I use the simple but specialized hypnotic inductions for regression to the energetic origin of a trauma pattern, the clients are able to access the essential information about the event easily. From there, we work together to resolve the trauma using various Dynamic Energetic Healing® strategies.

Determine the Components of the Traumatic Event

With the client now in the energy field of the origin, it is time to identify the individual components of the traumatic event, including (but not limited to) these disruptions:

- The affective residues of the trauma itself (shock, sadness, guilt, anger, fear, etc.)
- Soul loss
- A damaged or shattered energy field
- Supernatural intrusions
- Limiting beliefs (e.g., I will never trust anyone again as long as I live.)

Frequently, these components will organically unfold and be revealed as the client associates into the story. While your client is in the regressed state, you must use your knowledge of the many possible consequences of trauma to inquire thoroughly so as not to overlook any important component. The client's MMT will provide assistance in this part of the healing process.

In addition to trauma resulting from an experience of their own, individuals may also carry trauma from others in their energy field. I call this *collective trauma*. Collective trauma can occur when you are a witness to or a passive participant in someone else experiencing trauma. If you are overwhelmed by or overidentified with the trauma of the other, you may absorb their traumatic stress into your energy field quite unintentionally. For example, a child can absorb the trauma of her mother being beaten by her father and be affected by that trauma as if it were her own. This phenomenon of internalizing trauma from the field of others is very common in abusive or dysfunctional families. There may be compromised energetic boundaries with one or more individuals (often an entire family or group).

Having healthy energetic boundaries with another individual means you are in appropriate relationship to them and able to hold your own power within that relational context. At the energetic level, healthy boundaries mean that, in this relational context, your energy field is strong and has no holes or splits. For example, when a person who has healthy energetic boundaries is criticized, he is able to maintain his emotional equanimity instead of reacting as if he is replaying an early childhood trauma with a parent figure.

A traumatic injury may also result in an individual experiencing long-standing grudges, as described by NLP practitioner Cheri Brinkman in *Anchor Point* magazine (1993) and elaborated on by Swack. Such grudges can be against an entire community or even against God (which is much more common than you might think). In these cases, I use EFT or chakra tapping, TAT, Tibetan bell or bowl, F/O holding, and other energy strategies as indicated by MMT to dissipate and balance each aspect of the trauma.

31

DEALING WITH TRAUMA

The next step in the Dynamic Energetic Healing® protocol is what I call unpacking the trauma package at the energetic origin. At any given traumatic event, there are many possibilities for what traumatic residue the individual may have been left with. Trauma is a multifaceted phenomenon — it comes in many forms and can have many consequences. People experience trauma differently, and they respond in various compensatory or adaptive ways that affect their body, mind, emotions, and spirit. The Dynamic Energetic Healing® protocol has the flexibility to deal with whatever has affected a victim of trauma.

This chapter examines and catalogues the factors to keep in mind when confronting both individual and collective trauma. When unpacking the trauma package from a traumatic event at an energetic origin, there are many components or aspects of the trauma to be sensitive to. First, you must be vigilant in dealing with strong negative affective residue and associated limiting beliefs (which are discussed in chapter 30, "Working at the Energetic Origin"). Then assess what other disturbances may have been generated at the time of the traumatic event.

Soul Loss

As explained in chapter 11, "Soul Loss," soul loss is a common consequence of trauma. I always ask if soul loss was experienced and, if so, what intervention is required to bring the client back to wholeness. Western psychology refers to reintegrating an inner part that has dissociated, but the shamanic model regards soul retrieval differently. Shamans claim that when there has been soul loss, the lost part is completely inaccessible. Clients who have experienced soul loss often tell me that since a particularly traumatic event, they have felt as though something is missing—they have never quite been themselves since the event.

The Wish to Die

Another devastating consequence of severe trauma is the generation (mostly unconscious) of a wish to die, due to the severity and intensity of the pain suffered. This is true of a single incident trauma, such as an automobile accident or a rape, as well as a threshold trauma.

There are varying degrees of trauma. If a child on a bicycle or inline skates collides with a tree, this "single incident" trauma is unlikely to generate a death wish. There may be sufficient shock and physical pain experienced to generate soul loss, but it is unlikely that the child will have a wish to die at any level of their being. However, if a child or an adult is brutally raped, it would not be surprising for that individual to test positive for an unconscious death wish. The child colliding with a tree is an accident; the lasting effects of that trauma might well be serious indeed. But a violation to one's being through a rape is of a different order completely.

Why might someone wish to die? When an individual feels that their being is completely filled with shame and their essential value has been completely diminished by a violation such as rape, the core self is shattered. The experience of violation is so profound and so pervasive that the traumatized individual frequently feels worthless as a human being. The wish to die becomes a logical intrapsychic consequence. As well, it goes without saying that soul loss will also be present as part of the constellation of symptomatology arising from the traumatic event.

The wish to die is even more common among individuals who suffer what Swack calls a "threshold" trauma. Typically, threshold trauma occurs when the individual has been repeatedly subjected to abuse and degradation over a period of time. At a certain point, the person feels that they have reached their breaking point or threshold and that they cannot tolerate or cope with the abuse any longer. Examples include a woman who has stayed in a marriage to an alcoholic man who regularly beats her up when drunk, or a child who is regularly molested by an uncle who is visited once a month for the weekend.

In both cases, the individual suffers frequent repetition of single-incident traumas over a substantial period of time, and the effects of the traumas are cumulative. Regardless of the source of the ongoing traumatization, results for the victim include the affective and cognitive experience of helplessness and hopelessness, soul loss, and the understandable wish to die as a way to escape what feels like a living hell.

When an underlying death wish is present as part of the trauma package, the individual no longer experiences the joy of living. A common by-product is chronic, low-level depression accompanied by an overidentification with the Victim archetype. When these individuals come for treatment for depression, they will not heal until this trauma package is unpacked and cleared. If the wish to die is stronger than the will to live, the traumatized individual develops various unhealthy and self-destructive coping strategies that may include addiction to nicotine or alcohol, illegal drug us, and very often, a predilection for the darker side of life.

Just as people cannot be fully present in their beingness if they have substantial unhealed soul loss resulting from trauma, individuals who carry a repressed death wish cannot be happy or healthy in their mind, body, or spirit. And the individuals may have numerous death wishes operating independently of each other, each one the consequence of a separate traumatic event.

Even years after individuals extricate themselves from the threshold trauma pattern that tyrannized them in their past, the death wish continues to influence their psyche with the deleterious outcomes to their mind, body, and spirit. When a death wish finally gets cleared from the psyche, clients often report back that the low-level depressed mood which they couldn't shake finally dissipates. When a death wish clears, not only does a person's mood shift, but the strength of their protective immune system comes surging back as their will to live reasserts itself.

Feeling Abandoned by God

A feeling of unresolved and often repressed anger and resentment toward God often results from threshold trauma. This occurs when individuals have exhausted all of their personal and spiritual resources.

Children who are brought up in a healthy and supportive environment grow up feeling safe and having an overall feeling of interconnectedness. These children learn this sense of support and connectedness from their extended family and community.

But if children experience a trauma, they may experience a disconnection at the core level of their being. This disconnection often fosters an existential sense of aloneness that could lead to a general sense of meaninglessness and chronic low-level depression and a concurrent deficit in the apprehension of the sacred. For a child, the experience of the sacred is a normal, healthy part of the developmental process. If a child's well-being and personal development are fostered, nurtured, and lovingly supported, their sense of the sacred will not just be maintained, it will flourish! Yet, disruptions in the homeostasis of that child's early life can cause significant tearing of the fabric of their sense of the sacred. Trauma is a significant contributor to this tearing.

It is important to remember that trauma is not always violent and overt. If a parent or caregiver lacks the emotional capacity or resources to nurture a child's needs as he or she develops, the child will experience a feeling of neglect. If the neglect persists over time, the child will experience a feeling of abandonment. Abandonment trauma can be obvious (such as when parents divorce and only one of them is awarded custody), but abandonment can also result from insidious neglect that occurs over time. In either case, the child is often left with the scars of a more subtle and less overt trauma than that generated by an accident or violent action.

Severe single-incident trauma, threshold trauma, and the trauma that results from abandonment can leave the affected individual with a disconnection from God or Spirit that can have dire, lifelong consequences.

Some individuals, adults and children, are very conscious of their anger toward God and blame God for allowing their traumatic experience to persist. This anger or resentment toward God can occur at any age. Whether it is a projection onto God as the abandoning parent figure, or a more conscious and literal directed anger at God or Spirit, the consequences to the traumatized individual are the same. Chronic mental and emotional dysfunction can result and can ultimately be a major source of self-sabotage. Persistent depression and an inability to form lasting, emotionally intimate relationships are frequent. This syndrome can also include a lack of hope for a positive future and an absence of vision for personal success.

Individuals who are angry at God are disconnected from their Source of Being. It is not surprising that these individuals continually dream up conditions that prevent them from being in the right place at the right time and connecting with the right people, no matter how much effort they make to achieve this. As long as these individuals continue to experience and identify with their woundedness and anger toward God, their experience of feeling "on the out-side looking in" will persist. Where there is no connection to God, there can be no genuine trust in other people or in the future. What's more, those who have not healed their resentment toward God often conduct themselves as being separate from nature and the needs of the earth. Sadly, the consequences of this are revealed in the gradual deterioration of earth's ecological fabric and an increasing lack of appreciation of and sensitivity to the natural world.

Trauma's Inherent Irony

Trauma is a part of life. As growing numbers of us continue to learn about and integrate the wisdom of indigenous peoples and the awesome power of the human energy system, sensitivity to and awareness of the far-reaching consequences of trauma is slowly emerging. Yet there is an irony in the aspiration to be well and the hope that our species will evolve beyond violence and war. On the one hand, healing old psychic wounds is now possible with Dynamic Energetic Healing® (and other cutting-edge healing models). On the other hand, although trauma is a common and predictable experience in life, many of its devastating, far-reaching effects are below the level of conscious awareness—most individuals are unaware of how important it is to get help to heal their traumas. This is not to say that people do not recover from trauma without the help of an excellent therapist; many do. But the sad fact is that many do not.

The evidence of unresolved trauma is all around us. When the traumatic wounds experienced by individuals are ignored and remain unhealed, the energy from the disowned parts of millions of wounded individuals (for example, the parts that are angry about having been abused but have no support or safe context to process and express that anger) has to go somewhere. This enormously powerful emotional energy gets unconsciously and energetically rerouted. When it goes into the body, diseases such as cancer and autoimmune disorders result. When it goes out into the collective, it is channeled through the media and expressed in increasingly graphic films, "realistic" television dramas, and the violent, mind-numbing video games that are becoming increasingly popular. Many of our political leaders, who probably have not healed their own trauma, seem to believe that violent military action is more efficacious than diplomacy. And individuals in regions laden with ethnically-based hostilities, whose war-related traumas are never given the time to heal in the constant warfare that spans generations, are unlikely to stand down and reflect on healing their grief and loss rather than expressing their anger as a thirst for revenge. There is no easy way to resolve these dilemmas. However, I know that comprehensive healing is now possible for those who ask for it!

When individuals have suffered much pain and loss, many of their unconscious defense mechanisms (which are consequences of trauma) have already been engaged. Those who have an unconscious wish to die are unlikely to ask for help from a psychotherapist. People who have been subjected to multiple traumas over a period of years and have lost their faith in God to help them will probably not ask for help from a psychologist. It is unrealistic to expect individuals whose coping strategy is a chronic dissociation that precludes them from being present enough to deal with their daily problems to even notice that they need help.

Of course I am overgeneralizing. There are supportive, understanding families that have a high degree of awareness of the suffering of a family member and that try to do everything to support the individual's return to health. Church communities also do everything they can to care for their own, including offering pastoral counseling and support. But the inherent dilemma is much like what Gautama Buddha proclaimed immediately after his enlightenment: All life is suffering, and there is a way out of suffering (by following the eightfold path). Not everyone is inclined to a path of meditation and spiritual study, which often takes years to effect substantial self-awareness and success. But if enough people can acknowledge the essential truth that suffering is part of life and no one is immune from it, there will be sufficient openness to acknowledge our pain (rather than using defense mechanisms such as denial and minimization) and begin looking for healthy ways to address it (rather than the violent, self-destructive expressions that perpetuate the unhealed trauma).

I am giving so much attention to trauma because, through a lot of hard work and diligent research, I have developed a synthesis of ancient and modern techniques to reclaim and maintain our natural, God-given mental, emotional, physical, and spiritual balance. I want to share this synthesis with you so that you too can experience progressive feelings of hope, emotional balance, and increasing joy and love.

Energetic Boundaries as a Component of Trauma

I want to briefly revisit the subject of energetic boundaries because they are an important component of trauma. An individual who has experienced trauma has accentuated rawness and vulnerability in a variety of contexts. For example, if an individual experiences trauma from another car colliding with theirs, that individual's energetic boundaries with *driving a car in general* and with *other drivers on the road* will likely be compromised. As a result, the energetic boundaries of these two specific contexts will need to be restored. Children who have been molested by a parent while at home may have their energetic boundaries with *the molester, the home,* and *the family in general* compromised.

As a therapist, how do you know if your client is in an analogous situation? You develop a fairly accurate intuitive sense about it. In the two cases I have used as examples, the contexts that I identified were related to the victim's experience and/or perception of not feeling safe or of being somehow personally violated. In the case of molestation, I also check the context of the clients' *physical body*, since that is where the violation occurred. It is fairly predictable that the energetic boundaries these clients have with their physical bodies are significantly compromised—and need to be restored to 100 percent.

Blocked Emotions and Distorted Relationship to Emotions

It is important to note that *emotions* can be energetically compromised by trauma. Some traumatized individuals become blocked from accessing or experiencing particular emotions; others lose their natural relationship to a particular emotion. In both cases, the energetic boundaries with that particular emotion must be restored. For example, if Max (an adult client) grew up with a parent who was given to frequent angry yelling and criticizing, it is likely that Max's energetic boundaries with the emotions of anger and shame are significantly compromised. He is probably conflict-avoidant because of an energetic weakness or vulnerability developed over time with the emotion of anger. This weakness is with other people's anger directed toward him, and Max also has an inner conflict with respect to feeling safe to use his own anger openly, freely, and spontaneously. Consequently, Max has likely developed many limiting beliefs (such as "Anger is destructive—people always get hurt when there is anger") that affect his daily life in numerous ways. These beliefs have created an inner barrier to honest communication and emotional intimacy in relationships.

It is also likely that Max's limiting beliefs themselves further weaken his energetic boundaries with the emotion of anger, his own and others'. These beliefs (conscious and unconscious) are the cognitive outcomes that cement Max's compromised energetic boundaries with anger. This is a significant sabotage pattern vis-à-vis Max's ability to maintain emotional intimacy in a relationship, because over time he has developed a strong energetic habit of avoiding what he had earlier experienced as a very hostile and dangerous energy. Max experiences himself as having no defensive capabilities for dealing with anger. He is unable to represent his personal (emotional) truth when someone challenges him. Max's limiting beliefs (which were generated as a consequence of the erosion of his energetic boundaries with anger) have soundly compromised his ability to use the specific emotional energy of anger. Until Max's underlying beliefs, generated by the traumas of his past, are energetically balanced and his ability to use anger when he needs to are once again available to him, he is *chronically disempowered*. Until his energetic boundaries are restored and his trauma healed, Max is operating at a deficit, *perpetually emotionally handicapped in all his relationships*.

In effect, Max is constantly tyrannized by an unconscious double bind (a situation in which an individual believes that conflicting thoughts or ideas—in this case, limiting beliefs—are both true). In Max's case, the double bind is something like, "I feel very angry with you, and it's not safe to feel or express anger because someone always gets hurt." As Max's therapist, I need to help him identify the double bind and reconcile his limiting beliefs. Then I need to help him establish energetic boundaries with his experience of anger so he can come into greater vibrational energetic harmony with his own and other people's anger.

An important point to add relates to the nature of polarity or opposites. If Max's experience of anger is no longer available to him because of a traumatic event, I need to hold the possibility that the emotion on the other side of anger is also blocked. After doing the work to help restore Max's access to and comfort with anger, I will be sure to check his relationship to love and compassion.

It is often the case that when one side of a polarity has been compromised, the other side has also been compromised. In the Chinese medicine model, this is expressed as the balance of the yin and yang energies. Both sides must come into harmony. The good news is that it is not terribly complicated to restore homeostasis to the whole system and reempower individuals such as Max so they can stand up for themselves and speak their truth in relationships. With Dynamic Energetic Healing®, an individual's entire damaged energetic matrix can be easily reconfigured so healing can be effected.

Overidentification with a Negative Archetype

Another possible consequence of trauma is the overidentification with the negative aspect of an archetypal form.

As you may already know, Jung developed the theory that the collective unconscious is populated with all the possible archetypes. Jung understood an archetype as an ancient shared image or symbol that represents an energy or human experience. These images play an integral role in each person's journey and make it possible for us to live fully and completely. Jung posited that we are born with these archetypal patterns (not unlike Plato's "original forms") at an essential and energetic level and that they structure our imagination and make it distinctly human. He believed that archetypes shape matter (nature) as well as mind (the psyche). Archetypes are cross-cultural and recognized by everyone worldwide. Jung claimed that archetypes are so fundamental to humanity that they are best characterized as elemental forces which play a vital role in the creation of the world and of the human mind itself.

Jung would say that when you identify with an archetype, you are tapping into a powerful primal energy (an aspect or form of consciousness) that is neither of your own creation nor a random accident of your mind. It is as though the archetype speaks through you—it is your link to the human collective. Familiar examples of archetypes include Mother-Father, King-Queen, Lover-Beloved, Warrior, Magician, Judge, Victim, and Hero. There are times when identification with an archetype can be helpful—and other times when it can be very destructive. In my clinical practice, problematic archetypal over-identification frequently occurs with the Victim, Martyr, Scapegoat, or Judge (often a critic figure). Evidence of overidentification commonly emerges out of trauma and its subsequent codependent behaviors. As a therapist, you can recognize clients who are overidentified with an archetype by their thoughts, behaviors, and experiences.

Framing clients' experience within the conceptual map of the archetypes often helps them to appreciate that their "unique" experience is actually normative within the larger human family—we are all identified with archetypes all the time. It only becomes problematic when an individual becomes *overidentified* with the negative aspects of an archetype, which significantly limits their choices and behaviors.

For example, Loretta came in complaining of persistent, low-grade depression. She experienced some personal losses ten years ago, when she was in her mid-thirties. When she came for treatment, she was still trying to recover from an unfulfilling marriage in which she felt exploited and emotionally victimized by her husband, whom she had loved. After we cleared all of the trauma related to her abusive marriage and difficult divorce, Loretta was still unable to maintain 100 percent energetic boundaries with her ex-husband. As a result, in spite of her good looks and sharp mind, she continued to feel downtrodden and depressed.

Loretta admitted that she had been feeling like a victim for almost two years now. Whenever she heard about her ex-husband dating somebody else, she devalued herself for allowing herself to be seduced and tricked by a man who became abusive. As she described her experiences, I wondered which variable was continuing to compromise her energetic boundaries with this man. It occurred to me that Loretta was "possessed" by the archetype of the Victim. I use the term possessed because when an individual is *over-identified* with an archetypal form, it often feels as if they have been taken over by a spirit. When an archetype possesses someone, it has tremendous power because it is constantly being infused with the energy of the collective unconscious.

When we determined via MMT that Loretta had indeed been taken over by the Victim archetypal energy, I explained why her emotional reaction was so strong. It was as if the archetype's energy was supercharged—the experiences that every person ever born who identified with this archetype were being funneled into this archetypal circuit, which Loretta was now connected to.

I then used a metaphor to help Loretta release her connection to the archetype. I asked her to imagine an enormous circuit board (the collective unconscious) with countless plug-ins representing connections to the millions of individuals currently being influenced and affected by this archetype. Our task, using various energetic strategies, was to pull the plug and disengage her from the constant infusion of negative energetic influence from this circuit board. This image helped Loretta attune to her identification with the Victim archetype during the selected interventions, which effectively disconnected her from the overidentification. Once her manual muscle testing indicated that she was 100 percent free from any identification with the Victim archetype, Loretta's energetic boundaries with her ex-husband were spontaneously restored. In subsequent sessions, her energetic boundaries with her ex-husband remained solid.

Is not unusual for individuals who have been labeled codependent, and who have suffered threshold trauma and dysfunctional family patterning over many years, to occupy and eventually be taken over by the archetypes of the Victim, Martyr, or Judge. With respect to the Judge archetype, individuals may overidentify with an inner critic who tyrannizes them with critical internal self-talk, may constantly "dream up" people into their lives to be critical of them, or may even overidentify with a critical person who constantly puts others down.

In some cases, it is sufficient to correct psychoenergetic reversal and establish energetic boundaries with the archetype in order to stabilize the client's relationship with the archetypal energy. But in most cases, bringing energetic balance to the client's whole system requires making sure that all related trauma is completely cleared. This paves the way for the client to disidentify from the energy of that specific archetype.

The Impact of Personality

Clients' personalities can complicate matters when they are attempting to disidentify from a destructive archetypal energy.

As mentioned in chapter 22, "The Chakra Interventions," I find that the Enneagram model, which groups personalities into nine distinct types, is most useful and constructive for helping clients discover and acknowledge their personality type. Primarily because of its spiritual origins, the Enneagram provides a nonpathologizing model of personality that is devoid of DSM-IV personality-disorder jargon and is easily accessible to clients. Clients complete the questionnaire (144 questions) developed by Don Richard Riso, author of *Discovering Your Personality Type: The New Enneagram Questionnaire* (1995), and then we briefly discuss the two personality points that they come closest to.

For example, if the client's dominant Enneagram point is One, the perfectionist, I know it will be challenging for them to disidentify from the Judge or Critic archetype because individuals with this personality type are predisposed to overidentifying with the Judge or Critic. Similarly, if a client's strongest Enneagram point is Two, the helper or caretaker type, it will be challenging for them to disidentify from the Martyr archetype because this archetype tends to support the propensities of the caretaker personality.

The role of the individual's personality is just another factor in the complex combination of internal and external influences that must be carefully considered when addressing trauma.

CHAPTER

32

INTEGRATION AND COMPLETION

O nce all the traumatic components at the energetic origin have been cleared and resolved, there is some important finishing up work that needs to be considered. Manual muscle testing continues to be our guide, keeping us apprised of when the client's work at the energetic origin has been completed.

Additional Karmic Healing

Additional karmic healing is sometimes required to tie all loose ends up at the energetic origin. This is often the most important element in depotentiating an active dreaming-up process that has been responsible for perpetuating undesirable chronic disturbances in the client's present-day life. Some clients discover that they need to identify and bring back with them a gift in the form of an internal resource that will help them stay empowered while they integrate their healing as they come forward into present time.

Additional karmic healing is usually needed if the energetic origin occurs in a past lifetime or between lifetimes. An example of this is Denise, who experienced an intrusion while reading in bed (see case history 16). This intrusion was from a man who, in a past lifetime, could not reconcile with his loss and internalized feelings of shame, hurt, and anger. He was avenging the rejection, which resulted in a karmic attachment to the woman who was my client in this lifetime. This man remained stuck in his anger, harboring a powerful grudge that compelled him to pursue my client lifetime after lifetime.

This was truly a karmic healing because it involved taking care of unfinished business whose origin was prior to this lifetime. At the time I was working with Denise, I was not using energy psychology methods. My therapeutic focus was purely process oriented, and this approach was sufficient to elicit enough information to pursue and discover this karmic thread. Now that I use the Dynamic Energetic Healing® model, I use a different approach—one that puts more responsibility on the client for resolving any karmic leftovers.

After a client has completed all healing work at the energetic origin, I inquire via MMT if there is any karmic residue between lifetimes that needs to be addressed. If there is, I direct the client to orient him/herself to a place "in time" following the lifetime in which we found the energetic origin. This process is hypnotic; I am giving the client suggestions to go to the place at the soul level. There, they are to wait for anyone from the previous lifetime with whom there is unfinished business to appear. I suggest that in this karmic realm, they will be able to communicate easily with the soul of any individual they need to finish up with.

Every time I have facilitated this process for clients, the healing results have been profound. It amazes me how emotional people can get when communicating with other beings at this soul level to forgive or ask for forgiveness, explain why they did certain things, and let go of resentment that they still carry from the past lifetime. What's more, in 90 percent of cases both parties have a natural and great willingness to forgive, understand, and reconcile with hurts and angers from the past. At the soul level, where individuals are less identified with ego, clients have much more compassion and understanding. Their egoic sense of themselves as separate and entitled is greatly diminished in this heightened spiritual realm of soul dialoguing with other souls, and they have fewer self-interested concerns when you review and recapitulate events of a prior lifetime.

As to the remaining 10 percent of cases, it is just as surprising how intransigent and punishing beings can remain, even at the soul level. In my experience, these unforgiving souls are usually contaminated with dark energy and have malevolent intentions toward the individual (my client). Most of them are spurned lovers who feel humiliated or offended that, in a past lifetime, my client had dared to leave and pursue a life without them.

In these situations I have to do a great deal of direct intervening, which includes helping clients troubleshoot as they go inside and talk to the being at the soul level. Troubleshooting in this case means reminding the intransigent soul being that their intention to never release my client—to not allow them to be free and autonomous—is ultimately self-defeating. I interject, reminding the beings that they are keeping themselves stuck in their pain and anger, effectively blocking themselves from karmically moving on and evolving. Very often, I have to actively intervene in the dialoguing process to release the dark energy contamination from the angry soul being so it will no longer affect my client. Occasionally, the soul being gives me permission to release the dark energy contamination that has been its source of unforgiveness and desire to punish.

It surprises me how many clients fully understand this past-life connection and find it excruciatingly painful to extricate themselves from it. In every case in which I have facilitated the healing of unfinished business with clients at the karmic level, healing for my clients has been the ultimate outcome. However, there have been a few cases in which it was evident that the soul being was not ready to move into the light itself, even after it had reluctantly released the client.

I also encounter cases in which the client remains claimed by a religious cult that, in a previous lifetime, the client was affiliated with but broke free from. A collective or group curse has been intentionally generated and directed at the client. The originators of these curses (individuals now at the soul level of being) believe that the curse is necessary in light of the client's perceived betrayal and abandonment of the group. I have found that although this saddens me, the issue cannot be forced—free will is given to all. I have neither the hubris nor the divine omniscience to insist on healing the karmic destiny of beings who have their own idea of personal direction in life, even if I perceive it to be evil and destructive.

When karmic healing has been done to the extent possible, I gently ask if my client needs to pause and reflect out loud on any new understandings or insights they derived from having healed this energetic origin. Frequently, new awareness has organically emerged, step by step, throughout the healing process. Nevertheless, many clients have found it helpful to articulate new understandings as a way to begin the cognitive integration that gathers the fruits of their healing process into their conscious life.

Create a Power Resource

By this point, clients are feeling quite good. They have done an enormous amount of personal healing work by unblocking a significant obstruction that had been in the way of their achieving a particular goal. This is a good time to ask if the client has a particular image, feeling state, or symbol to refer to *internally* in the future as a way to reelicit these feelings of accomplishment and resolution with respect to personal healing.

In neurolinguistic programming (NLP) jargon, this is called an *internal resource state*. An internal resource state is an intentionally created positive association that can be linked to new experiences to augment them with positive emotional energy. When I intentionally support my client in creating a positive internal resource state, I am anchoring the internal image or feeling state to the positive feelings the client is experiencing now that a significant trauma has been eliminated. Thus, we are creating a power resource.

For example, a client may generate the image of a golden sword as his or her power resource. I direct them to remember all of their positive feelings associated with the healing experience every time they internally refer to that bright, glowing, golden sword. After leaving my office, they have a powerful associational link to the feelings connected to their successful healing experience. The client can now consciously picture the sword in future situations that are upsetting as a way to maintain equilibrium and reelicit the positive feelings of confidence that are now associated with this image.

Integrate the Healing

Using hypnotic language, I direct clients to integrate everything they have healed from this place and point in consciousness (i.e., the energetic origin) forward through time to the present and come 100 percent back into their physical body. I summarize the primary themes that were intended, healed, and resolved at the energetic origin they just visited. As they come forward through time to the present, I remind them in a soft voice that their energy field has been completely reconfigured because all significant limitations and trauma related to the starting intention have been permanently released. This energetic shift has already positively affected *every event they have already experienced*, from our present back to the energetic origin. In other words, I add conscious intent to the integration of what has been healed by reminding clients that there has been an instantaneous cascading or domino effect that has modified in a positive way their entire karmic history from the point of the energetic origin to the present. I also remind clients that their subconscious mind, that part of them which is the bridge to their soul, understands everything I am saying and will ensure that these changes are immediate and permanent. I ask them to visualize returning through time to the present in the same way that they had regressed to the energetic origin. I remind them that they are forever changed by the healing work they have just completed.

Whatever the theme of their intention was (personal health, intimate relationships, or chronic anxiety, for example), I emphasize that the integration process profoundly heals the theme of their intention (to varying degrees, depending on whether this was just one of many origins in a larger pattern of interconnected origins). This helps to refocus clients on their initial intention statement, which may have been established four or five sessions prior.

The integration process is deeply affirming and empowering. This is particularly true when manual muscle testing corroborates (when the client is back in the present) that the healing done at the energetic origin has been completely and successfully integrated through time to the present.

Check for Parts Left Behind

When the return and integration are completed, I always check to make sure that the client has not left any part of him/herself behind. Through muscle testing, I ask, "Are you 100 percent in your physical body in present time?" The answer is usually yes, but it is also true that clients frequently leave a part of themselves in a place and time in their past.

When this occurs, there are two approaches to take. The first is simply to ask clients if they know what part of themselves they left behind. If they know, I ask them to close their eyes and "go back" and retrieve that part so that when they return they are wholly in their body in present time. Muscle testing will corroborate this integration.

If clients don't know what part of themselves they left behind, I ask through muscle testing if there is an intervention we can use to help them to retrieve the part. Frequently, frontal occipital holding is selected, which often enables me to "see" what they are holding on to (from their recent regression experience) that prevents them from being fully present in their physical body. Although no more formal healing needs to be done pertaining to the energetic origin, clients occasionally discover that a part of them is somehow still attached to some aspect of the experience they just healed. This "revisitation" of the origin can be extremely helpful in reemphasizing to clients an aspect of their experience that they need to spend more time with in order to bring the experience to closure.

An important question to ask the client via MMT at this time is whether their active dreaming-up process has been completely depotentiated in the specific perceptual channels that were originally identified. Since all trauma has been cleared at the origin, the energetic link that kept the client connected to the origin has been severed. When the muscle testing confirms that the link is severed, I excitedly tell my clients that what they had been energetically eliciting from the past into their current life situation has been resolved. This is tremendously reassuring—it reinforces that chronic problems, whether they be physical, relational, or parapsychological, will be eliminated or significantly reduced by the healing work just accomplished. From now on, the past is only a reference point for a memory rather than a source of ongoing misery.

Future Pace

When muscle testing has confirmed that no parts of the client were left behind and the active dreaming-up process has been depotentiated, I ask my clients to close their eyes and, knowing what they now know to be true based on what they have just experienced with me, imagine a number of scenarios in their future that directly relate to their stated intention. In the jargon of neuro-linguistic programming, this is called *future pacing*. If a healing or power resource has been acquired at the energetic origin, I suggest that they bring it with them into each of the imagined future scenarios. Future pacing is a way of recruiting newly discovered or developed inner resources. Through the power of their subconscious, individuals merge these inner resources into possible futures to be better able to anticipate successful outcomes and recognize them when they occur. Future pacing is a way of mentally rehearsing (and thereby developing an integrated preparedness) for situations that would not have had positive outcomes prior to the healing.

Future pacing gives clients the ability to recontextualize experiences that were, in the past, difficult and disempowering. For example, for the client whose intention was to feel more comfortable and confident expressing anger, the future pacing is imagining different interpersonal contexts in which they successfully express their anger. But the healing that the client has accomplished at the energetic origin up to this point may not be enough, since he/she has no prior experiential reference points for successfully and confidently expressing anger. In fact, it might be extremely difficult for the individual to even imagine that expressing anger confidently could be possible.

In these cases, I make sure clients have 100 percent energetic boundaries *with their future*. Frequently, there is psychoenergetic reversal on the intention to establish these energetic boundaries. Once the reversals are corrected and the boundaries are installed, clients discover that it is quite easy now to imagine these possible future situations successfully.

In most cases, work on an energetic origin is now completed. Some intentions can be resolved in an hour. In other cases, it takes two or three sessions to eliminate all the blocks to actualizing the specific intention because there are a number of energetic origins related and connected to the specific intention. Regardless of how long it takes to complete the origin work on an intention, the benefit to clients is always immediate and noticeable.

CONCLUSION TO PART 3

It is important to remember that although Dynamic Energetic Healing® fits within the framework of energy psychology, there is much more going on when I am working with clients than there would be if I were using a single energy psychology approach. We (the client and I) establish a sacred space, request the presence of our respective spiritual resources, and allow ourselves to be swept up in the dreambody experience throughout the healing process. These factors are the main reason why intransigent and complex trauma is released and healed completely and why my clients consistently experience success and accelerated transformative change. Because these factors play an integral role in Dynamic Energetic Healing®, I see myself primarily as a facilitator working from my second attention; this allows me to be sensitive to multiple realities.

As a facilitator and process-oriented therapist, I never know what to expect when working with a client's process. Consequently, I use a nonlinear approach to assist clients in healing trauma from past events. The Dynamic Energetic Healing® protocol presented in this book is a guide to help trainees stay organized throughout their learning process. Once you understand and internalize the protocol, keep in mind that any point during a session is a viable point of departure.

For example, if your client reports having a difficult time with a specific individual, this might be an appropriate time to establish energetic boundaries with that individual. If the same client becomes distraught when describing how difficult it is to be around the difficult person, you might become directive in the moment and guide your client to begin EFT or chakra tapping to reduce or eliminate their emotional distress—another departure to interject a component of the protocol.

If I get the impression while talking to a client at the beginning of a session that they are dissociated (I can usually see a part of them hovering above their head), this is another point of departure. With the help of muscle testing, I determine to what degree they are embodied. For example, if they are only 62 percent in their physical body, I ask a series of questions (both with and without muscle testing) to determine whether this is the result of a single incident or part of a long-standing pattern of, for example, conflict avoidance or intimacy avoidance. Using the protocol as a loose guideline, I might establish an intention for this individual to be 100 percent in their physical body. I then check for elements specifically related to this intention, including psychoenergetic reversal, energetic boundaries with their physical body, objections on the intention, and any energetic origins that need to be healed. If there are origins to be healed, I identify the lead origin that should be attended to first (first and worst) and ask whether there is an active dreaming-up process associated with this origin. Then I inquire about which regression technique will most expeditiously lead the client to the energetic origin.

These examples illustrate that once you understand and have internalized the basic structure of the Dynamic Energetic Healing® protocol, you have the opportunity to be tremendously flexible and creative in how you use the protocol. You can follow the clients' needs as they are revealed to you and then return to the basic outline as a way of staying on track. In this process-oriented manner, you need never fear losing your way when assisting an individual to heal.

Dynamic Energetic Healing® is an integrative model that benefits from the synthesis of a variety of powerful healing modalities. Using this approach leads to rapid, consistent, positive therapeutic outcomes that are experientially verifiable in each session. For the most part, complete elimination of traumatic residue from old injury is a predictable outcome of the use of Dynamic Energetic Healing® techniques. I feel very excited to have this opportunity to share this new approach with you.

PART 4:
CASE HISTORIES

CASE HISTORIES

The case histories that follow have been culled from hundreds of Dynamic Energetic Healing® sessions that I have facilitated since 1998. My intent is to illustrate my process-oriented style of working with clients and the various steps and applications of Dynamic Energetic Healing®. As I describe each case history, it will become clear how the Dynamic Energetic Healing® protocol (see part 3) is consistently followed, albeit sometimes circuitously. To keep the length of these accounts manageable and to focus on the most important elements of each case, these case histories are summaries of what actually occurred. Consequently, as you read the account of each case, please keep in mind that although I always work within the step-by-step protocol described in part 3, the progress of each case may differ somewhat from the formal statement of the protocol. Work with clients in therapy sessions rarely follows structured protocols exactly, unlike training sessions that are designed to illustrate the sequential steps. The other important point to remember is that each of these case histories has been chosen and written to highlight particular aspects of the Dynamic Energetic Healing® protocol.

Nearly all of the themes and important elements of Dynamic Energetic Healing® described in this book are portrayed in these case histories. These cases will also give you a sense of how different interventions are combined to effect positive therapeutic outcomes. In addition, they provide many examples of how I work with my second attention in therapy sessions. You may wonder how I "see" the things that I describe in my interactive process with clients. It is a matter of having cultivated my second attention to the point that I now trust my impressions or intuitions sufficiently to bring what I learn from them into the therapeutic relational context.

The clients that I describe are everyday folks. The Dynamic Energetic Healing® approach gave them the feelings of safety and acknowledgment they needed in order to share their impressions with me as they emerged. It may surprise you that these everyday folks are capable of the extraordinarily intuitive and spiritual insights revealed in these case histories. I have been and still am always surprised by the incredible awareness and sensitivity that clients reveal as we do this work. The information that clients generate during past-life regressions always amazes me, and it is this information that is integral to their successful healing outcomes.

My experiences and those of my clients may seem unbelievable or fictitious, but I assure you that these experiences are simply descriptions of the subjective and interior perceptions that emerge from within us when we step into Process together. Dynamic Energetic Healing® integrates very different paradigms for how we know things to be true, and many people doubt their usefulness and efficacy because of their lack of familiarity with them. But these psychoenergetic and spiritual modalities are effective and powerful strategies for generating consistently positive therapeutic outcomes.

Though the names, professional circumstances, and descriptions of my clients have been changed to protect their privacy, their healing stories are absolutely true. I recommend that you suspend your disbelief while reading these stories so that you, too, can open up to new possibilities for healing and for living a healthy and happy life.

1

ELIMINATING PANIC ATTACKS
RELATED TO THE FEAR OF
HAVING A COLONOSCOPY:
CLEARING AN INTRUSION

Larry was a client of mine years ago when I was just beginning to use Dynamic Energetic Healing® with clients. I saw him alone as well as in a men's group I was facilitating. At that time, Larry was dealing with depression and marital issues. He achieved a favorable outcome after ten months of combined individual and group treatment, and I didn't hear from him for over six years.

Then I received a call from his wife, who explained that Larry had to see me immediately because he was experiencing debilitating panic attacks. She felt I was the only one who could help him because his treatment in the past had been so successful. Since he was in crisis, I agreed to fit him in the next day.

Larry arrived really stressed. He is a general contractor and a big guy — about six foot five and quite physically imposing. That day he looked like a frightened child, bent over and hardly able to look me in the eye. I asked him what had been happening and he told me the following story.

For the previous year, Larry had been experiencing irritable bowel syndrome accompanied by frequent diarrhea. This created a great deal of stress for him because he was frequently working outdoors and his guts were often "tied in knots," which created considerable pain. Larry's doctor recommended a colonoscopy, but the very idea of this intrusive procedure freaked Larry out completely. So his doctor sent him for a barium photograph x-ray instead. When this provided evidence that Larry had a polyp in his lower bowel, his doctor told him it was essential to have the colonoscopy to make sure he didn't have colon cancer or any malignant lesions. His next appointment was in one month.

It had been a week and a half since Larry had met with his doctor; since then Larry was unable to work at all. His doctor prescribed Paxil for stress. By his own admission, Larry had been in total terror since beginning to take the drug, so he quit taking it. Following that, he began experiencing classic panic-attack symptoms, such as fear of having a heart attack, difficulty breathing, fear that he would never be able to go back to work, and "every other fear I could think of." He had fears about not doing his job well enough (if he could ever get back to work), fears about not earning enough money, fear of the intrusive medical procedure, and fear of the panic attacks coming any time without warning. He described his life as hell on earth with unrelenting torment.

As I continued to question Larry, he told me that he experienced all of his fears in his solar plexus—that was where he felt his panic and terror.

We established an intention to eliminate all anxiety and feelings of panic associated with having a colonoscopy. As we muscle tested, Larry was psychoenergetically reversed on the intention itself. That is, when he stated the intention out loud his arm muscles tested weak. When Larry stated out loud that he did *not* want to eliminate his anxiety and panic feelings, he muscle tested strong. This energetic phenomenon frequently occurs when there is resistance to addressing something that is very frightening for the client. Larry's energy system was reversed with respect to the specific thought field associated with addressing the colonoscopy. This must always be tested for before doing any further energetic balancing; otherwise, what might appear to be completed could be sabotaged immediately after the work is done, effectively undoing the healing work.

There are many effective ways to correct psychoenergetic reversal. I had Larry rub what are frequently called the psychoenergetic reversal points (the sore points) a few inches below the collar bones (these are lymphatic drainage points, so they are often sore). As he rubbed these points for two minutes, Larry repeated out loud: "I completely love and accept myself, even though I do *not* want to eliminate my anxiety and panic feelings associated with having a colonoscopy." After two minutes, we muscle tested again and the psychoenergetic reversal was completely corrected.

I want to note briefly that this method for correcting psychoenergetic reversal is generic in the energy psychology community. It was initially taught this way by Dr. Roger Callahan. As mentioned in chapter 9, "The Mysterious Phenomenon of Psychoenergetic Reversal," I generally correct this in the same way that I approach any other problem—I ask the client's body what the very best intervention is at that moment to correct the reversal.

I next directed Larry to orient to his most present fear while tapping on the fourteen EFT points. Before he started tapping, Larry established a SUDS (subjective units of distress) of 4 on a scale of 1 to 10, with 10 being the most fearful feelings and 1 being neutral. After the first round of tapping, Larry noticed an empty feeling in his solar plexus; his SUDS level was still at 4. After the second round of EFT tapping, Larry was aware of a thought that this wasn't going to work; his SUDS level was now 3.5. He continued with two more rounds of EFT tapping and the feeling of dread in his solar plexus was relieved; his SUDS level dropped to 2.

As Larry continued to tap, he began experiencing various physical sensations after each round: some tension across his back, a tingle across his arms, and then a different tension across his back as though he was holding something in his arms. His SUDS level, which had stayed at 2, went back to 4 instead of progressively decreasing (as is usually the case), and his "tension" kept shifting around. I became suspicious and did some more muscle testing, this time inquiring whether there was any supernatural influence. To our surprise, there was indeed.

I carefully muscle tested and determined that Larry had contracted an intrusion that had established residence in his solar plexus area. I suspected that this was the cause of his irritable bowel syndrome and panic attacks. The best intervention for Larry was to hold the TAT pose while being aware of the tension from his solar plexus moving throughout his body. This was only partially successful, so Larry repeated the procedure to release the intrusion at the body level and the auric-field level. The muscle testing then indicated that the intrusion was 100 percent released from Larry at all levels and that there was no additional supernatural interference influencing him. What's more, after the intrusion was released, there was nothing else that needed to be done! The intrusion was the single causative factor responsible for Larry's panic attacks and the feelings of dread and terror. Once we corrected his psychoenergetic reversal about dealing with his fears of having a colonoscopy, it was a short road to completion. We used EFT as an interim albeit important first step in helping Larry to relax and creating the conditions needed to identify a supernatural intrusion.

As Larry prepared to leave, he commented that his solar plexus/stomach area felt more relaxed than it had in a very long time. He felt tired but calm, and I reassured him that the muscle testing showed that nothing else needed to be done.

The next day, Larry's wife called and sounded excited. She wanted to know what I had done, because Larry was back to work for the first time in nearly two weeks. That was pretty good feedback for me. Did Larry ever go through with his colonoscopy? My assumption is that he went ahead with it since he needed to rule out colon cancer, but neither Larry nor his wife has called for a follow-up appointment. In this case, no news is great news.

2

METAMORPHIZING
POST-SURGICAL DEPRESSION:
CONSCIOUS APPLICATIONS
OF CIRCULATING CHI

A middle-aged man was referred to me for residual pain and depression that resulted from a hernia operation he had had six weeks prior. Richard's doctor told him that he was one of the few (statistically, one in a hundred) who for unknown reasons did not have a normal, full recovery from what is considered routine hernia surgery. Consequently, Richard was left with ongoing "searing" pain around the surgery site and down his right leg.

Richard was becoming preoccupied with the fear that his pain would never abate. He was also very depressed because the doctor's assurance of a quick recovery and rapid dissipation of post-surgical pain had not been true for him. Richard was no longer able to hike, bike, lift, or even walk without pain. He had not been sleeping much at night, and he was quickly falling into hopelessness and despair. Life for Richard was relentless pain without any reassurance from the various doctors he had consulted. This coterie included the surgeon who had done the hernia operation, a pain specialist, and a specialist he had consulted for a third opinion. These doctors continued giving him injections of nerve blocks, which did not work. Richard was frightened, because the doctors continually insisted that this was the only thing they could do to help—aside from performing another surgery to try to improve the results of the first one. Richard was terrified that he might become paralyzed or worse if he had another surgery. At least one doctor told him that there might be nerve damage from the initial surgery, which exacerbated Richard's feelings of hopelessness of ever recovering from his chronic pain. He was beside himself from not knowing what his best option was.

Using Dynamic Energetic Healing®, we first cleared the surgery trauma residues, which included soul loss and a number of affective components (hurt and pain, fear, anxiety, depression) that composed his surgical trauma structure. We established energetic boundaries with his pain and his obsessive negative thoughts associated with feelings of hopelessness and despair. We used a combination of EFT, TAT, F/O holding, and other energetic strategies. By the end of our first session, manual muscle testing indicated that Richard had released all traumatic residue from the surgery itself. He later told me that he was much quieter internally by that evening and that he felt a great deal lighter emotionally.

After our second session, Richard decided to pursue acupuncture as an adjunct therapy. His results were good. During his third acupuncture session, he became aware of his chi (life-force energy) moving down from the surgery site through his leg and out his big toe. This was a new experience for him and quite reassuring, since it coincided with a mitigation of his pain.

This feeling and perception of his chi moving down his leg became a very important element in Richard's healing. We created a kinesthetic resource anchor with two of his fingers so he could access and stimulate the flow of his healing chi as often as he needed to. Richard said that this was perhaps the most powerful tool he had available to quickly change his attitude when he fell into despair.

In Dynamic Energetic Healing® I use a variety of strategies to help clients unblock or shift the state of their chi field so their energy can circulate freely again on many levels (conscious, unconscious, physical body, soul or karmic, aura or biofield, and the chakra system) *without* the traumatic or limiting information that was previously in their energy field. Creating a kinesthetic resource anchor is an NLP technique. I am a certified neurolinguistic programming (NLP) practitioner and I integrate NLP techniques into my work with clients when they are appropriate. In this case, Richard had already described his internal resource as the perception of the pleasant sensation of chi moving down his leg and out his big toe. This sensation assured him that his energy around the surgery site was no longer completely stagnant—in fact, it could be drained off and circulated. He understood that one of the most basic tenets of Chinese medicine is that blocked or stagnant chi is primarily responsible for illness.

I helped Richard establish the resource anchor by having him think of and remember the pleasant sensation of the flow of chi energy down his leg and his resulting feeling of hopefulness. As he was internally focused on these positive experiences, I instructed him to touch the tips of the thumb and little finger of his right hand together and hold them together for approximately thirty seconds, the duration of his internal focusing. After he established the chi resource anchor, I had him practice a few times by imagining himself in specific situations and contexts. In each new context, I directed him to fire off the anchor (touch his fingers together in the same way) while recalling the positive feelings and sensations. In this way, Richard built in a new, easy-to-access tool he could use whenever he started to feel depressed or fearful of ongoing pain. This made him feel in control of what had been his feeling of hopelessness.

In our next session we began to address Richard's limiting beliefs associated with suffering. These included beliefs that were directly connected with the surgery and his physical body as well as his more global, core beliefs. Again, we used a variety of Dynamic Energetic Healing® techniques, and at the end of the session, Richard remarked that he felt his chi moving down his leg, corroborating that energy-based therapies (including EFT and chakra tapping) move the chi in very noticeable ways. This successful therapeutic result was possible because the chi energy associated with his cognitive limiting beliefs about suffering contributed to keeping the chi at his surgery site contracted and blocked. The energy interventions helped to move the stuck chi, which dissipated the limiting beliefs, and so the pain from Richard's surgery site began to diminish. As he collapsed the energy fields (or thought fields) associated with fear and pain *at the belief level*, Richard experienced immediate energetic and proprioceptive relief as sensations of chi coursed down his leg from the surgery site. What a wonderful example of the power of thought to keep physical pain localized! Richard's experience is also a great example illustrating how Dynamic Energetic Healing® quickly and effectively releases *at the energetic level* information that perpetuates pain and suffering. Richard's biofeedback was immediate and undeniable.

A couple of sessions later, Richard selected (via manual muscle testing) a few other interventions from my repertoire. One of his selections was the meditation that involves using a mantra while visualizing golden divine light coming into the crown chakra and out through the third-eye point (sixth chakra) every time the individual chants a syllable of the mantra. We chanted together for four minutes. Afterwards, Richard reported that once again his chi was stimulated and moving down his leg from the surgery site and out his toe.

There are many explanations for why and how sacred sound current works its magic, from the frequency of the sound current (often called vibrational healing), to the Gurumuki language itself, and to Sheldrake's morphic resonance theories. I have used this meditation technique, called Kirtan Kriya, for over twenty years. I learned it from Yogi Bhajan. (See chapter 25 for a full description of this meditation).

I want to emphasize that through a variety of techniques, Richard experienced his essential energy system being activated for powerful self-healing. He now knows that he can fire off his NLP anchor, tap on EFT points, or chant a mantra to activate his circulating chi for self-healing. For me, this is empirically validating and exciting.

Richard terminated therapy with a larger perspective on what this trauma was all about for him. He is through his chronic pain, fears, and negative thinking, and now he knows that he will heal. He also knows he has an energy body that responds positively to specific stimuli. *Through his own healing process*, Richard eliminated his limiting core beliefs about suffering. He also strengthened his connection to his Higher Power or God, about which he was uncertain when we started his treatment. He discovered that he was angry at God and that he *carried a grudge against God that he wasn't even aware of*. We eliminated this grudge as a very important step toward Richard reconnecting to his spirituality, something he had been yearning for but had not identified as a problem when he first came to see me.

Richard needed only nine sessions to complete his treatment. Through Dynamic Energetic Healing® and acupuncture he was able to resolve the physical pain that his doctors had been unable to address successfully. What's more, he overcame the feelings of hopelessness that were taking him down the road to pharmaceutical drugs and the belief that life is pain. And finally, he strengthened his connection to Spirit through experiential validation that we are energetic beings with a connection to the Infinite. Richard's faith in God is restored, and he is now able to move forward toward a normal and productive life once again.

3

RESOLVING DEPRESSION, INSOMNIA, AND SUICIDAL THOUGHTS: HEALING THE AFTERMATH OF CHILDHOOD ABUSE AND TRAUMA

A friend of Amy's referred her to me for counseling. Amy was twenty-five years old, bright, pretty, and angry. She worked as an editor at a major publishing company—a great deal of responsibility for someone so young. She was controlling and a perfectionist, and she admitted to having a hot temper. She was athletic and active, yet she had been depressed for years.

Amy and her brother (who was two years younger) were products of divorce, and they had lived with their mother from the time Amy was five years old. About three years later, Amy's mother remarried and the three of them moved in with Amy's new stepfather. Amy remained with her family until the middle of high school, by which time the family had moved four times. She couldn't take her stepfather's cruel discipline, and finally she told him off during a particularly heated exchange. During her junior year, Amy's mother and stepfather decided that Amy needed to live elsewhere. She went to live with her biological father, and so was separated from her brother.

Amy was always very protective of her brother, and the separation from him was extremely painful and difficult for her. When Amy was a sophomore in college she received some bad news—her brother, who was still in high school, had been in an auto accident. He had been driving two friends; one was killed and the other was injured but recovered. Amy's brother was OK physically, but he never seemed the same to Amy afterwards. She believed he never recovered from the accident because he felt guilty about the death and injury of his friends. In addition, he admitted to Amy that their stepfather had physically abused him and that their older stepbrother had sexually abused him. He began to isolate himself and stopped calling Amy. All of this upset Amy tremendously. She told me her stepfather regularly hit her and her brother with a belt; he was affiliated with a fundamentalist Christian church and believed that parents should never spare the rod. Amy said that even though the whippings were painful, she never really *felt* traumatized by them—only angry at her stepfather.

Amy got on with her life, marrying and then divorcing. Three months before starting counseling with me, she married again. She said her husband was wonderful, and she felt lucky to have found such a compatible and gentle man. She came for psychotherapy because she had been depressed, felt hopeless much of the time, had constant suicidal thoughts, and woke up throughout each night. This made her feel even worse because she was exhausted all the time, and she was working forty hours a week.

I met with Amy fifteen times over the next year. She was very clear about her therapeutic objectives: she did not want to take antidepressants anymore, she wanted to get over her depression, and she wanted to stop thinking about suicide all the time. She had taken antidepressants in the past but they didn't help at all.

As Amy talked about her problems, it became quite evident to both of us that her starting goal or intention was to be free from feeling emotionally responsible for her brother. She worried about him all the time and always felt sick to her stomach—even vomiting because of her worry. She suspected that worrying about her brother was one of the main factors in her not sleeping through the night. Amy acknowledged being afraid of her feelings, and it was clear from her flat affect that she was emotionally detached in her relating to me.

At the beginning of the next session we established energetic boundaries with her brother using frontal occipital holding and TAT. We then used TAT and chakra tapping to establish energetic boundaries with her emotions generally. Next, I asked via manual muscle testing if there were any energetic origins specific to her starting intention (to be free of feeling emotionally responsible for her brother) that needed to be healed. The muscle testing indicated that there was a current-life origin from an event that occurred when Amy was three years old. As a consequence of a primary disturbance at the origin, Amy was blocking her ability to experience her sadness (i.e., she was repressing it). When I asked Amy if she had any awareness of limiting beliefs associated with this resistance to experience or express her own sadness, she immediately came up with three: it's a sign of weakness to feel sad; sadness is pointless and doesn't solve anything; and her mother was always crying and it drove her crazy.

During our next session, Amy told me that she became most aware of her sadness at night in bed, when she would, for no apparent reason, start sobbing and feel nothing but overwhelming sadness. As we talked about this phenomenon, Amy realized that there was a connection between her feelings of sadness and her brother not having called her in three years. She felt a great deal of loss.

We reviewed the three limiting beliefs Amy had identified in the previous session. Keeping those beliefs and her new awareness of the relationship between her sadness and her brother in mind, we used frontal occipital holding. This intervention cleared all the negative emotional charge from the limiting beliefs and restored Amy's ability to experience her own sadness.

Her muscle testing had identified another current-life energetic origin that occurred when Amy was twelve years old. When I asked her to reflect on what occurred in her life at that time, she knew immediately what the event was. She and her brother were in the next room while her mother gave birth, screaming, via a natural childbirth process without any drugs. This was a highly charged emotional event for Amy, during which she suffered a great deal of trauma, which she was still carrying. Her energy field had fragmented, and she experienced both soul loss and a degree of dissociation. Her muscle testing called for frontal occipital holding, which cleared the fragmentation of her energy field, the soul loss, and the dissociation completely. (Note that Amy's experience is a classic example of an overwhelming event that causes emotional trauma and PTSD. This type of experience is explained in detail in chapter 10, "Understanding Trauma within Dynamic Energetic Healing®.")

Next, we discovered that Amy's ability to experience fear had become blocked. Because of the traumatic event that occurred when Amy was twelve, her fear got stuck (in a manner of speaking). Since then, she had been unable to emotionally process her experience of fear—it had been frozen at the time of the traumatic event. At the unconscious level, the traumatic event was Amy's inner reference point for experiencing fear. At the time, she had been unable to process her fear in a healthy and complete way—the event was so overwhelming that Amy's fear simply paralyzed her. Once we had identified this aspect of Amy's condition, Amy drew some conclusions; these were her limiting beliefs about her experience of fear.

We identified seven specific limiting beliefs. Four of them were these:

- I can't control my feelings—I get overwhelmed by them and then get angry.
- I won't be able to think rationally or make good decisions.
- When I'm overwhelmed by fear, my whole body starts shaking and my heart begins to pound faster.
- I can't be in control—it's scary.

I directed Amy to reflect on the traumatic incident and the seven limiting beliefs so they would all be present in her collective thought field. We used frontal occipital holding and chakra tapping to balance out and neutralize all of the limiting beliefs 100 percent.

At our next session Amy was feeling better. She was sleeping a little better, and her suicidal thoughts had diminished significantly. She reported that her depressed mood was much reduced, and although she was still thinking about her brother, it didn't bring her down as much as before.

As various elements of early trauma are released through Dynamic Energetic Healing® methods, it is typical for clients to notice significant changes in their mood and attitude fairly quickly. A major principle of energy psychology is that information from past trauma is carried in our energy field at various levels. When I use energetic strategies to release trauma (the effectiveness of which is immediately corroborated through manual muscle testing), the information that has been causing various disturbing symptoms essentially evaporates as the energy fields that contained the information collapse. When the energy fields are collapsed, the client comes into homeostasis. Assuming that the client is not retraumatized, the symptoms that persisted for many years prior will disappear as a natural consequence. It is not necessary to ruminate for hours on end about traumatic events in our past. Insight is always satisfying to the intellect, but insight alone does not resolve trauma. Trauma must be released in order for homeostasis to occur.

At our next session, we continued pursuing the intention for Amy to free herself from emotional responsibility for her brother. We returned to the energetic origin when she was twelve because we had not completed our work on this. I had an intuition that Amy had no energetic boundaries with childbirth. I confirmed this using manual muscle testing and determined that EFT would be the intervention of choice. Amy had increasing awareness emerge as she tapped the meridian points. She realized that her vicarious and traumatic experience of childbirth had been painful and intrusive. She also realized that she had not only had to take care of herself but of someone else as well—her brother. What's more, she had felt a responsibility to do something to help her mother, who was screaming in the next room.

Her muscle testing indicated that Amy had established energetic boundaries with childbirth at all levels except throughout her chakras. We needed frontal occipital holding to complete the balance. As I made contact with her, I saw that Amy was contracted energetically at her second chakra. I asked for spiritual assistance and connected with the archetype of the Divine Feminine, which balanced her second chakra and restored her boundaries with childbirth to 100 percent.

Muscle testing next indicated that Amy had absorbed the trauma from both her mother and her brother. I refer to this as collective trauma, which happens when someone witnesses another person's trauma and absorbs that trauma into their own energy field due to a lack of firm energetic boundaries. In Amy's case, she was not able to stay emotionally separate from her mother or her brother because she was emotionally overwhelmed and had no boundaries with either of them. Instead of remaining an autonomous individual, being supportive and holding the field with her positive intention for her mother and brother, Amy had unintentionally merged with the energy fields of her mother and her brother during a time of extreme vulnerability. This is an excellent example of the importance of having solid energetic boundaries with the people we are in contact with day to day, especially family members.

Her muscle testing selected frontal occipital holding as the intervention of choice. As I gently contacted Amy's head, I saw the intense fear from her mother and brother as a gray area being held around her body in her auric field. As I continued to gently hold her head, the gray gradually diffused until I saw that finally there was balance in Amy's energy field.

The only thing left to resolve at this energetic origin was some residual shock, fear, and feelings of extreme vulnerability. Amy reflected on those feelings as she referred back to the event while tapping on the prescribed meridian points. After two cycles of tapping, she had released all residual negative emotional charge from the energetic origin. There was nothing left to do—the origin had cleared 100 percent. We both ended the session feeling good about what we had accomplished.

Amy's overall condition improved significantly over the next few months. She still thought about her brother but no longer worried about him. She described her experience as a sense of emotional detachment from her brother, though she still felt tremendous love for him. She was no longer obsessing about him or feeling guilty about all the things she should or could have done to help him. She no longer thought about suicide, and on a scale of 1 to 10, with 10 being the worst, she described her experience of depression at 2. She was sleeping four to five hours at a stretch every night and found that she could go back to sleep more easily after awakening early in the morning. Overall, she was feeling very satisfied with the work we had done together.

Amy had decided to go back to school to get out of her job, which she hated. Though she was concerned about the financial stresses that this would bring, she was feeling good enough about herself to know that she deserved to be happy. We identified and cleared some lingering psychoenergetic reversal connected to her fears of being unable to sleep deeply, and Amy used EFT to clear a few residual limiting beliefs that still generated some anxiety around sleep, including these:

- Because it has gone on for so long, I now believe I will have irregular sleep patterns forever.
- Any little sound will wake me up.
- My husband will always wake me up when he gets up for work early in the morning.

It took Amy about ten minutes to completely collapse the energy fields associated with these limiting beliefs. Her muscle testing indicated that there was nothing more that we needed to do to address her sleep issue because her sleep disturbance was tied closely to the trauma that we had released earlier.

As we met for Amy's last session, all of her initial therapeutic goals had been addressed to her satisfaction. Amy was ready to terminate therapy with me, and we briefly recapitulated the work that she had accomplished with me.

Amy had accomplished a great deal and felt very good about the work we had done together. As a footnote, when I first met Amy, she was vehemently against the idea of having children. This made sense because of the trauma she had experienced connected to her mother giving birth. Even though her husband wanted to have children, Amy wouldn't hear of it. About six months later, after she terminated therapy with me, another client (Amy's friend who had referred Amy to me) told me that Amy was pregnant and was excited about having a child.

All things are possible when old trauma is released from our energy field.

Neutralizing Present-Day Allergy Symptoms: Learning Psychopomp Work in a Past-Life Origin

Amy, who we met in case history 3, came for a follow-up session just to make sure that everything was remaining stable and in balance after all the work we had done. Amy muscle tested positive on this, so I asked her what she would like to work on for that last session. Amy was experiencing very bad allergies, and she wanted to get rid of them because they made her "suffer and feel tired." It was mid-June, the time in the Willamette Valley of Oregon when hay farmers harvest and cut their crop. Consequently, there was a lot of pollen permeating the valley air, and many people suffer from spring and summer allergies at that time of year in Oregon.

I began asking questions while muscle testing her. We determined that a past-life energetic origin was responsible for the allergy problem Amy was having in her current life. With some brief prompting, Amy regressed easily into the energy field of the past-life origin, which had occurred three karmic lifetimes ago.

As she was suspended above the scene in which the specific event occurred, Amy needed to visualize and channel healing white light down into the scene as her first intervention for soul-level healing. When she had done this, I asked through muscle testing if there was anything more that needed to be done prior to associating into the past-life scene—no. So I directed Amy to float gently down into the event, descending to exactly the right time and appropriate place in this past life as she associated into the experience.

I am able to share with you a verbatim account of Amy's past-life experience because I am a touch typist and recorded this on my laptop computer in the session. Here is Amy's story:

I see a teepee and it looks like it is brown, possibly animal hide. It looks like I'm in a camp. There are other teepees. It's daylight now. I see mountains and green all around. We are on a dirt area. It's a sunny day. I feel I'm a little child, maybe about six or seven years old. I am a girl. I feel like I'm walking around looking for something. There are other people around that are all busy with their chores. Looks like I find the other kids out in the trees, playing. I go over there to play with them. We all start running in a field. We start rolling around in the tall grass. We are trying to make designs like snow angels in the grass on our backs.

We are by a little creek. Some of them are playing in the water. A couple of them are trying to swim across, so it must be a river. I'm still on the shore throwing stuff in the water. Probably about eight kids, with two of them on the other side of the river. The two that swam across are coming back and both make it back OK. Some kids are jumping off a small rock ledge into the water. One of them slips and falls and hits their head on the rock on the way down. The older kids go to help. They find the boy who isn't waking up. They tell me and another child to run back and get help. We are running back through the fields back into the camp. We tell our parents and tell them to come and get the doctor, and we lead them back to the river. The kid is still unconscious with blood coming from his head. I'm just watching. I think I'm in shock. I'm just watching and curious about what's going on.

I muscle tested Amy to find out if she had indeed been traumatized by the incident. The muscle testing indicated yes and selected frontal occipital holding as the best intervention to address the trauma.

As soon as I made contact with her, the impressions began coming very quickly. I realized right away that the ground was cursed and that Amy carried an earthbound spirit from someone who had been buried at the place Amy had described in the story. The earthbound spirit indicated it needed to be in dialogue with Amy.

I stopped the frontal occipital holding and told Amy what needed to happen next. I asked her to close her eyes, go inside, and ask the earthbound spirit to talk to her. The following is Amy's verbatim description of their dialogue.

He [the spirit] wants to know why I think I can help it. Because I am aware of your presence. He says he doesn't know where else to go. He became very ill and died and was buried there. They buried him in a hurry for some reason. He's just confused. He was fifteen when he died. He got pneumonia. It was wintertime. He didn't mean the ground to be cursed.

I interjected to ask the spirit to remember his guardian spirit. He said it was a bear. Amy and he called his guardian spirit animal to take him to his spiritual family. Amy continued, "He sees it so he starts to follow it and says thank you. They kind of just fly away." When we muscle tested, all supernatural interference relating to the attachment by the earthbound spirit had cleared.

Next, Amy reidentified as the young girl in the past-life regression and needed the Tibetan bell and TAT to release all residual contamination from the past lifetime caused by being on the cursed ground. This residual contamination had been responsible for generating her allergy symptoms. When we next muscle tested, Amy was reassured that all contamination had cleared and there was no other old interference that had been causing her allergy symptoms.

Amy shared with me her two new awarenesses from having gone through this experience. The first was, "Don't roll on cursed ground." The second was the need to be sensitive to the dying process so she can help others to transition. This was a wonderful learning for her to share with me, because she had no previous awareness of the need for psychopomp work. As a footnote, the muscle testing indicated that Amy would be completely free of allergy symptoms in three days. When I spoke with her about three weeks later, I asked about her allergies—she had not had any problems since our last meeting. As Amy and I discussed her past-life experience, it was obvious to us that it wasn't just rolling around in the tall grass that was responsible for her allergy symptoms. Instead, it was being exposed to the cursed ground and an earthbound spirit that were responsible.

The last point I want to make is that Amy had never done any past-life regression or hypnosis before. I was impressed by the ease with which she was able to elicit and narrate her experience of this past-life origin. But I have come to recognize that nearly everyone who is directed by their own muscle testing to regress to a past-life trauma in order to heal a current problem manages to do this work remarkably well. Amy was no exception.

5

HEALING THE ROOTS OF
MELANOMA SKIN CANCER:
DISIDENTIFYING FROM TWO
NEGATIVE ARCHETYPES

Nadine is in charge of a corporate childcare center. Her doctor referred her to me for depression. Nadine was very clear about her therapeutic objectives, which she described to me during the intake session. She wanted to clear out some of her old patterns, which included being a victim and being abused. She characterized herself as having weak boundaries and described herself as often being "sucked dry" by people she spent time with, which included her colleagues, parents, and even the children where she worked. She further described herself as being "too empathic" and feeling a "codependent compulsion to join others and thus lose myself in relationship."

In addition, Nadine wanted to get healthier. She had developed melanoma, a skin cancer, on her back a year before. Since that initial lesion, the cancer had been popping up everywhere on her body. Her doctor cut out the lesions, but a new one always emerged somewhere else. Nadine told me that chemotherapy is not an effective treatment for this kind of skin cancer.

Nadine was also experiencing a great deal of despair. Around the time when she developed her cancer, her partner of five years, Steven, began pulling away. They were very close emotionally, and it came as a complete surprise to her when Steven left her to marry another woman two weeks before her first appointment with me. Since then, Nadine had been feeling suicidal and beside herself. She had started taking Paxil and thyroid supplements about six months before but found that they hadn't been helping her since Steven left. So she took her doctor's advice and called me for an appointment.

During our first session, we cleared Nadine's abandonment trauma that was generated by Steven's departure. There were a number of associated affective components, including shock, guilt, and pervasive sadness, as well as a limiting belief that we had to clear (i.e., that being abandoned is a traumatic loss). Nadine was convinced that it was completely her fault that Steven had left, and thus she felt totally responsible for what happened. Once the trauma was released, Nadine helped me to better understand that not only had she no energetic boundaries with Steven, but she had no boundaries with anyone! Through a variety of energetic strategies, she was able to restore 100 percent energetic boundaries not only with Steven *but with people in general.* Not a bad start for an initial intake session.

When Nadine came for her session the following week, she was furious! She hadn't recalled feeling that angry since she was a child. She was having violent dreams that were totally uncharacteristic of her, dreams that involved hurting Steven. She did not recall ever having that kind of imagery before. She was very nervous about all this anger that was surfacing, and she felt that things were getting worse. She used the words "I feel uncomfortable in my skin."

I wondered to myself whether this was an unconscious reference to her skin cancer. I had learned from my years of training in processwork that repressed emotional energy often gets rerouted into the body as a chronic physical symptom or disease process. Since I know that energy takes on different forms of expression, it made sense that the energy of anger could express itself as the energy of cancer. I wondered how this was going to play out in Nadine's therapy. But that was to be for our next session.

As we talked about what was going on right then and there, Nadine's starting intention became self-evident: "*I want to disidentify with the Victim archetype and regain full access to and expression of my anger while feeling safe with my anger* (i.e., establish 100 percent energetic boundaries with my anger)."

There was no psychoenergetic reversal on the intention, nor were there any objections from any internal part of her to continue on the intention. When I muscle tested Nadine to determine if there were any energetic origins, we found a current-life origin that had occurred fifteen years before when she was thirty-two years old. As she reviewed her own chronology, Nadine was able to pinpoint the event that was the energetic origin. Her then-husband, to whom she had been married for seven years, was having an affair with his secretary. When she had discovered this, she was in despair.

As I started inquiring on what might be part of this energetic origin, Nadine's muscle testing indicated that some kind of dark energy pattern was trying to mislead me (as is usually the case with dark energy forms). Supernatural interference that emerges during muscle testing immediately becomes the priority. I have found through the years that if supernatural interference is specifically identified and then released, a great deal of the rest of the matrix that is blocking the intention frequently falls away by itself.

After inquiring more deeply, it was determined that Nadine was carrying a *self-generated curse*. Most people can understand how someone else's anger toward them can be so penetrating—it feels like being cursed! The lingering negativity from someone's harsh words directed at you often feels like toxic residue that is hard to shake off. If the intent to hurt you by using words is intentional, it can feel like shards of glass penetrating your energy field. Turning thought forms into weapons like this is a malevolent use of consciousness. Though most people would not describe it as such, words can pierce you more deeply then a knife can.

In Nadine's case, her feelings of unworthiness were so great at the discovery of her husband's affair that she turned her shame inward, creating the power of a curse. Nadine's self-esteem was so poor at the time that she took on all the responsibility for what had happened and became overidentified with the Victim archetype. I asked her if she knew what this meant. She did— she had experienced being a victim all her life, and she was willing to do anything to free herself of this painful experience.

Nadine's manual muscle testing selected a series of interventions necessary to release this self-generated curse. First we chimed a Tibetan bowl, followed by Nadine applying two minutes of self-administered NAEM tapping. At this point, her muscle testing indicated that she was still holding this energy at the soul level and the unconscious level.

Then Nadine selected frontal occipital holding as the intervention of choice. As I made contact with her, I connected with the energy of the Divine Feminine. I received very rapid impressions of a large, flowing feminine angelic form, embracing Nadine's neglected, needy, sad inner child and infusing that child with love and nurturing. I felt that a part of Nadine had just become fortified with something that she never received enough of.

When we next checked her muscle testing, the self-generated curse was completely released, and Nadine had disidentified with the Victim archetype 100 percent.

As we continued to muscle test and inquire what else we needed in order to work on this intention, it quickly became evident that Nadine was somehow obstructing her ability to access and express her anger. Frequently, there are many limiting beliefs that support this pattern. But in Nadine's case, her muscle testing indicated that it was not necessary for her to identify what any of these beliefs were. All that was required was for Nadine to focus her thoughts on how difficult it was to feel and express her anger while I sustained the frontal occipital holding intervention.

As soon as I started my invocation, I connected with the healing spirit of Jesus. I started to feel his Sacred Heart energy infuse Nadine with the love that is beyond the polarities. I realized during this process that this love is nonconceptual and unconditional. It is the love beyond good and evil that includes good and evil. It is the love that transcends judgment, for judgment is of the conceptual, separating mind. This love is very pure, and because it is nonjudgmental, its healing powers run deep. This is what Jesus revealed to me.

When I asked Nadine what she had been aware of, her thought was that she wouldn't be loved if she expressed her anger. Spirit knew exactly what medicine Nadine needed at this time. When I next muscle tested Nadine, she was no longer blocked to experiencing her own anger. What's more, in the process she had established 100 percent energetic boundaries with her own and others' anger. This completed our session.

When Nadine came in for her third session two weeks later, she was feeling stronger inside herself, although she was still having her ups and downs. She had decided to lower her dosage of Paxil and intended to wean herself off it completely. After a brief discussion of the changes Nadine was beginning to notice, she decided she wanted to address her melanoma. After a bit of muscle testing, we came up with the following starting intention: "I want more conscious awareness of the dynamics involved in my cancer process and the underlying need for keeping it. I want to heal this disease."

To test for psychoenergetic reversal, I had her repeat the intention statement aloud and then muscle tested her. She was reversed on all five core psychoenergetic reversal statements associated with healing: I don't want to, I don't deserve to, It is not safe to, It is not possible to, and I won't heal from this cancer. Our muscle testing indicated that Nadine needed the frontal occipital holding intervention in order to correct the psychoenergetic reversals.

Shortly after making contact with Nadine, I saw a group of Native American women surrounding Nadine, their drums beating as they directed loving, nurturing energy into her very cells. I sensed their healing energy penetrating deeply into her being. When I asked Nadine what she was aware of, she said she thought she really needs people in her life rather than acting stoically. She elaborated by saying that she tends to push people away because of some need to be independent. Her illness was part of taking on Steven's issues; she made them her own. She had never considered this before, and it struck her as a revelation. The muscle testing revealed that she was still psychoenergetically reversed at the unconscious level and throughout her chakras.

The next intervention Nadine requested was the chiming of the Tibetan bell, followed once again by frontal occipital holding. As I made contact with Nadine, I got strong impressions of her *Shakti* energy (the Hindu term for the powerful feminine aspect of the life-force energy) being stimulated at her second chakra. The next impression I got indicated she had a blockage preventing her energy from opening up at the second chakra! I didn't know what this meant, but it was evident that there was a disturbance centered in her second chakra. When I asked Nadine what she noticed, she said she heard an affirmation in her head saying that she can be loved without having to be ill! Then she said she wondered if it was about Steven—they had had sex only five times during their five-year relationship. At the unconscious level, Nadine had carried a belief that she couldn't be loved without being ill. I realized that I was seeing Steven's sexual blockage.

As Nadine and I talked about this, she began to realize that she had been energetically absorbing Steven's pain and fear of his own sexuality, which was the reason for their compromised sexual relationship. Nadine had taken on Steven's sexual trauma. As we continued to discuss this, Nadine told me that because she still felt very protective of Steven, she didn't want to let go of his sexual pain and trauma if it meant that it would go back to him. I found her belief about this very interesting. I wondered how many other people carry the same limiting belief that if they let go of trauma they have absorbed from someone else, the trauma would go right back to the other person, like a rubber band snapping back into place. I used a computer metaphor to help Nadine to better understand this: it's like copying a file. When a file is copied from the computer hard drive onto a floppy disk, the original file still stays on the hard drive. Nadine needed to understand that Steven still had his sexual trauma, regardless of her intent to take it away from him.

I began to realize that Nadine was identified with the Martyr archetype. The Martyr ascribes value and meaning to suffering, and that is exactly what Nadine was doing. Before doing anything else, we needed to clear Nadine's identification with the Martyr archetype. Her muscle testing indicated that an energetic origin from a past lifetime was responsible for her identification with this archetype in her current life. Interestingly, the muscle testing indicated it was not necessary to regress back to the past-life energetic origin and get the story of the event in order to heal and resolve her identification with the Martyr archetype.

As part of the release process of the archetype, I had a strong intuition that I needed to first test Nadine for psychoenergetic reversal on her willingness to let go of Steven's trauma. She was indeed psychoenergetically reversed on the following three core reversals: It's not possible to, I don't deserve to, and I will not let go of Steven's trauma.

Next I asked through our muscle testing if it would be possible to select an intervention to address the psychoenergetic reversals and the Martyr archetype simultaneously—yes, and the intervention was frontal occipital holding. I believe we were able to do this because the deeply embedded beliefs that showed up as psychoenergetic reversals were part of the Martyr archetype that Nadine was identified with. During the intervention, I perceived an inner conflict within Nadine—her energy field was expanding and then contracting, expanding and then contracting, and so on. Eventually, her energy field came into homeostasis as a result of the intervention. When I asked Nadine what she had noticed, she said she had felt a lot of fear of what she would be if she didn't suffer. During the intervention she felt physical tightness, and then she felt it finally release. She had the thought that if she let go of this pattern of taking on the pain of others, her relationships would be totally different, and she didn't know what that would be like.

We were excited when muscle testing the intervention's results showed that everything had cleared completely. Each of the three psychoenergetic reversals was corrected. Nadine was no longer identified with the Martyr archetype at any level, and she now had 100 percent energetic boundaries with Steven. When I asked her if there was anything else that needed to be addressed on the initial intention, her muscle testing indicated there was nothing more. To me, this meant that there was no more energetic fuel generating melanoma. By clearing the energetic origins relating to her overidentification with two prominent archetypes, which were the primary causes of her dysfunctional relationships, Nadine dissolved the roots of her cancer. Having accomplished this, one would expect that the melanoma would disappear rapidly. She agreed to track this very carefully with her doctor. Two years later, Nadine reported being completely free of cancer.

6

TRANSFORMING THE FEAR
OF BULIMIC PURGING:
SHAMANIC SPIRIT RELEASEMENT

Elyce has been tormented by food and eating issues for most of her life. Elyce is now in her forties, and this troublesome pattern had reappeared. Though she was managing to control the urge to vomit after eating and maintain a healthy diet, she suspected that the recent death of her father had restimulated her latent bulimia. She admitted that even though she knew, objectively, that she is relatively slim, she continued to perceive herself as obese when looking in the mirror. This had not worried her because she had the self-destructive bulimic behaviors under control—that is, until a few weeks prior to coming to see me.

Elyce had been struggling with the inner compulsion to vomit after eating and had come for help on the issue: "There is a part of me that continues to resist letting go of my bulimia." When she came for her first session, she hadn't purged for a while, but until a few weeks before she was purging three or four times a week. It had frightened her that this old behavior might easily take her over and become out of her control. Elyce worried that she was damaging herself physically from the violent vomiting, particularly her throat. She admitted that it felt like a huge control issue. She didn't want to regress back to starving herself (which she almost did years ago when she fought with anorexia), and now she was also struggling to overcome her powerful bulimic urges.

Elyce's primary internal sensory focus was the feeling in her stomach. "If I feel any pressure in my stomach, I have to get rid of it." This proprioceptive perception was of a penetrating oversensitivity. Elyce shared that if she felt any pressure in her stomach after eating, her thoughts immediately turned to the need to purge. The pressure generated the fear that she had eaten too much and that she would get fat. So, her starting intention to address her concerns was, *"I want to stop the compulsive need to vomit if I feel any pressure in my stomach after I eat something."*

After clearing for psychoenergetic reversal and objections on the intention, our muscle testing indicated there was an energetic origin on her paternal grandfather's lineage that needed healing. As we talked about this for a moment, Elyce commented that she has had problems with her throat throughout her life. This was a curious interjection. I had her focus her attention on her throat and she described it as feeling sticky. We were following her second attention. As Elyce kept her awareness at her throat, her discomfort with the stickiness increased.

In the next moment, I had an impression that the frontal occipital holding intervention might be useful to gather more information before addressing the energetic origin. I was following my own second attention. I stayed with it and asked Elyce with muscle testing what the best direction would be to proceed at this point. The muscle testing confirmed my intuition and we proceeded with this intervention.

As soon as I made contact with Elyce, I was drawn to my upper-world Tibetan master, whose charge is to direct the spirits of the recently deceased to their next destination. He often assists me by directing healing energies to my clients in various ways. He began specific vibrational chanting while shaking his Tibetan rattle (or prayer wheel), focusing on Elyce's torso, particularly her solar plexus. I saw a dark cavern in it, followed quickly by a gargoyle-like being trying to retreat deeper into Elyce's body. But very quickly the chanting was too powerful to hide from, and this dark being was drawn out—along with two others just like it—as though pulled by a tractor beam. I saw my upper-world teacher directing these beings back to the universe from whence they came.

Next I saw what appeared to be an interdimensional portal that was very energetically active; it was expanding and contracting. It was evident that those beings had used this portal to enter Elyce's stomach, where they had then established residency. As my spiritual ally continued his very focused, directed chanting, the energetic movement of the portal froze and became inactive. The dark interior of the cavern became an azure blue. Soon, the cavern filled up with a white light and I knew that the healing was complete.

Just at that time, I heard a strange sound that lasted for about ten seconds. I couldn't identify it—I thought it might be coming from the waiting room outside my office. Internally, I bid good-bye to my helper and thanked him for his generous help. He had done an extraction on Elyce and sealed off the entry portal to block any other exploitative beings from occupying that inner space in Elyce. What a blessing!

When I asked Elyce what she had experienced, she said that the sound I heard had come from her, but she had no idea where it had come from. She was very startled by making the low, guttural sound and uncertain about what it might mean. I told her that we would have to wait and see what unfolded in the coming days and weeks. She felt good about the experience as we discussed its possible meaning for her.

In our follow-up session, Elyce shared that her fears associated with the purging were gone. This was a tremendous relief, but she admitted that there was still a part of her that didn't want to let go of that fear. She reasoned that if she truly let go of that fear of bulimic purging, she would be letting go of the behavioral mechanism that helped her to maintain control over how much she ate. This nagging fear is part of Elyce's obsessive-compulsive propensities, which tend to get restimulated and amplified by stress.

Elyce has more work to do on this issue. This work will include clearing psychoenergetic reversals and depotentiating shame as the core, organizing emotional energy that everything else is connected to. We also need to address the ancestral energetic origin identified in the first session. But by using Dynamic Energetic Healing® techniques, I helped Elyce to clear her field of fear and, based on my subjective perceptions, to release the intrusive beings that were responsible for that fear. That was an excellent first step in a successful integrated treatment approach to Elyce's complex problem.

TRANSMUTING THE TRAUMA
OF EARLY SEXUAL ABUSE:
CORRECTING A LIFETIME
OF DISEMBODIMENT

Tressa was referred to me by a friend who was a former client of mine. A lesbian, Tressa initially wanted to come to terms with a former lover named Sue. Five months after their relationship began, Tressa realized that for reasons she didn't understand she couldn't be vulnerable—so Sue left. A few months later, Tressa discovered that Sue was in another relationship. Tressa felt hurt and angry because she still loved Sue. In our first session, Tressa did some forgiveness work, established 100 percent energetic boundaries with Sue, and by the end of the session felt that all her negativity toward Sue had been resolved.

As we started our second session, Tressa acknowledged feeling much lighter toward Sue, no longer feeling the pain of the loss or any of the desperation she had been feeling before our first session. Her depressed mood was gone, and she was accepting of what had happened with Sue. Now she felt open for however her relationship with Sue might unfold.

Tressa's next issue was her relationship with her mother, who she described as very controlling and manipulative. Tressa was in her mid-thirties, yet her mother still "tracked her down" every day to check up on her and make sure she had her hand on Tressa's pulse. Tressa wanted her mother to honor her boundaries, but she felt guilty and uncomfortable about being direct and assertive with her. Because of her mother's pattern of intrusiveness and claiming ownership of Tressa and her two siblings, Tressa had internalized her anger. After some discussion with me about the issue, Tressa arrived at the following intention statement: *"I want a mutually respectful, adult relationship with my mom."* This was our starting point.

As we muscle tested for any form of interference on this intention, we determined that an energetic origin had occurred when Tressa was eleven years old. It didn't take Tressa long to identify that year as a pivotal turning point in her life. For the previous five years, she had been continually molested by her stepfather. While they lived with him, Tressa and her family enjoyed an upper-middle-class lifestyle in a well-to-do section of the city—something they had never had before. When Tressa was eleven, she finally told her mother what was happening. When Tressa's mother confirmed the truth, she divorced Tressa's stepfather. The family became destitute again.

As we continued to inquire via manual muscle testing, it became clear that some supernatural interference was associated with this energetic origin—specifically, an entanglement that was still active between Tressa and her mother. In this case, the entanglement was a toxic energetic connection that had persisted through time, carrying unresolved resentment, pain, and especially guilt about what had happened as a result of Tressa's admission to her mother. Tressa still felt responsible for the poverty that she felt she had brought upon the family, and these feelings were energetically linked directly to her mother.

The first intervention required to clear and dissolve this entanglement was frontal occipital holding. I began to experience images and impressions of Gaia, the spirit of the earth, as I saw Tressa's energetic boundaries with her mother expand outwards and become more robust. Gaia was infusing her with earth energy, helping to ground her and make her more solid. *Tressa became aware that she always blamed herself regardless of the situation.*

Muscle testing then indicated frontal occipital holding again. During the next three minutes, I saw a bright light come forth from nonordinary reality and move into Tressa's physical body, absorbing what I saw as old, stagnant, dark negative energy in her pelvis and reproductive areas around her ovaries. As we conducted the intervention for the third time, I saw the healing energy of Jesus come into her first and second chakras. This energy filled the chakras with golden light that was intended to replenish and restore energetic balance to those areas that had held the cumulative toxic energy from the sexual abuse from the years past.

Our next intervention was chiming the Tibetan cymbals, for clearing away any residual entanglement energy in Tressa's second chakra. Finally, our muscle testing directed us to use the frontal occipital holding intervention one last time.

During this three or four minutes, I shifted into the dreamtime experience and had a vision of the spirit beings of a Native American tribe becoming very active in their compassionate undertakings. As I held my hands gently around Tressa's head, I immediately saw a large medicine wheel with only the women of the tribe standing in a circle surrounding Tressa, who was standing next to a large, brightly burning fire. As they chanted softly on her behalf, each woman approached Tressa with healing food and other ritual gifts to affirm their love for her along with their blessing for her healing. They then took Tressa into their sweat lodge for purification. When this ritual was completed, the shaman of the tribe accompanied Tressa to his place and gave her some healing herb tea. She fell into a deep, feverish sleep for three days of further purification. During this time, she was attended to by the women.

When the three days were over, the women brought Tressa out to reconnect with the rest of the tribe. Tressa was healed of the toxicity of the entanglement with her mother *and all of the related sexual abuse.* The manual muscle testing corroborated this—there was nothing more to address related to the intention.

Tressa reported that at the end of the frontal occipital holding intervention, just before I removed my hands from her head, she felt a powerful surge of energy that originated in her pelvis and traveled up through the rest of her body. She felt energized and clear. This was where we ended our second session.

Tressa came to her third Dynamic Energetic Healing® session a changed woman. She had decided that Sue was not really good for her, and so she had begun dating again. Along with this conscious letting go of Sue, Tressa had begun to realize that she is an individual worth appreciating. She decided to get another dog (her former companion had died) so she could have someone to open her heart to again. She believed that the dog would help her to open her heart to another person and to be available for a committed relationship.

When I saw Tressa again three weeks later, I asked if she had noticed any other changes since our last session. She had, but she said that one of them was embarrassing to speak about. She decided to talk about it anyway. For the first time in over five years, her orgasms were as wonderful and stimulating as they used to be. I believe this was a direct consequence of all the second-chakra healing she had undergone in our last session.

The other positive change Tressa noticed was that her mother had not been contacting her as often. And Tressa now found herself somehow able to cut her mother off during a phone conversation by simply saying, "Mom, I've got to go now." To Tressa's great surprise, her mother ended the conversation respectfully, without any of her usual criticism. Tressa was happy to be able to set appropriate limits with her mother and have her mother respect them. This outcome dramatically illustrates what can happen when a long-standing entanglement, such as the one connecting Tressa and her mother, is released. It also illustrates the combined power of *energetic* strategies and *shamanic* practices when dark, negative, stagnant, toxic energy from sexual abuse is released from the body and from the chakras. Dramatic positive change happens very rapidly as a result.

Next, Tressa wanted to address a long-standing problem that she described as poor memory and the inability to integrate a lot of information at one time. She became easily flustered when having to deal with a lot of information and had difficulty staying mentally focused. At she described this, I began to wonder if soul loss or some variation of dissociation was involved. Tressa thought she might have had some kind of brain damage from a traumatic birth. She was born with pneumonia, and it had taken the doctors nearly four minutes to clear her lungs of fluid. At the time, they worried that she might be mentally challenged as a result of insufficient oxygen to the brain during these four minutes.

After this discussion, Tressa established the following intention: *"I want to be able to multitask effectively with a clear head, not get overwhelmed, and stay mentally focused and remember things easily."* I perceived that she was not fully embodied. So, after muscle testing determined that Tressa was congruent on her stated intention, I checked to what degree she was in her physical body. We discovered that Tressa was *only 25 percent in her physical body*, and the energetic origin was her own birth, as she had suggested! While muscle testing about the origin, we discovered that an energetic intrusion which occurred during her birth was occupying all seven major chakras. I know that we are most open to supernatural intrusion when we are in a vulnerable or powerless situation—Tressa's case certainly met this criterion.

The first intervention that her muscle testing called for was the Tibetan bell. This cleared the intrusion at the auric-field level, but it remained at all other levels. The next intervention called for was frontal occipital holding. As I gently contacted Tressa's head with my hands and recited my prayer, one of the elders from the Native American tribe appeared. I saw Grandmother performing an extraction ritual on Tressa in nonordinary reality. Grandmother drew a design, first around Tressa's belly and then opposite her belly on her back. These were black circles with small spokes sticking out around the outside every two inches. When this was completed, I could see the dark energy draining from Tressa's solar plexus down through her pelvis and legs, out her feet, and deep into the earth, where it was absorbed. This completed the extraction. When we muscle tested, the intrusion had been released at all levels 100 percent, and there was nothing more to do at this origin. Our muscle testing indicated that Tressa was now 45 percent in her physical body, a large improvement from 25 percent but still far from normal.

Upon further inquiry, muscle testing determined that an additional energetic origin had occurred when Tressa was twenty-six years old. She had been living with a man and his two young kids for nearly eight months and was planning to marry him. He told her he was worried that his kids would disturb Tressa with their chicanery, and so, to Tressa's dismay, he yelled at them quite a lot. Eventually, he began drinking a six-pack of beer every night and isolating himself in his workshop. Tressa became disenchanted by the deteriorating situation and decided to leave him. She left feeling unworthy and unappreciated, disappointed that the man she had planned to marry seemed not to value her needs and interests. For Tressa, this was a personal loss trauma that had never been addressed. The primary affective components of this loss trauma were the feelings of self-devaluation and sadness that she still carried. In addition, we discovered that Tressa's vulnerability had allowed another energetic intrusion to occupy all of her chakras.

Her muscle testing determined that frontal occipital holding would be the best intervention to start with. As soon as I placed my hands gently around Tressa's head, I immediately had a vision of my upper-world Tibetan master who began chanting blessing words and mantras for her healing. After one minute of this, the scene shifted to the transcendent energy of Lord Krishna. My perceptions were of a vast and cosmic vibration of the Allness that is. I fell into a deeply altered state as I momentarily merged with the Allness. After a moment or so, I saw energy coming through Tressa's chakras like multicolored spheres of cosmic color pulsing down her central channel to energize and nourish each of her major chakras. This continued for another moment until the energy slowly dissipated.

When we muscle tested, all traces of the trauma and energetic intrusion had been cleared and released—there was nothing more to address related to the energetic origin. Muscle testing determined Tressa was now 75 percent in her physical body, much better but still not fully embodied. It occurred to me that since she had been significantly dissociated from the time of her birth, Tressa probably had no energetic boundaries with her body; if she had, she would be in good relationship to her body. Muscle testing confirmed my intuition. She had absolutely no energetic boundaries with her physical body because she had been so disconnected from it for so long. Therefore, we needed to establish and work on this as a secondary intention (a sub-intention) that would bring Tressa closer to her overall goal *to become fully embodied*. I also checked and determined that there were no more energetic origins to address.

Tressa's first intervention was two minutes of tapping the temporal curve. Next, muscle testing determined that Tressa needed frontal occipital holding. While implementing this intervention, I connected strongly with the powerful healing energy of Gaia. An inner voice communicated to me that Gaia's energy is nurturing in all ways. Tressa would need to care for and nurture her physical body like she would that of a lover.

Next, we used the Tibetan bowl to establish energetic boundaries with Tressa's physical body at the soul level, and then to open her heart chakra. I could see that her energy was contracted there—opening the heart chakra allowed Tressa to be open to love and to nurture her physical body. Once this was completed, muscle testing determined that Tressa was finally 100 percent embodied and had 100 percent energetic boundaries with her body.

Our work was done for the day. I welcomed Tressa back to physical reality in a new, grounded way that she hadn't experienced since the time she took her first breath. As is often true with very rapid pattern changes, Tressa would need to continue to correct for psychoenergetic reversal about it being safe to be 100 percent in her physical body, as her habitual experience challenged this. But we had cleared out the information contained within her energy field that carried traumatic residue and supernatural intrusions.

It is left to Tressa to continually reaffirm her experience of being fully embodied and to notice the difference this makes for her every day. This will certainly take some getting use to, but what a joy it will be for Tressa to fully occupy her physical being and be completely present with her experience. Better orgasms were just the tip of the iceberg. An amazing journey indeed!

RELIEVING ACID REFLUX AND PREPARING FOR LABOR AND DELIVERY: ENERGETIC BOUNDARY WORK AND PAST-LIFE REGRESSION

Sally's family physician referred her to me for panic attacks. Sally was twenty-six years old, married, and working as a dental hygienist. She was experiencing anxiety about not letting her difficult, painful history sabotage her marital relationship. Sally had been molested by one of her mother's boyfriends during her elementary school years. As a consequence, she had difficulty trusting those close to her, fearing that they would hurt and abandon her.

Sally was very psychic, and she could access phenomena in the spirit world or supernatural realm easily. Many would consider this a gift to be grateful of, but Sally's history of abuse and neglect had done considerable damage to her energetic boundaries. She often felt and sensed various kinds of intrusive energies while trying to sleep at night.

One of the first things we did was identify the contexts in which Sally had poor energetic boundaries and restore these boundaries to 100 percent. These contexts included her husband, her psychic abilities (to prevent her from being flooded by unsolicited psychic information), her estranged mother, her past abuser (at this point, the "inner" abuser from her elementary school years), her sleep (she didn't feel safe while trying to sleep), and particularly, other peoples' anger. Sally had repressed her memories of the sexual abuse until she spontaneously began having flashbacks at age seventeen. She was in counseling for the next four years to address the abuse issues and get her life on track. She realized later that she began having panic attacks at the age of thirteen, but she never got help for her anxiety because all the adults in her life minimized her experiences.

I met regularly with Sally for one year, until she gave birth to her first child. I helped her to resolve her panic attacks and related anxiety, particularly in regard to the upcoming birth of her child. Six months into her therapy, when she was in the early stages of pregnancy, Sally was finally feeling safer in her own house. She continued to be aware of her gut being tense and of having a low level of general anxiety, but her panic attacks had dissolved. She was no longer holding her breath and stuttering when someone was short with her, having cleared old trauma and established energetic boundaries with her personal power. Sally had never felt that she had any personal power before, which is typical for those who are identified with the Victim archetype after being repeatedly molested over a period of years.

But at this point in Sally's progress, two new issues began to emerge. The first was her fear of giving birth and of not being able to control her body (generating the fear that her body "is going out of control, like exploding or throwing up and not being able to stop"). Her second fear was of not being able to control her persistent acid reflux, which prevented her from sleeping for more than two hours at a time. Sally was taking prescription medication four times a day and yet was still having very severe heartburn. She was exhausted from lack of sleep, and she had the perception at a feeling level that her old panic attacks were on the verge of returning.

We decided to deal with Sally's fear of acid reflux first. Her new intention was to heal and resolve the overproduction of acid in her stomach, which was responsible for producing excess acid in her throat. Connected to this was her desire to stop the nightmares of being hurt or left by someone she loves.

As we muscle tested, it was revealed that an inner part of Sally had an objection to her proceeding on the intention. This inner part was fearful that Sally might be exposed to information that could be upsetting to her. This fear was unconscious—Sally had no awareness of it. We used TAT and the Tibetan bell to balance the energy that was generating this objection, but Sally was still holding this conflicted energy at the physical body level. Further muscle testing determined that an energetic origin twelve lifetimes ago was responsible for keeping this conflict stuck in Sally's solar plexus. To resolve this conflict, she needed to regress into the energy field of this past lifetime and associate into the experience to get the story.

Using a simple hypnotic regression technique, Sally associated into the past-life story easily. She described the following:

I see this cabin where this lady is living by herself with a shotgun for protection. She looks very angry but more scared, actually. It's kind of a small community or town. I see water like a river nearby. I'm feeling anxious.

At this point, I directed Sally in EFT meridian point tapping (this intervention includes tapping on the fourteen points) to alleviate her growing anxiety.

I'm waiting for someone to come. I picture it being a man on a horse, not a welcome visitor.

Sally began crying, and once again I directed her to tap on the same meridian points. She described having an overwhelming sense of fear, which she felt in her stomach as a knotted tightness. She continued to use EFT tapping.

He's just done something in the past that was harmful to me in some way. He has arrived and is there with me. Can't see real clearly. I shoot him! I told him that I was fed up and not going to take anymore.

At this juncture, I muscle tested Sally while asking a number of questions. We determined that this man had cursed her with his abusive anger. Frontal occipital holding was called for, and it completely cleared the curse. Additional questioning determined that personal trauma, including shock, fear, anger, extreme feelings of vulnerability, and emotional contamination from this man, needed to be released. We used the frontal occipital holding intervention again, which cleared all the traumatic residue that remained at that energetic origin.

When Sally came back to present time, she had three new awarenesses that needed to be acknowledged.

- The curse was thought rather than said, but it was just as powerful as if it had been said.

- I need to trust my impressions and instincts. I often don't say things I see or think because I distrust myself and don't feel safe to say them. It is self-deprecating.
- I have always had a fear that I am psychic. These "knowings" have scared me, so I have dismissed them and never talked about them. I know now that it is important to accept this part of myself and make peace with it.

When we muscle tested once more, we found that these new awarenesses were accurate. And not only had Sally cleared the internal conflict on the intention, but by doing the past-life regression she had cleared everything that was preventing her from actualizing her stated intention.

Sally said she would email to let me know her results regarding her acid reflux symptoms and her nightmares of being hurt and left (the theme of the past lifetime). The next week I received this email from Sally:

Just wanted to drop you a quick line to let you know that my chronic heartburn is almost all gone (about 90% gone). It feels like it's been years since I felt this good with that constant irritation. I still have it a little at night, but my diet hasn't been the greatest the past week so that's probably my fault. I think if I weren't pregnant, it would be totally gone. I'm so excited!!!!!! I can't wait to tell Dr. _____.
Thanks again :) Sally

As her due date approached, Sally became increasingly anxious. Because of her years of molestation, she was uncomfortable trusting doctors, especially with respect to reproductive matters. Her obstetrician-gynecologist was well respected in the community and Sally liked him, but she still felt uncomfortable with the standard physical exams required during pregnancy. Her muscle testing indicated that she first needed to establish energetic boundaries with the doctor, the nurses who might assist him, and his office staff using EFT and F/O holding. Then we needed to establish energetic boundaries with her bodily experience of being pregnant, going through labor, and giving birth. Sally was very uncomfortable with the idea of her body growing in a distorted manner. She was also very fearful of "delivering a baby the size of a watermelon" through her vagina, even though she acknowledged that childbirth was a most natural thing.

We used F/O holding and TAT to establish these boundaries, which significantly reduced Sally's anxiety. In the conversation that followed, Sally mentioned that she kept hearing horror stories from women who, unsolicited, told her about the painful and intense experiences they had giving birth. We used the Tibetan bell to establish energetic boundaries with others' labor and delivery stories so that Sally would have greater emotional detachment from the horror stories. She also realized that she needed to be more proactive with these women and tell them flat out that she didn't want to hear their stories because she was protecting herself from any negativity. (This is an example of a cognitive-behavioral intervention.) As our session continued, Sally remarked that though this pregnancy should be one of the happiest and most joyful times in her life, she felt cut off from being able to experience these feelings. As we discussed her detachment from what she intuitively knew should be joy, she had an ah-ha awareness—she carried a limiting belief that blocked her ability to feel and experience her own joy. She described it as, "If I let myself experience or feel that joy or happiness, my fear is that it will be a farther place to fall from." Sally realized that she had absorbed this from her father, who always reminded her not to get too excited or get her hopes up about anything because he didn't want her to be disappointed. He tried to protect her from making any mistakes in life so she wouldn't experience any disappointments. Sally realized that he distrusted the basic goodness in life.

Once we framed this cognitive awareness as a limiting belief that was blocking her ability to access her experience of joy, Sally's muscle testing indicated that we needed F/O holding to balance this. After the intervention, her muscle testing indicated the limiting belief was completely cleared (the energy field which carried that information had collapsed), and she now had 100 percent free and open access to experience her joy, specifically related to her current experience of growing a baby.

Sally's last session was just two weeks before her due date. She was optimistic, relaxed, and relieved that she had just finished her last day of work. Sally still had some lingering concerns about labor and delivery. She wondered if we could ask some muscle testing questions to make sure she had sufficient energetic boundaries with all necessary and related contexts for the upcoming event. I was glad to accommodate her. The only contexts that were not energetically boundaried 100 percent were with the hospital and the pain associated with labor and delivery. To boundary her fears about the hospital, Sally used TAT while focusing on the room she would be in. To boundary her fears about the pain of labor and delivery, Sally needed a few chimes of my Tibetan bell. These two simple energetic interventions engendered the emotional confidence Sally needed to look forward to delivering her first baby.

Sally terminated her therapy with this session. The panic attacks she had suffered were completely gone. The nightmares she had experienced and the feeling of not being safe while sleeping in her bed at home had disappeared. Her acid reflux and heartburn, though still present, were minimal and occasional. They were no longer an ongoing disturbance that prevented her from sleeping. And with all the energetic boundary work Sally had done, she was not only confident but actually looking forward to her labor and delivery.

About a month later I received this email:

Howard, I can't believe it's already been a month, but I wanted to let you know that we had a baby girl. Muscle testing was right about the sex, but off on the birth date by 6 days. Maybe that's something God wanted to keep as one of His miraculous mysteries??? Anyway, I wanted to let you know that everything went well as far as labor and delivery. In fact, the nurses and doctor said they see few first-time moms as focused and calm as I was. I really was! I did it mostly natural too. I had to have a dose of Stadol, but it wore off long before I got to the pushing phase. I did ask for an epidural at one point, but it was too late. I went from 2 to 10 cm dilated in an hour! . . . I had three helpers and I needed all of them, but things couldn't have gone better. . . . Thank you for all of your help. I know the work we did preparing for labor and delivery made the difference. Happy Holidays!

Sally

9

ALLEVIATING THE LOSS AND GUILT OF GIVING A BABY UP FOR ADOPTION: FINDING POWER THROUGH PAST-LIFE REGRESSION

Corky was referred to me for depression. She was twenty years old and had lost her zest for life. She had become pregnant just after turning nineteen. She had a pattern of sleeping with a man once and never seeing him again. This is what had happened with Ronald. After their initial meeting, she never returned any of his phone calls.

Corky was raised a Catholic, so having an abortion was not an option for her. She was prepared to keep the baby and, in fact, that option was her first choice. However, her parents were very much against it—they threatened to withdraw their financial support for her college tuition and made it clear that keeping the baby as an unwed mother was unacceptable. Under this pressure from her parents, Corky put the baby up for adoption.

Initially, Corky liked the adoptive parents. She felt happy and relieved that her baby had a home with loving, caring parents. At the beginning, the adoptive parents told Corky she could visit her baby anytime, but things changed over the first six months. Corky perceived that Debra, the adoptive mother, was very controlling and insecure. This woman began making it clear that Corky wasn't welcome anymore. Corky was despondent—she felt tremendously guilty for giving up her baby. She was also angry and resentful toward her parents, and she felt ashamed that she could not express her anger outwardly. Her anger was being rerouted into her body. It was my opinion that this contributing to Corky's colitis and self-hatred.

When I asked Corky what her therapeutic objectives were, she was very clear:

- I want to feel completely free to be myself again.
- I want to be free of guilt.
- I want to like myself again.
- I want to reclaim my excitement for life and not be depressed.
- I want to feel love again.

I explained to Corky how manual muscle testing works in Dynamic Energetic Healing®. She was familiar with muscle testing from her chiropractor and felt pretty much at home with all this. We asked with muscle testing if we could put all of her therapeutic objectives together into one clustered intention—yes. When I asked through muscle testing if there were any objections from any part of her to going forward on the intention, we were told there was one.

Corky felt undeserving. I explained that this is not unusual for someone grieving a loss. We talked about this for a while so Corky could have a cognitive understanding of the larger ramifications of loss. Through our discussion, she finally gave herself permission to begin grieving. We confirmed this through muscle testing—she was congruent. Corky was finally on her way to begin processing her experience and her feelings about giving her baby up for adoption.

Corky's second session revolved around her relationship with her parents, especially her father. She felt a lot of resentment toward him and carried many negative messages from him. The first thing Corky needed to do was establish solid energetic boundaries with her father, but there were a number of limiting beliefs internalized from her father that had to be addressed first. These included "I won't love you anymore unless you do what I want" and "If you keep Jonathan [the baby] I will leave you." Corky remarked that she still got sick to her stomach when thinking about these beliefs. In addition to this visceral feeling of sickness, Corky also elicited a disturbing image of her father, his teeth bared, spitting at her with anger and pounding at her chest with his finger. As you can see, Corky was carrying an enormous amount of negative emotional charge—at multiple levels—that was connected with the limiting beliefs.

We used a variety of energetic strategies, including TAT, EFT, and Corky's willingness to forgive her father, to release the energy fields that were carrying the information which supported the negative emotional charge. When we were done, all the limiting beliefs were cleared 100 percent. The queasiness Corky had felt in her stomach had vanished. When I asked her to try to re-create the threatening image of her father, she couldn't do it.

Corky then selected frontal occipital holding as her intervention of choice to establish 100 percent energetic boundaries with her father. I saw a dark cloud that was completely around her slowly dissipate and completely dissolve. I asked Corky if she had any new understandings or new awarenesses from the process that we had done in the session. She had a number of them:

- My dad does love me.
- It's OK to face my past.
- I have my three angels with me.
- I'm starting to feel whole again.
- It's OK to have these internalized issues; I will be able to face them, and I have the power to come out OK.
- There is light at the end of this tunnel.

During the next couple of sessions, I helped Corky focus her attention on self-empowerment. Debra was no longer allowing Corky to visit. The court had scheduled a mediation session between Corky and the adoptive parents to discuss visitation issues. Debra and her husband were well into their thirties and established in their careers, and Corky felt very intimidated by them. Psychologically, Corky was relating to them as surrogate parents of her own. Her new intention was to have the strength and confidence to confront Debra in the mediation session without fear. She wanted to be congruent about believing that she could get her needs met before she went to the mediation session. She wanted to feel powerful enough to have the confidence to relate to the adoptive parents as another adult and not as a confused teenager.

When we next muscle tested, it was evident that Corky had no energetic boundaries with Debra. In order to establish 100 percent energetic boundaries with her, Corky selected four minutes of NAEM tapping followed by three minutes of chanting a specific mantra, *Ong*. This did bring Corky's boundaries with Debra up to 100 percent, but there was something else that was hanging her up. Her muscle testing determined that Debra had directed a curse at Corky that was affecting Corky's personal power. Corky knew right away what the curse was—the curse energy was directed at Corky to make her feel small, weak, bad, and powerless. This was not news to Corky, because she had felt cursed by Debra for months. Corky selected the Tibetan bell to be chimed numerous times while she reflected on her perception of the curse. This released the curse energy 100 percent. Corky then talked about how her fear, anger, and frustration had built up because of Debra's manipulation and deception.

In our next session, Corky said she still felt intimidated by the agency mediator. As she described her feelings, I told Corky that I perceived she was carrying some damaging limiting beliefs. When I asked her about this through muscle testing, she discovered three limiting beliefs:

- No matter how prepared I am, the adoptive parents and the mediator will not see my side or agree to what I want.
- If I have to take the matter to the court, the judge won't hear my position, or hear me.
- The judge will take Jonathan from me forever.

After Corky identified these limiting beliefs, I directed her to tap on the EFT meridian points for about three minutes to release the negative emotional charge. I next asked what the best intervention would be to clear all three limiting beliefs completely. It was the Kirtan Kriya meditation, which we chanted together for three minutes. When we were done, I asked Corky if she had any new awarenesses derived from our process during that session. She reported four new learnings:

- I will be OK.
- God will protect me on my journey.
- Jonathan will always know I love him.
- My relationship with Jonathan originated in a higher place, a place that is sacred, and will be protected there.

I was both astounded and impressed by Corky's emerging awareness. By releasing her fears from her energy field, her depression was lifting and her physical body was feeling more relieved. And somehow she was generating amazing spiritual insights that were very empowering.

When I asked if there was anything remaining that was blocking Corky from actualizing her intention, the muscle testing identified that there was a death wish present as well as some kind of supernatural interference. Upon further inquiry, I determined that Corky was carrying an archetypal pattern called the Wounded Holy One. I had learned about this pattern during a two-day seminar I took from Dr. Andrew Hahn, who co-developed, identified, and described this phenomenon with Judith Swack.

This archetype can best be understood as a story about a major betrayal that occurred in a past lifetime. There is always a death wish present, and there is always involvement of a supernatural intrusion. This archetype usually arises in the therapy process when clients are struggling with their purpose for being. To put it more succinctly, this archetypal pattern emerges when there is a disturbance in your ability to manifest your soul mission.

In the story, you [the protagonist] are either the healer, political leader, or spiritual leader of a community. You are serving your community and you are very congruent about doing God's work. At a certain point in the story, a trusted follower betrays you to the authorities in power. You are then put to death, but not before you, in your anguish, curse God for having abandoned you. You feel anger toward God because you don't feel supported by God. You were essentially serving God by serving your community, but now you are not able to complete your soul mission. By cursing God, you (the "holy one") fracture your connection to God; as a consequence, you become wounded because your soul flips to a new loyalty—with the dark side of Spirit. This generates horrific, murderous deeds in subsequent lifetimes. As a Wounded Holy One, you carry tremendous shame at the soul level for what has transpired.

Clearly, the influence of this archetype can be a major block to a client manifesting a fulfilling and meaningful soul mission in the current lifetime. The soul carries this information as karmic damage laden with self-loathing. In addition, these individuals are deeply resistant to reconnecting to God because of the shameful things they have done over the span of many lifetimes. Interestingly, it is very common for clients carrying this archetypal pattern to be quite spiritually sophisticated, with deeply grounded spiritual values. Yet for all their spiritual practice and devotion to God, they continue to feel sabotaged in their attempts to fulfill their life mission.

The first thing I needed to do with Corky was pin down the specific lifetime during which the Wounded Holy One event occurred. In Corky's case, there were two past lifetimes that were involved in this pattern. Muscle testing identified the sixteenth previous lifetime as the one in which the betrayal occurred. However, the supernatural intrusion occurred two lifetimes before that (her eighteenth), which set up the conditions for the betrayal to happen in the sixteenth.

Using a variation of the NLP timeline technique, Corky quickly and easily regressed through time into the energy field of her past lifetime number
eighteen. As she was suspended high above the scenario that she could not yet
see, we muscle tested and determined that her first task was to connect with
Source and visualize channeling healing energy down into the scene that she
would soon be associating into. When her muscle testing confirmed that she
had completed this first task, Corky visualized herself gently floating down
onto the timeline itself. The following is a verbatim transcription of her story.

I'm in trees. It looks like a jungle. It seems almost like there is a
storm, flashing light. Huts, like a village and meadow clearing. I see
kids and paths. It doesn't seem like I should be there, even though I
know it. I am a man with two other men walking on a path. We are
going deeper into the woods. We are wearing leather clothes. We are
going hunting. There's a big animal, like a tiger but not a tiger. I see
this big tiger/cat attacking me. It's chaotic. I can see it dead with
spears in it now. I see a picture of me really mangled . . . my legs . . .
and deep cuts in my chest. I'm not dead, though. I feel like maybe I
sit by myself and watch life because I'm mangled. Again the flashing
storm. I'm screaming because of the thunder—it's really loud. I'm
angry at my life. I was strong, now I'm nothing. I was beautiful with
smooth skin, now I'm just scarred. I'm afraid to look at the animal's
face because it's so evil looking. It's not like anything I've ever seen
before. Big head, tusks, big teeth. I see myself getting tossed by those
tusks. Its eyes are gold and they flash—wild. The tusks don't fit with
it but they go there. A mean mouth. If it could speak, it would be the
devil. Makes an awful growling and gnashing noise. Never encountered this kind of creature before. We are all scared. I'm trying to kill
it when it attacks me. It feels that part of me is angry at them because
they didn't help me fast enough. Dead, it's bloody and its mouth is
open—heat waves, evil, coming out of it.

At this point, I muscle tested and determined that we needed the frontal
occipital holding intervention to address this dark energy. The healing spirit of
Jesus descended into the room as Corky reflected on the feeling of evil that
her experience had just generated. Our intention was to release the darkness
that Corky felt emanating from the animal, that Corky as the protagonist per-

ceived as evil. Her muscle testing indicated that we had released all the dark energy that had contaminated her. She continued the story, still deeply associated with the protagonist:

> Next I felt a sucking coming out of my body, sucking all of the darkness out of my body. I was dead and so was the animal. As I lay dead, something like a vacuum sucked it all out from my soul. I feel pure now. I was already dead when I was screaming. I was angry because that thing had taken over me, and nobody saw me.

That was the end of Corky's story. When we muscle tested once more, she had released every trace of supernatural influence in that lifetime which was connected to the Wounded Holy One pattern. We muscle tested to find out if there was any residual trauma to release—no. The entire disturbance in the eighteenth past lifetime was the dark energy that contaminated her from the strange, evil animal. Nothing more was needed at that energetic origin.

With minimal prompting from me, Corky progressed forward to present time as she integrated the healing that had occurred from her past lifetime number eighteen forward to now.

By our next meeting, Corky was feeling more positive and less depressed. She had met with her attorney and found out what her legal rights were. Her attorney recommended that they draft an amendment addressing the visitation agreement. Corky felt back in control. She was sleeping better and feeling much better emotionally. She had enrolled at a university out of town to continue her undergraduate work. She had already selected an apartment and was hoping to get a job at a little clothing boutique close to the university. Her attorney had scheduled a mediation session to deal with the visitation issues for three weeks in the future. Although still a bit anxious about it, Corky was more confident of a positive outcome. In addition, she reported noticing that she was being more assertive in her relationships in general, particularly at her place of work. She no longer felt like a victim, and she had decided she wasn't going to let anybody treat her that way again.

After briefly updating me at her next therapy session, Corky continued on her quest to resolve the Wounded Holy One pattern that came into being during her past lifetime number sixteen. She regressed easily using the same modified NLP timeline technique that we had used previously. As before, she first needed to visualize directing healing light down into the scene below her, first for two minutes and then for an additional three minutes. Once this was completed, her muscle testing indicated that she could gently float down into the scene below and associate into the main protagonist of the story. The verbatim transcription of the story is as follows:

I see a dead person with their head cracked open. [As I questioned Corky a little bit more about this, I determined that she needed to skip back in time to the beginning of the story.] Now I see open prairie. There are lots of small homes ... a village ... children running around. I have long black hair and I am a male. It's like a Native American scene. I'm watering my horse. It's nighttime. Seems like there is dancing, lots of men, all very intense, like a ritual. I feel like I am watching, not connected. I have a family, a wife smaller than I am with little kids. I am very large and strong. She's pregnant again. I'm in a respected place, like a hunter and warrior versus a religious person. It's nighttime. It's a different scene. Three men are attacking me. I'm on the ground and they are above me with spears, stabbing into me. It's happening far away from my home. I know these men. It feels like one of them is my brother. I was too powerful in some way. My brother is the most vicious. He's screaming at me. He feels that my presence in some way is going to take his place. If I'm the one people respect, they won't respect him. He wants to take my wife and family as his. I have known some of his feelings toward me before. People are afraid of him. At the dance, he had some position of power there. It feels like I should have protected the people in the village from him. I felt he had broken off from the larger group. There aren't elders with respect there. When I was there I was in charge and in authority. Now he's ruling this group. It feels like I'm lying on the ground looking up. I'm so afraid.

At this point, I directed Corky to proceed with EFT meridian tapping to discharge her fear so she could continue.

I see his face over me. I'm almost dead. He's screaming at me. He stabs me in the gut while he's looking in my eyes. I can't believe I'm dying. I'm not going to see my family. He tricked me. I hate him! He's evil! How could God let this happen? I'm confused about God.

I'm done with God for allowing this to have happened. I hate God. I feel sick to my stomach with sadness.

I asked Corky to inquire within about the relationship that "he" had with his brother.

He's younger than me. He's just always negative. Thinks people are always out to get him. He's resentful, thinking I was more privileged, that people paid more attention to me and respected me more when we were younger. Always in my shadow. He also wanted my wife. He would just grab her and hassle her when I wasn't around. We even had a confrontation about him touching my wife. Now it seems that it wasn't with two others, just us, with him deceiving me about wanting to go for a walk. He's hateful and manipulative. When I have to see him with my wife, who's so scared, and with my kids, I cursed God after I died and saw this.

This was the end of the story. When I muscle tested Corky, we determined that she needed to return to the time just after that past lifetime—what the Tibetan Buddhists refer to as the Bardo realm—to complete unfinished business with the souls of the other participants in the story. We had run out of time, so it would have to wait until our next session.

At the beginning of our next session, Corky told me she continued to feel well. She was feeling stronger emotionally, with a growing confidence that she would do fine during the mediation session. She was eager to finish up the Wounded Holy One pattern in the Bardo realm from where we had left off. She closed her eyes and took a few deep breaths as she relaxed deeply. I prompted her to return back to her past lifetime number sixteen, floating high up out of her body over the timeline. When she perceived that she was in the energy field of that past lifetime, I muscle tested her to make sure.

When reassured that Corky was in the correct energy field, I explained again about the Bardo realm. This is where the Tibetan Buddhists describe the souls of the departed transitioning to. Using this conceptual framework, I suggested that Corky direct her consciousness to merge with this Bardo realm and the souls that resided in it from the past lifetime she had most recently visited. The presupposition here is that all of the people who were in that past lifetime would be present in the Bardo realm, but as souls rather than embodied individuals. Any of the soul beings with whom Corky still had unfinished business would be available to talk to. I directed Corky to simply set the intention internally to invite any of the soul beings with whom she needed to speak to come forward. The following is the verbatim dialogue that Corky experienced in the Bardo realm.

I see my wife. She was angry at me because my brother told her I ran off to leave her with him. They were miserable. She didn't know I loved her. I tell her I'm really sorry I left you. I watched you after I died. *She's saying that she is Jonathan!* This is my chance to show her that I loved her. She was miserable without me. *I'm telling her I'm not going to let her go again.* She forgives me. *She's going to be with me again!* I just tell her how much I love her. Everything is very bright and intense—lots of light. Looks like God. It is! I'm telling Him how I was scared and I didn't understand. I know it wasn't Him. He didn't have anything to do with my brother. I'm sorry! I thank Him for letting me love her soul again (my wife). I'm now in a good place with God. I feel like the members of my community and my kids are here, and my brother's off to the side. I tell them how much I loved them and how sorry I am, especially to my kids. I know how hard it was for them. I tried to get back to them but I just couldn't. I see my brother—I tell him I forgive him. I know his soul—he was driven to do it. He wouldn't really want to hurt me. My brother responds and tells me he didn't hate me, but there was something inside of him telling him to hate me, to kill me, that I was bad and I was always trying to be better than him. He said he was jealous. He's sorry. It was the devil in him.

At this point, I muscle tested Corky to find out what her brother needed in order to release the dark energy that still resided in his soul. First I rang the Tibetan bell; then I did frontal occipital holding on Corky. I saw lots of golden light surrounding both of us and many angels around the brother. When I next muscle tested Corky, all the dark energy had been released from the brother in the Bardo realm. Corky then continued with her story.

He's thanking God. He tells me he loves me and he's sorry, and it's good now. I tell him I just wanted it to be over. I understand it wasn't him. He's going to trust God too. He didn't know why he was acting evil. Now he will depend on God.

I muscle tested Corky to find out if there was anything more than needed to be done in the Bardo realm—her work was completed. There was no more unfinished business with anybody, at any level, from that past lifetime. I directed Corky to move out of the Bardo realm, but before progressing forward in time, I asked her if she had acquired any resources in the Bardo realm that she felt were important to bring back with her. She said yes, but she wasn't sure what they were. I had a pretty strong hunch, so I muscle tested her and asked if the resources were new understandings or awareness about her relationship with God and her son—yes. I asked Corky to think about it for a moment and to share with me the first things that came to her mind. These were the new understandings that came to her:

- Jonathan's spirit will always be connected to mine; he knows at his core who I am in his life.
- God is the divine healer.
- No wound is too deep for God to heal.
- I am able to carry out my soul's mission.

The next muscle testing indicated that nothing more needed to be done. I directed Corky to reflect on her new understandings as she progressed forward in time to the present and to being fully incorporated into her physical body. As she was imagining moving forward from the energy field of the past lifetime into present time, I suggested that everything she had healed and everything she had learned be permanently integrated into and positively affect each subsequent lifetime, up to and including the present one. I then gave her a moment, which was all it took for Corky to take a deep breath and open her eyes.

There was a huge smile on her face. She knew she is going to be OK with Jonathan—there was no doubt in her mind. And she knew she isn't walking alone anymore.

There are many things I can say about Corky's Wounded Holy One past lifetime(s) healing. Her past-life regressions were vivid and explicit. Corky was deeply associated with the protagonist of each story and experienced a great deal of emotion. Corky had never done any past-life regression work before. Other than having a rather loose conceptual understanding of the Wounded

Holy One archetypal pattern, Corky had no preconceptions about what to expect. I made no suggestions about what she might find in her past-life regression experience; the manual muscle testing was our guide throughout. What we defined as supernatural (i.e., the evil animal in Corky's eighteenth past lifetime) was unique to Corky's perceptual experience. I had never encountered this animal before. And in the Bardo-realm healing, her evil brother described the qualities of hatefulness—the devil inside of him that made him act in those ways. It's not really necessary to know anything more about the dark energy that consumed the brother, or the emanations of evil from the ferocious creature in her first past-life regression story. What Corky experienced and described is consistent with the archetypal pattern of the Wounded Holy One.

As stated earlier, betrayal is always a major theme of this archetypal pattern. It was easy now to make connections between betrayals in Corky's present-life experience, related both to her biological parents and to Jonathan's adoptive parents. What's more, I found it remarkable that in the Bardo realm healing, the wife acknowledged being the same soul as Jonathan!

You may be asking yourself whether Corky's perceptions and experiences in her past-life regressions were really true. The answer is that it doesn't matter. It doesn't matter because, first, it cannot be proven—it was her subjective experience. Second, the experience is only meaningful to Corky to the extent that it helps her to heal and resolve the dilemma that she wanted me to help her with.

Based on her new understandings, I would say that Corky's past-life regression experiences were especially meaningful. I theorize that betrayal was a core issue for Corky that came along with her soul into this lifetime. Consequently, Corky had a pattern of relationships with intimate others that precluded any kind of commitment. This is probably why she slept with her male partners only once. It may also explain why Corky felt betrayed by her parents for not supporting her in wanting to keep her child.

I also theorize that since Corky has now healed and resolved this archetypal pattern, her pattern of relationships is going to change dramatically. There will no longer be a deep, core-level sabotage pattern interfering with her ability to be vulnerable and honest in her relationships. This doesn't mean Corky has no more work to do, but it does mean that she will be more open to allowing people into her life in a more welcoming and fulfilling way. And that's completely separate from her acknowledgment that she will be able to accomplish her soul's mission in this life, whatever that may be. That's a very empowering statement for a person as young as Corky.

Our last two sessions were essentially finishing-up work. Corky still had some anxiety about the mediation meeting with the adoptive parents. We discussed strategies for conducting herself during the mediation in a way that would not threaten Debra. I then helped Corky establish a kinesthetic resource anchor (as described in case history 2). In this case, I had Corky close her eyes and recall specific experiences, one memory at a time, when she felt self-confident and powerful. As I prompted her to feel what she felt, see what she saw, and fully engage all of her senses, at the point of greatest association into the experience I prompted Corky to touch her thumb and right index finger together and hold them for thirty seconds. This was anchoring all her positive internal memories or resources at her fingertips. This is one of the most useful NLP strategies, and one that I frequently use with clients. It took us about thirty-five minutes to establish a well reinforced and reliable power resource anchor. I then directed Corky to purposefully and intentionally fire off the anchor by touching her fingertips together during her mediation meeting when she felt she needed to be confident and powerful.

Corky's last therapy session went well. Though her mediation meeting had been emotionally challenging, she felt relieved and confident that her visitation needs would be met. She was no longer threatened by Debra and had actually left feeling empowered by her ability to stay in the arena with her and not collapse emotionally. Manual muscle testing reflected that Corky still had 100 percent energetic boundaries with both adoptive parents, especially Debra.

Over the twelve-week period that I worked with Corky, she accomplished a great deal. On her own subjective rating scale, Corky reported that she was feeling between 70 and 75 percent better from when she had started therapy with me. She was ready to move on into the next phase of her life, knowing that she would always be involved in her son's life. In a very short time, she had accomplished an enormous amount of personal healing. She felt good about her relationship with her parents and, even more importantly, she felt good about herself. Corky wrote out the last two new understandings that summarized her work with me:

- I am powerful in ways that include every part of me—emotionally, physically, and intellectually.
- It is OK to let myself experience pleasure.

Nine visits in twelve weeks was a life-changing experience for Corky. She had very specific therapeutic objectives when she came in. She achieved those objectives, along with a great deal of new learning and understanding.

This clinical study is an excellent example of following the client's process. We used energetic strategies that included EFT meridian tapping, frontal occipital holding, mantric chanting, and past-life regression. Though Dynamic Energetic Healing® fits under the umbrella of energy psychology, there was a great deal of cognitive learning that came with Corky's new awarenesses throughout the process. Needless to say, I was elated by her success.

CASE   HISTORY

10

RELEASING OLD TRAUMA
AND ALLEVIATING SYMPTOMS
OF FATIGUE: ALLERGY
ANTIDOTING TECHNIQUES

I saw Julia once a month. She is a lawyer and, as is common with lawyers, she is overwhelmed by the demands of her senior partners to maintain a high level of billable hours. She had very little time for herself and was always tired. Near the end of the fall, Julia arrived for one session exhausted. Her presenting symptoms were fatigue, lack of mental clarity, and experiences of a dreamy state.

I had a strong impression that we should inquire (using MMT) if an energy toxin (etoxin) might be contributing to her symptoms. We got an affirmative response, so we proceeded with allergy elimination protocols that I learned from Sandi Radomski, LCSW, ND, at an international energy psychology conference.

I explained to Julia how certain foods and other substances can be responsible for all kinds of troublesome symptoms, such as hives, poor digestion, insomnia, depression, and anxiety. Every substance, including foods, perfumes, dust, and molds in the air we breathe, has a unique electromagnetic frequency or signature that interacts with our unique electromagnetic signature. If the frequencies are harmonious, there is no problem. But if something interacts with us that generates allergic symptoms at any level, it is considered an etoxin to us. Doctors who specialize in allergies use desensitization therapies—they introduce very small amounts of the offending substance, which creates antibodies that build up the body's resistance to the allergen. In the

371

field of energy psychology, we are learning that we can neutralize or antidote allergens or etoxins through the use of energetic strategies.

Dr. Roger Callahan, the developer of Thought Field Therapy, identified energy toxins as agents that affect the energy field and often cause psycho-energetic reversals (among various other problems). Acupuncturist Dr. Devi Nambudripad developed an allergy-elimination protocol called NAET, which is used primarily by acupuncturists to help patients eliminate their reactions to allergens. Sandi Radomski used Dr. Callahan's and Dr. Nambudripad's trainings, among other energy psychology trainings, to develop a comprehensive series of protocols that she calls allergy antidotes. It is from Ms. Radomski's training that I have begun to integrate the treatment of etoxins within the paradigm of energy psychology into Dynamic Energetic Healing®.

As I began briefly explaining to Julia how allergy antidotes work, I took out my kit of thirty vials. I had purchased this Core Collection of vials from Sandi. The vials, which are filled with water and alcohol, have been injected with the precise electromagnetic frequency of a particular substance. The frequency of the substance is amplified tenfold so that the contents of the vial strongly represent the substance to be muscle tested. I randomly picked up the vial labeled Blood to show Julia what the vials look like.

I muscle tested Julia's intention ("I want to completely alleviate my fatigue, dreamy state/lack of mental clarity") for congruency. There was no psychoenergetic reversal and no conflict to proceeding, so we began muscle testing using the vials in the testing kit.

Nine of the vials initially tested weak for Julia. They were vitamin C mix, toxic chemicals, vaccine mix, candida mix, mold mix, newspapers/ink, RNA/DNA, virus mix, and blood. We needed to prioritize, and since (coincidentally) the blood vial was the substance that weakened her the most, that's where we started.

Julia held the blood vial as we began muscle testing. The initial responses to our questions indicated that there was supernatural intrusion, specifically a generic intrusion. Using MMT, I determined that frontal occipital holding was the intervention of choice. Immediately after reciting my invocation, I saw a large area of dark contracted energy in her pelvis. As I continued to attune to the area, I saw that the intrusion was located there. Immediately thereafter, I had an image of a bright light coming into Julia's pelvis, scouring out the entire area to clean out the intrusion. After one minute, the light slowly lifted out of her and disappeared. I removed my hands. MMT corroborated that the intrusion was released 100 percent.

I next had Julia restate the intention to test for psychoenergetic reversal. She was indeed reversed (i.e., she tested strong) on all five statements:

1. I don't want to alleviate my fatigue.
2. It's not possible to alleviate my fatigue.
3. It's not safe to alleviate my fatigue.
4. I don't deserve to alleviate my fatigue.
5. I will not alleviate my fatigue.

MMT indicated that we could treat all five reversals together as a group, and all the psychoenergetic reversals were corrected after two minutes of tapping the temporal curve. However, as is often the case while applying energetic strategies, Julia had two unexpected and spontaneous thoughts relating to her first husband's death from a heart attack.

I just want to go into a deep coma and just sleep and when everything is OK I can then wake up. Wake me when it's over. I survived it. How could I have? I was supposed to die too. So somehow I have to do penance since I survived. Guilt.

It is significant to note that the anniversary of his death is in November, at which time fourteen years had elapsed. Julia reported that her fatigue has progressively worsened since the heart attack.

It became clear to Julia and me that these two spontaneous awarenesses were limiting beliefs. These beliefs contained so much self-devaluing energy (her relentless feelings of guilt) that they were also self-generated curses. Further inquiry bore this out and indicated that Julia was still carrying traumatic residue from the energetic origin of the events following her husband's death. Her limiting beliefs/self-generated curses were unresolved traumatic residue from the loss she suffered fourteen years prior.

We followed Julia's process and asked what intervention would be best to clear these two limiting beliefs. MMT indicated that frontal occipital holding was the intervention of choice. During the intervention, I elicited Jesus' healing energy; I also elicited the awareness that Julia required self-forgiveness. Julia's intense anger toward her husband for dying reemerged, and she recalled that at the time she didn't want to live because his death made her a single parent. Though she had been furious with him following his death, she had managed to repress these feelings over the years. As well, she had been angry at him because of his strange behavior just prior to his heart attack. He had stress-related emotional problems and was spending more and more time with his parents, going to their house almost every evening. He was avoiding Julia and their children due to his own fatigue and emotional problems.

Julia cleared the limiting beliefs at all levels except at the soul level, where she was still holding some of the traumatic residue. MMT indicated we needed to do frontal occipital holding once again. During the intervention I saw a constriction at Julia's throat chakra and her need to say something (that she had suppressed) to her dead husband. After some discussion and confirmation with MMT, we concluded that Julia had to say (out loud!), "I forgive you for choosing your parents over me." This statement released her anger toward her husband for dying on her *at the soul or karmic level* so she could learn to live on her own and learn certain life lessons. This clearing at the soul or karmic level allowed the compression of energy in her throat chakra to come into balance; I could see that her throat chakra energy was no longer contracted.

After Julia had verbalized this, MMT indicated that the curses were cleared 100 percent—there was no residue remaining from the energetic origin. MMT indicated there were no other etoxins weakening her and making her feel exhausted for which we needed to test.

Julia's body had chosen the blood vial to antidote, not because blood was toxic to her *but because her husband had chosen blood relations over Julia and her children.* The blood vial stimulated Julia's thought field to have those limiting beliefs emerge; it also revealed a most mysterious passageway to alleviate her symptoms of fatigue and exhaustion that stemmed from an old loss-trauma imprint. Amazing! Blood and its associated thought fields were already very present in our collective energy field even before we started doing the formal healing work. This is an example of following my second attention (trusting my impressions to inquire about etoxin possibilities and choosing the blood vial first) to connect with my client's dreaming process. Healing was the end result.

When we tested for completion of treating blood as an etoxin, Julia had antidoted it 100 percent through all time and dimensions (meaning her energy field no longer experienced blood as a toxin generating allergy-like symptoms in any form).

With respect to Julia's initial intention to alleviate her fatigue and lack of mental clarity, her energy progressively improved over the following weeks and months. This session was a turning point in healing her fatigue.

11

SHIFTING LIFELONG PERSISTENT DESPAIR: DREAMTIME AND FRONTAL OCCIPITAL HOLDING

Sarah, a reference librarian at a large university in Portland, had been seeing me for post-traumatic stress from childhood abuse. For the past three months, she had been sick with various ailments, from localized infections to aching joints throughout her body to pervasive exhaustion. She was worried about her immune system and did not understand why she had been unable to over-come or resist these physical problems.

As I now held the space for Sarah to talk and process her feelings and thoughts about the difficulties she was having, she realized that the central issue was despair. She felt there was nothing she could do when she got into this deep state of despair except hold on and wait until it passed, which was sometimes hours and sometimes days. She realized that this despair related directly to the time in her childhood when she felt a total lack of self-confidence. Sarah described her experience as "just completely giving up." She felt unable to follow through on any positive action, even if that meant not being able to take her medication to relieve her depression. She realized that this despair has always been about being unable to help herself and feeling profound anger toward herself as a consequence. She described her experience as being totally helpless. This, she said, is her Achilles heel. When she gets into this state of being, she knows that if something were to happen to her husband she could never take care of herself—she would just lie down and die.

Sarah described this experience as a progressive snowballing of hopelessness. When she gets discouraged enough she cannot use the tools that she knows and falls into this deep well of despair. I interjected at this point and suggested that we begin muscle testing to see if we could find an intervention that would collapse the energy fields carrying the information which perpetuates her despair.

Sarah's muscle testing elicited frontal occipital holding as the best intervention. I directed Sarah to reflect on everything she had shared with me and continue thinking about her despair. She became very associated and connected to her experience of despair—her thought fields were laden with the information that was perpetuating the problem state. As I gently made contact with her, I immediately began receiving impressions of an Old World community that struck me as European. Then information began to come to my awareness very quickly. I saw a dark cloud like a fog pervading this European village. It spread like exploring, probing fingers engulfing the entire community. I immediately knew that this was the Black Death of medieval times, consuming everyone who it came into contact with. As I had this knowing, overwhelming feelings of despair, tremendous grief, and hopelessness washed through my body.

As the scene changed, I started getting impressions of the despair and helplessness of victims of the Nazi death camps in World War II. It was the same feeling that came over me when I accessed Sarah's karmic memories of the Black Death. These karmic memory impressions contained all the qualities and features that Sarah had described feeling just a few minutes earlier.

Now that I had the information, I was praying for help from any spiritual resources either of us had. I had identified the source of the thought fields as being karmic and had determined that Sarah needed spiritual help (among other things). In what seemed like just a few seconds, I moved deeper into the dreamtime experience and saw my upper-world Tibetan master turn from his mountaintop meditation place and begin chanting, directing the very specific vibratory healing energies toward Sarah. Finally, what I saw made me shudder. As I realized that both of these past-life memories were representations of morphic resonance at the collective level, I saw dark ghosts emerging from Sarah. My Tibetan master took responsibility for redirecting them to wherever they needed to go next. I was overwhelmed with awe at what I had seen. I was tremendously grateful for the healing power of this spiritual resource, which released very old, powerful memories that were directly influencing Sarah to experience despair.

When I was finished I shared everything that I had seen with Sarah. Although this was not strictly necessary (since the results of the MMT would be the same regardless of Sarah's knowledge or lack of knowledge of my subjective experience), sharing my experience with Sarah enabled her to generate a very helpful and important cognitive awareness. My perceptions about these karmic influences seemed amazing to me, but Sarah said they made perfect sense to her. Although she had never had past-life memories of the medieval Black Death, she had had many intuitive intimations of having lived through the Holocaust in a death camp.

Sarah then began to make some current-life connections to her family of origin. She realized she could never get her parents to stop hurting her no matter what she did or what she said. She realized that as a child she could never have made them stop doing the terrible things to her that they did. She also realized in this moment of clarity that this is one of the main reasons why she often feels inadequate in making decisions about changing anything in her life. This was all about those feelings of helplessness and hopelessness that led her deeper and deeper into despair. Sarah continued to talk about the correlations between what I had seen while doing the F/O holding intervention and her growing awareness based on her experience as a victim of childhood abuse.

Just before ending our session, I wanted to reassure Sarah that the work we had done was complete. I wanted to let her know that she had made a profound change not only at her belief level but at her very core. I had her say out loud, "I'm a victim of my despair." I muscle tested her and her arms went weak. I then had her say out loud, "I now know I have resolved the experience of despair for myself." Her arms were as strong as steel. This was confirmation that the work we had done in that session, both cognitively through our initial dialogue and energetically through the F/O holding intervention, had been very powerful healing work.

The process we followed supported Sarah in two very important ways:

- The positive results of the manual muscle testing gave her very strong positive reinforcement (on the subconscious and conscious belief levels) that her despair was resolved.
- Sarah had a spontaneous cognitive awareness about her relationship to her family of origin and about her feelings of despair and helplessness that contributed to her inability to make decisions and take action.

Hearing about my experience facilitated this awareness, which provided her with more insight.

I so appreciate the fact that Dynamic Energetic Healing® addresses the problem state of the client at multiple levels, providing enhanced possibilities for permanent change. I knew I would continue working with Sarah, but the Sarah who would be coming for her next appointment would be a much lighter individual—she had released the terrible burden of very painful, fearful memories from her energy field. These memories would no longer be imposing themselves on Sarah, because we had depotentiated the deeply wounding layers of profound experiences of suffering that few of us can even imagine.

Sarah's next session was three weeks later. She was no longer feeling despair, even though she was still struggling with her health. She had experienced flashbacks (as would happen periodically) since our previous session, but to her great surprise she was "no longer rocked by them." She said she felt like a different person and hoped this would be permanent. She realized she could still have the awful memories and flashbacks of her parents' abuse without the despair of feeling that she will never heal from the abuse. She said she had "a feeling of something breaking, and the realization that I don't have to be afraid anymore."

Something in Sarah had shifted dramatically. Though the shift was energetic in nature, she was now integrating the changes and making sense of her new reality cognitively. This is often the process of change in Dynamic Energetic Healing®—the intellect needs time to "make sense" of the instantaneous change that happens in the office. Sarah was tremendously buoyed by this shift. She suspects that if she weren't working with me, she might never get over her "chronic fear syndrome." I just hold the space for her that she will.

12

OVERCOMING COMPULSIVE OVEREATING: HEALING THE WOUNDED INNER CHILD

Lisa, aged forty-four, is a physical therapist who came for help because her marriage of ten years had gone stale. During our initial interview, Lisa admitted that she suffered from a lifelong eating disorder. From as far back as high school, Lisa binged and purged in order to stay thin. As she got older and continued to struggle with this, Lisa was able to make some connections between how she was feeling in her primary relationship and her compulsive need to purge (vomit). She was smart, well educated, and aware of what a healthy diet requires, but she couldn't stop herself from frequently visiting dessert shops and eating enormous pieces of chocolate cake. Afterwards, she felt guilty for eating such sugary foods. Her guilt tormented her until her tension escalated to the point that she had to purge in order to experience calm. When Lisa was finished vomiting, she felt terribly ashamed for being so out of control.

Though Lisa didn't know exactly what the cause of this behavior was, she suspected that it was tied to her marriage and her unmet emotional needs. Her husband, Sal, was a nice man but "wasn't a communicator." During their ten-year marriage, they had gradually drifted apart as Lisa became bored and disenchanted with Sal. Her diet was terrible and she was increasingly aware of her compulsive overeating, particularly of sweets.

Lisa met another man with whom she became enamored. John had many qualities that Lisa admired—he was athletic and could keep up with Lisa; he was intellectual and challenged that part of Lisa which Sal never did; and he was very articulate and into personal growth, unlike Sal. Lisa found herself spending lots of time with John, and it was during this time that she decided she wanted to leave Sal for good. She knew this was the right decision for her, but because Sal had never done anything hurtful to her and was basically a nice guy, Lisa felt some guilt about abandoning the marriage. Her bingeing and purging became more out of her control, and she acted out emotionally with John in ways that she found embarrassing. Lisa processed everything through her emotions; she was a feeler. This was one reason why John, an intellectual, was so attractive to her—he personified the part of Lisa that she didn't identify with. Lisa was in a crisis right now. She was emotionally conflicted about leaving her husband, and she acted like a lovesick adolescent when she was around John. She admitted that her emotions were out of control and she wanted some help.

It was clear that Lisa needed to have stronger energetic boundaries with her emotions so she could feel more in control of her life. Establishing solid, consistent energetic boundaries would put her in optimal relationship with her own emotional reality. This would enable her to make more judicious decisions and give her more choices for how to respond to the challenges of intimate relationships.

Our starting intention was for Lisa to establish 100 percent energetic boundaries with her emotions. To check for psychoenergetic reversal, I had Lisa state the intention out loud while I muscle tested her arms. She was reversed on all five of the core psychoenergetic reversal statements; that is, her answers were as follows:

- I don't want to have energetic boundaries with my emotions.
- It's not possible to . . .
- It's not safe to . . .
- I don't deserve to . . .
- I will not establish 100 percent energetic boundaries with my emotions.

Muscle testing indicated we could cluster the five statements together and treat them as a comprehensive thought field, rather than addressing each statement separately.

The intervention Lisa selected was four minutes of NAEM tapping, which corrected all psychoenergetic reversal on the intention. However, further muscle testing indicated that there was an objection to moving forward on establishing boundaries with her emotions.

It didn't take Lisa long to figure out what this unconscious part of her was objecting to. Lisa was fearful of what would happen to her sense of self if she were suddenly able to manage her emotions. Throughout her life, she identified herself as an "overly emotional, extreme reactor." This had almost become a limiting identity in that Lisa used her emotionality as a self-indulgent strategy to elicit attention. She wasn't proud of this, but she didn't know any other way of getting her needs met in a relationship.

MMT indicated that frontal occipital holding was the intervention of choice. As Lisa settled in to reflect on this objection and fear, I made contact with her. I immediately connected to the Hawaiian volcano goddess known as Pele. Many years ago, after visiting Hawaii, I spent a great deal of time in the shamanic journey process connecting with Pele. I see her as a powerful spirit of the earth, one of the many manifestations of the goddess energy of the Divine Feminine. As the fiery spirit of the volcano, Pele is both creative and destructive. Her essence is generative; she brings to birth new land through the fiery lava of the volcano. But at the same time, her fire purifies and cleanses.

During one trip to the big island of Hawaii, I felt an overwhelming energetic stimulation at my second chakra. All my senses were heightened, and I had a strong physical drive to be sexual with my wife. I figured out what was going on in a couple of days, and I was then able to refocus my meditation and use a yogic technique to transmute and balance my second-chakra sexual energy, which had been overstimulated by the life-giving force of Pele. (I learned the technique, called Sat Kriya, from Yogi Bhajan.)

This experience demonstrated to me the power of the generative force of the living earth. When I visited Volcano National Park on the Puna coast of Hawaii, I walked on recent lava flows and saw pools of red-hot molten lava just feet from where I stood. The recently crusted-over lava I walked on was so hot that it felt as if the bottoms of my running shoes were melting. In my shamanic journeying, I recognized all of this as the manifestation of the spirit of Pele. Since that time, the spirit of Pele comes to me when a client needs strong purification. This was the case with Lisa.

When I made contact with Lisa, I saw the red-hot molten caldera of Pele. The next image was of Lisa's spiritual body being lowered gently into the center of the fiery caldera. My awareness was then flooded with impressions of Lisa's outer shell being infused with fire. This outer shell was her emotional body, where decades of pain, trauma, and abnegation had accumulated.

It was clear that Pele was purifying and purging Lisa's emotional body through fire. I had seen this before with other clients, but never so clearly as with Lisa. I felt Pele's heat channeling through her; my own body started to feel hot. After a moment, I saw Lisa's spiritual body ascending from the fiery caldera. I knew then that the purification process was done.

When I checked in with Lisa, she said she felt a shift happen in her body. She was a feeler, so her body was always her first reference point. She didn't see images the way I do, yet she knew that something had changed profoundly. She felt more calm than she had remembered feeling in a long time.

When we muscle tested, Lisa had cleared the inner conflict and the associated fear 100 percent. And as I had suspected would happen, she had also achieved 100 percent energetic boundaries with her emotions at all levels.

Psychotherapy is an involved process. Ideally, it is a collaborative one, with client and therapist working together to achieve the client's therapeutic objectives. In Dynamic Energetic Healing®, the client's awareness shifts on many levels because the model induces clients to access various internal resource states. When the client's awareness shifts at the cognitive or thinking level, it takes time for these changes to integrate throughout the whole person after they leave the session. This may take an afternoon or it may take many months. In Lisa's case, establishing solid energetic boundaries with her emotions was just one step in her healing process. It did not solve everything for her, but it did set up the conditions for Lisa to realize what the next step in her healing process would be.

Over the next three months, while Lisa's separation with Sal was proceeding, she had a few more sessions with me. Lisa and Sal made some financial decisions and agreed what to do about their assets, but Lisa's emotions about her separation and divorce process were still up and down. In addition, she found herself acting like that needy adolescent, literally throwing herself at John, who found her behavior off-putting. After spending a certain amount of time with John, Lisa felt overtaken by her very intense feelings. These feelings directed her behavior to become intrusive and disrespectful of John's personal boundaries.

Lisa felt ashamed for acting so immature and out of control. After some discussion about the ramifications of this behavior, Lisa established the following intention: "I don't want to act in that childlike way ever again, feeling needy and alone and just wanting affection." I had Lisa state her intention out loud. When I muscle tested her, both of her arms went weak, indicating psychoenergetic reversal. We then began a series of interventions and discoveries that hearkened back to Lisa's childhood and her family of origin.

The first intervention was chiming a Tibetan bowl, which corrected the psychoenergetic reversal at the unconscious level only. Lisa then selected frontal occipital holding. After centering and making contact with Lisa, my awarenesses came very quickly. I started getting impressions of energetic strands between Lisa and her mother. These strands were connected to Lisa at her heart chakra. As I stayed with my awareness, I saw very clearly that Lisa was holding a great deal of resentment in her heart center, the seat of compassion. As soon as I saw this, my black panther leaped into view and, in his mysterious and amazing way, absorbed and transmuted this residual dark energy.

An *entanglement* is a dark energy formulation that is usually the residual anger and resentment from an acrimonious interpersonal encounter. An entanglement can be between two individuals or an entire group of people.

When my black panther had completely absorbed all of this old resentment, the dark ring around Lisa's heart chakra had dissolved. I removed my hands and asked her what she had experienced during that two minutes. Lisa filled me in on the family dynamics that I had just become aware of on an energetic level.

Lisa described an old pattern of emotional abuse suffered at the hands of her father. Lisa's father was a misogynist. He would first target Lisa's mother with his verbal abuse; when he couldn't get to her mother, he would target Lisa instead—he found this entertaining. What I saw as an entanglement between Lisa and her mother was Lisa's anger and resentment toward her mother for not stopping her father's emotionally abusive behavior. Lisa was very emotional, and her father thought she was lots of fun to tease because he could always get a rise out of her. Lisa never stuck up for herself around her father. Even with all the teasing she endured, while she was growing up she still thought that her father was a cool guy and that he loved her. This was all very confusing and hurtful to Lisa. As is often the case in psychotherapy, unresolved hurts and trauma connected to Mom and Dad were still creating problems for the adult Lisa in her intimate relationships.

After Lisa shared this information with me, it struck me that she was being affected by another dark energy formulation that Dynamic Energetic Healing® calls the *cosmic void*. My colleagues Mary Hammond-Newman and Nancy Gordon developed the concept of the cosmic void as a metaphor to describe a dark energy formulation that individuals experience as a feeling of living in a void. When I connect with a client who has a cosmic void, I get strong impressions of deep sadness and aloneness, along with a feeling of isolation that has pervaded for a very long time. There is often the feeling of dispiritedness that comes from being cut off from Source. The image I get is of an astronomical black hole, far out in space, whose dense gravitational field is pulling everything into its black center of nothingness. Our cosmic-void metaphor extends an energetic cord from the black hole across the vast expanse of space and right into the crown chakra of the unfortunate individual. The result is a fracturing of the individual's connection to Source, as the gravitational pull from the black hole usurps the individual's connection to Source.

Lisa's muscle testing supported this metaphor as the interference pattern we needed to clear. Lisa selected frontal occipital holding as our starting intervention. Soon after making contact with her, I got the impression of a dark stain in the upper right area of her auric field. As my inner awareness focused on that, my vision became more clear. I saw what I can only describe as a hidden "cyst" that had been covered over in what appeared to be a fold in Lisa's energy field. I had never seen anything like this before. I discerned that there were numerous layers in Lisa's energy field, and this black splotch was hidden in a fold in one of the layers.

The impressions that followed informed me that this represented an old traumatic wound. It seemed like the grain of sand in an oyster shell that creates an irritation and eventually becomes a pearl. In Lisa's case, the irritation became a traumatic cyst that was no treasure at all—it was a family wound that had generated the feelings I associated with a cosmic void. To me, this was the energetic legacy of Lisa's unresolved pain and sadness that her father had never sufficiently loved her.

I called for help and asked the compassionate spirits to heal Lisa's pain. Within five seconds, I saw my upper-world Tibetan master turn from his seated, meditative stance and begin chanting in Lisa's direction. This went on for about forty-five seconds. To my utter delight and amazement, I saw the black cyst shrink down to nothing. By the time the Tibetan master was done and turned away from Lisa, there was no more blackness and her energy field in that area was the same as it was everywhere else. When we next muscle tested, the cosmic void had cleared 100 percent.

Lisa was convinced that her compulsive overeating was simply an effort to fill this empty space in her. She realized that the embarrassing, acting-out behaviors of the adolescent inside her were unconscious expressions of desperately trying to acquire her father's love. Lisa was tremendously relieved to have released this old pain. She was absolutely convinced that her eating disorder had spontaneously healed. Subsequent sessions confirmed this.

The last thing we needed to do in that session was restore Lisa's energetic boundaries with her mother and her father, since she had none. Lisa selected one minute of NAEM tapping, followed by the frontal occipital holding intervention. As soon as I established physical contact with Lisa, I heard drumming. As my vision became clear, I saw the women of Native American beings in nonordinary reality gathered together in a large circle. They were drumming healing, loving energy into Lisa, whose spiritual body was in the center of the circle. Interestingly, I could feel Lisa's body shuddering. This went on for some time, until the drumming circle broke up and the women approached Lisa to wrap her in a blanket. They took Lisa to the women's common area, where they exchanged stories for the rest of the night. This provided Lisa with the healing affirmation she needed in order to overcome the deficit from her parents.

When I finished, I asked Lisa what she had experienced. Though she did not have any of the imagery that I did, she felt her body shuddering and vibrating. When we muscle tested, Lisa had 100 percent energetic boundaries with both her mother and her father.

A number of months later, Lisa brought me up to date on how things had changed for her. I was very glad to hear that she was no longer caught in the compulsive cycle of bingeing and purging. Her relationship to food was healthy, without any of the out-of-control cravings to overeat. Just as importantly, Lisa felt in control of herself emotionally and was no longer acting out a wounded and needy child in her relationships with men.

Lisa had come in to check her energetic boundaries and make sure they were still as strong as before. To our mutual delight, her boundaries had stayed solid. Once she was able to integrate the adolescent part of her that continually acted out, she realized that John wasn't the best man for her. Shortly after, she met and fell in love with another man with whom she shared common interests. They were compatible in all the ways that Lisa desired, and they remain happily married to this day.

RESTORING HEALTHY IMMUNE FUNCTION: ESTABLISHING ENERGETIC BOUNDARIES WITH AN ANCESTRAL EARTHBOUND SPIRIT

Jay, who is in his late forties, suffered from chronic upper-respiratory, immune-compromised illnesses. Over the course of treatment, I helped him address and resolve a variety of traumatic experiences from which he carried residue.

At the time of this particular session, Jay was in a stable place emotionally and physically. He had just completed running a marathon, something he had done more frequently when he was younger. He had begun training a couple of months prior to the race and had paced himself well. However, one week before the race Jay became exhausted and started developing an upper-respiratory illness.

Jay completed the race the next week, finishing in the top ten for his age group, and he felt pretty good about his overall performance. But his upper-respiratory illness came back. Now Jay was feeling depressed—not just from the letdown of the race being over but also because he felt his immune system was "shot."

With my help, Jay set the intention to stay physically healthy and maintain a strong immune system.

As we talked about different ways to approach this, I got the strong feeling that I needed to do a brief diagnostic journey. I explained what this would involve and Jay was very interested in learning what this method might reveal. I darkened the room and began to rattle. I immediately connected to a Native American spiritual ally who, in nonordinary reality, began rattling around Jay.

I saw immediately that there was a thick line of energy a couple of inches in front of Jay's body that ran from his head to his toes. I realized that this was the energy of another being—a spirit that had attached itself to Jay's energy field.

That was all my ally was willing to reveal to me in nonordinary reality. He communicated that the rest of the healing work needed to be done in ordinary reality, so I ended my journey. I shared my experience with Jay. I asked him what he thought about it and, more pointedly, whether he had any awareness of a spirit attached to him. He surprised me by immediately suggesting that it might be his sister, Marla, with whom he had been very close before her death from cancer a few years earlier.

The fourth anniversary of Marla's death was the week following the marathon. Jay and Marla used to run races together, so Jay talked to her in his mind as he was running this race. As he began to tire during the last three miles (roughly the length of a 5-K), he thought of Marla and what *she* had gone through when she had tried to run her last 5-K during her fight with cancer. As Jay talked to her, he found himself becoming increasingly identified with her *during the time that she was sick.*

Jay told me that he always wished to be close to Marla and experience what she was experiencing when she was alive. During her bout with cancer (particularly the last two months of her life), his time with her was most poignant. So during the last three miles of the marathon, when Jay was struggling to finish the race, he knew his immune system was "totally shot"—just like Marla's had been during her last run.

Jay believed that a part of Marla gives him strength, but he had failed to realize that he was identifying with her cancer-weary body (i.e., her compromised immune system). Other times, when he was feeling strong and healthy, he imagined her next to him, healthy and running strongly, just as she had been prior to her cancer.

The information I received in my shamanic journey made it clear that this was a case of "spirit obsession." Marla's spirit was not possessing Jay, but he was regularly referring to her and inviting her into his energy field so he could be close to her. (I wonder how many people unwittingly keep their deceased loved ones attached to them, preventing the deceased from moving on and evolving.)

I next asked Jay a series of questions about his relationship with Marla. I also asked what he wanted for his sister and asked him to consider what path to take that would consider the best and highest good *for both of them.*

Jay thought about this for a moment. Then he smiled at me, looked me straight in the eye, and told me that Marla had just come to him. She said that now she understands how important it is for Jay to remember her when she was strong and when they were running together before cancer had so rudely intruded in her life. This is a wonderful example of how an internal resource—specifically, a spiritual resource—emerges during Dynamic Energetic Healing® treatment.

Jay realized that even with all the healing work we had done to remove the traumatic residue he had accumulated from Marla's illness and death, his desire to be close to his sister had overridden the benefits of the healing work. All of his manual muscle testing had indicated that Jay carried no more emotional or traumatic residue from the loss of his sister. However, it was evident to both of us that the relationship between Jay and Marla, *now better appreciated as an ancestral spirit*, needed to be processed and redefined.

This was not a typical case of earthbound spirit attachment because Jay wanted to keep her (as a spirit) with him; if it were, our goal would be to release the attached and interfering spirit because most of them cause all sorts of problems. Indeed, it was evident that Jay and his sister (now a deceased spirit) were both maintaining the relationship—the problem was that the relationship needed to be redefined in order for Jay to stay healthy.

Jay established the intention for his energetic boundaries with Marla to be at 100 percent. Via Jay's MMT, it became clear that he had an unconscious objection to fulfilling this intention and that this objection had created an internal conflict within Jay. His most poignant memories of Marla were from the last years of her life when she was struggling with cancer. He was afraid that Marla would feel betrayed if he stopped empathizing with her suffering and that she would perceive him as callous and insensitive. As a consequence, he focused on her weakness rather than her strength. When I asked Jay why he was doing this, he did not have an explanation. All he could say was that he just kept focusing on her dying process and how painful it was for him.

Now that we had clearly identified the internal objection, it was easy to eliminate these information fields with energetic strategies. After just two interventions, Jay's muscle testing determined that he was at 100 percent energetic boundaries with Marla. To complete the process, I had Jay future pace to imagine seeing himself with a strong, healthy Marla and seeing them running races together.

Jay shifted his internal reference points to remember and see Marla when she was at the height of her strength and good health. Not surprisingly, Jay acknowledged that her deceased spirit understood this and would support Jay by helping him to remember her vitality and strength. In addition, nothing more needed to be done to address any unresolved loss suffered from his sister's death.

Soon after this session, Jay's upper-respiratory problems gradually but completely disappeared. What had been out of Jay's awareness and negatively influencing him energetically had shifted. Jay was able to heal. Even more importantly, he now has a spiritual resource to support his physical well-being and help him to maintain a healthy immune system.

CONFRONTING PSYCHIC ATTACK: REESTABLISHING THE RELIABILITY OF MUSCLE TESTING

Vicki, who supervises security staff at a prison in Washington state, has been seeing me about some personal issues on and off for several years. She has worked for a number of correctional institutions over the last fifteen years. During that time, her intelligence and sensitivity allowed her to rise through the ranks to a highly paid supervisory position—she is one of the few female supervisors of security staff at the prison.

A significant amount of my work with Vicki over the last few years has been to support and empower her to keep her spiritual light bright in these places of darkness. Vicki has known for many years that she is a *light worker*. Light workers are aware of their spiritual mission or purpose in life, which is to bring healing energy and compassion to others in whatever ways they can. Although Vicki didn't really understand why she ended up working in prisons, she accepted and acknowledged her role as a light worker in these dark and often anger-filled institutions.

As a supervisor, Vicki does not have much direct contact with the inmates, but she has regular interaction with the employees of the prison, particularly the security staffers. Vicki told me that the correctional institutions she has worked in are sexist and misogynistic. This has made it particularly challenging for her to supervise security staffers who have been there for many years. She refers to this group of men as "the good old boys."

In one of our sessions, Vicki asked for help in dealing with a small group of the good old boys. As she described the interactions she had with these men, she realized she had fallen back into an old codependent pattern of trying to please them in order to avoid conflicts. Further discussion revealed that Vicki had unwittingly taken on the role of the good mother to these men. She felt guilty when any of them were unhappy and did everything she could to avoid making them angry. We discovered that this small group of men were projecting onto Vicki their desire for her to take care of them. This unconscious phenomenon, along with Vicki's old patterning, had caused Vicki to unconsciously take on the projection of being the good mother, which significantly compromised her energetic boundaries with them. Once Vicki realized the unconscious trap she had fallen into, we were able to establish 100 percent energetic boundaries with this specific group of men and with their anger in general. That was all that was required to get Vicki back on track.

Vicki's next appointment was eight weeks later. She described how she had been much more confident in her interactions with the staff since our last appointment. She was no longer taking care of them emotionally. In fact, she was being much more forthright and explicit, telling them that they have to take responsibility for their own problems since that is not her job.

Vicki started to chitchat with me about what she and her partner had been doing recreationally. I listened attentively and very quickly realized that I was going into a trance. I started feeling very tired—to the point that I could hardly keep my eyes open—even though it was only three in the afternoon. Many thoughts went through my mind, including that I might have to excuse myself and take a break from this session. I felt drugged, and I didn't know how much longer I'd be able to last. I felt as though my mind was in a fog, and I couldn't concentrate on or attend to what Vicki was saying. It must have lasted about fifteen minutes, and then when Vicki started talking about her work situation again, my mental clarity returned to normal instantly!

In retrospect, I realized that this has happened to me many times in the past with other clients. I believe that this phenomenon is energetic and that clients do it unconsciously when they are afraid of addressing something threatening. I've always described it as "psychic interference," as though an invisible energetic barrier is thrown up by the client's unconscious to defend a part of themselves against an anticipated confrontation.

I always experience this phenomenon in the same way as I did with Vicki. I feel as though I'm going to go to sleep, and I have difficulty attending to what my client is telling me. I start thinking I need some caffeine or I need to take a nap, and I wonder how I'm going to get through the session. The psychic fog I experience feels as though I'm being pushed away from staying in contact with my client. It's an amazing energetic phenomenon. But if I stay with the process, I always experience an instantaneous shift—my mind clearing and returning to normal heightened awareness—at some point in the client's dialogue with me. That's when I realize that the client is talking about something which they find very threatening.

This is a classic example of what Mindell calls a double signal. He says that double signals are *unconscious mixed messages which are intended to confuse*. Some obvious examples include a person who is smiling at you as they are expressing anger and a person who is sitting with their hands scrunched up into fists on their legs and telling you that they are relaxed. The person is not consciously aware of trying to confuse you with their communication, which means that double signals are an example of what Freud called a defense mechanism generated by the unconscious mind.

Because it is the nature of double signals to confuse, I didn't notice Vicki's conflicting communication at the time—it was veiled. Only afterwards did I realize that as she was talking calmly about her partner, inside she felt very threatened by some employees at the prison. During our session, she was too scared to even consider raising the issue with me. When I emerged from the trance that Vicki's double signal had triggered in me, I realized I needed to tread very delicately with whatever would occur next.

Consistent with her double signaling to avoid the threatening issue, Vicki's initial intention was to establish 100 percent energetic boundaries with sugar (since she was feeling somewhat out of control with sugar) and then determine if sugar was an energy toxin and whether or not she needed to antidote it.

As soon as we began muscle testing, confounding things started to happen. I first muscle tested to determine whether Vicki's chi field was balanced or switched. (This is my first step in muscle testing any client.) Uncharacteristically for Vicki, her chi field was switched, so our first step was to rebalance her chi field so that we could confidently rely on her muscle testing. I directed Vicki to stimulate a series of three acupressure areas (the small of her back, her kidney meridian points under her collarbones, and her Governing and Central Vessel points just above and below the lips) by gently rubbing each area for thirty seconds. This simple correction is sufficient for 98 percent of my clients whose energy fields are switched, but Vicki's chi field remained switched.

I next directed Vicki to do Cook's balance, another energy-balancing strategy often used by energy psychologists (Gallo, 1999). I rarely need to use it, but Cook's balance is a very reliable method for rebalancing the client's chi field if the intervention just described does not. I did these corrections with her, to make sure that my own chi field was balanced properly. Once again, Vicki's chi field remained switched.

I knew from working with Vicki in the past that this situation was not caused by neurological disorganization. I asked Vicki if she had been doing anything unusual within the last twenty-four hours or if she had been in an environment that was unusual for her—she had not. She said that she had been eating more healthily (i.e., eating less sugar) for the past two days.

I was perplexed, to say the least. Because I had been unable to correct Vicki's switched chi field, I resorted to surrogate muscle testing—I knew I could not trust my muscle testing of Vicki. Standing four feet across from her, I began asking questions and muscle testing my own fingers. I quickly determined that Vicki was contaminated with dark energy intrusions. It all began to make sense—the earlier foggy state of my awareness and inability to attend to Vicki, and now this confounding problem with her muscle testing. Some kind of dark energy formulation had malevolent intentions for Vicki, and it was preventing me from balancing her chi field. As a result, her muscle testing responses were unreliable and none of the normally effective balancing interventions worked. I continued to surrogate muscle test and determined that frontal occipital holding was the intervention of choice to eliminate these intrusions.

As soon as I made contact with Vicki, I moved into dreamtime. One of my power animals, a panther, was circling around her. My attention was next drawn to her chest, where I saw a large mass of gooey black tar deep in her chest cavity. I saw my black panther jump into her chest, absorbing most of the black tar. Shortly thereafter, he jumped out of her chest into his own realm, vomiting onto the ground what he had absorbed. He then bounded back into her chest and absorbed the rest of the gooey tar.

Then the scene changed, and Vicki's spiritual body was in the realm of my black panther. Vicki was buried in this primordial earth realm up to her neck, which enabled the earth to drain the residue of the poisons that she had absorbed into her body from the dark energy intrusions.

When this was completed, the scene changed again, and my black panther ally had given her a small piece of fruit from a nearby bush, very reminiscent of a rose hip. After that, Vicki was taken to a small pond of pristine water and offered a few sips to further purify her physical body.

That was the end of my compressed-time shamanic journey. I surrogate muscle tested Vicki and determined that we had released and cleared the dark energy intrusions at all levels except that of the physical body.

The next intervention selected was the Tibetan bell. After chiming it several times, I muscle tested Vicki again and discovered she was still holding some kind of dark energy in her physical body. Surrogate muscle testing determined we needed to use frontal occipital holding once more. Shortly after making contact, I perceived the powerful loving energy of Jesus coming into the room as rose-quartz light. It infused me completely and then focused intensely on Vicki. The energy was being directed at her heart center, which somehow squeezed out numerous dark, slug-like creatures from her back, as if they were coming out of her pores. I continued to just hold the space, knowing that I had nothing to fear with the powerful spiritual energy of Jesus doing the healing. I'm never afraid of becoming contaminated myself when I'm working with the compassionate spirits; I trust them completely to keep me safe.

After this, it was very evident that there was no more dark energy left in Vicki. I decided to muscle test her directly this time. She was no longer switched, and she was clear of dark energy contamination at all levels. *I had been unable to muscle test Vicki because she was contaminated with dark and malevolent energy.* That had never happened to me before. I am always learning.

Naturally, I was curious about how Vicki had been contaminated by this dark energy. I asked if she had any speculations about it. She did. There were a few security staffers who had been at the prison for many years. She said they were pretty scary individuals, and everyone at the institution danced around them. Another supervisor who had been on the job for a number of years confided to Vicki that nobody wanted her position because they would have to supervise these guys.

Vicki told me that one of her core values is fairness. When she had examined the scheduling for all the employees she supervises, she discovered that these three guys had managed for years to preserve an eight-to-five workday for themselves. Their schedule remained consistent while all the other staff was regularly rotated. Vicki brought this to everyone's attention at a staff meeting and told everybody that she intended to revise the schedule so it would be fair for everyone.

After the meeting, these three men confronted Vicki and told her in no uncertain terms that there would be hell to pay if their schedules were messed with. Vicki interpreted this as an overt threat and acknowledged to me that she didn't trust these guys or what they might be capable of doing. Clearly, she was under psychic attack (through fear and intimidation) by these men who were furious with her for daring to challenge the world they had created for themselves at this institution. As we talked more about this situation, Vicki realized that these men had cursed her with their negative thought forms.

In indigenous societies, one of the shaman's roles is to protect the community from the negative thought forms of aggressive neighboring communities and hostile shamans. The power of these negative thought forms to cause actual physical damage and harm is well understood. Shamans call these negative thought forms *intrusions*. Intrusions are particularly effective when the intended victims are filled with fear. When shamans do extractions to release these intrusions from the victims, they see the intrusions in nonordinary reality as darts, malevolent insects, and other fierce, aggressive energies. In the world of spirit, it is well known that the negative effects of these cursed thought forms are an energetic reality. As Dr. Larry Dossey pointed out in *Prayer Is Good Medicine* (1996), people can be hurt as well as healed through the power of focused and intentional thought.

This was certainly the case for Vicki. She admitted to being intimidated by and afraid of these men. She acknowledged that they were capable of acting out malevolently toward people they didn't like.

When I next muscle tested Vicki to see if she had any energetic boundaries with these men, it was no surprise to discover that she had none. Her energy field was not even close to being robust vis-à-vis them. What made the situation even worse was that Vicki was psychoenergetically reversed on all five core statements associated with the intention to have any boundaries at all with these men! That is, she muscle tested strong on the following statements:

- I don't want to have energetic boundaries with these three men.
- It's not safe to have energetic boundaries with these three men.
- I don't deserve to have energetic boundaries with these three men.
- It's not possible to have energetic boundaries with these men.
- I will not have energetic boundaries with these three men.

Vicki's psychoenergetic reversal and lack of energetic boundaries had made her vulnerable to energetic intrusion.

The first intervention that Vicki selected to resolve this situation was sounding a Tibetan bowl. Following that, Vicki needed to use the NAEM tapping intervention for four minutes to correct all psychoenergetic reversals and establish 100 percent energetic boundaries with all three individuals. With that, our work was done.

What a circuitous route we took, from the trance state I fell into from the double signaling to the intention to establish energetic boundaries with sugar, which resulted in becoming aware of the supernatural phenomena that were creating obstructions for accurate and reliable muscle testing.

You may be wondering how to protect yourself and keep yourself safe from dark energy intrusions. This is an important question to consider. The answer is very simple and comes from the shamanic tradition: You make sure that you are power-filled. This means that you acknowledge to yourself that there are forces in the world that can hurt you, you accept that there is evil in the world, and you accept that people can choose to do evil things.

The shamanic tradition teaches us to do the same thing that I reminded Vicki to do: Honor and walk with spirit every day so you will be always protected.

15

MITIGATING DEPRESSION: UNCOVERING AN ENERGETIC ORIGIN OUTSIDE OF WORLDLY TIME

April is thirty-eight, single, and a certified public accountant in private practice. She came to see me for help with a number of difficult issues—she just couldn't figure out what was wrong with her life and her health. She was suffering from ongoing fatigue and, as a result, cancelling a lot of her appointments. Although she is a very reputable accountant, April was having trouble keeping her practice full enough to pay the bills. This was creating some anxiety, and she was constantly worrying about her income.

But what was even more disconcerting to April was the deepening exhaustion that was overcoming her. After some blood tests and a consultation, her doctor identified an imbalance in her thyroid. But April knew this wasn't all of the story. We had crossed paths briefly in the past, and she felt comfortable with my therapeutic orientation. She is a very spiritually sensitive woman and felt that I could help her.

We spent our first three sessions doing some boundary work, some relationship work, and releasing some spirits that had attached themselves to her and been clinging to her from a past lifetime. By our fourth session, April was feeling much better generally, and her energy was slowly beginning to return. She was still experiencing a depressed mood, and her doctor had so far been unsuccessful in finding the right antidepressant. I suggested that our goal for this session be to heal her depression. As we established this intention, we needed to acknowledge that her endocrinologist had made a causal link between her thyroid imbalance and her depression.

I began by muscle testing April for the presence of any energetic origins. There were none in her current lifetime, in her past lifetimes, in her ancestral lineages, or between any lifetimes. I asked if there was any supernatural influence—yes. I then asked if we needed to name this supernatural interference in order to clear whatever it was—yes. We discovered that one aspect of the interference was a curse. Another aspect was something on a collective level that I had not encountered before. I asked if there were energetic origins of the supernatural interference—no. I had never experienced this dilemma before, and frankly, I was perplexed.

April began to get some intuitive shivers, and she said this related to a group of people living in her area who had come together with a unified purpose. She didn't know much more than that. Not knowing where else to go with this, I asked her through muscle testing if doing the frontal occipital holding intervention would be the best step to take next—yes. As I made contact with April, I began to get some fascinating impressions.

It seemed that April was connected to a group of spiritually intrepid people who had agreed as a collective to explore the spiritual realms of nonordinary reality. These individuals were trying to time travel. April got the impression of a figure that, like a time-lapse photograph, had a number of silhouettes of itself behind it. She suspected that these people were trying to learn how to manifest or project themselves from one place to another via spiritual means.

I received some additional information: the process that this group was practicing had transformed into a curse, and this curse was somehow seducing April. The members of the collective had made an implicit agreement among themselves. They were abandoning their involvement in the physical world in favor of an ascetic, life-denying existence in order to develop their spiritual nature. The altered states of consciousness that were generated by participating in this group experiment seduced April and the others into denying the value of being in their own physical body and of their connection to the earth.

As April and I talked about this, I realized that her muscle testing had indicated that there was no energetic origin because this origin was an agreement made *outside of time*! Temporal time was irrelevant—this group had evolved its collective consciousness to the point that they could communicate with each other "out of time." They were practicing group methods to develop their souls shamanically and evolve into a collective soul.

I had never encountered this kind of energetic origin before. I had done some reading on what aboriginal people call dreamtime, and I had studied this with Dr. Arnold Mindell within the context of processwork. I knew in theory and through anecdote that individuals could communicate wordlessly with each other over vast distances. This is what the aboriginal people claim they do. This was problematic for April because of the agreements she made with this group. These agreements were generated by this seduction of the collective consciousness of this group, which was experienced by April and the others as a more desirable altered state than individual autonomy. In present time, April was having problems in the physical world with her job and physical health. No matter how hard she tried, she couldn't get her life to work right.

I suspected April might be psychoenergetically reversed on her willingness to cancel her agreements with this group. When I had her say out loud, "I now want to cancel my agreements with this group," her arms muscle tested weak; when she said the opposite statement her arms were strong. She was clearly psychoenergetically reversed.

Frontal occipital holding was selected again. As I made contact, I saw that this group was spiritually self-indulgent and had an unconscious fear of dealing with the suffering of the world. They had abandoned their commitment to the earth and had compromised their heart centers as a consequence. This intervention balanced and corrected April's psychoenergetic reversal.

Next I muscle tested April to determine if she had any energetic boundaries with the suffering of the world—she had none. Using muscle testing, she selected the Tibetan bowl and ten minutes of tapping the NAEM points. These interventions restored her boundaries to 100 percent with the suffering of the world. Muscle testing then confirmed that April now had 100 percent energetic boundaries with her body, chronological time, and her work in the world. In addition, she had 100 percent boundaries with the collective that she had been part of. I muscle tested April to find out if the curse generated by the seduction of the collective was still present—it had spontaneously dissolved.

April and I were curious to know when her association with this collective had begun. But we determined through her muscle testing that we could not find this out. Apparently it was something that was not for us to know, at least at the conscious level.

Community is an important value for April. She puts a lot of energy into nurturing and being nurtured by her community. This is clearly one of the positive residues from the time when she was connected to this spiritual collective. When we finished our work and were reflecting on the session, it made sense to April that the agreements she had made with this group to deny the value of her physical body in the physical world were a very strong negative influence on her in this lifetime. It was now easy to make correlations between the problems she was having in this life and the revelations we had discovered about her agreements with this collective.

We reflected back to our first session, when April was significantly dissociated and needed to spend some time working with me to help restore full embodiment. She felt strongly that in *this* session we had begun an accelerated healing process. She sensed that her physical energy would soon be restored — and it was. April also knew intuitively that she was now much more connected to the world than she had been before our session; she felt that she was back. She also knew that by releasing this collective curse, she was finally going to start manifesting what she desired in her life. It was an amazing session for both of us.

16

VALIDATING EMPIRICALLY THE EXISTENCE OF PAST LIVES: RECOVERING POWER AND TERMINATING THERAPY

About thirteen years ago, while I was learning processwork, I was working with Denise to help her with relationship issues. After a few months, Denise mentioned that she was on a very restricted diet because of her many food allergies. We talked about it a little bit but then returned to the work on relationships. When Denise was a child, her controlling mother often invaded her personal boundaries. As a consequence, Denise was very slow to trust other people (including me) and reluctant to disclose much about herself. In our sessions, she parceled out information in bits and pieces when she felt safe enough to do so.

After another two months and once again out of the blue, Denise described a very traumatic, mysterious incident that happened about ten years earlier. She was reading in bed late one night when she felt the room getting very cold. As she bundled herself up in her blankets, she saw and felt a dark form moving toward her from the other side of the room. As this form moved closer to the edge of her bed, Denise was overwhelmed with fear and felt tremendous dread. She pulled the covers over herself and hid underneath them, shaking with fear of this dark, unknown force. Eventually she turned the light off and fell into a fitful sleep. Ever since that experience, Denise had lived with what she called a "tight gut" and had developed numerous food sensitivities. I was the first person that she had ever told this to. This sounded like some kind of spirit intrusion, but since I had never encountered this before, I told her I would like to share this with my friend and mentor

Michelle for consultation, emphasizing that any personal information would be kept confidential. She gave me permission to consult.

Michelle told me it could very well have been some kind of spirit intrusion, but the only way to be certain would be to journey shamanically and find out for myself. At that time, I had been studying with Michelle and journeying under her guidance for about nine years. There were devoted and powerful helping spirits to assist me, so I pursued this with Denise.

Though she was generally mistrustful, Denise was very spiritually sensitive and willing to explore and consider shamanic intervention. I explained that I would try to establish contact with the being that had apparently intruded into her personal space and possibly attached itself to her. I would start with a journey to the upper world, guided by my devoted horse, a guardian spirit that had been working with me for many years. I explained that with the help of drumming music to facilitate my journey, I would narrate to Denise everything that I saw in order to keep her apprised of my experience.

My horse took me very quickly to an upper-world realm that I saw as gray rock outcroppings with a dense forest brush surrounding a small clearing. In the middle of the clearing was a dugout area with a fire burning in it. Though it was dusk, I could see the area clearly. I moved close to the fire for warmth as my horse stood behind me next to the brush. I did not know what to expect but continued to assert my intention to contact the being that intruded into Denise's space, if indeed a being were responsible for her experience.

In the spiritual realms of the upper and lower worlds, there is no time. Even so, the other part of me imagined that I had been waiting a few minutes when darkness fell upon the scene. Suddenly, I saw a large, imposing, black form moving slowly toward me. At first glance, it appeared to be a tall, broad gargoyle-like creature—almost insect-like—with a cloak that reminded me of large wings. As it got closer to where I was sitting, I slowly stood up, faced it square on, and told it in no uncertain terms that what it had done to Denise was not OK with me. I was about to demand an explanation when it suddenly lunged at me! As it made contact with me, I experienced a force field of light surrounding me that I instantly knew was the protective light of the healing spirit of Jesus, with whom I had recently done a lot of shamanic work. My physical body jolted reactively as I saw this creature bounce off me back into the rock outcroppings. I was pretty shaken up, and since this creature was nowhere to be seen, I decided to end my journey there and return with my horse the same way that I had ascended.

I shared with my client everything that I had not been able to report during the assault. I told Denise that I had no conclusive explanation for what happened. I added that I hoped for a positive outcome from my journey, but we would have to wait to see whether she noticed any difference before her next session. I again asked Denise if she would grant me permission to consult with my shamanic supervisor as to a possible next step. She said that would be fine.

I met with Michelle the next day and explained what had happened. She told me I needed to go back to find out what happened to the being so I could help it to heal. I needed to find out why this being was interested in Denise. She said that this being was probably in pain, and I needed to help it first in order to help my client. My initial response was dismay! I had been attacked and was quite apprehensive about having another encounter with this being. Michelle reminded me that because I had devoted, loyal, and strong spiritual allies, I would be protected. It is my responsibility as a shamanic practitioner to do what I can to help all beings that need assistance, regardless of which realm they reside in.

At Denise's next session, I explained to her what needed to happen. I told her I would journey to reconnect with the being that assaulted me. I reminded her that once again I would narrate my experience as it was happening. I put in the drumming tape and prayed to my helping spirits for help, guidance, and protection during my journey. I set my intention and waited for my horse to appear. Within seconds, he was by my side and we were going up to that same upper-world realm where I had encountered the being the first time. We arrived at the same place very quickly, and everything appeared as it had before. There was a small fire burning in the center of the clearing, but this time it was already dark. I was apprehensive and vigilant, and I asked my horse to stay close. After a couple of minutes, I began to call for the being. Almost immediately, I saw an indistinct shape coming toward me. I was shocked at what I saw—what had been a large, threatening, black gargoyle-like being now appeared as a collapsed, smallish, gray being. As it moved toward me, I felt deep sadness and a sense of defeatism emanating from it. It stopped when it was about ten paces from me.

Suddenly, I saw a cascade of pictures in front of my inner eye. A story began to unfold like a newsreel. The setting was in medieval times. I saw a nobleman courting a lady dressed in a beautiful gown. As the pictures continued, the nobleman's overtures were rejected; the lady chose someone else as her suitor. The nobleman was humiliated in front of the whole community. His shame was so great that he felt compelled to leave the community. In his hurt and anger, he vowed to avenge the affront to his dignity. I then saw that he had been following her soul for lifetimes, finally finding this opportunity to get his revenge.

I was amazed by what I had just seen. I had received phenomenological evidence for the transmigration of the soul! In this shamanic state of consciousness, I had received corroboration for what I had heretofore simply taken on faith. As I reflected on this internally, I remembered my charge from Michelle to do everything I could to help this being.

I was suddenly back at the clearing by the fire, with this ashen, pathetic, hollow soul in front of me. I now had some context in which to relate compassionately to the being's sadness and feelings of defeat. I told him I understood his shame and anger; I was sorry for his pain and for how long he had suffered. I asked if he wanted to be free of his suffering—yes. I told him there was a way I could help him, but first he needed to release Denise from his malevolent curse. I reminded him that what had occurred was many lifetimes ago. His soul had its own destiny to fulfill, and the grudge he was carrying kept him stuck, preventing him from moving on and evolving. There was a pause and then, with a sigh of deep resignation, he said OK. I asked him if he knew where he needed to go—no. I asked my horse if it could help him find his way, and my horse nodded affirmatively. I told my horse I would wait by the fire while it guided this being to the next stop on its long journey. The next thing I knew, there was a whoosh as my horse moved swiftly past me, and the being was gone. After what seemed like a few minutes my horse returned, nuzzled me on the cheek, and we were on our way back.

When I debriefed with Denise, she was surprised by the story and relieved at the way it ended. She had no conscious awareness of any past-life experience, let alone the one I had described. We talked for a while about the possible ramifications of this healing. *She felt validated to know that her experience many years earlier was not something she had just made up.*

At our next session, Denise reported that sometime during the first week following the healing journey, she began to notice that an area around her solar plexus felt very different. She described it as a belt of muscles all the way around her midsection that spontaneously relaxed. She had felt tightness inside her gut but had never realized how tightly bound up this band of muscles had been through the years. It was good to hear that she had physical confirmation of positive and noticeable change from the healing journeys we had shared. I continued to see Denise over the next few months. Perhaps not so coincidentally, the relationship issues that she was struggling with also loosened up.

As a process-oriented therapist, it is sometimes my job to take on the role of provocateur in relation to the victim part of my client. So, during a process-oriented weekend workshop, Denise and I wrestled—a common technique used in processwork. Process-oriented wrestling allows people to experience their feelings physically and bring them out more strongly without the fear of being physically hurt. They remain aware that this is essentially a psycho-drama for psychotherapeutic benefit, so these wrestling matches usually feel almost staged.

Although Denise normally presented as a shy, unassertive woman (some-times she said nothing to me for minutes at a time, eyes gazing downward at the floor), she wrestled with me in a very aggressive way. This wrestling match was much more than a psychodrama for her. In a sense, it was the cul-mination of all the work she had done with me to reclaim her power from her controlling mother. As we rolled on the floor, with the other participants cheering for Denise from the sidelines, I could feel myself struggling against the growing strength of this petite, small-framed woman. The match ended with her pinning me on my back, aggressively grabbing my shirt with both of her hands and yelling, "Are you ready to stop now?!"

Maintaining my meta-awareness, I understood the dream figure that I was enacting with Denise. When the lifetimes-old curse was finally released in our healing journey, the grip that her resentful past-life suitor had tenaciously held on her power center had finally been released. She knew this physically by the release of her solar plexus muscles and by a gradual diminution of her food allergies. The goal of her therapy was to reclaim the power that her mother had taken from her as a child. At the moment when Denise was yelling at me, I knew she was reclaiming her power from her mother in an undeniably physi-cal way. I told her I was ready to stop, and then I watched her very carefully. She allowed just a hint of a smile to be revealed before getting off me. At that moment, I knew that her victory was mine as well. Very shortly after that weekend workshop, Denise said she was ready to terminate therapy with me. I was most happy to hear that and agreed with her decision.

Spirits? Past lives? My own experience confirms over and over again that these things are indeed real.

17

TREATING LONG-TERM PANIC DISORDER: RESOLVING RECURRENT SPIRIT INTRUSION AND LEARNING TO HONOR ALL PARTS OF THE SELF

The events described in this case history took place over two years. This case was extremely complex and had many unexpected turns. The subject, Don, made continual progress toward achieving his initial intention, which was to rid himself of constant panic attacks. In addition, many other important but seemingly unrelated issues emerged as we progressed through Don's treatment. As you will see, at times even I harbored occasional doubts about whether Don would heal. Those times of doubt always reminded me of my need to reassess my own feelings of self-importance and defer to Process, the streams and currents of which we moved into and were guided by.

As is reflected in many of my case histories, Don has a strong spiritual imperative. Don's treatment turned out to be not just a spiritual crisis of sorts for him but also a developmental crisis. He had to confront the strong—even demanding—inner insistence from his soul that refused to leave him alone. His dreamingbody had to be acknowledged and supported, and this had to be accomplished in a way that his personality and religious convictions could accommodate.

To make it easier to follow what may appear to be Don's circuitous path to healing, I have (with the recommendation of my editor) included headings in this case history. The headings identify many of the important links in this case, but not every single issue Don and I addressed. Many of the elements of the Dynamic Energetic Healing® protocol are recognizable, as are many of the interventions I use.

At first glance, it may appear that Don and I addressed one thing after another, but this was hardly the case. Process has its own logic—if you can stay with it long enough—and Don ended up exactly where he needed to, though it was not an easy road. Nothing done with Don was gratuitous; each issue and piece of his process presented itself organically as I followed my second attention and honored Process.

At the end of this two-year course of therapy, Don had accomplished a tremendous amount vis-à-vis the initial presenting problems that he had hoped to resolve. But to say that Don is now complete would be presumptuous and irresponsible. Yes, he was able to discontinue his medication. Yes, he no longer suffers from panic attacks or dark energy intrusions. But Don has come to realize that he has to take personal responsibility for managing his anger and his tendency to want to be in control, which is something he'll have to work on continually in the future.

Don also knows that he must acknowledge his spiritual nature, which demands to be heard. Our sessions taught him that he must work harder to accept and feel compassion for all parts of himself in order to be in harmony with his family and work life. Interestingly, this is not at all what he thought was important when he began this healing journey.

In December, a medical researcher named Don was referred to me by his chiropractor, who had correctly diagnosed Don's problems as mentally/emotionally based. Twelve months before, Don's family doctor had prescribed three medications—Klonopin, Zoloft, and Trazodone—for severe anxiety, panic disorder, and the accompanying inability to sleep at night. Don was trying to get off these drugs but had been unable to do so. He complained of panic attacks (three or four a week), heart palpitations, back and neck pain, waking up in the morning with his jaw and hands clenched, nausea, dizziness, and general muscle tension.

Establishing the Intention

At our first session, Don told me that when he tried to wean himself from these drugs, he experienced side effects including excruciating headaches, anger flare-ups, exacerbation of his anxiety, and an inability to sleep at all during the night (these side effects are common in cases such as Don's). He felt hopeless about getting off the drugs and resolving his panic attacks. What's more, he had tried a variety of complementary medical approaches, including acupuncture, change to a natural diet, regular exercise, and four months of chiropractic, all to no avail. In the end he was told his problems were stress related.

After taking Don's complete history, I explained the conceptual framework of Dynamic Energetic Healing® and asked him if he felt uncomfortable with any of this "nontraditional psychotherapy." Though it was all very new to him, Don was open to trying anything that might help, especially since he had already explored some alternative methods for healing. Being a medical researcher, he understood the fundamentals of how acupuncture works, so it was not too much of a stretch for him to grasp the underlying presuppositions of an energy-based psychotherapy.

Initially, Don wanted to stop clenching his jaw, fists, and arms; he also wanted to sleep more soundly. But after some deeper inquiry with the help of manual muscle testing, we determined that his soul's wisdom was directing him to set these issues aside temporarily and hold the intention to resolve his panic disorder first; this is where we started. Thus, rather than deciding for Don what I believed was most important to address first, I became the facilitator to his soul's wisdom, the part of him that knows from the very core of his being what his most important need is at that moment. Don's process would guide us throughout his course of treatment, which took two years to complete.

Restoring Access to Repressed Feeling States

Over the next three months, we worked on clearing trauma from a variety of energetic origins, starting with an origin from when Don was twenty-six years old. In response to these traumatic events, his access to his own feelings of shame and sadness was blocked. Though he hadn't realized it, Don had developed the unconscious habit of overcompensating behaviorally for his inability to feel and experience shame and sadness. Using a variety of Dynamic Energetic Healing® strategies, including EFT tapping, Tibetan bell, chakra stimulation, F/O holding, and TAT, we were able to restore Don's access to those feeling states. This restored access brought Don immediate and noticeable emotional relief. He perceived a lightness to his general beingness that he had all but forgotten.

Establishing Energetic Boundaries with Driving

At our next session we addressed a panic attack Don had experienced just a few days prior while driving on a snowy freeway after sundown. We used energy strategies to restore 100 percent energetic boundaries with the experience of driving (anywhere, in any weather conditions). By the time we were finished, Don was once again in right relationship with driving. The vibrational frequency of his energy field and his thoughts about driving were brought into optimal alignment with his experience of driving, which created the boundaries he lacked. Don hasn't had any further anxiety while driving since that session.

Clearing a Family Curse

At the next session, Don confided that he had always believed that he would die of a debilitating disease when he turned forty-six. He had been told that cancer and heart disease run in his family, and since he was now forty-four he had been thinking about it a lot lately.

Using manual muscle testing, we tested for a limiting belief—there wasn't one. But upon further inquiry, we determined that he was carrying a family curse (a form of collective trauma he had absorbed in his energy field)—he had significant amounts of toxic energy in his energy field from his family of origin. Don almost felt relieved to be told he was cursed, because we were able to release the curse using energy strategies.

If Don were consulting a practitioner who worked within a different therapy model, they might discuss this as a family myth or story that has been reinforced from generation to generation. Don and his doctor might decide to confront this family story proactively and develop a plan for Don to reduce his risks of disease. Don might be told that he needs to create a new story and perhaps reframe his initial understanding from the perspective of multigenerational family systems. Hypnosis might be used in conjunction with a cognitively based reframing approach so Don could change *at the belief level*.

But in Dynamic Energetic Healing®, manual muscle testing identified this as an *energetic* phenomenon that was part of his energy field. It was the information from family members who held this self-destructive belief (unconscious implant) in their collective field that was truly toxic. By addressing this curse energetically, we would also clear the information at the belief level. We used F/O holding, TAT, and the Tibetan bell to release this collectively held trauma or curse. We cleared the family curse that Don had worried about for the whole of his adult life in fifteen minutes, but Don was skeptical.

We next needed to establish energetic boundaries with Don's immune system because he had no faith that it would maintain his good health and protect him from cancer and heart disease. We used frontal occipital holding again and his boundaries were restored to 100 percent. At our next session two weeks later, Don acknowledged that in some way that he could not explain, he no longer worried about dying from a disease. The curse had truly been released.

By May, Don was sleeping well but still woke up with his jaw and hands clenched with tension. His panic attacks were occurring only twice a month now, and he was feeling more relaxed with people generally. But he still wanted to be off the medications. Now his intention was to have good mind/body health—this was our new starting point.

Establishing Energetic Boundaries with the Future

Don also discovered that he had no energetic boundaries with his own future. As mentioned earlier, he believed he would die when he turned forty-six. He also felt that since his wife, Susan, spent nearly all of their discretionary income, there wasn't enough money to invest in IRAs for retirement. To Don, his future looked abysmal and ultimately hopeless. Using frontal occipital holding, we were able to restore his energetic boundaries with his wife, his relationship to money, and his relationship to his future. This gave Don a sense of optimism about the things to come.

Experiencing the Side Effects of Discontinuing Medication

Don's next appointment was five weeks later. During our previous session, MMT had indicated that *all* significant prior trauma (related to his panic-attack symptoms) had been resolved, and I had referred him to another doctor for a medication evaluation, since Don was insistent about getting off his medications. He had now cut his medication dosages in half and was sleeping through most of the night for the first time in years. Due to complications in his schedule, Don never did coordinate with the doctor. Instead, he went online to research the drugs that he was taking. He found that he would need eight to ten weeks to completely wean himself off these drugs. But when he read the postings from other people who were on the same drugs, he found that many of them could not get off the drugs! When they tried to do so, the side effects were so terrible that they acquiesced to their fate. As Don was tapering off his intake of Zoloft and Trazodone, he had horrific nightmares for three or four nights and terrible, penetrating headaches that lasted for days.

(However, he did notice that the clenching of his fists significantly improved when he cut his intake of the drugs in half; he found this very encouraging.)

Don's experience reflects an enormous oversight made by the pharmaceutical companies that market their drugs to physicians. Don was certain that if he hadn't learned from others that they suffered the same side effects as he did, he would have succumbed to the drugs.

During the last two sessions, Don reported that each time he cut back his drugs by another quarter, he suffered some kind of severe side effect. The latest was extreme rage that lasted for three days. It was only with Susan's encouragement and support that he persisted. Finally, his irrational fits of anger disappeared. Following this, he had crushing headaches that finally subsided, as did his clenching fists, and he began sleeping deeply through the night. How ironic that he could sleep soundly only after he weaned himself off the drugs that were, in part, supposed to help him sleep.

Don was now completely off all his medications. He was sleeping better and no longer had persistent anxiety. His relationship with Susan had improved and his outlook on life was optimistic. So far, he had been in treatment with me for six months.

Over the next few months, Don continued to come in occasionally for reassurance and check-ins to ensure that his energetic boundaries were firm. His sleep fluctuated from very good to poor as a new pattern started to emerge. Though his panic attacks were gone, he still had occasional bouts of situational anxiety and would also become aware of his heart pounding, especially when he woke in the middle of the night.

A New Pattern of Dissociation Emerges

About January of the following year, Don began describing symptoms that fit the diagnostic criteria for dissociation. These included feelings of detachment, inability to concentrate and recall information, dizziness, and episodes of depersonalization or derealization—times during his normal activities when he felt as though he was not integrated with his physical body.

Manual muscle testing indicated he was indeed only 70 percent in his physical body. Our interventions included treating psychoenergetic reversal associated with limiting beliefs such as "It's not safe for me to be in my physical body," "My body will not support me now," and "I'm not happy being in my physical body." We also needed to establish energetic boundaries with his physical body. We used the Tibetan bell and F/O holding to accomplish 100 percent reembodiment (see chapter 11 for the "Protocol for Ensuring That Your Client Is 100 Percent Embodied"). But this was only the beginning of a new and most interesting pattern that began to unfold.

Though Don no longer suffered from panic attacks, he was beginning to manifest symptoms related to his dissociated out-of-body experiences and a proclivity to regularly attract dark energy into his energy field. Whenever he felt dissociated, he became vulnerable to dark energy intrusions and a host of other symptoms, including waking at 2:30 A.M. He was also experiencing a recurrence of some of his earlier panic-attack symptoms, including achiness in his hands, arms, jaw, and back; weakness in his knees; headaches; dizziness; awareness of his heart pounding throughout his body; and general bodily tension. He was experiencing numerous dark energy intrusions, which we cleared easily with energetic strategies as they arose. But this developed into an ongoing pattern, a very frustrating and discouraging experience for Don. It took many months for us to determine and resolve the underlying cause of these recurrent dark energy intrusions.

Spiritual Intrusions and the Emergence of Psychic Phenomena

Don was also perceiving psychic phenomena, such as visions in the middle of the night after he awoke and occasional perceptions of "a dark thing looking like a vague human form" moving around him and threatening him as it moved toward him. This scared him tremendously. After each of these experiences, our muscle testing indicated that Don was not fully embodied. He empirically corroborated this by describing many of the symptoms of dissociation outlined previously. After releasing the dark energy intrusions and being restored back to 100 percent embodiment, Don always felt great.

Don was going through what I describe as a spiritual crisis, and what Stanislav and Christina Grof call a spiritual emergency. The Grofs edited a number of articles written by experts and published them in *Spiritual Emergency: When Personal Transformation Becomes a Crisis*. These experts explain how a variety of spiritual and transformational crises can cause hallucinations, seizures, panic attacks, pain, and severe depression—all of which are symptoms of physical and mental illness. When people suffer in this way, they often feel as though they are going crazy, and their doctors may agree. But Grof and Grof claim that this kind of diagnosis is mistaken in many cases. They strongly recommend that "spiritual emergency" be adopted as a new category of clinical psychiatric diagnosis (Grof and Grof 1989).

Don and other Christians believe it is unacceptable to deal with spirits or mediums, as admonished in various passages in the Bible. Yet Don's healing process consistently revealed that he needed to deal with supernatural phenomena that were disturbance factors affecting many aspects of his life. This created personal and marital conflicts about belief and value systems for Don, which in turn created boundary issues that we needed to address on and off over the next six months.

Don needed to establish energetic boundaries with his physical body, Susan (and her spiritual beliefs), supernatural phenomena, his astral body, and *the emerging spiritual part of him that he was denying*. Don does not use alcohol, but when he went to a bar with a friend to socialize briefly, he picked up a dark energy intrusion. When he went for a brief visit to a cemetery with Susan to pay respects to a relative, he picked up disembodied earthbound spirits that then needed to be released. He perceived this the following night—in the middle of the night he woke up feeling dizzy, with his back hurting and his whole body aching. He tried to relax and let his mind wander. He saw a blue background, and then a face passed by his internal imaging sensors quickly. He next saw "a diamond like on a ring and then the face like a gargoyle." Don said to it, "You are from the graveyard," and then his whole body went cold with goose bumps.

These trapped spirits communicated to Don that they were not malevolent; they just wanted to be released. Manual muscle testing indicated that they came into Don through his first chakra. First we establish 100 percent energetic boundaries with his first chakra using the Tibetan cymbals and Tibetan bowl. Then MMT indicated that prayer would be the best intervention to release the earthbound spirits. We both prayed for their release for three to five minutes. Our muscle testing corroborated their complete release from Don. Finally, Don needed to restore his energetic boundaries with supernatural phenomena by tapping on the chakras, starting with the crown chakra and moving down to the root chakra, for three cycles. This completely restored his boundaries with supernatural phenomena to 100 percent.

In the middle of the night some weeks later, Don had a vision of Susan's grandmother smiling. Then he felt himself being picked up and slammed down on the bed a number of times, but Susan did not perceive the bed moving. Then Don saw "a dark thing moving from right to left that stopped right in front of me." Afterwards, he felt shaky, jittery, and anxious, and subsequently he had headaches. Once again, we needed to clear and release a dark energy intrusion using various energetic strategies.

Accepting Spiritual Gifts and Spiritual Destiny

During one of Don's sessions in March, we determined that in light of all that he had been experiencing, Don needed to accept and embrace his own gifts. This starting intention was an effort to reframe the fearful events of the past four to five months.

First we needed to establish 100 percent energetic boundaries with the emerging spiritual part of Don by doing F/O holding, three minutes of heart-center tapping, and more F/O holding to complete the boundary balance. During this last intervention, I saw one of my guardian spirits approach as I went into a compressed-time shamanic journey. In nonordinary reality, I saw Don being dismembered and experiencing an initiation ritual; after being spiritually cleansed in the dismemberment process, he was reintegrated (put back together). I was told that Don must work with his own compassionate spirits. When we muscle tested, he had 100 percent energetic boundaries with his emerging spiritual part.

Don's muscle testing next determined that there was an energetic intrusion occupying his fifth and sixth chakras. The intervention chosen was the Tibetan bell. As I chimed the bell, I clearly "saw" that Don was blocking access to his karmic legacy from a past life in which he was a shaman. He needed to access this karmic legacy by becoming proficient in the shamanic journey process.

After extensive questioning, Don's MMT determined that his next intervention was to take his "first" shamanic journey to the lower world. I accepted this because Dynamic Energetic Healing® is process oriented and because I had had the intuition months earlier that Don was a shaman who needed to come out of the karmic closet, so to speak. Even though the ramifications of his spiritual emergency were causing Don cognitive dissonance with his Christian beliefs, Process was honored and Don consented to journey. Don's journeying process into the lower world was very smooth. He discerned and contacted a waiting guardian spirit (power animal) easily and without incident. His description of the lower-world landscape was vivid and extensive. None of this surprised me, given the depth of Don's affinity to supernatural phenomena (which, unfortunately, had become a negative component of his life).

Five weeks later, Don had an endoscopic examination followed by a colonoscopy procedure, during which a small polyp was removed. Don felt quite anxious prior to both procedures, but with energetic support he got through them OK—but not without incident.

I have found that it is very common for clients who undergo intrusive medical interventions (such as surgery or radiation treatment) to end up with dark energy intrusions. This is because of the fear and vulnerability that accompanies these procedures. This extreme vulnerability creates a weakening in the individual's auric field and energetic boundaries because they must consent to have their most personal space (their physical body) violated. As a consequence, the middle-world energy beings in nonordinary reality have a greater opportunity to attach to the person's energy field like parasites, sucking on their life-force energy through their fears. The consequences to the individual vary, but they are always weakening in one way or another. Don was already feeling fragile from his ongoing dissociation and emergent psychic episodes, so he succumbed energetically to dark energy intrusion from these medical procedures.

A couple of weeks later, Don began experiencing his familiar symptomatic distress, including waking up at 2:30 A.M., feeling pounding in his chest at various times during the day, waking up with his hands and jaw sore from clenching during the night, and headaches. His symptoms quickly intensified when he became anxious about anything, something that he hadn't experienced for a long time.

Manual muscle testing indicated he was being affected by a "black hole" occupying all seven major chakras; frontal occipital holding was selected as the best intervention to release this. As I stood over Don (who was seated in a chair) with one of my hands lightly contacting his forehead and the other cupping the occipital region of the back of his head, I began to experience a compressed-time shamanic journey as the compassionate spirits that I work with emerged in my interior awareness. These guardian spirit helpers are the tribe of Native Americans that include both men and women. Depending on the needs of the client, the healing work is sometimes done by just the women, just the men, or the tribe's shaman.

In this case it was the tribe's shaman who appeared. He directed me to clean the room with burning sage and chime the Tibetan bell, which I did. When I reconnected with Don in the F/O holding position, I perceived the tribe's shaman (in nonordinary reality) surround Don with a circle of fire in the configuration of burning torches. The shaman stepped into Don's energy field and, with his knife drawn, sliced into each of Don's four sides to create tears or openings in his field. Then I saw the shaman stick his arm through these openings and pull out revolting, black tar-like substances that he threw into a bucket next to him. When he was finished, he sealed each cut with a torch, smudged Don with sage, and sprinkled him with water for cleansing.

I next saw the shaman with his eagle sitting on his left shoulder. As the scene changed, he led Don into the woods. The shaman retched there, and then he led Don into the nearby river to be cleansed. That completed the journey and the intervention. As is becoming more common in my work with clients, the spirits had accomplished the healing.

I smudged the room to clear any residue from the extraction process that I witnessed and then confirmed via MMT that Don had released all traces of the intrusion 100 percent at all levels. The only thing left to do in that session was reestablish 100 percent of Don's energetic boundaries with sleep, which we did easily using the Tibetan bowl and frontal occipital holding.

The Habit of Dissociating

As the weeks passed, Don became very sensitive to the difference between being fully embodied and being dissociated. Once his many energetic intrusions were cleared, he noticed how remarkably present he felt now that he was fully in his physical body again. He noticed how easy it was to recall information accurately and how relaxed he felt in his interactions with people. This was in stark contrast to how stressed and anxious and drained he felt when he was frequently dissociated. It made him wonder just how long he had been dissociating.

Don's experience made me wonder how many of the mental and emotional problems that people suffer from are a direct result of being dissociated, with or without dark energy intrusions. As I tracked this more attentively with my other clients, I realized that many people tend to dissociate from early childhood trauma as an unconscious adaptive strategy—what Freud called a defense mechanism. For many people like Don, this tendency becomes an unfortunate habit of being (or not-being when dissociated!) responsible for all kinds of chronic symptoms. Once clients learn to notice the difference between how good it feels to be fully embodied versus how painful dissociation (with all of its attendant symptomatology) is, life and the prospect of healing become more hopeful. But as you know, bad habits of any kind are difficult to break. Individuals need ongoing therapeutic support to break the habit of dissociating and thereby prevent the soul loss that accompanies this habit or tendency.

Between the frustrating incidents of intrusion, Don was becoming progressively more hopeful. Yet the pattern persisted, occasionally blindsiding Don into temporary despair. Even I began to have occasional doubts about the comprehensiveness of our work together.

Uncovering a Karmic Contract

Over the next two months, Don would be well for a while and then begin dissociating again, with the full complement of symptoms tyrannizing him until we got together to balance his energy. Don was affected by dark energy intrusions so often that he began to believe that he was some sort of magnet for them. The therapy continued with me wondering if and when we would find the key to it all after such a long and difficult struggle to heal.

It was determined in one session that a past-life energetic origin was responsible for Don carrying three earthbound spirits. After Don died in this past life, he had made a karmic contract with these spirits at the soul level. When I helped Don to talk with them in a regressed state, we discovered that they did not want to leave him. We needed to use the Tibetan bowl and frontal occipital holding. During the latter intervention, I accessed my upper-world Tibetan Buddhist teacher, who facilitated the release. When we were done, Don was once again 100 percent in his body and free of all distracting symptoms.

A Soul Retrieval

In a subsequent session, I was directed to do a soul retrieval to bring back a part of Don. This part did not want to return because of the stress of Don's interpersonal conflicts and the demands of his life. Don had to agree to provide more relaxation time in his current life before the split-off part would leave its safe environment in nonordinary reality. When this part integrated back into Don, the intrusion we had identified earlier cleared; after doing two minutes of heart chakra tapping, Don was 100 percent in his physical body again.

Absorbing a Partner's Unhealed Sexual Trauma

A month later, Don arrived at a session feeling awful, but he could not identify any precipitating events that could have caused his aching arms, headaches, poor concentration, and weak knees. So, through the diagnostic tool of manual muscle testing and my energetic merging with my client, I began asking questions—that's what I often do in these cases. The answers revealed that Don had no sexual boundaries with Susan or his own sexual energy, and he was being affected by an intrusion at his second chakra.

I surmised that these difficulties could result from the sexual abuse Susan had experienced as a child. She had not healed the related trauma, and Don— a very empathic person and caring husband—was energetically picking up her sexual shame, fears, and any unresolved dark energy at his vulnerable second chakra. At the beginning of the session he was only 40 percent embodied. By the time we were finished, he was back to being 100 percent in his physical body. MMT indicated that Don should refrain from sexual activity with Susan until she came in to clear up her unresolved sexual trauma.

This is a wonderful example of what occurs in collective fields. Your energy field is always overlapping those of others. These groupings can be large (such as families) or small (such as two people who form a couple). When your energetic boundaries are solid and firm, you maintain your personal autonomy and energetic integrity. When your boundaries are weak, you become vulnerable to the energies of those around you and may unwittingly internalize their trauma energetically.

I have seen this time and again with clients who are going through post-operative cancer radiation treatment. Without exception, the clients who endure weeks of radiation treatment regularly come back negatively affected by dark energy intrusions. Upon inquiry, we usually find that these intrusions are in the waiting room area, feeding on the physically weakened and anxious cancer patients who have had surgery (and often chemotherapy). Dark energy feeds primarily on fear, and there is plenty to go around in these waiting rooms. I have also had many occasions to release dark energy or trauma from people who had energetically absorbed it from others. I have even discovered many adults still carrying their own unreleased birth trauma as well as their mother's (during their birth, they internalized their mother's pain and trauma from the labor and delivery). No wonder so many people are confused and unhappy!

The following week Susan came in for a session to restore her energetic boundaries with her own sexuality and with her sexual relationship with Don. We discovered at the outset that there was a conflict related to this intention: Susan's fear of revisiting the many years of sexual abuse and shame that had occurred in her childhood. We cleared unresolved trauma and the associated dark energy and completed the session by restoring her energetic boundaries. Since that session, Don and Susan have had a vital and healthy sexual relationship.

Retrieving a Power Animal and Releasing a Spirit

Don's next session was a turning point. It was only a few days after his previous session, but Don was once again experiencing dissociation symptoms: his knees felt weak, he felt jittery, he had trouble sleeping through the night, and he awakened with his arms aching. He was also noticing tightness in his chest and labored breathing.

I decided Don would benefit from a power animal retrieval and the infusion of spiritual power that this would provide. He was agreeable, so we dimmed the lights and I rattled to the four directions and to the lower and upper worlds to call in the helping spirits. I turned on the drumming tape and sat down next to Don. I journeyed down to the lower world and connected with a large black bear, who I perceived was an elder who wanted to teach Don "bear medicine." The bear told me that he had been trying to merge with Don but just couldn't.

As the bear and I ascended from the lower world and approached this middle world, I saw scenes of another occurrence related to Don. We were at a rest stop along a freeway somewhere out of state, and I saw the wandering soul of a thirty-four-year-old man who had been the victim of foul play at the rest stop. He was scared and disoriented—and he came into Don.

I communicated with this earthbound spirit and discovered aspects of his spirituality that helped me to give him the spiritual assistance he needed to make the transition to the next phase of his soul's journey. When this depossession journey was complete, I energetically infused the large bear, which had waited patiently for this other errant soul to leave, into Don.

After the journey I asked Don for his reactions. He remembered that one night nearly ten years earlier he had been exhausted while returning from a business trip many hundreds of miles from home. At around 3 A.M., he pulled over into a rest stop to try to catch a few hours of sleep. He awoke suddenly from a terrifying nightmare. He was so scared that he left the rest stop immediately. We inquired via MMT if this incident had precipitated Don being possessed by the earthbound spirit—yes. The muscle testing also indicated that all supernatural influence had been neutralized and Don was again 100 percent in his physical body.

Correcting Psychoenergetic Reversals

Don's next session was a week later. When he arrived, many of his familiar symptoms were present: weak knees, nausea, headache, and general body aches. I muscle tested him by asking the questions that had become so familiar, and to our delight we found no dark energy and no dissociation! But upon further inquiry, we discovered that Don was being affected by three powerful psychoenergetic reversals (beliefs that have a significant limiting influence because the energy fields associated with the specific beliefs are reversed). Our job was to correct the psychoenergetic reversal for each of the limiting beliefs and thereby depolarize the specific energy fields.

Don's psychoenergetic reversals were as follows:

1. I don't believe I will be safe when I come home.
2. I don't deserve to be 100 percent in my physical body.
3. I don't believe that I am finally healed of all this stuff I have suffered from all these years.

For the first psychoenergetic reversal, we used the Tibetan cymbals and TAT. This established 100 percent energetic boundaries with Don's home and corrected the reversal. For the second reversal, we used the F/O holding intervention for two minutes. During this period I experienced a compressed-time shamanic journey in which I saw Jesus baptize Don in nonordinary reality and then bless him. This was sufficient to correct the reversal and establish 100 percent energetic boundaries with his physical body. For the third reversal, we used F/O holding again, but this time I channeled healing energy to Don's third chakra. This corrected the reversal.

As we discussed how Don was feeling afterwards, he mentioned that years earlier he had consulted his physician about heart palpitations that he was experiencing. His physician had told Don that he suspected Don had a heart problem, which was not reassuring news to a worrier like Don. Since then, he became anxious whenever he perceived his heart beating or pounding. Don declared an intention to establish 100 percent energetic boundaries with his internal auditory portal and his inner perception of his heart beat/pulse.

Don's MMT selected the frontal occipital holding intervention. Over the next two minutes, I connected with the energy of Krishna. To me, Krishna personifies the transcendent and interconnected aspects of the Universe as vibration. This reference point of mine is somehow transformed into energy that gets linked to my client, in this case Don. That energy channeled into Don. When it stopped, we muscle tested and Don was sufficiently boundaried in all the contexts we had intended. He felt whole again and our session was finished.

A Final Spirit Intrusion Episode

Our next session (about a week later) was the last session in which Don had to deal with supernatural phenomena, particularly dark energy intrusions. He arrived with many of his familiar, oppressive symptoms.

Don told me a disturbing story of something that had happened since our last session. He had driven out of state on business. While staying at a motel, he woke up in the middle of night and became aware of steps behind him. As he turned to look behind the bed, he saw "this dark thing" that moved to the foot of the bed. It was in the shape of a person but amorphous. Don felt the room go cold. He tried to scream but was too scared to make any noise; he tried to move but was frozen in place. After what seemed like an eternity, the dark thing disappeared. Don tried to go back to sleep, but he was very agitated. When he awakened in the morning, all of his symptoms had returned.

Don wondered aloud whether he was taking on the fears of his father who, in his latter years, never wanted to leave his house. I wondered silently whether I could do anything to help Don resolve this pattern.

But I trust Process completely. I muscle tested Don to inquire what was needed to resolve these symptoms. Our answers indicated that this was another earthbound spirit possession and that another shamanic depossession journey was required. All of my previous work with Don had been effective in releasing all supernatural intrusions and possessions, so I couldn't understand how this had happened yet again. I had asked Michelle, my friend and shamanic mentor, about persistent spirit possession. She said that it is well known in indigenous societies that sometimes a spirit has a certain affinity or attachment to a particular individual. Occasionally in these cases, the intruding spirit keeps returning—even after being released—while it tries to figure out the healer's "medicine" or healing techniques. I realized this might be the case with Don, but I was undeterred—my relationship to my helping and guardian spirits is solid, reliable, and honorable. I trust them completely.

I proceeded to journey, this time rattling for one of my guardian spirits to guide me to the upper world so I could connect with the intruding spirit. After learning its story I went down to the lower world to retrieve a power animal that would guide the earthbound spirit back to its rightful place. I retrieved a red-tailed hawk who energetically and happily took the fearful and disoriented spirit to its spiritual family. That was the last Don ever saw of it.

We then had to establish energetic boundaries with the intruding spirit, which Don accomplished easily with two minutes of TAT. That ended our session and Don's experiences with supernatural intrusion.

Since that session, supernatural interference is no longer an issue in Don's psychic life. His years of anxiety and panic were largely caused by supernatural negative intrusions. These intrusions were now resolved once and for all.

Reconciling Christianity with the Soul's Desire to Journey

For the next couple of months, Don came in still complaining of dissociation symptoms. We discovered that now that the supernatural influence was resolved, this persistent dissociation was caused by Don ignoring the part of himself that needed to journey shamanically so he could connect to and acknowledge his spirituality. Don's troublesome, persistent problem with supernatural intrusions was a way for his dreamingbody to keep him connected to Spirit, albeit in a way that disempowered him. Don is a conservative Christian and prayer is a regular part of his life, so he was conflicted about journeying to connect with compassionate spirits. He was willing to journey to satisfy the demands of this part of him, but he acknowledged that he would have to wrestle with reconciling his Christianity with what his soul was requiring of him. After a while, Don figured out that he could journey to connect with the spirit of Jesus and satisfy both his soul's spiritual desire for him as well as his conscious mind's wish to honor Jesus in a traditionally Christian way.

While Don still occasionally becomes dissociated and experiences some of the symptoms that plagued him in the past, the energetic adjustments he needs to completely reembody are now brief and simple. He is aware of his tendency or habit to dissociate when he feels out of control with his work or his home life (for example, when Susan brought home a new puppy who soiled the Persian rugs throughout their house). But Don's process has changed, and he is now working on being more deliberate in his decisions and actions in all aspects of his life. He knows that if he acts impulsively or reactively he sets up conditions that may lead to a dissociation response and the return of some of his old symptoms. That happens much less often now, as evidenced by his infrequent visits to my office (months rather than weeks between appointments).

Don's spiritual struggle and his learning to be an integrated human being were intense during his two years of therapy. The particulars of his experience are unique, but his basic story is not—we all have old patterns that sometimes feel like they get the best of us. Don no longer uses mind-numbing drugs and he feels more secure in his relationship to Spirit, even though he continues to search for the way that feels most congruent for him. He no longer has panic attacks, and he acknowledges that having a personality bent on controlling people and events outside of himself doesn't agree with living a harmonious life. Don is healing and becoming more peaceful, living a life progressively free of fear. He knows his process is ongoing and requires daily attention and vigilance—he is committed to living more wholly. He is grateful for the Dynamic Energetic Healing® strategies, as I am for the healing and awareness that unfolded in Don's treatment process.

Don's successful outcome is not unusual. As clients finally experience the relief from long-standing emotional problems that other therapies were unable to help with, they recognize that Dynamic Energetic Healing® is a way to grow and evolve into the person they have always wanted to be.

CONCLUSION

Dynamic Energetic Healing® is an innovative and remarkably effective model for helping people move beyond the constrictions caused by past trauma. By weaving together core shamanic practices, energy psychology applications, and processwork principles in a psychotherapeutic setting, Dynamic Energetic Healing® enables clients to experience profound healing that emerges from a paradigm shift in the client–therapist relationship.

Dynamic Energetic Healing® does not have a cognitive-behavioral bias, so constructive altered states of consciousness generated by the treatment modalities described in this book become not only possible but integral to achieving consistent positive therapeutic outcomes. It is no coincidence that trainings for senior managers in the largest and most successful Fortune 500 companies continually emphasize the need to "get out of your head" to achieve creative solutions to complex problems. As Albert Einstein said, "We can't solve problems by using the same kind of thinking we used when we created them."

In my work with clients, it is my intention to be sensitive to and support all parts of them, instead of simply entertaining their cognitive queries and narratives in an attempt to understand a problem whose roots go deeper than the limits of the rational mind. It is our Western cultural bias to make sense of the world through our rational intellect only. This is an important part of who we are, and when I work with clients I acknowledge and support the rational intellect—I never devalue it. But we are so much more than our intellect. Practicing psychotherapy from a strict cognitive-behavioral orientation would be much like trying to paint natural settings with only the three primary colors.

Dynamic Energetic Healing® acknowledges that we are multidimensional beings. It actively supports the unique complexity of each client by acknowledging that we carry and process information at multiple levels: cognitively through our rational intellect; somatically in our physical bodies; subconsciously below the level of our conscious awareness; unconsciously as part of the collective unconscious populated with archetypal forms; energetically through our chakras, meridian system, and biofield; and spiritually through our nonrational incursions into the invisible worlds of nonordinary reality. Dynamic Energetic Healing® integrates principles and practices of non-Western paradigms, and thus the energetic and spiritual realities become powerful internal reference points. The therapist and client become transformed by these reference points that become energetic and spiritual resources, and rapid and seemingly unexplainable healing is empirically validated in the psychotherapy session.

As I connect to and access my spiritual resources, I encourage and allow clients (through my modeling and sharing) to discover and connect to their spiritual life. This process of the therapist and client working together and with their respective spiritual resources brings deep compassion into the psychotherapeutic context.

Dynamic Energetic Healing® makes this possible because it is an inter-subjective model of psychotherapy. An old myth of psychotherapy is that the therapist can and should maintain a neutral orientation when with clients. Because so much of my model is based on the therapeutic relationship, it is fair to ask how much you (the therapist) should disclose before you invite clients to take care of you. I have examined this important issue in this book. In the end, perhaps what is most important is to be real enough to be fully present with your clients. If you succeed in this, your clients will feel free to be themselves more fully and they will access those places deep within themselves where profound healing emerges.

Traumatized clients frequently negotiate life from an experiential place of loss of personal power. Through the methods described in this book, the various components of traumatic residue are discharged from the various levels on which the client was carrying them. Once clients are freed from the binding trauma that regulated and determined their lives, they can more easily generate spiritual resources and recover previously inaccessible ones. Thus, they become power-filled and ready to move in the direction of embracing a life that is now rife with possibilities. The religious or spiritual tradition that the client comes from or currently embraces is always available to draw upon. These spiritual resources do not need to fit neatly into the category of the numinous—they can be identified and retrieved anytime a strong sense of wonder or positive feeling experience reveals itself in a person's day-to-day life. They become the means whereby people become empowered and open more to come from a place of compassion.

While clearing and releasing old traumatic residue is central to the success of Dynamic Energetic Healing®, this model also teaches clients that becoming more sensitive is not about becoming more vulnerable. On the contrary, as clients develop an awareness to follow their second attention, their sensitivity to the deeper process of their lives begins to stimulate parts of them that had lain dormant. This allows their personal dream—which is always unfolding if they allow it to—to start to piece together.

Like anything worth learning and discovering, uncovering the big dream that came in with your soul—your soul's purpose—requires a certain strategic intentionality that you can only learn in Process. In other words, it's about finally waking up! To discover your life's dream or purpose for being is to become self-realized. Dynamic Energetic Healing® supports this dreaming process through the interactions that occur in the psychotherapeutic relationship.

If you are interested in learning about training opportunities in Dynamic Energetic Healing®, I invite you to consult my website:

www.DynamicEnergeticHealing.com

Also posted on this site are contacts and links to other energy psychology, processwork, and core shamanism resources.

FINAL THOUGHTS

As an integrative model of psychotherapy, Dynamic Energetic Healing® combines three distinct healing methodologies—core shamanism, energy psychology, and processwork. Practitioners require substantial training to become proficient in each of these methodologies in order to practice Dynamic Energetic Healing®. The work described in this book (particularly the case histories) reflects many years of supervised training and practice in these methodologies. The notion that anyone can become a powerful healer is perhaps an overstated and irresponsible New Age platitude promulgated by marketing gurus and popular seminars. But I do believe that people who have the sincerity of heart and the commitment to help other people and the planet can learn to be helpful in a psychotherapeutic context using Dynamic Energetic Healing®.

But no single model of healing works for every client, and it would be arrogant and presumptuous of me to claim that every client treated with Dynamic Energetic Healing® gets completely well and achieves their desired healing outcomes. Some clients are not ready to heal, and some clients are not supposed to heal. It must also be remembered that my clientele does not generally include people suffering from schizophrenia or serious personality disorders. Mental illness encompasses a wide spectrum of problem states with varying degrees of severity. Dynamic Energetic Healing® successfully addresses many mental and emotional conditions, but it remains untested with various mental illnesses. I have fundamental concerns about the overuse of psychoactive medications, but I acknowledge that many people suffering from major mental illness are functionally sustained by using their medications regularly. I also realize that not all individuals who could benefit from psychotherapy are motivated to pursue it.

It would be wise for those interested in learning Dynamic Energetic Healing® to reflect upon these matters deeply. For aspiring practitioners who have not done sufficient personal healing work, attempting to assist a severely traumatized individual is irresponsible at best. When the therapist–client relationship includes significant discordant countertransference, therapists who lack psychological and spiritual integration are in over their heads and courting personal illness.

I encourage readers to experiment with and try out many of the techniques I have described, and I hope that lots of people learn how to apply these techniques for the benefit of the many in need. But I must sound two cautionary notes.

The first is that attempting to apply these techniques and strategies without sufficient training and supervision can be dangerous to yourself and your clients. The second is that an unscrupulous individual who has been seduced by power could easily use these techniques and methods to take advantage of vulnerable, needy, and disempowered clients.

Therefore, it is extremely important to do your own spiritual work if you are to implement Dynamic Energetic Healing® from a place of integrity. Impressing others with your newly acquired psychic abilities as you move between the visible and invisible worlds is not at all what healing is about. As therapists, we must remain aware that it's a privilege to assist someone in their healing process and acknowledge that love accomplishes the healing. Let us always remember this as we become more effective and successful healers.

APPENDIX 1

CONCERNS REGARDING THE PHARMACOLOGICAL MODEL

"There will be in the next generation or so a pharmacological method of making people love their servitude and producing dictatorship without tears, so to speak, producing a kind of painless concentration camp for entire societies so that people will in fact have their liberties taken away from them but will rather enjoy it."

—Aldous Huxley

Psychopharmacology is becoming an increasingly important component in the treatment of mental and emotional stress. Most statistics reflect that more Americans are being treated for mental and emotional disorders compared to ten years ago. But it's important to note that the treatment model most often used is psychopharmacological.

I suspect that expedience and convenience are two of the main reasons for this. More people are becoming educated about the benefits of counseling and psychotherapy, but there continues to be a preponderance of naïveté and ignorance about the psychotherapeutic process. Consequently, people in need usually go to their family doctors first for stress-related complaints (i.e., anxiety and depression). These doctors are frequently overworked, and they tend to support the medical model of treatment for mental and emotional disorders. The result is their increasing use of and reliance on powerful pharmaceutical drugs as the first (and often only) intervention to support their patients' health and well-being.

While it is true that many people benefit from time-limited psycho-pharmacological interventions, too many family doctors are inadequately informed and insufficiently networked to augment drug treatments with referrals to counselors and psychotherapists. This situation is continuing even as current research shows that the combination of medication and cognitive-behavioral therapy is more effective than medication alone.

An important question is this: Why aren't more people seeking psycho-therapeutic help? Part of the answer may be the stigma that is still associated with mental-health issues. But a great deal of responsibility must be assigned to the cozy relationship between the American Medical Association and the large pharmaceutical corporations. Drug companies continue to spend more and more on marketing, health insurance premiums continue to rise, and so do drug prices. Meanwhile, doctors, who are still captive to HMOs, tend to spend less and less time on each patient appointment. Drug manufacturers and pharmacies have a vested interest in increasing the usage of prescription drugs—their markups and profits are considerable. As a result, manufacturers spend millions every year marketing their products to doctors (*Money*, September 2001, 122).

Doctors are revered and sanctioned as our nation's healers. When patients complain of depression or anxiety due to life stressors such as parenting, overwork, or lack of personal fulfillment in their forty-plus hours a week at work, doctors want to be helpful. Physicians can provide some palliative care quickly by prescribing a magic bullet, no matter what the origin of the stress-induced depression or anxiety may be.

I have treated many clients who have become addicted to pharmaceutical drugs for their problems, thanks to their family doctor. In Dynamic Energetic Healing®, it usually does not take long to discover the underlying trauma pattern and to release clients from what has been tyrannizing them for years. Most clients must also make significant changes in their lives in order to eliminate their old patterns, and they are generally willing to do this rather than stay on brain-modifying drugs for the rest of their lives. Ironically, new clients who are on an antidepressant always know that the underlying problem is still there, along with the accompanying hopelessness. Clients often feel "broken" because nobody has been able to help them heal their problems. Clients often feel tremendous shame that they are addicted to their brain-modifying drugs because it makes them feel like victims of something they do not understand. Add to this their family doctor's ongoing recommendation that this is the right treatment because it is the best the doctor can do for them! Most doctors do not want to admit defeat, so they collude with the pharmaceutical corporations to medicate the general population. This is happening right down to children, who are now increasingly being prescribed antidepressants for depression:

From 1998 to 2002, prescriptions for kids had increased by 49%. (*Los Angeles Times*, March 21, 2005, F1)

Since the late 1980s, big drug companies, the psychiatric establishment—including the American Psychiatric Association and the National Institute of

Mental Health—and the Food and Drug Administration (FDA) denied any link between antidepressants and increased suicide. But the Salem, Oregon *Statesman Journal* (June 3, 2004, B4) reported that according to a lawsuit filed in June 2004 by New York Attorney General Eliot Spitzer, GlaxoSmithKline PLC

> committed fraud by withholding negative information and misrepresenting data on prescribing its anti-depressant Paxil to children.... Filed in New York State Supreme Court, the suit said Glaxo suppressed four studies that failed to demonstrate the drug was effective in treating children and adolescents and that suggested a possible increase in suicidal thinking and acts.

Clinical studies by other large drug manufacturers were also suppressed and crucial information about the safety and effectiveness of the drugs was determined to have been withheld from public scrutiny. Two-thirds of the trials conducted by drug manufacturers before the late 1990s found that these medications performed no better than sugar pills, but details of the negative trials were kept from doctors and parents (*Washington Post*, August 10, 2004, A06). By the second half of 2004, a groundswell of complaints from parents of children who had taken these antidepressant drugs along with congressional hearings pushed the FDA to respond.

In October 2004, the FDA finally issued a Public Health Advisory to warn about the increased risk of suicidal thoughts and behavior in children and adolescents being treated with antidepressant medications. This action was taken in response to the results of controlled clinical trials and a multiplicity of case reports, which showed that children and adolescents who were given an antidepressant were twice as likely to become suicidal as those who were given a placebo and that in most cases the drugs provided no clinically significant benefit beyond what a placebo provided. As stated in the announcement, the FDA now requires manufacturers to include a "black box" warning on the labeling of all antidepressant medications. This warning must identify the risk of suicide as being a possible side effect and emphasize the need for close monitoring of patients who start these medications. Dr. Lester M. Crawford, Acting FDA Commissioner, was quoted as saying that

> today's actions represent FDA's conclusions about the increased risk of suicidal thoughts and the necessary actions for physicians

prescribing these antidepressant drugs and for the children and adolescents taking them. Our conclusions are based on the latest and best
science. (http://www.fda.gov/bbs/topics/news/2004/NEW01124.html,
October 15, 2004)

The new warnings are now carried on thirty-two antidepressants, including Prozac, Wellbutrin, and Zoloft. Finally, parents are being alerted to the
causal relationship between suicidal behavior and antidepressant drugs. For
the first time, they are able to make an informed decision on how to proceed
when their child is experiencing depression.

Dispensing drugs for behavioral, emotional, and mental disturbances is
fast becoming the most prevalent of the many models of treating psychological issues that are available today. Unfortunately, this medical model is
not helping patients feel more alive, more loving, and more sensitive. On
the contrary, after they wean themselves off their prescribed drugs, my
clients say they knew the drugs blunted their ability to feel, but they got
so used to being half numb that they forgot what it is to feel happy and
alive to the ups and downs of day-to-day life. I am deeply concerned about
the proliferation of prescribed brain-modifying drugs that medical doctors
are all-too-willing to promote, particularly since biotechnology and
synthetic pharmaceuticals are being hailed as the next new wave of medical progress.

Psychiatrist Joseph Glenmullen has done significant research into the
dangerous side effects of antidepressants, which are largely unknown to the
patients who take them and to the doctors who prescribe them.

In recent years, the danger of long-term side effects has emerged in
association with Prozac-like drugs, making it imperative to minimize
one's exposure to them. Neurological disorders including disfiguring
facial and whole body tics, indicating potential brain damage, are an
increasing concern with patients on the drugs. Withdrawal symptoms
are estimated to affect up to 50 percent of patients, depending on the
particular drug. Sexual dysfunction affects 60 percent of people.
Increasing reports are being made of people becoming dependent on
the medications after chronic use. With related drugs targeting serotonin, there's evidence that they may effect a "chemical lobotomy" by
destroying the nerve endings they target in the brain. . . . And startling

new information on Prozac's precipitating suicidal and violent behavior has come to light. (Glenmullen 2000, 8)

Over years of practice, Glenmullen (2000, 11) noticed the emergence of disturbing trends associated with patients taking Prozac and other serotonin boosters, such as Zoloft, Paxil, and Luvox. A number of Glenmullen's patients developed tics and twitches that would often persist for months after stopping the drug.

The tics may be facial, like fly-catcher tongue darting or chewing-the-cud jawing, or involve the whole body, like involuntary pelvic thrusting. The tics are the dread side effect in psychiatry. With earlier classes of drugs that caused these kinds of tics, they are disfiguring, untreatable, and permanent in up to 50 percent of cases.

With pharmaceutical giant Eli Lilly aggressively marketing Prozac in the late 1980s as a "designer medical bullet targeting serotonin," Prozac became an instant success. *New York Magazine* touted Prozac as a "wonder drug" (*Newsweek*, March 26, 1990). Psychiatrist Peter Kramer became a cultural icon with *Listening to Prozac*, in which he lavished praise without reservations on these serotonin-boosting drugs. Kramer (1993, 15) claimed these drugs could transform people by actually changing their personalities. Using the phrase "cosmetic psychopharmacology," he proclaimed, "Some people might prefer pharmacologic to psychologic self-actualization." Glenmullen noticed that it was just about this time that managed care insurers (HMOs) were pressing doctors to cut costs with their patient appointments and persuading them to prescribe more drugs for mental-health issues instead of referring patients to therapists. With little concern for the consequences to patients, these powerful brain-altering chemicals began to make significant inroads into how doctors dealt with mental-health and stress-related issues. It wasn't too long before primary care family doctors were writing up to 70 percent of all the prescriptions dispensed for Prozac, Zoloft, and Paxil.

To the already long list of conditions treated with the drugs were added anxiety, obsessions, compulsions, eating disorders, headaches, back pain, impulsivity, sexual addictions, premature ejaculation, attention deficit disorder, and premenstrual syndrome. Serotonin boosters are all-purpose psychoanalgesics, not just "antidepressants," which was merely the first application for which they were approved. (Glenmullen 2000, 14)

Prozac became the number two best-selling drug in America, closely followed by Zoloft and Paxil. In 1998 alone, more than 60 million prescriptions for the drugs were written. It is estimated that at least 10 percent of the American population has been exposed to serotonin boosters. What is particularly troubling to me is that at least half a million children have been prescribed the drugs, "with pediatric use one of the fastest-growing 'markets,' this in spite of the fact that repeated studies have shown antidepressant drugs are no more effective in children than placebos" (Glenmullen 2000, 15). One reason these new drugs have become an overnight success with the American public is the general perception (promulgated by the prescribing doctors) that they have virtually no side effects. In Kramer's (1993, 10) glorification of Prozac, he proclaimed, "There is no unhappy ending to this story. . . . The patient recovers and pays no price for the recovery."

Subsequent research has revealed that one of the most prominent reactions to artificially elevated serotonin levels in the brain is a compensatory drop in dopamine levels. The dangerous and varied side effects now emerging from the use of Prozac and other drugs that produce a dopamine drop are quite well known among the psychiatric community. The profound secondary effects that boosting seratonin has on other neurotransmitters were unknown when these drugs were introduced, in spite of the FDA trials that preceded their warm welcome by the psychiatric community. Many researchers now believe that this dopamine compensatory response is responsible for the severe side effects emerging with the drugs' use (Glenmullen 2000, 20).

While the dominant medical model is luring us into increasing prescription drug use, our culture is having another serious affect on us. I am very concerned about how many of us are falling prey to the consensus reality trance of the dominant culture—what Don Miguel Ruiz (1997, 2) refers to as "society's dream or the dream of the planet." Fortunately, even as we move forward into the twenty-first century with our growing understanding of the human genome, ancient spiritual and healing technologies and principles are becoming more widely available. Energy psychology models—and Dynamic Energetic Healing® in particular—are some of the major beneficiaries of this widening application of ancient wisdom. It is my hope that despite the convenience of taking a daily pill to enhance one's ability to cope with the stresses of modern life, people will wake up and realize that they are not ill. They don't need medication just because the pace of life and its many responsibilities can feel overwhelming. There are other options, if only people would choose them. We have the ability to bring our lives into balance and to be happy—and it is my prayer that we will.

APPENDIX 2

DSM-IV DESCRIPTIONS OF DISSOCIATIVE DISORDERS

For those interested in just how the DSM-IV characterizes and defines dissociative disorders, Kaplan and Sadock (1988, 345–48) provide these abbreviated definitions:

1. **Dissociative Amnesia** (formerly called **Psychogenic Amnesia**): Defined as a sudden inability to recall important personal information already stored in memory. The capacity to learn new information is retained. The disorder usually begins abruptly, and the person is usually aware that he has lost his memory. A few people, however, report a slight clouding of consciousness during the period immediately surrounding the amnestic period.

2. **Depersonalization Disorder**: Characterized by a persistent or recurrent alteration in the perception of the self to the extent that the feeling of one's own reality is temporarily lost, of feeling mechanical, being in a dream, or feeling detached from, and as if one is an outside observer of, one's mental processes or body. "Studies of incidence indicate the transient depersonalization may occur in as many as 70 percent of a given population, with no significant difference in incidence between men and women." "An occasional and particularly curious phenomenon is that of doubling: the person feels that his point of conscious 'I-ness' is outside his body, often a few feet overhead, from where he actually observes himself, as if he were a totally separate person. Sometimes the person believes he is in two different places at the same time, a condition known as reduplicative paramnesia or double orientation."

3. **Dissociated Fugue** (formerly called **Psychogenic Fugue**): Defined as sudden unexpected wandering, often far from home, and an inability to remember one's former life or identity. The person may take on an entirely new identity and a new occupation.

4. **Dissociative Identity Disorder** (formerly called **Multiple Personality Disorder** or **MPD**): This disorder is characterized by a person's having two or more distinct and separate personalities each of which determines the nature of his behavior and attitudes during the period when it is dominant. The original or host personality is usually amnestic for the other personalities.

DYNAMIC ENERGETIC HEALING®
PROTOCOL CHECKLIST

Client: _____

Prepare to Work on the Specific Intention

☐   1. Create a sacred space
☐   2. Calibrate MMT
☐   3. Test for hydration
☐   4. Ensure energy field is circulating normally
☐   5. Troubleshoot (if necessary) for negative transference, etoxins, or supernatural influence

Verify That the Intention Is Ready to Be Worked On

☐   6. Test for psychoenergetic reversals (general and specific)
☐   7. Prioritize and ensure accuracy of intention statement
☐   8. Verify that no inner parts have objections to the intention

Work at the Energetic Origin

☐   9. Identify and treat the energetic origin(s)
☐   10. Identify linkages (if any) between energetic origins
☐   11. Determine if an active dreaming-up process is linked to an energetic origin
☐   12. Check if energetic boundaries with the energetic origin are required
☐   13. Determine the best regression technique to the energetic origin
☐   14. Identify specific components of traumatic event (if one is present at origin), including: affective residue, limiting beliefs, soul loss, damaged energy field, collective trauma, supernatural phenomena, etc.
☐   15. Track and follow client's process

Unpack the Trauma Package at the Energetic Origin

☐   16. Unpack the trauma package at the energetic origin by inquiring more deeply about: possible death wish, feeling abandoned by God, compromised energetic boundaries, distorted relationship to emotions, overidentification to a negative archetype, impact of client's personality, etc.

Complete and Integrate the Healing

☐ 17. Inquire if any additional karmic healing is required
☐ 18. Determine if spiritual resources can be elicited
☐ 19. Integrate the healed trauma through time to present
☐ 20. Ensure that no part of the client is energetically left behind
☐ 21. Verify that any active dreaming-up process in all perceptual channels is depotentiated
☐ 22. Future pace

BIBLIOGRAPHY

Achterberg, Jeanne. "The Wounded Healer." In *Shaman's Path: Healing, Personal Growth and Empowerment*, edited by Gary Doore. Boston: Shambhala, 1988.

American Psychiatric Association. *Diagnostic and Statistical Manual of Mental Disorders*, 4th ed. Washington, D.C.: American Psychiatric Association, 1994.

Baldwin, William. *Spirit Releasement Therapy: A Technical Manual*. Terra Alta, W.V.: Headline Books, 1992.

Beijing College of Traditional Chinese Medicine. *Essentials of Chinese Acupuncture*. Beijing: Foreign Languages Press, 1980.

Bhajan, Yogi. *Kundalini Yoga Manual*. Pomona, Calif.: Kundalini Research Institute, 1971.

———. *Kundalini Yoga Manual*. Pomona, Calif.: Kundalini Research Institute, 1972.

Blake, Dudley D. "Treatment outcome research on post-traumatic stress disorder." *NCP Clinical Newsletter* 3, no. 2 (spring 1993): 14–17.

Bohm, David. *Wholeness and the Implicate Order*. Boston: Routledge and Kegan Paul, 1980.

Brinkman, Cheri. "Letting Go of the Grudge." *Anchor Point*, August, 1993.

Buhner, Stephen Harrod. *The Lost Language of Plants: The Ecological Importance of Plant Medicines for Life on Earth*. White River Junction, Vt.: Chelsea Green, 2002.

Bynner, Witter, trans. *The Way of Life According to Lao Tzu*. New York: Capricorn Books, 1944.

Callahan, Roger, and Richard Trubo. *Tapping the Healer Within: Using Thought Field Therapy to Instantly Conquer Your Fears, Anxieties, and Emotional Distress*. New York: McGraw-Hill, 2002.

Campbell, Joseph. *This Business of the Gods: In Conversation with Fraser Boa*. Caledon East, Ontario: Windrose Films Ltd., 1989.

———. *The Hero with a Thousand Faces*. 1949. Reprint, Princeton, N.J.: Princeton University Press, 1973.

Castaneda, Carlos. *The Power of Silence*. New York: Simon & Schuster, 1987.

———. *The Active Side of Infinity*. New York: HarperCollins, 1998.

Childre, Doc, and Howard Martin. *The HeartMath Solution*. San Francisco: HarperSanFrancisco, 1999.

Classic Yoga for the Antelope Valley. "Tibetan Bells—Himalayan Singing Bowls" [online]. Revised December 5, 2003. http://www.classicyoga.org (accessed November 17, 2004).

Clinton, Asha. *Matrix Work Manual*. Princeton, N.J.: Energy Revolution Press, 1999.

Cowan, Tom. *Shamanism as a Spiritual Practice for Daily Life*. Freedom, Calif.: Crossing Press, 1996.

Cowley, G. "The Promise of Prozac." *Newsweek*, March 26, 1990.

Craig, Gary, and Fowlie, Anrienne. *Emotional Freedom Techniques™: The Manual*. (self-published), 1995.

Dossey, Larry, M.D. *Prayer Is Good Medicine: How to Reap the Healing Benefits of Prayer*. San Francisco: HarperSanFrancisco, 1996.

————. *Reinventing Medicine: Beyond Mind-Body to a New Era of Healing.* San Francisco: HarperSanFrancisco, 1999.

Durlacher, James V. *Freedom from Fear Forever.* Tempe, Ariz.: Van Ness Publishing, 1994.

Easwaran, Eknath. *The Mantram Handbook: Formulas for Transformation.* Petaluma, Calif.: Nilgiri Press, 1977.

Eden, Donna. *Energy Medicine.* New York: Jeremy P. Tarcher/Putnam, 1998.

Einstein, Albert. *The Meaning of Relativity.* Princeton, N.J.: Princeton University Press, 1955.

Eisenberg, L. "Commentary: What should doctors do in the face of negative evidence?" *Journal of Nervous and Mental Disease* 184: 103–5.

Eliade, Mircea. *Shamanism: Archaic Techniques of Ecstasy.* Translated by Willard R. Trask. Princeton, N.J.: Princeton University Press, 1972. Quoted in Sandra Ingerman, *Soul Retrieval: Mending the Fragmented Self* (San Francisco: HarperSanFrancisco, 1991), p. 28.

Fisher, R. L., and S. Fisher. "Antidepressants for children: Is scientific support necessary?" *Journal of Nervous and Mental Disease* 184: 99–102.

Fleming, Tapas. *You Can Heal Now: The Tapas Acupressure Technique.* Redondo Beach, Calif.: TAT International, 1998.

Freud, Sigmund. *Civilization and Its Discontents.* 1929. New York: Norton, 1955.

Fuentes, Starr. *Divine Intervention Dimensions/Hertz Training Manual.* Navasota, Tex.: (self-published), 2000.

Gallo, Fred P. *Energy Psychology: Explorations at the Interface of Energy, Cognition, Behavior, and Health.* Boca Raton, Fla.: CRC Press, 1999.

———, ed. *Energy Psychology in Psychotherapy: A Comprehensive Source-book*. New York: W. W. Norton, 2002.

Gallo, Fred P., and Harry Vincenzi. *Energy Tapping*. Oakland, Calif.: New Harbinger Publications, 2000.

Gaynor, Mitchell. *The Healing Power of Sound: Recovery from Life-Threatening Illness Using Sound, Voice, and Music*. Boston: Shambhala, 2002.

Glenmullen, Joseph. *Prozac Backlash*. New York: Simon & Schuster, 2000.

Good News for Modern Man: The New Testament and Psalms in Today's English Version. New York: Thomas Nelson, 1972.

Grof, Stanislav, and Christina Grof, eds. *Spiritual Emergency: When Personal Transformation Becomes a Crisis*. Los Angeles: Jeremy P. Tarcher, 1989.

Harner, Michael. *The Way of the Shaman*. New York: Bantam Books, 1982.

Hillman, James. *The Soul's Code: In Search of Character and Calling*. New York: Random House, 1996.

Hong Liu, Master, with Paul Perry. *The Healing Art of Qi Gong*. New York: Warner Books, 1997.

Huxley, Aldous. *Brave New World*. 1932. New York: HarperCollins, 1998.

———. *Island*. 1962. New York: Harper & Row, 2002.

Ingerman, Sandra. *Soul Retrieval: Mending the Fragmented Self*. San Francisco: HarperSanFrancisco, 1991.

———. *Medicine for the Earth: How to Transform Personal and Environmental Toxins*. New York: Three Rivers Press, 2000.

Jahnke, Roger. *The Healing Promise of Qi: Creating Extraordinary Wellness through Qigong and Tai Chi*. New York: Contemporary Books, 2002.

Jung, C. G. *Memories, Dreams, Reflections*. New York: Vintage Press, 1961.

Kaplan, Harold I., M.D., and Benjamin J. Sadock, M.D. *Synopsis of Psychiatry: Behavioral Sciences, Clinic Psychiatry*. Baltimore, Md.: Williams & Wilkins, 1988.

Kharitidi, Olga. *Entering the Circle: Ancient Secrets of Siberian Wisdom Discovered by a Russian Psychiatrist*. San Francisco: HarperSanFrancisco, 1996.

Koestler, Arthur. *The Ghost in the Machine*. London: Hutchinson & Co., 1967.

Kramer, Peter D. *Listening to Prozac*. New York: Penguin Books, 1993.

McCraty, Rollin. *Science of the Heart: An Overview of Research Conducted by the Institute of HeartMath*. Boulder Creek, Calif.: HeartMath Research Center, 2001.

Mindell, Arnold. *Working with the Dreaming Body*. Boston: Routledge and Kegan Paul, 1985.

———. *The Dreambody in Relationships*. New York: Routledge & Paul, 1987.

———. *Working on Yourself Alone: Inner Dreambody Work*. New York: Penguin Books, 1990.

———. *The Shaman's Body: A New Shamanism for Transforming Health, Relationships, and the Community*. New York: HarperCollins, 1993.

———. *Dreaming While Awake: Techniques for 24-Hour Lucid Dreaming*. Charlottesville, Va.: Hampton Roads, 2000a.

———. *Quantum Mind: The Edge between Physics and Psychology*. Portland, Ore.: Lao Tse Press, 2000b.

Mitchell, Stephen. *The Gospel According to Jesus*. New York: Harper Perennial, 1991.

Modi, Shakuntala, M.D. *Remarkable Healings: A Psychiatrist Discovers Unsuspected Roots of Mental and Physical Illness*. Charlottesville, Va.: Hampton Roads, 1997.

Narby, Jeremy, and Francis Huxley, eds. *Shamans through Time: Five Hundred Years on the Path to Knowledge*. New York: Jeremy P. Tarcher/Putnam, 2001.

Pearce, Joseph Chilton. *Magical Child*. New York: Plume, 1992.

Pellegrino, E. D. "Commentary: Clinical judgment, scientific data, and ethics: antidepressant therapy in adolescents and children." *Journal of Nervous and Mental Disease* 184: 106–8.

Prabhavananda, Swami, and Christopher Isherwood, trans. *How to Know God: The Yoga Aphorisms of Patanjali*. New York: New American Library, 1953.

Radin, Dean I., Janine M. Rebman, and Maikwe P. Cross. "Anomalous organization of random events by group consciousness: Two exploratory experiments." *Journal of Scientific Exploration* 10, no. 1 (1996): 143–68. Quoted in Larry Dossey, M.D., *Reinventing Medicine: Beyond Mind-Body to a New Era of Healing* (San Francisco: HarperSanFrancisco, 1999), p. 83.

Ray, Sondra. *Celebration of Breath: Rebirthing*. San Francisco: Celestial Arts, 1983.

Rinpoche, Sogyal. *The Tibetan Book of Living and Dying*. San Francisco: HarperSanFrancisco, 1994.

Riso, Don Richard. *Discovering Your Personality Type: The New Enneagram Questionnaire*. New York: Houghton Mifflin, 1995.

Ruiz, Don Miguel. *The Four Agreements*. San Rafael, Calif.: Amber-Allen, 1997.

Schwartz, Gary E. R., and Linda G. S. Russek. *The Living Energy Universe*. Charlottesville, Va.: Hampton Roads, 1999.

Shapiro, Francine. *Eye Movement Desensitization and Reprocessing*. New York: Guilford Press, 1995.

Stevenson, Ian. *Twenty Cases Suggestive of Reincarnation*. Charlottesville, Va.: University Press of Virginia, 1974.

———. *Where Reincarnation and Biology Intersect*. Westport, Conn.: Praeger Publishing, 1997.

Three In One Concepts. *Participant's Manual, Third International Conference in Energy Psychology*. San Diego, Calif.: Association of Comprehensive Energy Psychology, 2001.

van der Kolk, Bessel A., M.D., ed. *Post-Traumatic Stress Disorder: Psychological and Biological Sequelae*. Washington, D.C.: American Psychiatric Press, 1984.

———. *Psychological Trauma*. Washington, D.C.: American Psychiatric Press, 1987.

van der Kolk, Bessel A., M.D., Alexander C. McFarlane, and Lars Weisaeth, eds. *Traumatic Stress: The Effects of Overwhelming Experience on Mind, Body, and Society*. New York: Guilford Press, 1996.

Villoldo, Alberto. *Shaman, Healer, Sage*. New York: Harmony Books, 2000.

Watzlawick, Paul. *The Language of Change: Elements of Therapeutic Communication*. New York: Basic, 1978.

Weiss, Brian L., M.D. *Through Time into Healing*. New York: Simon & Schuster, 1992.

Wesselman, Hank. *Spiritwalker: Messages from the Future*. New York: Bantam Books, 1995.

Zukav, Gary. *The Seat of the Soul*. New York: Simon & Schuster, 1989.

INDEX

abuse
  childhood, 323–28
  emotional, 204, 379–85
  sexual, 203, 345–50, 375–78
acupoints, 188–90
in EFT, 190
addiction
  ancestral energetic origins of, 273
  behaviors associated with, 203, 204–5
  soul loss and, 244
adrenal glands, 200, 201
affective residue, 288
alexithymia, 99
allergies, 206, 329–32, 371–74, 403–7
ancestral energetic origins, 272, 273
ancestral spirit, 387–90
antidepressants
  increasing use of, 69
  links to suicide, 435–36
  risks of, 94–95
  side effects of, 436–39
anxiety, 409–26
archetypes, 296–99

codependency and, 298–99
Divine Feminine, 323–28
Jung's theory of, 148, 297
Martyr, 333–39
negative, 333–39
overidentification with, 297–99
Scapegoat, 149
Victim, 152, 202, 210, 291, 297–98, 333–39
Wounded Holy One, 357–70
attention. *See* first attention; second attention
auric field, 379–85, 418
autoimmune disorders, 244

Bardo realm, 153, 154, 357–70
Berne, Eric, 28–29
Bhajan, Yogi, 6, 9, 121, 212
  on discipline, 130–31
  on keeping chakras balanced, 200–201
  on Kirtan Kriya, 231
  on Sat Kriya, 204, 229–31
  White Tantric yoga and, 12–16
Biological Basis of Religion and Genius, The, 8

birth trauma, 409–26
body-centered therapies, 28, 54
boundary issues, 77
boundary work. *See* energetic
    boundaries
Brave New World, 69–70
brow point. *See* sixth chakra

Callahan, Roger, 83, 172, 187, 216
    development of TFT, 35–36
    on psychoenergetic reversal,
        85–88
Callahan Techniques®. *See* TFT
Castaneda, Carlos, 3, 56, 61, 72–73
Central Vessel, 188, 190, 262,
    391–97
    in NAEM, 215
    in TFT, 20
chakra, 122
    defined, 33, 199
    fifth, 200, 209–11, 409–26
    first, 200, 201–2, 345–50, 409–26
    fourth, 200, 206–9, 215, 345–50,
        379–85
    interventions, 199–214
    life-force energy and, 122
    second, 200, 203–4, 323–28,
        333–39, 345–50, 379–85
    seventh, 200, 212–13
    sixth, 200, 211–12, 319–22,
        409–26

Soaring Crane qigong, in, 125
    stimulation, 409–26
    tapping, 58, 89, 181, 319–28,
        409–26
    third, 199, 200, 204–6, 409–26
Chen, Hui-xian, 125–26
chi, 119
    defined, 33, 119
    flow of, 126–27, 319–22, 391–97
    meridians, 145, 190–91
    stimulation of, 190
    See also life-force energy
childhood, trauma, 323–28
chronic fatigue, 206
chronic pain, 232
Clinton, Asha, xxv, 39, 79, 178
codependency, 139, 204, 391–97
    archetypes and, 298–99
cognitive therapy, 28, 41
collective energy field, 174, 409–26
collective trauma, 288, 323–28,
    409–26
compassionate spirits, 67–70, 239
    role of, xxv, 19, 23–24
Conception Vessel. *See* Central
    Vessel
core shamanism. *See* shamanism
countertransference, 49, 134,
    223–24
Craig, Gary, 178, 187–88
crown chakra. *See* seventh chakra

current-life energetic origins, 272,
409–26
curses, 149–51, 399–426, 333–39,
371–74

dark energy, 44, 158, 224
case histories involving, 333–39,
357–70, 391–97, 409–26
detecting via MMT, 163–64
entanglement, 379–85
intrusion, 147–48, 158–59, 163, 245
darshan, 51
death wish, 290–91, 357–70
defense mechanisms, 409–26
Freudian view of, 27, 107
overcoming via MMT, 261
depression, 157, 244, 291, 319–28,
333–39, 357–70, 399–402
ancestral origins of, 273
mainstream treatment of, 69,
94–95
soul loss and, 111–12, 117
Diamond, John, 35
directive tapping, 193–94, 214, 236
dissociation, 345–50, 409–26
defined, 107
DEH approach to, 109
effects of, 267
Freudian view of, 108
mainstream treatment of, 108
PTSD and, 96–97

shamanic approach to, 109
trauma as outcome of, 267–68
See also soul loss
divination, 64, 239–42
Divine Feminine archetype, 323–28
divine separation, 272, 274–75
Doors of Perception, The, 3
Dossey, Larry, 249
dreambody, 55–57, 59, 76,
161–62, 180
dreamingbody. See dreambody
dreaming-up process, 277–80
dreamtime, 222
drumming, 181, 227, 235–37, 403–7,
409–26

eating
compulsive over-, 379–85
disorders, 206, 341–43
Eden, Donna, 195, 197, 287
EFT (emotional freedom
techniques), xxiii, 22, 39, 161,
178, 180
acupoints, 190
case histories involving, 315–28,
351–70, 409–26
DEH protocol, 192–93
directive tapping, 193–94
modified for DEH, 187–94
regression via, 283
TFT, relationship to, 187, 190

embodiment, 345–50
concept of, 113, 114
protocol, 116
verifying completeness of, 305
EMDR (eye movement
desensitization and reprocessing
technique), 197
emotional freedom techniques.
See EFT
emotions, effect of trauma on,
295–96
energetic boundaries, 114, 115,
117, 152
case histories involving, 319–22,
333–39, 345–70, 379–402,
409–26
codependency and, 139
defined, 140
effect of trauma on, 294–95
establishing, 280–82
importance of, 288
restoring, 140, 141–43
role in dealing with trauma, 140
energetic origins, 77, 114, 271–88
ancestral, 272, 273
case histories involving, 345–50,
399–402
current-life, 272, 409–26
defined, 275
divine separation, 272, 274–75
karmic. *See* past-life

links between, 276–80
past-life, 103, 152, 246–47, 272,
273, 276, 329–43, 409–26
regression to, 282–87
types of, 272, 273, 276
energetic practice, benefits of, 130
energy, concept of, 37–38
energy field
collective, 174, 409–26
damaged, 288
strengthening, 165
energy flow, testing client's,
262–63
energy psychology, xxiii, 32–34,
53–54
scientific explanation of, 36–37
variations of, 39
Enneagram Model of Personality
Types, 207, 299
entanglement, dark energy, 379–85
Erickson, Milton, 16, 21, 54–55, 133
extraction, 64, 102, 240, 245–46,
409–26
eye movement desensitization and
reprocessing technique.
See EMDR

fifth chakra, 200, 209–11, 409–26
first attention, 56–57
first chakra, 200, 201–2, 345–50,
409–26

Fleming, Elizabeth Tapas, xxv, 178, 183
Flight of the Eagle, The, 3
focused prayer, 181
F/O holding (frontal occipital holding), 58, 89, 181, 219–25
  case histories involving, 319–85, 391–402, 409–26
  in shamanic extraction, 246
  teaching of, 223–25
fourth chakra, 200, 206–9, 345–50, 379–85
  in NAEM, 215
Freud, Sigmund
  on dark energy, 147
  on defense mechanisms, 27, 107
  on religion, 66
  on transference, 48–49
  on trauma, 27
frontal occipital holding.
  See F/O holding
future pacing, 306–7

Gallo, Fred, xxv, 39, 215
Gaynor, Mitchell, 232
Gestalt therapy, 29
God, anger toward, 291–93
Goodheart, George Jr., 34, 195
Gordon, Nancy, xxiii, 383
Governing Vessel, 183, 188, 190, 391–97

in NAEM, 215
in TFT, 20
Grof, Stanislav and Christina, 415

Hammond-Newman, Mary, 20, 114, 383
  contribution to DEH, xxiii
  tunnel of light technique, 284–85
Harner, Michael, 68, 239
healing from the body level up, xxiii, 22
Healy, David, 95
heart-center tapping, 409–26
heart chakra. *See* fourth chakra
HeartMath, Institute of, 208
Hillman, James, 75, 76, 80
Hong Liu, Master, 124
Huxley, Aldous, 3, 4, 69–70
hydration, 261–62
hypnosis, 16, 21, 30

Ichazo, Oscar, 207
Ingerman, Sandra, 44
inner parts, 152–55, 267–69, 305–6. *See also* soul loss; soul stealing
insomnia, 323–28
integrating healing, 304–5
intention
  achieving alignment with, 78–80
  defined, 72

intention (*continued*)
  establishing client's, 265–69
  objections to, 267–69
  prioritizing, 266–67
  therapist's, 50
intrusion
  dark energy, 147–48, 158–59,
    163, 245, 391–97, 409–26
  past life, from, 301–2
  shamanic view of, 102
  supernatural, 264, 288, 315–18,
    329–39, 345–50, 357–74,
    399–402
intuition, 211
Island, 4, 69–70

Jnana yoga, 119–20
Jung, Carl, 145
  on archetypes, 148, 297
  on collective unconscious, 41

karmic energetic origins.
  See past-life energetic origins
karmic healing, 301–3
kinesiology, 32–33, 182
  applied, 34
  behavioral, 22, 35.
    See also MMT
Kirtan Kriya, 181
  mantra, 120–21, 123
  meditation, 228–32, 357–70

Kohut, 30
Kramer, Peter, 173
Krishna, Gopi, 8
Krishnamurti, J., 3, 119–20
kriya
  defined, 120
  Kirtan. *See* Kirtan Kriya
  Sat Nam, 204, 229–31
Kundalini yoga, 6, 120–21, 199, 212

life-force energy, 6, 7
  Shakti, 7, 333–39
  Shaktipat, 15–16
  terms for, 33
  See also chakra; chi; prana
limiting beliefs, 77, 150, 288
  case histories involving, 319–28,
    351–74, 409–26
  curses, distinguished from,
    148, 151
  first chakra and, 202
  inner conflicts and, 296–97
  objections by inner parts, 268–69

mainstream medical model, 171
mantra, 120–21, 123, 181, 227–32,
  319–22, 357–70
manual muscle testing. *See* MMT
Martyr archetype, 333–39
meridians
  acupuncture, 188, 201

energy, 145, 190–91
tapping on points, 323–28
TFT, in, 20, 32–33
See also life-force energy
midline energy treatment. See NAEM
midline points, 215.
  See also Central Vessel;
  Governing Vessel
Mindell, Arnold, 31, 41–42, 146
  on double signal, 393
  on dreamingbody, 55–56,
    162, 180
  on dreaming-up process, 277–80
  on perceptual channels, 124
  processwork training, 17–18
MMT (manual muscle testing), 22,
    34, 35, 50
  accuracy, ensuring, 258, 391–97
  best intervention, selecting, 235
  calibration, 259–61
  curses, identifying, 149, 150
  dark energy, detecting, 163, 164
  defense mechanisms,
    overcoming, 261
  description, 259–61
  embodiment protocol, 116
  energetic boundaries,
    determining, 140
  energy flow, testing, 263
  guide, using as a, xxvi
  hydration, importance of, 261–62

hypnotic trance, 136–37
  importance in DEH, 181–82
  lost soul part, recovering, 153–55
  psychoenergetic reversal, 87, 89
  specific intention, identifying,
    77–80
  surrogate, 391–97
  therapeutic goal, establishing, 71

Naad yoga, 122–23, 228
NAEM (negative affect erasing
    method), 89, 180, 215–17
  case histories involving, 333–39,
    357–70, 379–85, 391–402
naval chakra. See third chakra
negative affect erasing method.
    See NAEM
negative archetypes, 333–39
NLP (neurolinguistic
    programming), 135–36, 319–22
  future pacing, 306
  internal resource state, 304
  representational systems, 136
  timeline regression technique,
    283, 357–70
  transderivational search, 135, 137
nonordinary reality, 61, 239
  realms of, 62–63
  soul loss and, 112

ovaries, 200, 203

pancreas, 200

panic attacks, 315–18, 351–56, 409–26

parathyroid, 200

past life, 224, 357–70

  empirical validation of, 403–7

  intrusions from, 301–2

  memories of, 375–78

  regression to, 273–74, 283–86, 351–70

past-life energetic origins, 103, 152, 246–47, 272, 273, 276

case histories involving, 329–43, 409–26

Perls, Fritz, 29

pineal gland, 200

pituitary gland, 200

possession, 409–26

post-traumatic stress disorder.
  See PTSD

power animal

  case histories involving, 391–97, 409–26

  in shamanism, 23, 67

  retrieval of, 239–40, 242–43

power resource, creating, 303–4

power spots, 167–68

PR. See psychoenergetic reversal

prana, 33, 119, 122, 127.
  See also life-force energy

pranayama, 6, 122

prayer, 249–50

pre-birth trauma, 272

Process, 39, 76, 134

  concept of, 32, 55, 58

  defined, xxiv

  importance of following, xxiv–xxv, 123, 309–10, 409–26

  working in, 89

process-oriented psychology.
  See processwork

process-oriented therapy, 42–44

processwork, 17–18, 49–50, 124, 225

protocols

  DEH, 255–311

  EFT, DEH version of, 192–93

  embodiment, 116

  recovery of stolen soul part, 153–55

psychic ability, 211

psychodynamic therapy, 30–31

psychoenergetic reversal (PR), 77–79, 83–89

  case histories involving, 315–18, 333–39, 371–74, 379–85, 391–402, 409–26

  effects on practitioners, 223

  testing for, 265–66

psychopharmaceuticals, 173

  limitations of, 433–39

  PTSD and, 94, 100–101

psychopomp work, 64, 240,
246–47, 329–32
PTSD (post-traumatic stress
disorder)
case histories involving, 323–28,
375–78
DEH approach to, 95–96, 101–2,
103, 105
dissociation and, 96–97
generation of, 287
mainstream approach to, 93–95,
100–101, 105
role of memory in, 103–4
shamanic approach to, 102–3
soul loss and, 103
symptoms and features of,
98–100

qigong, 124–26, 127–28, 201, 225
quantum physics, 36–38

regression to past life, 283–86,
273–74, 351–70
resource anchor, 319–22, 357–70
root chakra. See first chakra

sacral chakra. See second chakra
sacred space, 24, 167–69
creating a, 258–59
importance of second attention
to, 169

Sat Kriya, 204
mantra, 229–31
Sat Nam, 121–22, 204, 229–31
Scapegoat archetype, 149
second attention, 56–57, 59
creating sacred space and, 169
importance of cultivating, 165
therapist's development of,
57–58
therapist's use of, 246
second chakra, 200, 203–4,
323–28, 333–39, 345–50,
379–85
seemorg matrix model, xxv, 39,
178. See also Clinton, Asha
self psychology, 30
seventh chakra, 200, 212–13
sexual abuse, 203, 345–50, 375–78
Shakti. See life-force energy
shamanic healing and interventions,
181, 239–47
divination, 64, 239–42
extraction, 64, 102, 240, 245–46,
409–26
power animal retrieval, 239–40,
242–43
psychopomp work, 64, 240,
246–47, 329–32
soul retrieval, 64, 240
shamanic journeying, 62, 68–69,
110–13, 225

shamanic journeying (*continued*)

  case histories involving, 341–50,
    375–97, 403–26

  purpose of, 23

shamanic spirits, 61–65

shamanism, 18–19, 37, 61–66,
  127, 146

  on dissociation, 109

  on intrusions, 102

  Western civilization versus,
    65–66

silent mind, 75, 128–29

sixth chakra, 200, 211–12, 319–22,
  409–26

smudging, 162, 169, 409–26

solar plexus chakra.

  See third chakra

soul, importance of, xxv

soul loss, 107–18, 288

  addiction and, 244

  causes of, 244

  defined, 110

  DEH approach to, 113–16, 118

  depression and, 111–12

  PTSD and, 103

  symptoms of, 111–12, 117

  trauma and, 244–45, 289–90

soul retrieval, 64, 112–13, 117, 240,
  243–45, 409–26.

  See also soul loss

soul stealing, 151–53

recovery protocol for, 153–55

  shamanic approach to, 153

sound

  healing with, 227–38.

  See also vibrational healing

  role of, 123

Source, 73, 75, 78

  connecting to, 78–80, 179

spirit. *See* compassionate spirits

spirit intrusion, 403–26

spirit obsession, 387–90

spirituality, 250

Stevenson, Ian, 273

stress, 91

Stringham, Michelle, 18, 409–26

subconscious, 158

suicide, 323–28, 435–36

supernatural intrusions, 264, 288.

  See also dark energy intrusions

  case histories involving, 315–18,
    329–39, 345–50, 357–74,
    399–402

supernatural phenomena, 409–26

Swack, Judith, 22–23, 39, 195, 197

Tapas Fleming, Elizabeth, xxv,
  178, 183

tapping

  chakra, 58, 89, 181, 319–28,
    409–26

  directive, 193–94, 214, 236

heart-center, 409–26

meridian points, 323–28

temporal curve, 180, 195–97,
   345–50, 371–74

TAT (Tapas acupressure technique),
   xxv, 39, 178, 180, 183–85

case histories involving, 315–32,
   351–70, 409–26

testes, 200, 203

TFT (Thought Field Therapy®),
   xxiii, 20, 32–33, 35–36, 187,
   190, 196

therapeutic contract, 51

therapeutic field, 56

therapeutic goal, 71–72

therapeutic presence, 47–48, 223

therapeutic relationship

   development of, 134, 137

   importance of, 133–35

   issues arising in, 48–49, 223–24,
      263–64

therapeutic touch, 221

therapist's role in DEH, 49

Thie, John, 34–35

third chakra, 199, 200, 204–6,
   409–26

third-eye chakra. See sixth chakra

third-eye point, 215, 319–22

Thought Field Therapy®. See TFT

Three In One Concepts, 39, 219

throat chakra. See fifth chakra

thymus, 200, 209

thyroid, 200

Tibetan bell, bowl, and cymbals,
   89, 123, 163, 181, 227, 232–35

case histories involving, 329–39,
   345–70, 379–85, 391–402,
   409–26

toning, 227, 232

Touch for Health, 34–35

transactional analysis, 28–29

transference

   in DEH, 48–49

   effects of negative, 263–64

trauma, 97

   birth, 409–26

   childhood, 323–28

   collective, 288, 323–28,
      409–26

   components of, 287–88

   defined, 92

   degrees of, 290

   dissociation caused by, 267–68

   effects of, 44–45, 92–93, 279,
      286–87, 289–99

   energetic boundaries, addressing
      via, 140

   Freudian view of, 27

   pre-birth, 272

   shamanic treatment of, 239–40

   soul loss and, 244–45,
      289–90

trauma (*continued*)

    types of, 292

    See also PTSD

van der Kolk, Bessel, 92, 93, 97, 99, 278

vibrational healing, 123, 181, 227–38. *See also* sound

Victim archetype, 152, 202, 210, 291, 297–98, 333–39

Weiss, Brian, 273–74

Western psychotherapy, 36, 38–39, 44

White Tantric yoga, 12–16, 123

Wounded Holy One archetype, 357–70

yoga, 33–34

    Jnana, 119–20

    Kundalini, 6, 120–21, 199, 212

    Naad, 122–23, 228

    White Tantric, 12–16, 123

Yogiji. *See* Bhajan, Yogi

Zukav, Gary, 128

TO ORDER ADDITIONAL COPIES OF

Dynamic Energetic Healing®

Integrating Core Shamanic Practices with Energy
Psychology Applications and Processwork Principles

Call toll-free at 1-877-370-4546 or use your credit card
to order online at *www.DynamicEnergeticHealing.com*.

NOTES

NOTES

NOTES